A Mediator in Matthew

A Mediator in Matthew

An Analysis of the Son of Man's Function in the First Gospel

Craig D. Saunders

FOREWORD BY
Joel B. Green

◆PICKWICK *Publications* · Eugene, Oregon

A MEDIATOR IN MATTHEW
An Analysis of the Son of Man's Function in the First Gospel

Copyright © 2021 Craig D. Saunders. All rights reserved. Except for brief quotations in critical publications or reviews, no part of this book may be reproduced in any manner without prior written permission from the publisher. Write: Permissions, Wipf and Stock Publishers, 199 W. 8th Ave., Suite 3, Eugene, OR 97401.

Pickwick Publications
An Imprint of Wipf and Stock Publishers
199 W. 8th Ave., Suite 3
Eugene, OR 97401

www.wipfandstock.com

PAPERBACK ISBN: 978-1-5326-9704-3
HARDCOVER ISBN: 978-1-5326-9705-0
EBOOK ISBN: 978-1-5326-9706-7

Cataloguing-in-Publication data:

Names: Saunders, Craig D., author. | Green, Joel B., foreword.

Title: A mediator in Matthew : an analysis of the son of man's function in the First Gospel / by Craig D. Saunders ; foreword by Joel B. Green.

Description: Eugene, OR: Pickwick Publications, 2021 | Includes bibliographical references.

Identifiers: ISBN 978-1-5326-9704-3 (paperback) | ISBN 978-1-5326-9705-0 (hardcover) | ISBN 978-1-5326-9706-7 (ebook)

Subjects: LCSH: Bible. Matthew—Criticism, interpretation, etc. | Son of Man | Jesus Christ—Mediation

Classification: BS2575.52 S38 2021 (print) | BS2575.52 (ebook)

02/25/21

*This book is dedicated to
My parents, David and Alberta Saunders
My wife, Rebekah J. Saunders
My sons, Josiah D. and Nathan A. Saunders*

Contents

Foreword by Joel B. Green | xi
Preface | xiii

CHAPTER 1
Introduction | 1
   1. Introduction   1
   2. Review of Research   2
      2.1. The Development of Son of Man Research from Past to Present   2
      2.2. Varied Perspectives on the Meaning of *Son of Man* in the Gospel of Matthew   12
      2.3. The Origin and Meaning of the Expression *Son of Man*   27
   3. The Method: New Redaction Criticism   29
   4. The Role of the Son of Man as *Mediator*   32
   5. Filling in the Gaps: The Thesis of This Project   34

CHAPTER 2
The Son of Man's Mediatorial Significance on Earth: Revealing God's Will to Genuine Disciples | 36
   1. Introduction   36
   2. The Son of Man as Mediator of God's Will on Earth in Matthew   37
      2.1. The Inclusio: ποιήσῃ τὸ θέλημα τοῦ πατρός μου τοῦ ἐν οὐρανοῖς in Matthew 7:21 and 12:50   37
      2.2. God's Will to Genuine Disciples: Self-Relinquishment (Matthew 8:18–22)   37
      2.3. God's Will to Genuine Disciples: The Necessity of Faith (Matthew 9:1–8)   44
      2.4. God's Will to Genuine Disciples: Faithfulness in Following after Jesus the Son of Man (Matthew 10:16–23)   51
      2.5. God's Will to Genuine Disciples: The Revelation, Call, and Response of God's Salvific Plan (Matthew 11:11–19)   57
      2.6. God's Will to Genuine Disciples: Mercy Redefines the Sabbath Law (Matthew 12:1–8)   70
      2.7. God's Will to Genuine Disciples: The Need of Spirit-Empowered Ministry (Matthew 12:22–32)   77

2.8. God's Will to Genuine Disciples: Imitating Jesus's Self-Sacrificial Ministry (Matthew 12:38–42)   82

3. Conclusion   89

Chapter 3

The Son of Man's Mediatorial Significance in His Passion: Fulfilling God's Will through Obedience | 93

1. Introduction   93
2. The Son of Man as Mediator of Fulfilling God's Will through Obedience   94
    2.1. God's Will Obeyed: Jesus the Son of Man's Fidelity to God's Revealed Confession (Matthew 16:13–28)   94
    2.2. God's Will Obeyed: Jesus the Son of Man and John the Baptist as Examples of Genuine Discipleship (Matthew 17:9–13, 22–23)   104
    2.3. God's Will Obeyed: Jesus the Son of Man as the Sacrificial Servant of All People (Matthew 20:17–28)   110
    2.4. God's Will Obeyed: Jesus the Son of Man Accepts Rejection and Death (Matthew 26:1–5, 14–56)   119
3. Conclusion   132

Chapter 4

The Son of Man's Mediatorial Significance at His Parousia: Judgment, Vindication, and Reward for Fulfilling God's Will | 135

1. Introduction   135
2. The Son of Man as Mediator of the Father's Judgment at his Parousia   136
    2.1. The Parable of the Wheat and Weeds: Separating the Children of the Kingdom from the Children of the Evil One (Matthew 13:24–30, 36–43)   136
    2.2. The Promised Eschatological Rewards for Following Jesus (Matthew 16:21–27; 19:16–30)   143
    2.3. The Events Surrounding the Parousia of Jesus the Son of Man: A Call for Endurance and Watchfulness in Light of a Disciple's Promised Coming Reward (Matthew 24:3–51)   152
    2.4. The Parousia: The Division of the Sheep and the Goats Based on Love for God and Neighbor (Matthew 25:31–46)   170
    2.5. The Son of Man's Judgment of Caiaphas at the Parousia: Vindication for All Faithful Disciples Who Follow God's Will (Matthew 26:63–66)   178
3. Conclusion   184

CHAPTER 5
Conclusion: The Son of Man as Mediator in Matthew | 187
    1. A Brief Comparison between Matthew's Christological Titles   187
    2. The Term *Mediator* in Relationship to Matthew's Son of Man   190
    3. Conclusion   198
        3.1. Filling the Research Gap   198
        3.2. The Son of Man's Earthly Ministry: The Mediator of God's Revealed Will in Matthew   199
        3.3. The Son of Man's Passion and Death: The Mediator of Demonstrated Obedience to God's Will in Matthew   207
        3.4. The Son of Man's Parousia: The Mediator of Promised Vindication and Reward for Faithful Obedience to God's Will in Matthew   214

Bibliography | 223

Foreword

Is THE SON OF Man problem solvable? I remember puzzling over this question as a student in the 1980s. I had read so many treatments, often in larger discussions of New Testament Christology (Oscar Cullmann, James D. G. Dunn, Joachim Jeremias, I. Howard Marshall, and C. F. D. Moule come to mind) but also in more focused studies of the Son of Man (Maurice Casey, A. J. B. Higgins, Morna D. Hooker, Barnabas Lindars, Heinz Eduard Tödt, and Geza Vermes, among others).[1] No real consensus emerged. We could not speak of the assured results of modern scholarship.

By and large, the debate revolved around two interrelated questions—the one centered on the etiology and tradition-critical development of the phrase, the other on its significance for the historical Jesus. The significance of these desiderata aside, what is so inviting and important about Craig Saunders's work is its alternative interest. Rather than center on concerns with prehistory, he quite rightly asks: How has the First Evangelist made sense of Jesus's identity as Son of Man? Irrespective of semantic origins or historical referents, what does the identification of Jesus as Son of Man in Matthew's Gospel tell us about Jesus, and about Matthew's Christology? This is an eminently useful question to pose, and Saunders pursues it with vigor.

Also important about this project is *the way* Saunders presses his interpretive agenda. Obviously, the story of Jesus's life and mission could be told in more than one way—the presence of four such narratives in the New Testament demonstrates this easily enough. In the mid-twentieth century, a number of interpreters explored the First Evangelist's distinctive theological aims by carefully, sometimes elegantly, separating his sources (tradition) from his own words (redaction). This form of redaction criticism evolved over the ensuing three decades as those interpreters allowed that the simple decision to include those sources, those traditions, indicated the evangelist's

---

1. My question was helped along by the title of A. J. B. Higgins's essay, "Is the Son of Man Problem Insoluble?" John R. Donahue provides a critical survey of research from that period in "Recent Studies on the Origin of 'Son of Man.'"

general agreement with or approval of them. If this is so, it followed, we might speak less of redaction criticism and more of composition analysis, and then of various forms of literary study. This metamorphosis was hurried along by a growing unease over common descriptions of the nature of the relationships among the Gospels and the putative identity of their various sources. Saunders's analysis moves beyond those methodological machinations, but retains awareness of that initial and key observation, namely, that similar episodes (and other story elements) can be combined and linked in diverse ways, serving various commitments and aims. Among the diverse and sometimes competing ways of construing Jesus's life and ministry, how has Matthew portrayed Jesus as Son of Man? Saunders responds not by tossing out work with a Gospel synopsis, nor with recourse to sources and tradents. Instead, he moves forward by comparing the relevant synoptic parallels—not to show how Matthew has altered this or added that (as though we could be certain of his sources) but to grasp how Matthew's distinctiveness is thrown into sharper relief when his account is read alongside other ways of recounting the same episode, dialogue, or monologue.

Taken together, this focus and this interpretive approach leads to a sustained argument concerning the function of Jesus's identity as Son of Man in the First Gospel. Saunders urges that, as Son of Man, Jesus relates to God and Jesus's followers as the go-between: teaching his disciples by word and example what it means to know and do God's will. All sorts of questions about the phrase "Son of Man" remain, of course, but this study presses the conversation forward with its theological focus on Matthew's Son of Man Christology.

Joel B. Green
Fuller Theological Seminary

Preface

THE FUNCTION OF THE Son of Man in the Gospel of Matthew is not settled. The majority of the research on the Son of Man in Matthew has been focused on the latter part of the Gospel, that is, Matt 21–25. A gap still needs to be filled in the research—a consistent, theological understanding of the role of the Son of Man throughout the entire Gospel. This thesis argues that Jesus the Son of Man serves as the *mediator* of God's will to his genuine disciples. The primary research method used is new redaction criticism, together with literary and social-scientific emphases. All thirty Son of Man logia are studied in their respective literary contexts and in relationship to the entire Gospel. In chapter one, a general review of Son of Man research is provided along with a sketch of representative literature on the Son of Man in Matthew. In chapter two, the Son of Man logia that relate to Jesus's earthly life are studied (Matt 8–12). In these passages, the Son of Man *mediates* God's revealed will to his genuine disciples through his message and works. In chapter three, the Son of Man logia that relate to the Son of Man's suffering, death, and resurrection are analyzed. The Son of Man's journey to the cross demonstrates his obedient response to his Father's will, which *mediates* for his disciples the self-denial and sacrificial allegiance to God's plan necessary in genuine followership. In chapter four, the Son of Man logia that relate to Jesus's parousia are investigated. The purpose of the Son of Man's parousia will be to *mediate* promised vindication and reward disciples who have proven their fidelity to Jesus and God's will. In chapter five a conclusion of research findings are addressed.

There are many individuals who deserve recognition for their assistance in this doctoral thesis. The support, encouragement, and prayers I have received from others throughout the duration of this project are so numerous I cannot possibly name them all. I would especially like to thank my primary advisor, Dr. Joel B. Green, for his wise council, recommendations, and constructive emendations throughout the entirety of my thesis work. My secondary advisor, Dr. David R. Bauer, has also been very helpful in working through the sections in Matthew and making suggestions on literary and compositional methodology of my work. I would like to thank Judith A. Seitz for her aid in editing each chapter of this thesis. I cannot adequately express my appreciation to my wife, Rebekah J. Saunders, for her support of God's call on my life. She has been a constant encourager throughout my educational pursuits and has challenged me to yield to God's leadership in every step of my doctoral work. Her prayers and friendship have strengthened my resolve. Since the day of my birth, my parents, David R. Saunders and Alberta I. Saunders, have committed my life to the Lord. They have supported, encouraged, and offered endless prayers in every stage of my personal and academic life. Their faith in God and His will for my life has been a constant respite in the midst of the challenges, joys, and many times of needed perseverance. I would like to recognize my two wonderful sons, Josiah D. and Nathan A. Saunders, who have also kindly persevered with me on this long road of thesis work. My prayer for them will always be that God's holy Word will be the light, peace, and hope which directs their lives in accordance to God's will, as it continues to be for me. Most of all, I am eternally grateful for my Lord and Savior Jesus Christ, who has been my guide and strength throughout my life. He is our Savior, the Son of Man, who came δοῦναι τὴν ψυχὴς αὐτοῦ λύτρον ἀντὶ πολλῶν (Matt 20:28).

Craig D. Saunders
Wilmore, KY
June 2020

Chapter 1

Introduction

1. Introduction

THE ROLE THE SON of Man sayings play in the Gospel of Matthew has received inadequate attention in Matthean studies. Scholarship has focused on (1) the specific role of the Son of Man as eschatological judge in Matthew, (2) a predominant focus on the source-critical investigation (i.e., the priority of Mark's Gospel and the influence of Q upon the Gospel) of the Son of Man in Matthew, and (3) studies that have been published on the influence of Dan 7:13–14; 1 Enoch; and 4 Ezra to the significance of the person and function of the Son of Man in Matthew (and, more generally, the Synoptic Gospels as a whole). However, these studies generally neglect a consideration of Matthew's own perspective on the Son of Man.[1] More needs to be said about the Son of Man sayings related to the earthly ministry and passion predictions and material in Matthew. These important contexts of the

---

1. Only two unpublished dissertations address the Son of Man in Matthew. First is Glazener, *Investigation of Jesus' Usage*. Glazener provides a helpful source-critical investigation of the Son of Man in Matthew. He briefly compares Matthew to the other Synoptics, but does not provide an exegetical analysis of any of the Son of Man logia in the Gospel. He posits that Matthew's picture of the Son of Man is as "the authoritative representative of God and God's elect ones" (197). The second is Witte, *Son of Man*. Using compositional-critical and narrative-sensitive methods, Witte analyzes each of the Son of Man sayings in Matthew and argues that Jesus's function as the Son of Man is to deal with the conflict between the unbelieving Jews and the Matthean community as it initiates their Gentile-inclusion mission. According to Witte, the Gospel of Matthew anticipates Jesus the Son of Man's resolution of this conflict at his parousia (20–21). He states, "The Matthean Son of Man sayings are not a heterogeneous mixture of christological statements that recall 'the whole of the history of Jesus'—his life, death, and after-life generally"; rather, "the Son of Man sayings in Mt refer specifically to Jesus' role in developing conflict between Kingdom community and those who oppose its establishment" (21). Even though Witte's conclusions are possible, it seems dubious to dismiss the meaning of the Son of Man's role from Jesus's whole history (i.e., his life, death, resurrection, exaltation, and parousia) in Matthew's Gospel, since every Son of Man saying is connected to Jesus's history. Consequently, conflict ideology takes precedence over a consistent theological meaning of Jesus the Son of Man's role in Matthew.

Matthean Son of Man material have been neglected in comparison to the parousia passages in Matt 21–25. An understanding of the function of the Son of Man for the entire Gospel is needed.

The goal of this monograph is to help fill in these gaps by concentrating on a thorough examination of the Son of Man passages in Matthew. This project will examine all of Matthew's Son of Man sayings, demonstrate how the mediatorial function of the Son of Man is resident in each, and synthesize the mediatorial function of the Son of Man in Matthew as a whole. I will utilize new redaction criticism as the primary method and literary, compositional, and social scientific as secondary methods for studying the theological implications of the function of the Son of Man in Matthew. I will study the Son of Man passages by categorizing them in light of three main ways they function in Matthew: (1) ὁ υἱὸς τοῦ ἀνθώπου in the earthly ministry of Jesus (chapters 8–12); (2) ὁ υἱὸς τοῦ ἀνθρώπου in the passion, resurrection, and exaltation of Jesus (chapters 16–17; 20; 26); and, (3) ὁ υἱὸς τοῦ ἀνθρώπου in the eschatological judgment of Jesus (chapter 13; 16:27; 19:28–29; chapters 24–25; 26:64). Within each of the contexts of the Son of Man material, I will prove the function of Son of Man in Matthew's theology is as *mediator*, the go-between between the Father in heaven and his present and future disciples.

2. Review of Research

2.1. The Development of Son of Man Research from Past to Present

The scholarly opinions regarding the Son of Man problem are far-reaching. In this review I will discuss the seven main opinions that represent the broad range of research.[2]

2.1.1. *The Expression* Son of Man *as an Indication of Jesus's Incarnation*[3]

A. W. Neander argues for the incarnational meaning of the Son of Man in his monograph *The Life of Jesus Christ in Its Historical Connection and Historical Development*. In his view, Jesus referred to himself as the Son of Man to emphasize his conscious relation to humanity. Neander asserts, "He called himself the 'Son of Man' because he had appeared as a man;

---

2. These main seven scholarly opinions regarding the Son of Man have been generated from the monograph by Müller, *Expression*. This monograph provides a detailed analysis of the various historical views on the expression *Son of Man* in NT literature.

3. This view is similar to the Patristic understanding of the expression Son of Man in the Gospel literature. See Müller, *Expression*, 9–92.

because he belonged to mankind; because he had done such great things for *human* nature (Matt 9;8); because he was to glorify that nature; because he was himself the realized ideal of humanity."[4] All of human nature is glorified in Christ the Son of Man because he is the incarnation of divinity. As the Son of Man, Jesus is elevated above all other humans due to his divine nature yet can relate to humankind because he is fully *human*. Neander emphasizes this elevation when he states, "It would have been the height of arrogance in any man to assume such a relation to humanity, to style himself absolutely MAN. But He, to whom it was natural thus to style himself, indicated thereby his elevation above all other sons of men—the Son of God in the Son of Man."[5] Neander argues that in the Gospels, Jesus used the expression Son of Man to designate his human personality and Son of God to designate his divinity. However, even though Jesus the Son of Man was completely human, he was different than humanity because he glorified that nature being the Son of God.

G. F. Wright also affirms the incarnational view of the Son of Man. According to Wright, when Jesus designated himself as the Son of Man, he was referring both to his humanity and his divinity:

> The divinity is *assumed*, while the humanization of that divinity is *asserted*. Before his hearers Jesus stands in human form and nature, calling himself the Son of Man, while he performs works, or predicts operations, which demand the attributes of the Godhead. The title "Son of Man" equals God manifest in the flesh, or the Word who was God become flesh; or God with us.[6]

Therefore, Jesus is asserted as the second person of the Trinity. In consciousness of his divinity, Jesus called himself the Son of Man; while in the consciousness of his humanity, Jesus called himself the Son of God. "Deity always lies at the basis of the title and gives it significance."[7] As the Son of Man Jesus is a perfect human, one who is much higher than a human but at the same time is still a human with all human weakness. In Wright's opinion, this understanding of Jesus as Son of Man runs through all the Gospels, providing a unity in the underlying thought of the term. Jesus is the everlasting (divine) Son who became incarnate and so has become the Son of Man. As the Son of Man, Jesus gives complete reference to humanity; he is the Son of Man who brings the kingdom of heaven to earth. As Son of Man, Jesus is wholly conscious of his greatness and position as

4. Neander, *Life of Jesus Christ*, 99.
5. Neander, *Life of Jesus Christ*, 100.
6. Wright, "Term 'Son of Man,'" 585.
7. Wright, "Term 'Son of Man,'" 585–86.

Messiah yet as a companion or mediator for humans and helping servant among humans.[8] The humanity in Jesus is not to be distinguished from other humanity except in its divine connections. Jesus used the Son of Man as his self-designation to emphasize that divinity had joined itself to humanity; the Word has become flesh.[9]

2.1.2. *The Expression* Son of Man *as Synonymous with "Man"*

Hans Lietzmann is most known for asserting the First Aramaic Stage into the investigation of the meaning of Son of Man. Lietzmann argues that the Greek phrase ὁ υἱὸυ τοῦ ἀνθρώπου received its meaning from the Aramaic equivalent בר נשא. According to Lietzmann, בר נשא is a "generic name" meaning *man*—a simple circumlocution for "I," the first person demonstrative pronoun.[10] Since בר נשא is the source of the Greek phrase ὁ υἱὸυ τοῦ ἀνθρώπου, then the expression is not a particular self-description of Jesus; rather, it is in the general sense as *man* (i.e., *jemand*—anyone). Lietzmann argues against the assertion that in apocalyptic texts ὁ υἱὸυ τοῦ ἀνθρώπου is a self-description of Jesus or is a messianic title. In his opinion, ὁ υἱὸυ τοῦ ἀνθρώπου is only a circumlocution for "Jesus the Messiah."[11] Any messianic meaning of ὁ υἱὸυ τοῦ ἀνθρώπου was forced later into the text as a secondary meaning; it was not part of the original generic meaning derived from the Aramaic בר נשא. The lack of messianic meaning is demonstrated by an examination of the variations of the parallel Son of Man texts in the Gospels.[12] Therefore, Lietzmann finds no theological meaning in the Greek expression ὁ υἱὸυ τοῦ ἀνθρώπου, nor does he view it as a self-designation of Jesus's identity or mission. He only finds meaning in the generic Aramaic expression בר נשא, meaning, "man" or "anyone."

2.1.3. *The Expression* Son of Man *as Jesus's Eschatological Self-Understanding*

Albert Schweitzer and Johannes Weiss are main proponents of the view that Jesus had in mind merely an eschatological meaning to his self-designation as Son of Man. In other words, the Son of Man was Jesus's understanding of his future role in the coming kingdom of God rather than his present role

---

8. Wright, "Term 'Son of Man,'" 593.
9. Wright, "Term 'Son of Man,'" 594.
10. Lietzmann, *Menschensohn*, 82–83.
11. Lietzmann, *Menschensohn*, 84–85.
12. Lietzmann, *Menschensohn*, 86.

during his earthly ministry. Schweitzer states, "When Jesus uses the term Son of Man to describe himself, he does not mean that he is an incarnation of a preexistent being, but that he is the man of David's line who will be the Son of Man in the Kingdom of God."[13] According to Schweitzer, the messianic secret revealed to Peter in Matt 16:13–17, 20 meant that Jesus would appear in the future upon the clouds of heaven coming as from heaven as the Son of Man, the Messiah. Thus Jesus had two entirely distinct personalities. The one is terrestrial, belonging to the age that is now. The other is as a celestial figure, belonging to the future messianic period.[14] Only through Jesus's suffering, death, and resurrection will he one day be the future messianic Son of Man. The Son of Man sayings in the Gospels, which are of a futuristic character (i.e., always suggesting a "coming upon the clouds of heaven" relating specifically to Dan 7:13–14), are considered authentic Son of Man sayings because Jesus is speaking in the third person, referring to himself as an eschatological figure. Schweitzer states, "All those passages are historical which show the influence of the apocalyptic reference to the Son of Man in Daniel: all are unhistorical in which such is not the case."[15] Without Jesus's own self-description of a future messianic Son of Man, the Gospels would have no authentic Son of Man sayings.

Weiss argues that when Jesus referred to himself as the Son of Man during his earthly ministry, he was making a *claim* rather than a self-designation. Jesus called himself the messianic Son of Man after his exaltation, and only then all people unmistakably understand that he was the Son of Man.[16] Therefore, Jesus did not regard himself as the Christ (i.e., Messiah and Son of Man) during his earthly ministry but believed that he would *become* the Messiah. In regards to Jesus's earthly ministry, Weiss states, "Since Jesus is now a rabbi, a prophet, he has nothing in common with the Son of Man, except the claim that he will *become* the Son of Man."[17] The expression Son of Man was given to Jesus at his exaltation when, at that time, he became the figure of the Messiah—the Son of Man of Daniel and Enoch. During his earthly ministry, Jesus was a prophet before all people who would one day in the future fulfill his eschatological role as the messianic Son of Man. When speaking about Jesus's eschatological role in the emerging kingdom of God, Weiss states, "The messianic consciousness of Jesus, as expressed in the name Son of Man, also participates in the thoroughly transcendental

---

13. Schweitzer, *Kingdom*, 106.
14. Schweitzer, *Mystery*, 118–19.
15. Schweitzer, *Mystery*, 124.
16. Weiss, *Proclamation*, 119–20.
17. Weiss, *Proclamation*, 82.

and apocalyptic character of Jesus's idea of the kingdom of God, and cannot be dissociated from it."[18] Like Schweitzer, Weiss understands Jesus's self-designation as Son of Man as only a future realization, not as a title Jesus would attain during his earthly life and ministry.

2.1.4. *The Expression* Son of Man *as a Prototype of Humanity*

In his article "Neglected Features in the Problem of the Son of Man,"[19] C. F. D. Moule implies that the expression Son of Man is not a self-designation of Jesus but emphasizes his representation of humanity. Moule argues that Dan 7 is the reliable guide for understanding the meaning of the Son of Man in the Gospel literature. In his view, the Son of Man in Dan 7 represents or symbolizes the persecuted loyalists (of the Maccabean days) in their vindication in the heavenly court. In other words, the Son of Man in Dan 7 emphasizes Israel's function and destiny in particular and humankind's function and destiny in general.[20] Moule argues that Jesus used Dan 7 to emphasize his ministry and similarly the ministry of his disciples. He states, "This symbol that Jesus adapted was to express his vocation and the vocation he summoned his followers. Jesus used the term *the* Son of Man . . . to apply it alike to his authority . . . in his present circumstances and in his impending death, and to his ultimate vindication."[21] Therefore, as the Son of Man, Jesus represented the kind of ministry that his disciples will be doing. The Son of Man expression in the Gospels is a *descriptive* term, emphasizing Jesus's ministry on earth (i.e., life, suffering, and death) and his heavenly vindication in the future (i.e., exaltation and second coming).[22] Similarly, Jesus, destined through suffering one day to be exalted, represented the ministry and future of God's chosen people. One might say that Jesus as the Son of Man portrays the prophetic vision and hope of what God's chosen people can expect in their present circumstances and future victory.

J. Y. Campbell asserts that the origin of the term Son of Man comes from Jesus himself. The term is a self-designation relating to his humanness, not necessarily to a messianic figure. Campbell states, "The Son of Man was used only for Jesus himself. He used it of himself as a phrase which expressed and even emphasized his real humanity and his solidarity with mankind, and that especially when speaking of his sufferings and of the victory and glory

---

18. Weiss, *Proclamation*, 129.
19. Moule, "Neglected," 413–28.
20. Moule, "Neglected," 414–15.
21. Moule, "Neglected," 414–15.
22. Moule, "Neglected," 424.

won through his sufferings."[23] Jesus identified with humanity and provided hope of vindication through the suffering and pain associated with living as God's people in an ungodly world.

2.1.5. *The Expression* Son of Man *as a Symbolic or Collective Understanding*

T. W. Manson is one of the strongest proponents of the symbolic or collective understanding of the Son of Man. Manson believes that the expression ὁ υἱὸυ τοῦ ἀνθρώπου in the Gospels is nothing but a rendering of the original Aramaic term *bar nasha* (בר נשא or בר אנשא), which was translated to ὁ ἄνθρωπος, meaning *the man*. The term *man* was used in a symbolic sense in apocalyptic literature.[24] According to Manson, the only Son of Man sayings that reveal Jesus's significance occur after Peter's confession, which were addressed to the disciples. Manson states,

> Son of Man in the Gospels is another embodiment of the Remnant idea. In other words, the Son of Man is, like the Servant of Jehovah, an ideal figure and stands for the manifestation of the Kingdom of God on earth in a people wholly devoted to their heavenly king. His mission is to create the Son of Man, the Kingdom of saints of the Most High.[25]

Manson's thesis is substantiated by Jesus's quotations from Daniel, which emphasize that the Son of Man is said to represent the people of the saints of the Most High. In relationship to the suffering Son of Man sayings, Manson asserts that these sayings emphasize that Jesus together with his disciples will be the Son of Man, that remnant that saves by service and self-sacrifice the means of God's redemptive purposes in the world.[26] Thus, the corporate sufferings will lead to a glorious consummation because to share the sufferings of Christ is to share in his glory. Through his death, Jesus brought the Son of Man into existence as a corporate body of believers known as the church.[27]

Lloyd Gaston is another proponent of the symbolic or collective understanding of the Son of Man. Gaston asserts that the original source for the NT understanding of the Son of Man comes from Dan 7. Therefore, correct understanding of the Son of Man in the NT must be interpreted in

---

23. Campbell, "Origin and Meaning," 154–55.
24. Manson, *Teaching*, 212.
25. Manson, *Teaching*, 227.
26. Manson, *Teaching*, 231.
27. Manson, *Teaching*, 235.

light of the original meaning in Dan 7. In Daniel, the Son of Man is a collective concept referring to the suffering and vindication of Israel. In Gaston's estimation, the genuine Son of Man sayings of Jesus refer back to Dan 7 and emphasize the original collective interpretation (of a group) and not necessarily to an individual.[28] Therefore, the messianic secret (i.e., the Son of Man) is not necessarily about Jesus but about believers who accept for themselves the necessity of suffering as a ransom for many and of future vindication. During the Gospel accounts of his transfiguration, Jesus emphasized that the disciples were not to tell the messianic secret until he had risen from the dead. According to Gaston, "The Son of Man rising from the dead is fulfilled in Jesus's resurrection, but in doing so he reflects his knowledge of an earlier understanding . . . in which the Son of Man rising from the dead refers to the general resurrection (Dan 12:2)."[29] All future Son of Man sayings are dependent upon the suffering-exaltation pattern of Daniel. In Dan 7:22, "judgment is given for the saints of the Most High." Therefore, the characterization of Jesus the Son of Man as judge refers back to the original understanding of judgment conferred upon the "saints of the Most High." Gaston argues that such judgment is clearly illustrated in Mark 8:38 and Matt 25:31–46, where the Son of Man is understood as a collective witness at judgment in which all will see the rewards/punishments given to those based on their deeds. In conclusion, Gaston states,

> It is always very difficult to try and reconstruct the teaching of Jesus when this differed from that of the church. Insofar as we can do, we conclude then that for Jesus the term Son of Man was a collective concept, referring to the community he had come to call into existence, the eschatological Israel, which would pass through from suffering to vindication.[30]

Gaston does not see the Son of Man designation as referring to Jesus himself, but only to the disciples, specifically, and the community of faith, in general.

2.1.6. The Expression Son of Man *as an Exclusive Circumlocution*

Geza Vermes is credited with initiating a new era of Son of Man research called the Second Aramaic Stage. Vermes uses material based from the whole of Talmud Yerushalmi, the Aramaic parts of *Genesis Rabba*, the *Genesis*

---

28. Gaston, *No Stone on Another*, 401–2.
29. Gaston, *No Stone on Another*, 402–3.
30. Gaston, *No Stone on Another*, 408.

Apocryphon from Qumran, a great deal of material from the Palestinian Targum, including the Geniza fragments and the Neophiti Codex, various types of Aramaic writings, and a variety of speech forms, to substantiate his thesis that the Aramaic expression (א)נש(א) בר (*bar nasha*) could be used with the meanings *a human being, a man, the man, one, anyone*, or *someone*, and also to prove that בר (א)נש(א) had a circumlocutional use, similar to the Hebrew *hāhū gabrā*, meaning *that man*. This Hebrew expression is located in examples where the reference is to self in the third person used in relationship to humility or modesty. Vermes mentions that בר (א)נש(א) can be contrasted with *hāhū gabrā* because *hāhū gabrā* can mean both *I* and *you*, while בר (א)נש(א) always relates to *I*, the circumlocutional self-reference. Vermes argues that the Aramaic expression *bar nasha* is behind the meaning of Son of Man in the Gospels; therefore, in his estimation, it was never employed as a messianic designation.[31] In *Jesus the Jew: A Historian's Reading of the Gospels*, Vermes differentiates the Son of Man sayings in the Gospels based on their connection to Dan 7:13. The first group includes thirty-seven sayings which are unconnected to Dan 7:13. These are circumlocutional references which refer to the speaker (i.e., Jesus) and which Jesus undoubtedly uttered. The second group includes six sayings which are directly connected with Dan 7:13. These sayings are a product of Christianity and were not spoken by Jesus (e.g., Matt 24:30; 26:64). The final group includes twenty-one sayings which indirectly relate to Dan. 7:13. These sayings allude to the OT text and refer to the Son of Man's parousia (his glory, kingship, on the clouds).[32] The relevance of the authenticity of the Son of Man sayings in the Gospels does not disqualify Vermes's conclusion:

> If only half of these sayings are authentic, it would still be justifiable to infer that the *son of man* circumlocution belonged to the stylistic idiosyncrasies of Jesus himself. The formal association of "the *son of man*" in the Synoptics with Daniel 7:13 appears to be derivative and can only scarcely be ascribed to Jesus himself. Nevertheless, it is most remarkable that even at this stage its use as a form of self-designation still survives. The only possible, indeed probable, genuine utterances are sayings independent of Daniel 7 in which, according to the Aramaic usage, the speaker refers to himself as the *son of man* out of awe, reserve or humility.[33]

31. Vermes, "Use of בר נש/בר נשא," 320–28.

32. Vermes, *Jesus the Jew*, 178–86.

33. Vermes, *Jesus the Jew*, 182, 184, 186. For the full discussion, see 160–91 (esp. 177–86). Vermes responds to more recent critics of his position in "Son of Man Debate," 193–206.

Therefore, Vermes does not see a problem with using the Aramaic expression בר נש(א) as evidence in support of a circumlocutional understanding of the Son of Man. Extra-biblical material that uses the Aramaic expression emphasizes a circumlocutional meaning. Even if some of the Son of Man references in the Gospels are not authentic, Vermes contends that all of the Son of Man references can still be seen as a circumlocutional reference; Jesus is speaking of himself.

2.1.7. The Expression Son of Man *as a Particular Person in the Greek Language*

Maurice Casey is the strongest proponent of the Second Aramaic Stage in Son of Man research and has expanded the work of Vermes. While Casey agrees with Lietzmann's emphasis on the generic meaning of the Aramaic idiom בר נש(א) (*bar anasha*), he asserts that this idiom may also have a particular meaning in the Gospels. In his most recent monograph, Casey argues that the most accurate way to discover the meaning of the Son of Man logia is through the reconstruction of the Aramaic term בר נש(א) (*bar anasha*).[34] According to Casey, previous scholars have ignored the Aramaic significance due to ignorance compounded by ideological bias. Such a criticism is manifested when reading primary sources in translation rather than in the languages in which they survived (i.e., focusing upon the Greek rather than the Aramaic). To educate scholars on the stability of the Aramaic language, Casey spends the second chapter of his monograph discussing the use of the Aramaic term, which he believes the historical Jesus used when the Gospels attribute to him the Greek term ὁ υἱὸς τοῦ ἀνθρώπου. Casey demonstrates the development of the Aramaic language to emphasize the significance of its idiomatic usage, which is apparently central to appreciating the term's usage by the historical Jesus. The degree of variation in the meaning of the term בר נש(א) is important in assessing the sayings of the historical Jesus. For example, the term may have both a general and specific level of meaning. Sayings related to a general level of meaning may be true of all human beings, or a person may generalize from his or her own personal experience. Sayings which represent a specific level of meaning may refer to an individual speaker and/or a group of associates.[35] According to Casey, since scholarship has minimized or ignored this idiom, serious mistakes have been made in relationship to the Son of Man concept. A careful study of how the Aramaic term בר נש(א) was used in the Aramaic sources used by the Evangelists, a normal term for *man* is needed. Casey

---

34. Casey, *Solution*, 81, 116–19.
35. Casey, *Solution*, 314.

demonstrates the legitimacy of בר (א)נש(א) through a comparison between the Greek and Aramaic sources by offering an Aramaic reconstruction of six genuine Son of Man sayings (Mark 2:28; 9:12; 10:45; 14:21; Matt 11:19// Luke 7:34; Matt 12:32//Luke 12:10). He argues that each case has a general level of meaning, referring to the disciples, as well as a particular reference to Jesus.³⁶ In relationship to the predictions of Jesus's death and resurrection (Mark 8:31; 9:31; 10:33-34), Casey argues that only Mark 8:31 is a genuine saying and 9:31 and 10:33-34 were created by the evangelist on the basis or Mark 8:31. In Mark 8:31, Casey finds a general level of meaning: All people die and will be part of a general resurrection. However, the text also has a specific reference to Jesus, who was speaking about his own death and resurrection. According to Casey, in the secondary sayings of the Synoptic Gospels, ὁ υἱὸς τοῦ ἀνθρώπου is used by all three evangelists as an important title for Jesus alone in the Greek. The result is a major christological title (i.e., the Son of Man), expressing the centrality of Jesus. The secondary sayings underwent a transition process from the original Aramaic בר (א)נש(א) to ὁ υἱὸς τοῦ ἀνθρώπου. Whenever the Gospel writer thought that the primary reference was to Jesus, ὁ υἱὸς τοῦ ἀνθρώπου was used in the singular. Whenever the Gospel writer encountered בר (א)נש(א) referring to anyone else, a different term such as ἄνθρωπος was used, and when בנ' (א)נש(א) was in the plural, the writer used other terms such as ἄνθρωποι.³⁷ Casey argues that the oldest Gospel was Mark and the writer made a midrashic use of Dan 7:13 in combination with other scriptural texts to create the new christological title, ὁ υἱὸς τοῦ ἀνθρώπου: in those passages referring to the second coming. Matthew carried this process further, especially in eschatological contexts, creating new Son of Man sayings. Luke also used ὁ υἱὸς τοῦ ἀνθρώπου as a major christological title. Casey asserts that John derived ὁ υἱὸς τοῦ ἀνθρώπου from the synoptic tradition, especially from Matthew.³⁸

36. Casey demonstrates the general and particular meaning in his discussion of the story of the healing of the paralytic and other isolated Son of Man sayings. He offers the same conclusion: they have a general meaning, referring to the disciples or other people, and a particular meaning, referring to Jesus himself.

37. Barnabas Lindars understands the Son of Man idiom similarly to Casey. Lindars asserts that the Son of Man expression in the NT must start with those sayings which preserve the Aramaic idiom. Thus, he views the Son of Man sayings as having a generic meaning while, at the same time, asserting that ὁ υἱὸς τοῦ ἀνθρώπου was used as an oblique way of referring to Jesus. Contrary to Casey, he does not view the expression as a major christological title in the Greek. He states, "According to the Jewish evidence for this usage, he must have spoken generically, so that there must have been a sense in which his words need not refer to himself exclusively. On the other hand the self-reference was intentional, and the point of the saying would be lost without it" (Lindars, *Jesus Son of Man*, 24-27).

38. Casey, *Solution*, 314-18.

Earlier Son of Man research was not interested in my central question. They did a theological assessment of the Son of Man relating to the incarnation, studied how the Aramaic expression בר נשא or בר (א)נש(א) influenced the meaning of the Greek phrase ὁ υἱὸς τοῦ ἀνθρώπου (whether referring to a generic or collective meaning, an exclusive circumlocution, or to a particular person), assigned Jesus's self-designation as Son of Man to a purely eschatological meaning, or viewed the expression *Son of Man* as simply a representation of humanity. However, none of these studies was interested in the use of the Son of Man in Matthew. They provide potentially helpful ruminations on background, sources, philology, and theology, but they do not try to read how Matthew's Gospel develops the phrase *Son of Man*. Therefore, I will concentrate the remainder of this chapter on how scholars have understood the expression *Son of Man* in the Gospel of Matthew.

2.2. Varied Perspectives on the Meaning of *Son of Man* in the Gospel of Matthew

The second section of this literature review describes the various primary scholarly perspectives on the meaning of the Son of Man in Matthew. I will include the views of Jack Dean Kingsbury, John P. Meier, Margaret Pamment, Heinz Geist, and Ulrich Luz as representatives of the various views on the Son of Man in Matthean research.

2.2.1. *Jack Dean Kingsbury*

Jack Dean Kingsbury examines the role of the designation the *Son of Man* in Matthew. He asserts that in Matthew, the Son of Man is a technical term and not a confessional christological title *per se* because Matthew did not use this term to emphasize the identity of Jesus. Instead, Matthew used confessional titles (i.e., Messiah, King of the Jews, the Son of David, and the Son of God) to reveal Jesus's identity. Throughout Matthew, the Son of Man never appears as a formula of identification. Kingsbury argues that the term the Son of Man is a self-identification of Jesus and never appears on the lips of the disciples or other figures/groups within the Gospel.[39]

Kingsbury asserts that the christological terms Son of God and Son of Man stand out most predominantly in Matthew: the first as a preeminent predication for Jesus in this age and the second as the sole predication for him beginning with the parousia. Therefore, the title Son of God in

---

39. Kingsbury, *Matthew as Story*, 96–97.

Matthew is the preeminent title in the rest of the Gospel, with the exception of the parousia in which Son of Man takes precedence. Kingsbury argues that unlike the term Son of God, which is confessional in nature, the Son of Man is public in nature, designating Jesus during his earthly ministry as he interacted with his opponents and the crowds or told his disciples what his enemies would do to him. According to Kingsbury, the term Son of Man does not occur until 8:20 because it is the term used when Jesus encountered the world, first Israel and then the Gentiles, and particularly his opponents and unbelievers.[40] Following the resurrection, Jesus the Son of Man stood before the world as the ruler and will come at the parousia to judge the nations. Therefore, the term Son of Man is the counterpart of the title Son of God. Only at the parousia does the Son of Man supersede the Son of God (cf. 25:31–46); this side of the parousia the Son of God is the ranking title (cf. 16:13–20).[41]

Kingsbury believes that Jesus as the Son of Man fulfills the role of judge in Matthew. The Son of Man will come to judge the church and the nations. The Son of Man will usher in the future consummation of the kingdom of heaven. After his resurrection, Jesus, on the one hand, resided "in the midst of his disciples as the Son of God (28:20; 18:20), but on the other, stood before the world as the Son of Man (13:37–38a)." Matthew depicts the world in post-Easter times as the "kingdom of the Son of Man" (13:41), the realm over which the Son of Man rules. In Matthew's perspective, after Easter "God reigns over the world in the person of Jesus Son of Man and, beyond the parousia, will continue to reign through this agency."[42] Therefore, Jesus as the Son of Man highlights the themes of repudiation and vindication in Matthew's theology. As far as Jesus and the righteous are concerned, the future kingdom means, respectively, vindication and the perfect realization of hope. With respect to Jesus, it is ironic that "the Son of Man who suffers crucifixion at the hands of Jew and Gentile and is utterly despised and rejected is the very one whom God has chosen to return at the consummation as Judge and Ruler of all (cf. 17:22–23; 20:17–19; 13:41–43; 16:28; 25:31–46)."[43] Therefore, in Kingsbury's estimation, the significant role the Son of Man plays in Matthew's theology is that of judge and ruler at the time of the parousia. Prior to the parousia, Kingsbury argues that Jesus is known and confessed by all as the Son of God.[44]

40. Kingsbury, *Matthew*, 117–22, 162.
41. Kingsbury, *Matthew*, 162–63.
42. Kingsbury, *Matthew*, 143.
43. Kingsbury, *Matthew*, 145.
44. In a recent article written by Kingsbury he minimized the significance of the

Kingsbury's understanding of the Son of Man in Matthew is helpful and, at many points, congruent with the Gospel's witness. His claim that the Son of Man in Matthew is not a confessional title is correct except in Matt 16:13–16 and 26:63–64, where the Son of Man is identified as the Christ, the Son of God.[45] The Son of Man is predominantly a functional title emphasizing what the Son of Man does and how his actions will affect the disciples and their future ministry. I agree with Kingsbury that one learns who Jesus the Son of Man is by what he does. In other words, Matthew reveals the function of Jesus through the actions of the Son of Man. In Matthew, the Son of Man revealed and demonstrated God's will on earth. At the parousia, the Son of Man will come to judge the disciples (and others) in regards to their faithful (or unfaithful) obedience to God's will. Kingsbury is correct to emphasize the future role of the Son of Man as judge and ruler. In Matt 13; 16:27; 19:27–29; 24–25; and 26:64, Jesus the Son of Man is the eschatological judge and ruler at his parousia. However, Kingsbury fails to examine the theological significance of the Son of Man sayings throughout the whole Gospel, thereby not providing a complete understanding of the meaning of the Son of Man. Kingsbury argues the Son of Man designation is only a post-Easter, eschatological figure that appears to have no influence over the present. His role is one of future vindication, in which the crucified Christ returns to establish the kingdom of the Son of Man. However, Kingsbury does not account for the contexts in Matthew where the Son of Man sayings reveal the function Jesus plays on earth before his return as coming judge (bypassing Son of Man references in Matt 8–12; 16:13–21; 17:22–23; 20:17–28; 26). Another concern with Kingsbury's view is that he claims that the title of Son of God is more prominent throughout Matthew than Son of Man. He argues that only in the parousia teachings does the Son of Man have precedence over the Son of God in Matthew. However, Kingsbury does not take into account the structural argument of repetition. Throughout Matthew, the Son of Man designation appears thirty times, while the Son of God only appears nine times. The Son of Man title should receive at least equal if not greater importance in Matthew in comparison with the Son of God. I argue that one gains a greater understanding of the Christology of Jesus as Son of Man than from Jesus as Son of God. Kingsbury minimizes

---

Son of Man in Mark. He makes two main claims: (1) Jesus's self-designated title Son of Man is not attributed to a messianic title of majesty, but (2) is simply a "solemn and forceful self-referential term that is used exclusively by Jesus to point to himself" ("Christology of Mark," 60, 69–70). Kingsbury, unfortunately, has not assigned the Son of Man title any theological meaning at least in Mark. He has not indicated whether his views on the Son of Man in Mark extend to his position in Matthew.

45. I discuss my interpretation of 16:13–16 in chapter 3 and 26:63–64 in chapter 4.

the prevalence of Son of Man sayings by emphasizing its absence in Matt 1:1—8:19. However, by examining the Son of Man's function throughout Matthew, one gains understanding of how the theology of the Son of Man influences the beginning section of the Gospel.[46] I do not think Kingsbury's argument from absence in Matt 1:1—8:19 is strong in light of the theological development of the Son of Man in the entire Gospel. Kingsbury is unsuccessful in providing a thorough examination of the function the Son of Man plays in the entire Gospel of Matthew. In this monograph, I examine all of the Son of Man sayings in their given contexts, emphasizing a more holistic understanding of this all-important designation in the Matthew.

2.2.2. John P. Meier

John P. Meier does not agree with Kingsbury's view that Jesus as the Son of Man relates only to the parousia in Matthew. Unlike Kingsbury, Meier strongly argues that the references to Jesus as Son of Man are more significant than the references to Jesus as Son of God. Meier states,

> Is the title Son of God *the* central title in Matthew's Christology, as Kingsbury claims? . . . Contrary to Kingsbury, I would consider Son of Man just as central to Matthew's Christology as is Son of God. And I would also see the bond between Christ and his church as *the* characteristic mark of Matthew's Christology.[47]

Contrary to Kingsbury, who sees Jesus's role as the Son of Man preeminently relating to his parousia, Meier believes that the Son of Man has the widest conceivable span of meanings: humble servant; possessor of divine power to forgive sins; friend of sinners who is exposed to reproach, mockery, and blasphemy; Lord of the Sabbath; the suffering, dying, and rising servant; the cosmocrator; the judge of the last day; and the one who will come in glory with his angels. Such roles of Jesus the Son of Man form a continuum of meaning, spanning public ministry, passion and exaltation, rule of the world, and final judgment. This span ties together the various aspects of the Son of Man and the Son of Man with the church.[48] Therefore, the term Son of Man becomes an essential component of the Christology of Matthew. Meier states,

---

46. I will comment on the influence the Son of Man has on the beginning of the Gospel in chapter 2.
47. Meier, *Vision of Matthew*, 1.
48. Meier, *Vision of Matthew*, 217–18.

> The connection between the teachings of the earthly Jesus, the turning point of Jesus' death-resurrection, the commission of the risen and reigning Jesus to his church, and the coming of Jesus to judge the end of the age—all these interlocking Christological and ecclesiological dimensions of Christian morality suggest that the overarching concept of Son of Man is vital to Matthew's Christology and total message. It is just as important as the title Son of God.[49]

Kingsbury argues that the absence of the title Son of Man in Matt 1–2 is a reason that Jesus's title as Son of Man is not as predominant as Son of God. However, Meier suggests that what Matthew says about the Son of Man as a humble yet powerful servant (8:17; 12:18–21; 27:39–43) is already prefigured in the proleptic passion narrative (i.e., Matt 1:21). In the Gospel as a whole, there appears a *bending* of the title Son of God in the direction of obedient service and humble suffering—that is, toward some of the meanings of the Son of Man.[50] This bending in the direction of obedient, redemptive suffering—one aspect of the Son of Man concept—is emphasized in Matt 3–4. In Jesus's reinterpretation of the law in Matt 5–7, Matthew emphasizes the Greek term ἐξουσία (authority, power) of Jesus's word. Throughout the Gospel, ἐξουσία is linked to the title Son of Man. The connection between 7:13–26 and the Son of Man is apparent. The importance placed on good deeds and doing the Father's will is connected to the eschatological Son of Man as judge who judges people according to their deeds (16:24–28, 34, 37, 39; 24:42, 44; 25:31–46). From chapters 7 to 14, Jesus the Son of Man title encompasses all three meanings: "lowly yet powerful servant on earth, dying and rising savior, eschatological judge who returns to save his own."[51] From chapter 13 onward, the Son of Man is κύριος (Lord), emphasizing his role as cosmocrator who presently reigns over the world (especially in 13:34–38 [alluded to in 28:19]). Therefore, the Son of Man cannot be restricted to the parousia (as Kingsbury states); the exalted Jesus is now the Son of Man reigning over the world. The present world, for all its mixture of good and evil, is even now the kingdom of the Son of Man (13:41; see also 24:1—25:46).[52] Within chapters 20–21, 26, the Son of Man exercises his rule in the form of service unto death. The death of the Son of Man is not an ordinary death; it is a sacrificial death, a giving of his life as a ransom on behalf of and in place of humankind. Matthew's

---

49. Meier, *Vision of Matthew*, 43–44.
50. Meier, *Vision of Matthew*, 57.
51. Meier, *Vision of Matthew*, 64–68.
52. Meier, *Vision of Matthew*, 92, 173–78.

Gospel understands the Son of Man's passion as a vicarious sacrifice for humankind but also views his sacrifice as a renewal of the fellowship Jesus will have with his disciples at the messianic banquet in the kingdom of his Father. The eucharist is a foretaste of the final banquet the Son of Man will have with his disciples after the parousia. "The Son of Man concept serves to bridge different epochs of salvation history and different theological motifs in Matthew."[53] Chapters 27–28 are Matthew's way of affirming that because of the death of the Son of Man, a new age has been broken into the old. The themes of delay, sudden return, and need for preparation or vigilance (in chapters 24–25) all point to the new age where the Son of Man will gather Gentiles into the church, declaring (as the Gentile soldier/other guards did): "Truly this was God's Son" (27:54). Throughout this new age, Matthew portrays a proleptic parousia, in which the exalted Son of Man comes to his church with cosmic power to inaugurate his universal reign and issue his worldwide commission. As the exalted Son of Man, Jesus is ruler of the universe and the universal church. Jesus's worldwide commission provides an allusion as to what happens when the Son of Man comes on the clouds of heaven (cf. Dan 7:14; Matt 26:64).[54] Meier thus provides a developed understanding of the role of the Son of Man in Matthew.

Meier offers a refreshing examination of the function of the Son of Man in Matthew. Unlike many scholars, he provides a careful exegesis of the variant ways the Son of Man designation is described in the Gospel. I agree with much of his argument. I especially appreciate his insistence (contra Kingsbury) that the Son of Man designation is "just as central to Matthew's Christology as is Son of God"[55] in Matthew. In addition, unlike Kingsbury, Meier correctly asserts that the Son of Man has a wider span of meaning in the Gospel, considering his public ministry, passion and exaltation, rule of the world, and final judgment. Meier is right in arguing that a connection exists between the Son of Man figure and the church in Matthew, especially in relationship to the disciples. Meier is correct to argue that the Son of Man is already prefigured in the proleptic passion narrative (cf. 1:21–23) and, therefore, cannot be dismissed from Matt 1–2. Meier provides substantial evidence in support of his claim that "the Son of Man concept serves to bridge different epochs of salvation history and different theological motifs"[56] in Matthew. He demonstrates how the Son of Man figure can be understood throughout the Gospel. Meier's proleptic

---

53. Meier, *Vision of Matthew*, 143, 185.
54. Meier, *Vision of Matthew*, 37, 204–5, 213.
55. Meier, *Vision of Matthew*, 1.
56. Meier, *Vision of Matthew*, 185.

parousia strengthens his connection between the Son of Man figure and the church. His view is helpful when considering the Son of Man's calling to inaugurate his universal reign, including both believing Jews and Gentiles. The Son of Man's cosmic power provides the church with the ability to continue his mission in the future.

The main weakness of Meier's argument is that he does not provide a specific role of the Son of Man in Matthew. Meier's "widest conceivable span of meanings"[57] of the Son of Man seems too broad, preventing a particular theological understanding of the Son of Man's role in the Gospel. He does not demonstrate how the Son of Man's role specifically guides the disciples's theological understanding of how to fulfill God's will in their future ministry. By viewing the Son of Man's role as mediator of God's will in Matthew, one can discover the ways the Son of Man reveals and demonstrates God's will to his disciples and, consequently, provides ways for them to emulate God's will in their present and future ministry. In addition, in reference to the Son of Man logia, one learns the motivation for the disciples's following God's will until Jesus's parousia, namely, vindication from death and future reward. Meier touches on the Son of Man's mediatorial role but does not develop this theological argument in Matthew.

2.2.3. Margaret Pamment

Margaret Pamment argues that the weakness of previous scholarly work on the Son of Man problem has been "the failure to provide a full picture of the teaching about the Son of Man in any particular Gospel."[58] She asserts that the Son of Man sayings are taken out of context and there is a lack of clarification in the Christology of each Gospel. Pamment attempts to solve this problem by urging that a "consistent meaning of the term 'Son of Man'" as it "emerges from an examination of its use in a Gospel as it stands,"[59] is needed, namely, in Matthew. From her study, Pamment concludes, "On a general level, what is said about the work and destiny of the Son of Man is also said about the disciples."[60] Pamment agrees with Reginald H. Fuller in his interpretation of Dan 7. He claimed that the Son of Man symbol is not to be understood as collective but representative. In Dan 7, the Son of Man represents both the saints and their ruler.[61] Similarly, Pamment believes that

---

57. Meier, *Vision of Matthew*, 217.
58. Pamment, "Son of Man," 117.
59. Pamment, "Son of Man," 117.
60. Pamment, "Son of Man," 117.
61. Fuller, *Foundations*, 35–36.

in Matthew the Son of Man is a representative figure who calls humans to follow his example and share his destiny. Consequently, ὁ υἱὸς τοῦ ἀνθρώπου functions differently from the other christological terms in Matthew. The term Son of Man draws Jesus and his disciples together into a shared destiny. While terms such as ὁ υἱὸς τοῦ θεοῦ and ὁ χριστός define who Jesus is, the term ὁ υἱὸς τοῦ ἀνθρώπου defines who humans are.[62] Pamment believes that the title Son of Man is absent in Matt 1–7 because only from chapter 8 onwards is the response to Jesus's teaching described and the meaning of discipleship unfolded. In chapters 8–9, the most reasonable way to understand the term Son of Man is as emphasized in 8:20: "every righteous man." Therefore, the emphasis on the authority of the Son of Man is shared with the disciples and potentially all people.

According to Pamment, even though such representative authority is available to all, only the disciples choose to exercise it. For example, the Son of Man has been given authority to forgive sins, demonstrating God's forgiveness and mercy. Similarly, all humans have been given the ability to forgive sins and demonstrate mercy to others, but in Matthew, only the disciples exercise it. In chapters 9–10, "the righteousness that is to exceed that of the scribes and Pharisees" (5:20) is to be demonstrated by the disciples.

Since the Son of Man exemplifies a way of life that is merciful to others, so the disciples are to live characterized by mercy (substantiated by Hos 6:6, in which merciful acts honor God). Mercy is also demonstrated in Matt 12 in which the Son of Man's act of mercy makes clear the lordship envisioned for the Son of Man. Jesus embodies the conception of humanity, conceived in the image and likeness of a God of mercy.[63] The sign of the Son of Man in 12:40 is emphasized further in Matt 16–17. Peter's confession of the Son of Man, leads to the prediction of the Son of Man's suffering, death, and resurrection. In the Matthean version, this prediction moves immediately into the disciples's requirement to "pick up the cross and follow him" (16:13–24). The way of suffering is represented by the Son of Man to the disciples as their future way of life. Jesus's teaching on rewards for following the Son of Man and his emphasis on the Son of Man's future role as eschatological judge in 16:24–28 draws together 10:23 and 13:41–43 with an emphasis on rewards for deeds. Since the Son of Man's destiny involves suffering, death, and vindication, similarly, the disciples will also share the same destiny. In 19:28, Jesus reassured his disciples that as a reward for leaving everything to follow him, they will share the role of judge with Jesus the Son of Man. With regard to 20:17–28, Pamment argues that in Jesus's teaching on his suffering

---

62. Pamment, "Son of Man," 118.
63. Pamment, "Son of Man," 120–21.

and death, the phrase λύτρον ἀντὶ πολλῶν indicates a "representative rather than a substitutionary meaning." In other words, the fate of Jesus the Son of Man represents the fate that awaits the followers of Jesus. Finally, in chapters 24–25, the sudden unexpectedness of Jesus's return draws attention to the effects of the events upon earth. The Son of Man's death, resurrection, vindication, and oneness with the needy of humanity emphasize his mercy. Jesus the Son of Man represents to all people how mercy should be revealed in one's conduct. At the time of judgment, reward is given to those who have acted mercifully towards others.[64] In conclusion Pamment states,

> A consistent picture emerges. Only Jesus uses the term "the Son of Man" and he does so to define his destiny and to call his disciples to participate in it. The Son of Man is a representative and exemplary figure.[65] Jesus as the Son of Man exemplifies the meaning of righteousness and mercy and leads the way dictated by righteousness and mercy, through suffering and death to vindication. The disciples are to follow his example.[66]

The Son of Man becomes for the disciples the one whom they are to emulate and follow. His life mission and destiny is to represent the present and future ministry of followers of Jesus.

Like Meier, Pamment offers a helpful discussion of the function of the Son of Man in Matthew. Like Meier, she presents a more holistic understanding of the Son of Man's function in the Gospel. I agree with Pamment that the weakness of scholarship in the Son of Man problem has been the "failure to provide a full picture of the teaching about the Son of Man in any particular

---

64. Pamment, "Son of Man," 123–27.

65. Kirk's recent monograph, *A Man Attested By God*, follows a similar argument to Pamment. Kirk compares Jesus with the idealized human figures recorded in early Judaism. According to Kirk, Jesus as Son of Man is an idealized human figure who is God's representative human being during his time on earth; the chief agent of God, in the Synoptic Gospels (272, 274). Unfortunately, Kirk argues that the Son of Man sayings do not depict both divine preexistence and a human being. In other words, the Son of Man is only God's agent not identified as God himself (339, 342). Kirk claims, "The son of man sayings do not meet the threshold established for claiming a divine identity Christology" (357). I will demonstrate in this study that the Son of Man *is divine*, in other words, God and the Son of Man *are* one; thus, a higher Christology than Kirk assigns. However, in Kirk's defense, he correctly states the following regarding the Gospel of Matthew, "But if the Christology of any of the Synoptic Gospels stands poised to *transcend* the mold of idealized human figures and stake a claim to divinity, it is Matthew" and "If there is a Synoptic Gospel whose recounting of Jesus' life might show the *insufficiency* of the idealized human paradigm for fully encompassing the narrated identity of Jesus, it is Matthew" (573, 574 [emphasis mine]).

66. Pamment, "Son of Man," 126–27.

Gospel."⁶⁷ Unlike Pamment, I do not base Matthew's interpretation of the Son of Man logia solely on Dan 7, but understand a possible connection between the Son of Man and Dan 7. Pamment's argument that Jesus's ministry and destiny represent the ministry and destiny of his disciples is plausible, but how she develops her argument may be questionable. She emphasizes that the Son of Man's authority, deeds of mercy, way of suffering, and rewards for deeds represent the present and future ministry the disciples are to emulate. In response to the absence of the Son of Man reference in Matt 1–2, Pamment asserts that only from chapter 8 onwards is the response to Jesus's teaching described. Even though her argument is tenable, I prefer Meier's view that the culmination of the Son of Man's ministry is already prefigured in the beginning section of Matthew (esp. 1:21–23).

Pamment's essay fails to provide a cohesive argument that draws these different themes together, which is its main weakness. She could have strengthened her position by carefully examining how the author of Matthew has developed the comparison between the Son of Man and his disciples in the Gospel. In other words, how do the Son of Man logia in Matthew lead to the discovery of what the disciples are to emulate in Jesus's ministry? How are they to demonstrate Jesus's actions in their own present and future ministry? I will answer these questions by demonstrating how Jesus the Son of Man's role as *mediator* reveals and demonstrates the present and future ministry the disciples are to engage in to be successful in obediently fulfilling God's will. The disciples's motivation for emulating the Son of Man comes from the vindication and promised reward given to them at his parousia.

2.2.4. *Heinz Geist*⁶⁸

Heinz Geist uses Rudolf Bultmann's classification of the three groups of Son of Man sayings⁶⁹ and begins by considering where the majority of Son of Man sayings occur in Matthew. He concludes that the meaning of the term Son of Man is located after Matt 16:13, since the majority of the sayings

---

67. Pamment, "Son of Man," 117.

68. Geist's *Menschensohn und Gemeinde* is the first monograph published on the Son of Man in the Gospel of Matthew. A more recent work is Walck, *Son of Man*. Walck researches similarities between the parables of Enoch and Matthew's Gospel and argues that they represent the Son of Man as judge (especially over those who have mistreated the poor and disfranchised [e.g., Matt 25:31–46]). See Walck, *Son of Man*, 1–2.

69. According to Rudolf Bultmann, "the synoptic Son of Man sayings falls into three groups, which speak of the Son of Man (1) coming, (2) suffering death and rising again, (3) as now at work" (*Theology*, 1:30). I will also use Bultmann's general classification of the Son of Man sayings in this book; see following.

(twenty-three times) occur after Peter's confession of Jesus as the Son of Man-Messiah (i.e., sayings attributed to his suffering, death, vindication, and eschatological judgment).[70] Geist does not agree with Kingsbury that the title Son of Man is only public but also sees it as a private title, providing meaning to Jesus's disciples and the Christian community in general.[71] Geist argues that the Son of Man idea stands in connection with the Son of Man's public activity and how the "personal way of Jesus" forms an alliance in the group of disciples and in the growing confrontation with Jesus's adversaries.[72] The meaning of the Son of Man is not located with the term itself but from the wider contexts in which the Son of Man sayings are located—particularly in the context of addressees of the Son of Man sayings and among the disciples, community of faith, and Jesus's adversaries. The Son of Man sayings are instructions to the addressees (i.e., most often the disciples, but also with the crowds, Pharisees, scribes, and other community officials).[73] Geist argues that the disciples are most often the addressees to the Son of Man's instructions because, possibly, the Son of Man sayings are historically identified with the twelve as valid representative church leaders and representatives of the wider members of the community.[74] The purpose of the Son of Man sayings is to educate the disciples and the wider church community of the ways of Christ. Geist also believes that the favored verb ἀκολουθεῖν (twenty-five times) in Matthew strengthens the emphasis of community in the Son of Man thought. This verb is meant to be interpreted metaphorically, emphasizing the growing number of followers of Jesus. In Geist's view, ἀκολουθεῖν substantiates his claim that there is an intentional connotation between the Son of Man texts and the disciples, community of disciples, and the community at large. In opposition to those who hear the Son of Man and his message are the Pharisees, scribes, high councilors, and high priests who represent the Jewish people altogether.[75] According to Geist, these adversaries are highlighted to demonstrate the counterpart of the disciples/community of followers, those who doubt the message of the Son of Man and reject him. In this way, the disciples, community of faith, and followers of Jesus stand out as those who hear the message of the Son of Man. Geist concludes his argument by arguing that, in Matthew, the disciples represent a clear picture of the community. Where the Son of

---

70. Geist, *Menschensohn und Gemeinde*, 18–19.
71. Geist, *Menschensohn und Gemeinde*, 21.
72. Geist, *Menschensohn und Gemeinde*, 23.
73. Geist, *Menschensohn und Gemeinde*, 24–26.
74. Geist, *Menschensohn und Gemeinde*, 26.
75. Geist, *Menschensohn und Gemeinde*, 28–29.

Man has spoken, these Christological sayings have produced an obviously particular description of the community."[76]

Geist offers a helpful study of the contextual principles that emerge from the Son of Man sayings. I agree with Geist that meaning comes from a wider context in which the sayings are located rather than from a source-critical or terminological emphasis. Geist is probably right to question Kingsbury's notion that the Son of Man is only a public title, since some places in Matthew describe the Son of Man speaking privately to his disciples (e.g., 13:36–43; 16:13–28; 17:22–23; 20:17–19, 25–28; 24:3–51; 25:31—26:2, 17–25). The Son of Man is both a public and private title in Matthew. I disagree with Geist that the locus of meaning for the Son of Man designation comes only as instructions to the addressees, whether they are the disciples, community in general, or Jesus's adversaries. Against Geist, the Son of Man designation means more than simply instructions to the recipients; the Son of Man has other contextual and theological meanings when analyzing the whole Gospel. Geist's argument that the true meaning of the Son of Man idiom can be discovered only after Peter's confession in 16:13 is untenable. The Son of Man logia are located in contexts prior to Peter's confession, and each designation is pregnant with meaning. These Son of Man sayings relate to Jesus's earthly ministry; they emphasize the Son of Man's role as mediator of God's will to his disciples (see chapter 2). Geist's notion that the purpose of the Son of Man designation is only to educate the disciples and wider church community in the ways of Christ limits the role of the Son of Man in Matthew and ignores all of the Son of Man sayings dormant in Matthew. A more complete meaning of the Son of Man can be revealed through a study of the whole Gospel (e.g., the characteristics of Jesus the Son of Man and the specific role[s] he plays throughout the Gospel). Such an analysis can determine what implications the Son of Man might have for the disciples, community of faith, and even Jesus's adversaries. I agree with Geist that the Son of Man passages have an intentional focus on the separation between those who reject the Son of Man's person and message and those who readily embrace the Son of Man's person and message. Such responses have important implications for the Son of Man's role as eschatological judge and ruler in Matthew (see chapter 4). Geist argues that the christological Son of Man sayings have "produced an obviously particular description of the community."[77] I agree with Geist only to the extent that the Son of Man's function as mediator in Matthew reveals God's will to his disciples, and, like Jesus, they are committed to obey God's will even if it requires suffering and

---

76. Geist, *Menschensohn und Gemeinde*, 31.
77. Geist, *Menschensohn und Gemeinde*, 31.

death (see chapters 2–3). The disciples and community of faith are to obey what the Son of Man reveals and demonstrates regarding God's will in their present and future ministry; consequently, they will receive the Son of Man's vindication and promised reward at his parousia (see chapter 4).

2.2.5. Ulrich Luz

Ulrich Luz shares with Geist the belief that the Son of Man sayings in Matthew are to be understood with respect to the disciples, specifically, and to the community of faith, in general. Unlike Geist, Luz defines the meaning of the title "Son of Man" in narrative not theological categories.[78] Luz argues that the Son of Man logia are not placed at crucial points in Matthew's narrative—neither in the beginning or end of the Gospel nor in texts that open or close a main section in the Gospel. Rather, the title Son of God is reserved for such crucial parts of the narrative.[79] Since the majority of the Son of Man logia are located after 16:13, Luz chooses to concentrate his discussion in contexts subsequent to 16:13. Almost all Son of Man logia concerning his coming and all regarding the suffering, death, and rising of the Son of Man are private instructions to the disciples. Luz states that "the bilingual readers of Matthew are not likely to have associated the Greek expression ὁ υἱὸς τοῦ ἀνθρώπου with the Aramaic usage" of בר נש, but would have interpreted ὁ υἱὸς τοῦ ἀνθρώπου "in a generic sense ('the species man')"; meaning for "everybody" not a particular individual.[80] Therefore, these readers would have been surprised by Jesus's use of the expression in sayings which predicted Jesus's particular history. Luz does not assume that Matthew was familiar with Dan 7:13–14 and would have automatically associated the Son of Man with a Jewish apocalyptic concept (i.e., with an assumed apocalyptic meaning). In his estimation, the meaning of the Son of Man concept came from "the Christian tradition, the words of Jesus, which are decisive for Matthew and his readers."[81] The expression was part of the Matthean church's own tradition and would have been familiar to his audience. Luz draws upon Paul Hoffmann's understanding of the Son of Man logia in Q, which argues that the title functions as a kind of common denominator, meaning, that the Son of Man reminds the readers that Jesus is both the human, homeless, persecuted Christ, and the coming judge of the world.[82] The Matthean

---

78. Luz, "Son of Man," 11, 17.
79. Luz, "Son of Man," 5.
80. Luz, "Son of Man," 5, 7.
81. Luz, "Son of Man," 8.
82. Hoffmann, *Studien zur Theologie*, 147–58.

church understood the expression the Son of Man as part of their language and understood it as referring to Jesus's destiny and future.[83] In light of this evidence, Luz argues that the Gospel is an inclusive story, reflecting the experiences and history of the post-Easter church. Matthew is a two-level drama: Jesus and his church began as a mission to the Jewish people but, due to their rejection of Jesus and his message, turned with a new orientation towards the Gentiles that strengthens the universal mission already existing in the church. Luz argues that the term ὁ υἱὸς τοῦ ἀνθρώπου does not appear in the prologue (1:1—4:22) because this term does not say who Jesus is but describes his way and future. Therefore, the Son of Man is more strongly connected to the narrative of the Gospel than the title Son of God. Throughout Matthew, the term Son of Man discloses the fate (suffering, death) and future realization (future judge and victor) of the Son of Man, which was already understood by the disciples (contra to the opposing Jewish leaders and certain Jewish people) and intensified the development of the disciples's understanding of the Son of Man's mission. The disciples alone joined in the Son of Man's earthly ministry, participated in it, and were attacked by the Jewish leaders and others along with their Lord. The disciples were willing to follow the Son of Man because they had narrative reminders of the present and future fate and actions of Jesus; they alone knew what kind of future awaits Jesus.[84] From the author's viewpoint, continuous and repeated instructions in the narratives where the Son of Man logia are located develop the understanding of the disciples, enlarging and deepening the disciples's knowledge and preparing them for what lies ahead. The history of Jesus narrated by Matthew determines the significance of the expression the Son of Man in an entirely new way. The Son of Man sayings do not so much interpret, but they pre-tell Jesus's history from his humility until his final exaltation and vindication.[85] In conclusion Luz states,

> There is no stage in the history of Jesus which is not commented upon by a son of the man saying. The "son of the man" therefore is a christological expression with a *horizontal dimension*, by means of which Jesus describes his way through history. . . . Closely connected with this horizontal dimension is its *universal dimension*. The story of Jesus the son of the man tells of his way from earthly life in Palestine until the point where he appears as judge over the whole Gentile world (24:30–31; 25:31–46).[86]

83. Luz, "Son of Man," 9–10.
84. Luz, "Son of Man," 10–14.
85. Luz, "Son of Man," 16–17.
86. Luz, "Son of Man," 18.

As the disciples and the community of faith were given these narrative reminders of the life and mission of the Son of Man, they grew in their understanding and practically fulfill his commission concerning these horizontal and universal dimensions.

With Geist, Luz is incorrect to assume that the locus of meaning of the Son of Man designation comes only with respect to the disciples and the community of faith. Luz also assumes that the meaning of the Son of Man logia occurs only after Peter's confession in 16:13 and, therefore, ignores Son of Man logia prior to 16:13. Like Kingsbury, Luz argues that Jesus's designation as Son of God plays a greater role in Matthew than the Son of Man, since, in their estimation, the term occurs in the most crucial contextual locations. However, as I stated previously, the structural argument of repetition highlights the importance of the Son of Man logia (thirty times) in contrast to the Son of God designation (nine times). I agree with Luz that the locus of meaning for the term is not solely located in Dan 7:13–14, since immediate and broader-book contextual evidence should have precedence over possible OT echoes. Luz suspiciously assigns Q as the main locus of meaning for the Son of Man designation. However, first, one should not be confident in Q as a certain source for the Son of Man designation; second, the Son of Man logia ought to gain their primary meaning from the context of individual Gospels rather than the Christian tradition. Luz's insistence on Q leads him down a faulty path by assigning a very broad understanding of the Son of Man in Matthew. The Son of Man sayings have a specific function in Matthew that is not congruent with such a mere general meaning. In addition, the Son of Man logia are not meant to "reflect the experiences and history of the post-Easter church";[87] rather, they emphasize Jesus's theological function in Matthew and the implications the Son of Man has for the disciples and community of faith. I will prove that the theological function of the Son of Man as *mediator* of God's will provides a holistic understanding of Jesus's ministry in Matthew and its implications for the present and future ministry of his disciples.

The previous scholarly views on the Son of Man designation in Matthew have not successfully provided a holistic, theological understanding of the Son of Man. A study that accounts for the entire Gospel of Matthew by providing a more complete understanding of the function of the Son of Man and the implications his ministry has for his disciples is needed.

---

87. Luz, "Son of Man," 10.

2.3. The Origin and Meaning of the Expression *Son of Man*

2.3.1. The Question of Origin

The origin of the expression *Son of Man* has not been conclusively proven among scholarship. Michael Goulder provides a strong argument that Ps 8:4-6 is behind the expression *Son of Man*. In his view, Ps 8 is the likely origin of the Son of Man because the answer was sought in Scripture, especially the Psalms, which he surveys in the Pauline epistles, Hebrews, and the Gospels. In his judgment, the Pauline epistles and Hebrews were written earlier than the Gospels. Therefore, since Ps 8 was used in earlier Christian tradition, it could be the source of the Son of Man in the Gospels.[88] Goulder states, "Ps 8 covers the Son of Man's whole history from before he was made briefly lower than the angels till his ultimate crowning with glory and honour, while Dan 7:13 speaks only of his authority and coming on the clouds."[89]

In regard to the Gospel of Matthew, the author records many OT prophetic fulfillment statements and uses the OT frequently; therefore, it would make sense that the expression *Son of Man* might find its background in Ps 8:4-6. Matthew uses the Psalms frequently in his Gospel and uses Ps 8:2 in 21:16.[90] In the LXX of Ps 8:5, "human" (ἄνθρωπος) is connected poetically with "son of humanity" (υἱὸς ἀνθρώπου). However, the verse suggests two different humans with "human" in v. 5a and with "or" (ἤ) preceding "son of humanity" in v. 5b. In vv. 6-7, the son of humanity is described as one who is temporarily ("for a short time" [βραχύ τι]) made lower than the angels and then crowned with glory and honor. He stands over the works of God's hands and all are subject to him under his feet. Such an understanding of the Son of Man (i.e., Son of Humanity) would fit well into Matthew's Gospel. In Matt 1:21-23, the author emphasizes Jesus's incarnation and highlighted his divine origin—he is God in human form, who came to earth to save his people from their sins. As Son of Man, he has the authority on earth to forgive people of their sins (Matt 9:6).[91] The humility suggested in being made temporarily

---

88. Goulder, "Psalm 8," 22-28.

89. Goulder, "Psalm 8," 29.

90. Other examples: Ps 91:11-12//Matt 4:6; Ps 78:2//Matt 13:35; Ps 118:25-26 and 148:1//Matt 21:9 and 23:39; Ps 118:22-23//Matt 21:42; Ps 110:1//Matt 22:44 and 26:64; Ps 22:18//Matt 27:35; Ps 22:1//27:46. Indirect references to the Psalms appear in other contexts: Ps 72:10//Matt 2:11; Ps 37:11//Matt 5:5; Ps 24:3-4//Matt 5:8; Ps 107:20//Matt 8:8; Ps 107:3//Matt 8:11; Ps 89:10 and 107:25-32//Matt 8:26; Ps 41:9//Matt 26:23; Ps 22:7-8, 16-18//Matt 26:24; Ps 42:6 and 43:5//Matt 26:38; Ps 27:12//Matt 26:60; Ps 26:6//Matt 27:24; Ps 22:7-8//Matt 27:29; Ps 69:21//Matt 27:34, 48; Ps 22:7 and 109:25//Matt 27:39.

91. See chapter 2 for further connection between Matt 1:21-23 and 9:1-8.

lower than the angels is clearly seen in the Son of Man's earthly ministry (cf. Matt 8:20; 11:19; 12:7–8 [9:13]); 12:40). In addition, the Son of Man's suffering and death emphasize his humility—his willingness to obey his Father's will and suffer and die to save his people from their sins (cf. Matt 16:21; 17:12, 22–23; 20:17–19, 28; 26:2, 24–28, 39, 42, 45, 54, 56). The Son of Man is crowned with glory and honor by being vindicated through his resurrection and exaltation (cf. 10:23; 16:21, 28; 17:9, 23; 20:19; [28:18–20]; 26:64). The Son of Man will stand over the works of God's hands and all will be subject under his feet when he comes as king, the eschatological judge of all humanity (cf. 13:36–43; 16:27; 19:28; 24:30–31; 25:31–34, 40; 26:64).

If the author of Matthew understood the origin of Jesus the Son of Man from Ps 8, this would align with the Christian tradition which made this connection already (esp. Heb 2:6–9), and established the notion that the expression *Son of Man* is a christological title since it indicates a divine origin. In my judgment, this is quite plausible as I have indicated in the context of Matthew. However, one should not rule out the possible connection to Dan 7:13–14, when viewing Jesus the Son of Man as the eschatological judge. Daniel 7:13 mentions "one like a son of man" coming with the clouds of heaven and given an eternal kingdom (v. 14). The historical Jesus knew Aramaic and the context of Matthew mentions Jesus the Son of Man coming on the clouds of heaven, establishing an eternal kingdom (cf. Matt 13:36–43; 19:28; 24:30; 26:64). In addition, the parousia of the Son of Man is more prominent in Matthew than the other Gospels.[92] The main problem with Dan 7:13–14 as the only origin of the Son of Man expression is the lack of connection to the Son of Man's earthly ministry and his suffering, death, and resurrection.

2.3.2. The Question of Meaning

The meaning of the expression *Son of Man* has been debated endlessly among scholars with no real consensus. In terms of etymology, it is important to mention that in Hebrew (בן אדם), Aramaic (בר נשא), and Greek (ὁ υἱὸς τοῦ ἀνθρώπου), the idiom can be translated "Son of Humanity," since אדם, נשא, and ἄνθρωπος can all be translated "human." In my estimation, the Son of Humanity is intimately connected with Jesus's relationships with humanity. In Matthew, God's relationship with humanity is mediated through Jesus who will save his people from their sins (cf. 1:21–23). Therefore, Jesus the Son of Man represents humans before God the Father. In Matthew, this representation is

---

92. Additional Son of Man references regarding the parousia which are not found in Mark or Luke: Matt 13:36–43; 19:28; 25:31.

emphasized in two main ways: (1) The Son of Man (i.e., Son of Humanity) is the mediator of salvation for human beings. Through his forgiveness of human sin which is culminated in his sacrificial death, he restores humanity's relationship with God the Father, which is God's will for all humanity (e.g., 1:21; 9:6; 20:28 [26:28]). (2) The Son of Man (i.e., Son of Humanity) is the mediator of God's will to a specific group of human beings, his present and future disciples. However, in many contexts in Matthew, the Son of Man's revelation of God's will through his message, works, and sacrificial death is offered indirectly to all humans. Those who accepted Jesus the Son of Man's message and works chose to follow him and were recipients of God's will through the mediatorial work of the Son of Man. Those who obeyed God's will as revealed through the Son of Man will be vindicated when he comes as eschatological judge at his parousia.

In regard to this thesis, the historical and traditional-critical line of inquiry is unimportant except in so far as it sets something of the parameters for the expression *Son of Man* as Matthew took it up and began to use it. However, the meaning of the expression as I have described it above is important in recognizing that the Son of Man is most likely a christological title which identifies him with humanity—the mediator of salvation for the purpose of restoring human's relationship with God the Father, and the mediator of God's will revealed to humans (specifically the disciples) for the purpose of their obedience to the divine will which prepares them for the eschaton.

3. The Method: New Redaction Criticism

Scholars have normally used source or redaction criticism to guide their interpretation of the Son of Man logia in Matthew. Because of their methodological commitments, they have argued for a reliance on Mark and Q, restricted the meaning of Son of Man logia from 16:13 onwards, emphasized the Son of Man's role primarily as judge, were unable to assign a specific role to the Son of Man, viewed the Son of Man simply as a representative figure of his disciples's mission, or interpreted the Son of Man logia as instructions to Jesus's addressees. I have already begun to show my hand, methodologically, by referring to the determinative role of Matthean context and the importance of a holistic grasp of Matthew's use of the phrase. Nevertheless, an emphasis on Matthew's unique contributions will provide interpretive guidance in my understanding of the Son of Man logia in the Matthean context. Therefore, I am using a newer form of redaction criticism in my analysis of the Son of Man references in Matthew. I will also utilize literary, composition, and social-scientific criticism.

New redaction criticism is concerned with how the writer has arranged his material in the Gospel to form his theology while comparing that arrangement with the other Synoptic Gospels. The main advantage of new redaction criticism lies in its emphasis on discovering the writer's own distinctive theological understanding of the material he has included and the implications of its meaning in the Gospel.

The older version of redaction criticism emphasized how an author utilized specific sources and then arranged and/or modified those sources into his material. New redaction criticism is focused primarily on how the author arranged his own material to form its theological meaning(s), while comparing the author's arrangement with the arrangement of other Synoptic writers.

Source criticism is concerned primarily with the different sources an author uses to arrange his material (e.g., the influences of the Gospel of Mark, Q, and other ancient Jewish literature), and what theological implications are discovered through the author's utilization of these sources. In contrast, new redaction criticism does not rely on source material but is concerned with how a writer arranged his material irrespective of his putative sources. In other words, the author has his own voice and, through his own contextual arrangement, provides his own theological interpretation of Jesus's life and ministry, and the implications of Jesus's life and ministry for readers and hearers of his material.

New redaction criticism is different from reader-response criticism because readers do not produce the meaning of the text; the writer does. Through the arrangement of his material, comparison with other Synoptic Gospels, and the particular emphasis on the author's distinct contribution to meaning, new redaction criticism concerns the context of his own literature and not the reader's viewpoint as the means of discovering meaning. Reader-response criticism places too much emphasis on the role of the reader, possibly leading to faulty interpretation based on the reader's own cultural, social, and belief systems, which may not have been the original intention of the author when composing his Gospel.[93]

An important overlap exists between new redaction criticism, literary criticism, and compositional criticism. In literary criticism the emphasis is on the literary conventions of the biblical material and the significance of these conventions for meaning. The way the author structured his material, the form he employs, the terms he chose to use, and the literary

---

93. Vanhoozer, "Reader in New Testament," 301, 302, 304–5.

arrangements he uses all contribute to textual meaning.⁹⁴ In compositional criticism, the concern is directed to the author's organizational schemes (e.g., placement of pericopes) and how they help to establish meaning. New redaction criticism focuses on all these interpretive strategies since they stress the author's role in developing meaning in the text; they allow the author's own voice to be heard. New redaction criticism is concerned with how the author has arranged his material to form his theology—very close to the aims of literary and compositional criticism. However, new redaction criticism is additionally concerned with the distinctive theological understanding of the author *in comparison* to the other Synoptic Gospels. The differences between the Gospels are highlighted, while special attention is given to the material not found in the other Synoptic Gospels. Any Synoptic difference located in the context of the material is where the author's distinctive theological message especially shines.

Mark Goodacre critiques older forms of redaction criticism when he says, "Redaction criticism without consideration of broader narrative context in the Gospels, and the literary agenda of the evangelists is, in the end, a blunted instrument that can only detract from our appreciation of the Gospels and their writers."⁹⁵ When speaking about the Gospel writers, Goodacre states, "Whether or not one believes that Luke read Matthew, all agree that these two evangelists had different aims, different perspectives, different theological tendencies, and different literary techniques. Naturally they order their material differently—this is, after all, one of the things that make a work distinctive."⁹⁶ The aim of new redaction criticism is to examine what makes an author's message distinct, different, and his own. A clear access to meaning can arise from analyzing the author's material in comparison with the other Synoptic Gospels.

I have chosen new redaction criticism for the interpretive method of this monograph because I am convinced that the writer of Matthew had a distinctive understanding of the function of the Son of Man in his Gospel. This method of interpretation will help in highlighting the differences between the Synoptic Gospels and, consequently, emphasizing the unique contributions that Matthew's Gospel brings to the function of the Son of Man in the contexts analyzed. By utilizing new redaction criticism, along with literary, compositional, and social-scientific methods, I will be equipped to study the Son of Man logia in Matthew in a way which will help provide answers to how the author develops his theology of the Son of

---

94. McKnight, "Literary Criticism," 473, 478.

95. Goodacre, *Case against Q*, 145.

96. Goodacre, *Case against Q*, 85–86.

Man in his entire Gospel. New redaction and related literary criticisms will allow me the needed freedom necessary to pursue my analysis of the theological implications of the Son of Man's mediatorial role; namely, how Jesus reveals and demonstrates God's will and the implications his mediatorial role has for the disciples and their future ministry. Specifically, Jesus's role as mediator will provide greater understanding of the reasons for obedient discipleship which is so significant in Matthew's theology of the Son of Man.

In utilizing the new redaction criticism method, I will examine the contexts surrounding the Son of Man logia in Matthew. A study of the contexts in which the Son of Man is discussed in Matthew is essential in discovering the function of Jesus as the Son of Man. A concern for how the contexts of the Son of Man logia in Matthew are different from the other Synoptic Gospels is important for highlighting the author's distinctive theology of the Son of Man. Literary, compositional, and social-scientific approaches will aid in understanding the contextual material surrounding the Son of Man sayings and will also help highlight the arrangement of the author's material and the social implications that helped tailor his theological thought.

4. The Role of the Son of Man as *Mediator*

I argue that Matthew emphasizes Jesus the Son of Man's mediatory role more and differently than the other Synoptic Gospels. With the prevalence of the Son of Man logia in Matt 8–26, Jesus's mediatorial role can be discovered in his earthly ministry, his passion predictions and other material relating to his suffering, death, and vindication, and in light of his imminent parousia. The Son of Man's role as mediator in Matthew emphasizes how the disciples can fulfill God the Father's will through a close, obedient relationship with his Father in the heavens. Jesus the Son of Man is the go-between in the relationship of the disciples and his Father the one in the heavens. He revealed and demonstrated what is necessary in obeying God's will. In addition, the Son of Man's mediatorial role is accentuated in revealing and demonstrating God's grace and mercy to his disciples specifically and to humanity generally throughout his earthly ministry, finding climax in his sacrificial death.

A mediator's role is to establish an eternal relationship with God and exemplify a holy character that would be imitated by his followers. Jesus becomes the source and model of how his ministry is to be emulated in the present and future ministry of his disciples. He presents his own redemptive mission as the prototypical ministry of the disciples. Jesus is deliberately set on inaugurating a new priesthood different from the old; the cultic service is linked to upbuilding a community nurtured by the life of its Savior.[97] Through Jesus's mediation, God's action and presence are disclosed to all. Jesus manifests divine holiness and seeks, by entering the world, to transform it. Jesus characterizes the function of the priestly minister, who carries out ritual and a cultic role, through his sacrificial death and as the universal judge by establishing representatives on earth who will lead a new community of priests.[98] The power and authority of Jesus is emphasized not in seeking his own advantage but in giving of his own life unreservedly for the sake of others. In contrast to what is expected by the Son of the Man as portrayed in the book of Daniel (e.g., 7:13–14), Jesus the Son of Man makes his life a service for humankind; for him, service entails the sacrifice of his entire life. As Son of Man, Jesus's role is to reveal to the disciples how they are to conduct themselves in the world; describing the way in which they are to exercise authority.[99]

Unlike the OT where the priestly functions are separate, in the NT Jesus conjoins the prophetic, cultic, and royal functions. Jesus's prophetic role is emphasized through his mission to teach the good news of redeeming love.[100] This work of proclamation culminates in the supreme witness of Jesus's ultimate sacrifice. Jesus's cultic role is demonstrated through offering his whole life as a sacrifice for humanity, which reaches climax in Jesus's sacrificial death. Jean Galot states, "Mediator, the new title applied to Jesus, is grounded precisely upon the act in which he gives himself as a ransom for all. It is because of this gift of his own self that he is the universal mediator."[101] Jesus's life-giving mission reaches its climax in his suffering and death.[102] His royal role is emphasized through his function as messianic king. Jesus expressed this through his authority to lead and establish his disciples, in a general sense, the church, and to provide a nonexclusive love through his sacrifice and life. Jesus's mission entails gathering a community that will continue to increase in numbers and will reach out to those who are still on the outside.

Jesus's covenantal promise is expressed through Jesus's dedication to the Twelve but is extended to all of humankind. The Twelve were the embodiment of the covenant. They were assigned the mediating position, by imitating the life of Jesus, and were the first recipients of this new priesthood.

97. Galot, *Theology*, 25, 34–36.
98. Galot, *Theology*, 38–41.
99. Galot, *Theology*, 43–45.
100. I will argue that Jesus's prophetic role is emphasized primarily through revealing the necessary requirements in obeying God's will.
101. Galot, *Theology*, 142.
102. I will argue that the Son of Man's passion predictions and passion material demonstrates the self-denying lifestyle required in obeying God's will.

Jesus intended to hand over this priestly power to the Twelve, so they could evangelize the world with the life and message of Jesus.[103]

Throughout Matthew, the Son of Man's presence, authority, and power among the disciples and the community as a whole are clearly portrayed. Matthew's Son of Man clearly demonstrates the conjoining of the roles of a mediating figure. In his life, death, resurrection, and exaltation, the Son of Man is the Father in heaven's chosen and anointed prophet, priest, and king. The Son of Man is preparing his disciples to take over his mediatory role as they emulate his words and deeds of redeeming love in the world.

5. Filling in the Gaps: The Thesis of This Project

I have demonstrated the need to extend the scholarly conversation about the Son of Man in Matthew. Much of the scholarly discussion regarding the Son of Man in Matthew has tended to assume a minimal significance for Jesus's function as the Son of Man or confined his role to eschatological judge. If these theological gaps are not filled, then one is left wondering what contribution, if any, the Son of Man logia have in Jesus's earthly ministry, passion predictions and the other passion literature, and what they suggest about Jesus's function as the Son of Man in Matthew. This monograph will fill these gaps by providing a clearer and more specific study of the function of the Son of Man in Matthew and how such an analysis will further the theological implications for this all-important designation.

I will argue that Jesus the Son of Man's function in Matthew is as *mediator* of God's will to his disciples. The Son of Man is the go-between in relationship to God the Father and the disciples, teaching them God's will and demonstrating the kind of lifestyle necessary in obeying God's will. When the Son of Man returns at his parousia, promised vindication and reward will be granted to faithful disciples who have emulated the Son of Man in their obedience to God's will. The Son of Man encourages his faithful disciples to endure in their obedience of God's will throughout times of persecution and temptation to disregard God's will for their lives and ministry.

My investigation into the function of the Son of Man in Matthew will be organized in three subsequent chapters. In each chapter, I will structure each section as follows: First, provide a textual orientation to situate the Son of Man saying in its immediate context. Second, compare the Son of Man saying(s) in Matthew with the other Synoptic Gospels. Third, present an exegetical analysis on the function of the Son of Man in that particular section, and fourth, summarize the role the Son of Man plays

---

103. Galot, *Theology*, 45–50, 74–77, 87.

in mediating God's will to his disciples. In chapter 2, I will investigate the Son of Man sayings that refer to Jesus's earthly ministry (Matt 8–12). I will argue that the Son of Man's function as mediator involves revealing God's will to his disciples. The Son of Man prophetically teaches his disciples the kind of behavior necessary to fulfill God's will in their present and future ministries. In chapter 3, I will investigate the Son of Man sayings that refer to Jesus's suffering, death, and exaltation (Matt 16:13–28; 17:1–23; 20:17–28; 26:1–56). I will argue that the Son of Man's function as mediator involves demonstrating God's will to his disciples. The Son of Man's priestly function of self-denying sacrifice and servanthood for the sake of others in obedience to God's will demonstrates to his disciples the kind of self-denying sacrifice and servanthood necessary in obeying God's will in their present and future ministry. In chapter 4, I will investigate the Son of Man sayings that refer to Jesus's imminent parousia (Matt 13:24–30, 36–43; 16:13–27; 19:16–30; 24:3–51; 25:31–46; 26:57–68). I will argue that the Son of Man's function as mediator involves promising future vindication and reward for faithful disciples who have obeyed God's will in their ministry and life. The Son of Man's kingly function as judge will occur at his imminent parousia when he will vindicate and reward his faithful followers for their obedience to God's will and will punish those who have rejected God and his will throughout their lives. In chapter 5, I will summarize how the present study has expanded Matthean research on the Son of Man, and how I have effectively argued that the Son of Man's function in Matthew is as mediator of God's will for his disciples.

Chapter 2

The Son of Man's Mediatorial Significance on Earth

Revealing God's Will to Genuine Disciples

1. Introduction

PREVIOUS SCHOLARSHIP IN MATTHEAN studies demonstrates a limited understanding of the Son of Man passages relating to Jesus's life on earth. Many times, concentrating on the latter part of the Gospel, scholars emphasize the Son of Man's role as judge in Matthew rather than expressing a holistic comprehension of the Son of Man's role in the entire Gospel. An analysis of the Son of Man passages in Matt 8–12, relating to his earthly ministry, and Matt 16–17, 20, and 26, relating to his suffering and death, provides a more holistic view. This chapter examines Matt 8–12, concentrating on a Matthean understanding of the role of the Son of Man as mediator of God's will to his genuine disciples during his life on earth.

As Son of Man in Matthew, Jesus fulfilled the role of mediator of God's will on earth to his disciples. Many of Matthew's passages identifying Jesus as the Son of Man on earth relate to the theme of discipleship. Jesus fulfilled God's will throughout Matthew and revealed it to his disciples through teaching and praxis, emphasizing what was necessary to follow the Father's divine will. Similarly, if the disciples adhere to God's will by following the example of the Son of Man, they will continue his mission effectively. However, apart from the Son of Man, the disciples could neither know nor understand God's will for them in the present or future and were, therefore, unable to practice God's will. I will demonstrate the Son of Man's revelation of God's will to his disciples by specifically examining Matt 8–12, while showing how this theme is demonstrated in the Gospel as a whole. Moreover, I will also show how Mark and Luke fail to present this revelation of God's will with the same emphasis and intentionality as in Matthew.

2. The Son of Man as Mediator of God's Will on Earth in Matthew

2.1. The Inclusio: ποιήσῃ τὸ θέλημα τοῦ πατρός μου τοῦ ἐν οὐρανοῖς in Matthew 7:21 and 12:50

The phrase ποιήσῃ τὸ θέλημα τοῦ πατρός μου τοῦ ἐν οὐρανοῖς is unique to Matthew; Mark and Luke do not use it. Matthew 12:50 is a structural *inclusio* with 7:21. In 7:21 the phrase ὁ ποιῶν τὸ θέλημα τοῦ πατρός μου τοῦ ἐν τοῖς οὐρανοῖς is almost identical to 12:50 and found nowhere else in Matthew. Matthew 7:21-27 is the last teaching unit of the Sermon on the Mount (5:1—7:29). Therefore, it serves as Jesus's final teaching of this discourse and as an introduction to Jesus's public ministry section, which culminates in 12:46-50. Since Matthew's Son of Man occurrences relating to his earthly ministry occur within this section (8:1—12:50), the will of God the Father can be seen as the central theme in Jesus the Son of Man's earthly ministry. Matthew highlights that the Son of Man serves as the mediator of God's will on earth. Those who obey God's will through Jesus's ministry are his true family (i.e., genuine disciples) who can thus authentically claim him as their Lord.

2.2. God's Will to Genuine Disciples: Self-Relinquishment (Matthew 8:18–22)

2.2.1. Textual Orientation

A scribe and a disciple approached Jesus, claiming they wanted to follow him. Jesus the Son of Man told the scribe that following him meant leaving one's home behind. He told the disciple that he could not bury his father and insisted that following him meant leaving behind one's family obligations. Following Jesus requires leaving everything and everyone behind.

2.2.2. Synoptic Comparison: Matthew 8:18–22 and Luke 9:57–62

The description of following Jesus in Matt 8:18-22 is paralleled in Luke 9:57-62 and absent in Mark. Luke's account has a different agenda from Matthew's since its primary focus is on the kingdom of God (Luke 9:60, 62). Luke stresses the need to preach the kingdom of God and the lack of preparedness for the kingdom of God.[1] From Luke's perspective, following Jesus means focusing on the work and readiness for the kingdom of God. However, Matthew's account focuses primarily on the term *follow* (ἀκολουθέω). Although Luke's account uses the term ἀκολουθέω three times (9:57, 59, 61), Matthew forms an *inclusio* with ἀκολουθέω (8:19, 22). This *inclusio* emphasizes following the Son of Man as the pericope's central theme. Matthew does not mention the missional focus regarding the kingdom of God, which is prevalent in Luke's account. David R. Bauer helpfully demonstrates that one of the main structural features in Matthew is the repetition of comparison between the ministry of Jesus and the ministry of his disciples.[2] This comparison strengthens my argument that Jesus the Son of Man is the mediator of God's will in Matthew. As the Son of Man relinquishes all earthly resources to follow God's will, the scribe and disciple are to do likewise if they are to be genuine disciples. Leaving behind earthly resources demonstrates the call of itinerant missionary work, which, seen in Matt 10, is the call to genuine discipleship.

In addition, Luke does not mention the Father's will. Luke includes Matt 6:10 and 7:21–23 in Luke 11:1–4 and 6:46–49, but in Matthew, unlike Luke, knowing the Father's will is essential in understanding the life of discipleship. In Matt 7:21–23, being under Jesus's authority requires that one does the Father's will. The only way a disciple of Jesus can accomplish the Father's will is to follow Jesus the Son of Man wherever he may go.[3]

A unique emphasis resides in the structure of chapter 8. Matt 8:18–22 is placed in the middle of stories of miraculous healing (e.g., the cleansing of the leper, 8:1–4; the healing of the centurion's son, 8:5–13; the healing of Peter's mother-in-law, 8:14–15; the healing of demon-possessed and sick people, 8:16–17) and, after 8:18–22, the exorcism of the demon-possessed

---

1. Green, *Gospel of Luke*, 407; Johnson, *Gospel*, 163. Johnson provides an important exegetical marker from the broader book context, namely, that the emphasis on preaching the kingdom of God is central to the disciples's commission in 9:2, 6, which is demonstrated to them by Jesus in 9:11. Marshall, *Gospel of Luke*, 411–12; Bock, *Luke*, 2:982, 984. Carroll says, "A distinctive feature of the Lukan presentation of the kingdom is its association with verbs of proclamation. Fully one-fourth of all Lukan occurrences of the expression 'kingdom of God' take this form" (*Response to the End*, 81).

2. Bauer, *Structure of Matthew's Gospel*, 57–60.

3. Note the emphasis on the immediate (εὐθέως) response of Peter, Andrew, James, and John when Jesus called them to follow him in 4:18–25 and 9:9. They left their earthly attachments and immediately followed Jesus. Jesus's disciples are called to come under his authority as Lord. In 4:25; 8:1, 10, the crowds also followed Jesus because of his miracles. In 8:2, 6, 8, 21, 25; 9:28; 14:28–30; 7:15; 20:31–33; 21:30; 25:11, 20–24, 44; 26:22, sick people called Jesus Lord (κύριε), indicating their need to submit to his authority. Jesus's authority and lordship are substantiated through his earthly ministry and are prominent in Matthew.

man (8:28–34). However, Luke 9:57–62 focuses more on mission as Jesus commissioned his disciples to emulate his ministry by proclaiming the kingdom of God and healing people. Luke also highlights Jesus's mission in the near future—his upcoming sacrificial death on the cross. Once again the agendas of the Gospels are different. The healing stories in Matt 8 are meant to highlight the authority and lordship of Jesus. In 8:4, 13, 32, *go* (ὑπάγω) is in the imperative, emphasizing Jesus's command that the leper go see the priest, that the centurion return home to his servant, and that the demons flee the demon-possessed man. Their immediate obedience to Jesus's command "to go [away]" demonstrates the authority of Jesus. In 8:2, 6, 8, 21, 25, the leper, centurion, and Jesus's disciples called Jesus "Lord" (κύριε) when speaking to him and requesting his help. Different from Luke, Matthew points to Jesus the Son of Man's authority and lordship, an important emphasis in this Gospel.

2.2.3. *Exegesis*

One of the primary ways to understand the call to genuine discipleship is in considering the difference between the scribe and disciple who came to Jesus. In Matthew, the identity of these individuals is important; however, in Luke's account, the individuals are generic and unknown.

The scribe made a promise to follow Jesus wherever he went. Scholars debate the legitimacy of the scribe's discipleship, holding three main views. First, many believe the scribe was a genuine follower of Jesus.[4] Matthew does not connect the scribe in 8:19 with scribes who were enemies of Jesus (i.e., "one of *their* scribes" in 7:29). Matthew implies that the scribe was a genuine follower from the matching phrase "and *another* of his disciples" (i.e., ἕτερος in 8:21). In 13:52 and 23:34, scribes (γραμματεύς) have a positive association with Jesus's disciples. The scribe addressed Jesus in a positive manner by calling him "Teacher" (διδάσκαλε), a reference Jesus used of himself in 10:24–25; 23:8; and 26:18. Finally, in 8:19 and 21, the scribe's and the other disciple's intent was to follow Jesus, which is characteristic of a genuine disciple. The scribe made the promise to follow him. Second, some scholars believe the scribe was a would-be follower of Jesus.[5] Jesus

---

4. Gundry, *Matthew*, 151–52; Lagrange, *Évangile*, 171; Hummel, *Kirche und Judentum*, 27; Fenton, *St. Matthew*, 128; McNeile, *Gospel according to St. Matthew*, 108–9; Walker, *Heilsgeschichte*, 27; Grundmann, *Evangelium nach Matthäus*, 258; Hill, *Matthew*, 162; Schweizer, *Good News*, 218–20.

5. Manson, *Sayings of Jesus*, 72; Morris, *Gospel*, 200; Turner, *Matthew*, 238–39; Harrington, *Matthew*, 119; Osborne, *Matthew*, 304; Hagner, *Matthew*, 1:216.

did not call the scribe "one of their scribes" (7:29). In 8:21 the scribe may be combined with "another [ἕτερος] of his disciples," but by calling Jesus "Teacher" in 8:19, he placed himself outside the disciples's circle since he did not call him Lord (κύριε) as did the disciple in 8:21. The term *another* (ἕτερος) in 8:21 seems to suggest that the scribe in 8:19 might have been a follower of Jesus in some sense of the word. However, Jesus's response in 8:20 indicates that the scribe had not counted the cost of discipleship, making his commitment superficial. Matthew 8:18–22 connects the issue of self-relinquished discipleship with 8:23–27 when the disciple apparently followed Jesus into the boat, which the scribe did not seem to do. Finally, the scribe's statement, "I will follow you wherever you might go," in 8:19 appears initially to be genuine (as in 13:52; 23:24) but is uncertain in light of Jesus's response in 8:20.

Third, some scholars believe the scribe was not a genuine follower of Jesus.[6] This view is the most plausible explanation for the following reasons. Except for 13:52 and 23:34, every reference to scribes in Matthew portrays them as Jesus's enemies. Prior to Matt 8:19, scribes were associated with King Herod who assembled them with the chief priests and asked them what the prophets said about where the Christ was to be born (2:1–6). The angel told Joseph that King Herod sought to kill Jesus (2:13). When deceived by the magi, King Herod gave orders to kill all male children two years old and younger, hoping to kill Jesus (2:16). Finally, the angel reappeared to Joseph and told him that King Herod was dead (2:19). Their association with King Herod indicates that the scribes were joining King Herod in opposing God's will. In 5:19–20, Jesus warned his disciples that the scribes and Pharisees exemplify those who break the commandments and teach others to do the same. Such people are called "least in the kingdom of the heavens" (v. 19). Then he told the disciples that their "righteousness must exceed that of the scribes and Pharisees" if they want to "enter the kingdom of the heavens" (v. 20). Jesus's warning suggests that the scribes and Pharisees did not have the kind of righteous character that genuine disciples must have; specifically, they opposed God's will through breaking his commandments and teaching others to do the same. In 7:29, the crowds contrast the scribes with Jesus. They were amazed because Jesus taught with authority (ἐξουσία) unlike their scribes. Such a contrast portrays the scribes in a negative light. After 8:19, the broader book context continues to place the scribes in a negative light as those who oppose Jesus and God's will. They participated in challenging Jesus's teaching (15:1–9), miracles (12:38–39), divine claims

---

6. Kingsbury, "On Following Jesus," 45–59; France, *Matthew*, 325–26; Gnilka, *Matthäusevangelium*, 1:310–11; Gibbs, *Matthew 1:1—11:1*, 430; Davies and Allison, *Matthew*, 2:41–42; Luz, *Matthew 8–20*, 17; Byrskog, *Jesus the Only Teacher*, 240.

(21:15-17), and authority (9:3-7); they killed divine messengers (17:10-12; 23:29-39); attempted to prevent others from accepting Jesus (23:13-15); planned Jesus's execution (16:21; 17:10-13; 20:18-19; 26:57-59); and mocked him while on the cross (27:41-44). Jesus warned his disciples not to follow their evil actions (23:1-7, 23).

In 8:19 a scribe promised to follow Jesus even though doing so would require self-renunciation. The scribe must follow the Son of Man by relinquishing present status, position, and livelihood to follow him. Jesus condemned the Pharisees and scribes for their thirst for status and recognition in 23:6-7, and revealed that their hearts are filled with greed[7] and self-indulgence in 23:25-26, which would indicate the scribe's unwillingness to follow Jesus. The scribe in 8:19 did not commit to following Jesus's obedience to God's will, since he would then be required to renounce his status and position and submit to Jesus's self-relinquishing lifestyle.[8] The scribe had not thought out the commitment of discipleship; therefore, he had no comprehension of a long-term commitment.

Kingsbury believes the key evidence against the scribe's genuine discipleship is that Jesus did not call him to become a disciple (as he initiated in 4:18-20, 21-22; 9:9); rather, the scribe initiated the desire to follow Jesus himself.[9] In my judgment, the Gospel's characterization of scribes as persons who reject Jesus and oppose God's will is a stronger argument. Jarmo Kiilunen states, "In der Kingsburyschen Deutung . . . doch künstliche Gegenüberstellung in den Text projiziert wird. Kingsbury ist zu seiner Interpretation aufgrund eines Vergleichs von 8:18-20 mit 4:18-22 und 9:9 gekommen. Es werden aber dabei Texte gegeneinandergestellt, die unterschiedliche Intentionen verfolgen."[10] Kiilunen is correct to question whether Kingsbury can adequately compare 4:18-22 and 9:9 with 8:18-20 based on their contexts.

---

7. The Greek phrase ἔσωθεν δὲ γέμουσιν ἐξ ἁρπαγῆς could be interpreted with reference to the Pharisees and scribes: "But inside they are full of robbery or from plunder," emphasizing their desire for accumulating goods or money in an unjust manner—consequently highlighting their self-absorption and greedy hearts.

8. The scribe can be compared with the rich man in 19:16-30 who appeared faithful in obeying the Mosaic law but was told by Jesus to also sell everything he had, give to the poor, and then follow him. The rich man refused to obey and follow Jesus due to his possessions. In contrast, the disciples had given up everything to follow Jesus. Jesus stated that anyone who gives up everything, including material and relational attachments, to follow him would receive the reward of eternal life. Genuine followers are those who "do the will of the Father in the heavens" (cf. 7:21-23; 12:46-50).

9. Kingsbury, "On Following Jesus," 49.

10. Kiilunen, "Nachfolgewillige Schriftgelehrte," 272-73.

Kingsbury's case is stronger when stating that by calling Jesus "Teacher," the scribe has positioned himself "outside" those who are considered followers of Jesus. Those who call Jesus "Lord" are usually those "inside" the discipleship circle.[11] Therefore, the scribe is characterized differently from the disciple who wants first to bury his father (8:21).[12] Unlike the scribe who referred only to Jesus as Teacher (διδάσκαλε), this disciple referred to him as Lord (κύριε). In Matthew, the vocative κύριε is a title given to Jesus by those who had faith in Jesus and responded to him positively (cf. 8:2–13; 9:28–29; 15:21–28; 17:14–21; 20:29–34), including those who were part of his disciple circle (cf. 8:23–27; 13:27; 14:28–30; 16:22; 17:4–8; 18:21–22). In 26:17–25, Judas, the one who betrayed Jesus, called Jesus "Rabbi" (ῥαββί; 26:25, 48–49) while the other disciples referred to Jesus as κύριε (26:22). Therefore, the scribe's desire to follow Jesus does not seem genuine.

The disciple asked Jesus the Son of Man if he could first go and bury his father. Even though the disciple's request seems forceful (ἐπιτρέπω is in the imperative), this command appears to be due to the desire to honor his father.[13] Therefore, Jesus's disciple deliberately put himself under Jesus's authority by asking if he could first care for his family. The context does not reveal whether this disciple did leave his family and follow Jesus. However, the disciple's reference to Jesus as "Lord" suggests that he was prepared to follow Jesus and leave the dead behind. Günther Bornkamm properly identifies Matt 8:23–27 as a practical expression of genuine discipleship: "The story becomes a kerygmatic paradigm of the danger and glory of discipleship."[14] Genuine disciples followed Jesus into the stormy sea (8:23–27) and, when in trouble, called out to him as "Lord" for help (8:25). Since the disciple in 8:21

---

11. Kingsbury, "On Following Jesus," 51–52. See also Byrskog, *Jesus the Only Teacher*, 240.

12. The term ἕτερος can indicate a difference in kind and translated as "another man, one of his disciples" (Davies and Allison, *Matthew*, 2:54). Schweizer states that the term πρῶτον in 8:21 indicates that this disciple will follow him later (*Good News*, 220). Nolland argues that ἕτερος indicates a different person since the scribe is never identified as a disciple (*Matthew*, 367, 367n85). Byrskog asserts that "in correlation to εἷς γραμματεύς, the narrator uses ἕτερος δὲ τῶν μαθητῶν in 8:21, not, as would be more consistent, ἕτερος δὲ μαθητής. This could imply that only the second actor is one of the disciples" (*Jesus the Only Teacher*, 240).

13. Kingsbury says, "The obligation of a son such as the disciple to look after the burial of his parents was a particularly sacred one in ancient Judaism (cf. Tob 4.3; 6.16). It derived from Moses's command to honor one's father and mother (Exod 20:12; Deut 5:16)" ("On Following Jesus,"54). Ben Witherington III surmises that various Jewish texts indicate that the duty to bury someone supersedes even the most binding of religious obligations (*m. Ber.* 3:1; Tob 6:13), all the more when dealing with a member of one's own family (*Matthew*, 188).

14. Bornkamm, "Stilling of the Storm," 57.

also called Jesus "Lord," this comparison may substantiate the possibility that he left his father behind and followed Jesus into the boat. Matthew's different characterization of the scribe and the disciple seems to highlight the Son of Man's insistence that genuine disciples follow God's will by abandoning previous attachments of family, status, position, and location in order to go where he leads (cf. 4:18–22; 9:9; 16:24–26; 19:16–30). The call to obey God's will is apparent in Jesus's missionary commissioning in 10:5–15, 37–39 when Jesus insisted that the disciples were not to bring possessions with them and were to place missionary work ahead of family members. In this way, Jesus the Son of Man becomes the mediator between God's will and genuine discipleship by instructing the disciples what following him entails. A genuine disciple must be willing to abandon all for the sake of following Jesus to obey God's will. The emphasis on God's will for genuine discipleship was highlighted previously in 6:10 and 7:21–23.

The Son of Man's statement that he has no place to lay his head in 8:20 serves as an invitation to discipleship. To follow after the Son of Man in self-renunciation is to experience his grace—a divine opportunity to discover God's will as mediated through Jesus the Son of Man's own praxis. The decision to receive this grace is dependent upon an individual's response: the scribe appeared to reject the Son of Man's offer, while the genuine disciple seemed to accept his invitation and followed the other disciples into the boat.

The contrast between the titles "Teacher" and "Lord" spoken by the scribe and the genuine disciple highlights the Son of Man's identity. He is the Lord. In the context of chapter 8, an emphasis is placed on Jesus's authoritative word. In 8:8–9, the statement of the centurion regarding Jesus's authority emphasizes the importance of obedience to his word. In 8:16, Jesus cast out spirits by his words. In 8:18, Jesus told his disciples to go to the other side and they obeyed his word (cf. 8:23–28). In 8:26, Jesus spoke a word of rebuke against the storm and stilled the wind and waves. Even nature obeyed Jesus's authoritative word. In 8:20, the Son of Man spoke the word—his self-renunciation and focus on itinerant ministry demonstrated his obedience. Therefore, genuine disciples were to follow his lead. The disciple recognized, at some level, that the Son of Man is a person of authority. To come underneath the Son of Man's lordship would require following him *first*, leaving all behind to enter into genuine discipleship. The Son of Man could reveal God's will to his disciples as they recognized his identity—he is the Lord. To follow the Son of Man is to submit to his authority, who reveals God's will that discipleship entails a life of self-renunciation. The Son of Man mediated to his disciples that genuine discipleship is an invitation to submit to God's will—namely, complete self-renunciation of earthly concerns to follow after Jesus in his earthly ministry.

Later in Matthew, the Son of Man's passion predictions (cf. 16:21; 17:22–23; 20:17–19; 26:2) and his role as the servant who gives "his life as a ransom for the many" (20:28 [cf. "the blood of the covenant shed for many for the forgiveness of sins" in 26:28]), emphasizes his mission of self-renunciation of worldly interest and sacrificing his life to serve others, delivering them from sin. Similarly, the disciples will be called to be willing to relinquish not only home but life to follow God's will (cf. 16:21–26). Matthew 8:20 helps to solidify Jesus the Son of Man's role as the mediator of God's will on earth.

Matthew 8:18–22 identifies the role of Jesus the Son of Man as mediator of God's will on earth. In Matthew, a genuine disciple of Jesus obeys him by following the requirement of self-relinquishment of all earthly attachments in doing the Father's will on earth. By calling Jesus the Son of Man "Lord," the disciple recognized at some level that Jesus was the Lord and, consequently, most likely accepted his invitation of grace—to follow him by committing to a life of renunciation. In addition, in light of his own upcoming suffering and death, Jesus taught his disciples and the crowds that giving up everything and everyone to follow Jesus is required to accomplish God's will on earth.

2.3. God's Will to Genuine Disciples: The Necessity of Faith (Matthew 9:1–8)

2.3.1. Textual Orientation

Jesus and his disciples entered his own city. Some people brought Jesus a paralytic. When Jesus saw their faith, he told the paralytic that his sins were forgiven. Some scribes said among themselves that Jesus was blaspheming. Jesus perceived their evil thoughts and healed the paralytic to demonstrate that he had authority on earth to forgive sins. After Jesus commanded the paralytic to rise up, pick up his stretcher, and go home, he did so immediately. The crowds were afraid and glorified God for giving such authority to humans.

2.3.2. Synoptic Comparison: Matthew 9:1–8; Mark 2:1–12; and Luke 5:17–26

The narrative of a paralytic's need for healing and Jesus's gift of forgiveness of sins is recorded in all of the Synoptic Gospels (Matt 9:1–9; Mark

2:1-12; Luke 5:17-26). However, in Mark and Luke the paralytic is lowered through the roof of the house. Only Matthew mentions that the paralytic was brought to Jesus with no mention of his being in a house. The Matthean account of this narrative is much shorter than the others. Unlike Mark and Luke, Matthew emphasizes the evil in the scribes's hearts, does not mention the scribes's claim that only God forgives sins, and places a stronger emphasis on the Son of Man's authority (twice in 9:6, 8).

2.3.3. Exegesis

Throughout Matt 8-10, the themes of human faith (πίστις) in Jesus (8:1-13; 9:18-34) and the authority (ἐξουσία) of Jesus as the Son of Man (8:14-17, 23-34; 9:9-13; 10:1-31) are strongly emphasized. Both provide a broader understanding of Matt 9:1-9.

Matthew 9:1-2 emphasizes Jesus's seeing the faith of those who brought the paralytic (and possibly the paralytic himself).[15] In 9:2b-4, Matthew contrasts the faith of those who brought the paralytic (and possibly the paralytic himself) with the thoughts of evil in the hearts (ἐνθυμεῖσθε πονηρὰ ἐν ταῖς καρδίαις ὑμῶν) of the scribes. Jesus affirmed the faith of those who brought the paralytic and believed in his ability to heal, and condemned the evil of the scribes who charged him with blasphemy for claiming that he could forgive sins. As stated previously, Matthew does not mention that the authority to forgive sins comes from God alone. However, God's authority is implied through his negative response to blasphemy by the scribes when Jesus claimed and then demonstrated that he has "authority to forgive sins" in vv. 6-7.[16] Throughout Matthew, the Pharisees, Sadducees, scribes, and

---

15. Scholars are divided in their view of τὴν πίστιν αὐτῶν in 9:2. Some believe that τὴν πίστιν αὐτῶν refers only to the ones who brought the paralytic. See Gundry, *Matthew*, 162; Harrington, *Matthew*, 121; Blomberg, *Matthew*, 153; Nolland, *Matthew*, 380; Luz, *Matthew 8-20*, 27; Hare, *Matthew*, 99. Others argue that τὴν πίστιν αὐτῶν refers both to the ones who brought the paralytic and the paralytic himself. See Hagner, *Matthew*, 1:232; France, *Matthew*, 344; Keener, *Gospel of Matthew*, 288; Morris, *Gospel*, 214; Osborne, *Matthew*, 327; Turner, *Matthew*, 248; Davies and Allison, *Matthew*, 2:88; Wilson, *Healing in Matthew*, 142.

16. The basic meaning of blasphemy in the Hebrew scriptures and in Judaism is to revile the very name of God. The rabbis believed only God could forgive sins, and the way they bestowed forgiveness was in line with divine instructions. See Bock, *Blasphemy and Exaltation*, 42, 110-11, 188. Therefore, when Jesus the Son of Man claimed he could forgive sins, he aligned his own authority with God. See Hagner, *Matthew*, 1:233. Regarding the charge of blasphemy, Bock says, "The charge seems to revolve around Jesus's taking up an exclusively divine prerogative with such directness based on his own authority. The offense appears to revolve around the fact that forgiveness comes outside any cultic requirements in a mere declaration, an approach that points to Jesus's

teachers of the law are considered unresponsive to Jesus; their lack of faith is apparent. They are presented as those who oppose Jesus through their negative reaction to him and they encourage others not to believe in him. Therefore, the religious leaders are usually portrayed as having evil in their hearts. In 12:35, 38–45; 16:4, the religious leaders are representatives of the evil generation due to their lack of faith in Jesus as demonstrated in their demand that he perform a sign to prove his power and authority. They also represent those whose "hearts [are] far away from God" (15:8) due to their hypocrisy and lack of faith. They do not share the characteristics of those who respond positively to Jesus by having "justice, mercy and faith" (23:23), exhibiting a lack of allegiance to God and his kingdom. This evidence accentuates the contrast between those who brought the paralytic and the scribes who accused Jesus of blasphemy. In addition, the implication exists that Jesus could see the intentions of evil in people's hearts that led them to sin (e.g., the intentions of lust [5:28]; stored treasure [6:21]; and the lack of faith to comprehend and follow the ways of the kingdom [13:14–15, 19; 15:8–9; 24:48]). The intentions of the scribes are important as they reveal their sin of lack of faith in Jesus's authority and power.

The emphasis placed on πίστις[17] highlights Jesus's role as the mediator of God's will on earth. God's will is mediated through Jesus's positive reaction to the faith of those bringing the paralytic (and possibly the paralytic himself). Their faith led Jesus to heal the paralytic and grant the forgiveness of sins. Healing and the forgiveness of sins became manifestations of God's will through the authoritative work of Jesus. Jesus taught his disciples/the crowds that having faith is necessary to manifest God's will on earth. The many healing episodes in Jesus's ministry emphasized the necessity of people's faith. Consequently, faith in Jesus's authoritative power resulted in the desired healing (cf. 8:5–13; 9:20–22, 27–31; 15:21–28). However, several times in Matthew, Jesus rebuked (or warned) his disciples because they were acting like ones of little faith (ὀλιγόπιστοι; cf.

---

own authority" (*Blasphemy and Exaltation*, 188).

17. Some scholars minimize the emphasis of πίστις in this pericope (e.g., Hagner, *Matthew*, 1:231–32; Schweizer, *Good News*, 224; Luz, *Matthew 8–20*, 27; Davies and Allison, *Matthew*, 2:88; Meier, *Matthew*, 91). Gibbs says, "That Jesus spoke because he saw the faith in both the paralytic and his friends is of no small significance. Even though their faith in Jesus cannot as yet have been what we would call 'fully informed' about his person and work, nevertheless, these men were trusting that Jesus is the one who has authority from God to heal and restore—and to forgive sins! To such faith Jesus speaks his word, 'Your sins are being forgiven' (9:2), which bestows the forgiveness that is the heart and center of salvation and that restores fellowship with God" (Gibbs, *Matthew 1:1—11:1*, 459). See also Gibbs, *Matthew 1:1—11:1*, 454, 458–59; France, *Matthew*, 344–45; Keener, *Gospel of Matthew*, 288–89; Carter, *Matthew and the Margins*, 215.

6:25–33; 8:25–27; 14:22–33; 16:5–12; 17:14–21). Through Jesus's teaching and praxis, he mediated to his disciples that exercising one's faith is mandatory for those who want to follow God's will.

The contrast between those who brought the paralytic and the scribes provides the essential connection between forgiveness and mercy. Those who brought the paralytic had faith that Jesus could heal him. Jesus, seeing the intentions of their hearts, completely healed the paralytic through physical healing and the forgiveness of his sins. Within chapters 8–9, people sought Jesus out because of his concern/mercy for the sick and had faith in his ability to heal them (8:5–13; 9:18–19, 23–26, 32–33). In contrast, the scribes accused Jesus of blasphemy because of their lack of faith in his ability to forgive sins[18] and their lack of mercy towards the paralytic who needed healing. From the beginning of the Gospel, Jesus's ministry of forgiving sins was a manifestation of God's will. In the birth narrative, the angel told Joseph that he was to name his baby Jesus because "he will save his people from their sins" (1:21). The ministry of forgiving sins is mentioned as the main mission for Jesus's coming to earth. Therefore, God's will for Jesus's ministry is demonstrated in his forgiving the sins of the paralytic. In addition, in 3:2, 6, the ministry of John the Baptist is described as the preaching of repentance, leading to people confessing their sins and receiving baptism. In 4:17, the same ministry is emphasized through Jesus; he began to preach the message of repentance. From the angelic declaration in 1:21 to the comparative ministry with John the Baptist in 3:2, 6 and 4:17, Jesus's role on earth was to mediate God's will through his ministry of forgiving sins. Since the culmination of Jesus the Son of Man's ministry was to save people by suffering and dying for humanity, physical healing and the forgiveness of sins are manifestations of the Son of Man's love and mercy for this paralytic. The Son of Man mediates his desire for a restored relationship between this paralytic (and all humanity) and God the Father through his sacrificial death—the means of forgiveness of humanity's sins (cf. 20:28; 26:28).[19] Similarly, the ministry of

---

18. The charge of blasphemy might also relate to the scribes's jealousy. Bock suggests that Jesus's claim of having the authority to forgive sins was a claim of independent authority, which would be a "risk to all current socio-political structures and a potential source of public instability" (*Blasphemy and Exaltation*, 231). The scribes probably thought Jesus's claim was "so close to God that he possesses authority even over the nation's highest religious authorities" (231).

19. In reference to Matt 20:28, Wilson states, "Unlike the Danielic Son of Man, the Matthean Son of Man is a servant who suffers on behalf of others (cf. Isa 53:4–5, 10–12, and note the quotation of Isa 53:4 in Matt 8:17)." Also, in relationship to Matt 26:28 he states, "Jesus' entire ministry can be summed up as saving people from their sins (1:21). . . . The forgiveness that the paralytic bears on his healed body is bestowed by one on whose own body will be broken and blood shed for the forgiveness of sins" (*Healing in*

forgiveness of sins would need to be an integral part of the disciples's future ministry, which is illustrated by Jesus's insistence that Peter forgive another person seventy times seven (i.e., unlimited forgiveness) in 18:21–35 (and forgiving enemies in 5:43–46). Forgiving others of their sins would reveal to them the love and mercy of Jesus and the Father, culminated in the Son of Man's suffering and death for the forgiveness of sins. Therefore, the Son of Man is the mediator of God's will to his disciples—forgiving others of their sins would be an integral part of the disciples's mission.

The comparative response between those who brought the paralytic to the Son of Man and the paralytic himself is important. Like those who brought the paralytic to Jesus with faith in his healing power, the paralytic demonstrated his faith in Jesus's authority to heal him by obeying Jesus's commands to take up his stretcher and go to his home (v. 7). The responses of those who brought the paralytic and the paralytic himself, contrast with the negative reaction of the scribes and accentuate their lack of faith when they rejected Jesus the Son of Man's authority and charged him with blasphemy.

The other theme brought out in Matt 9:1–9 is the authority (ἐξουσία) of Jesus. Jesus demonstrated his authority to forgive sins on earth by healing the paralytic, which is emphasized by the imperative verbs used in 9:5–6: "Rise up, walk, take, and go." Jesus's commands to the paralytic highlighted his authority to heal and forgive sins. The paralytic was healed because he obeyed Jesus's commands—he rose, walked, took his stretcher, and went home (vv. 6–7). The focus on Jesus's directives in 9:6–7 is similar to that in 10:1–31, when Jesus gave his authority to the disciples and commanded them to display their message and works to the Jewish and Gentile peoples.[20] Ironically, the scribes who questioned Jesus's authority in their hearts (9:3–4) are contrasted with the religious leaders who recognized his authority while inquiring concerning the source of his authority (21:23–27). Jesus the Son of Man's mission on earth was to bring salvation—the forgiveness of sins—to all people for the purpose of restoring their relationship with God the Father. The Son of Man mediated the means of a restored relationship between God and humanity through his death and resurrection which is prefigured in his healing ministry.[21] The connection between Jesus the Son

---

Matthew, 150–51).

20. Throughout 10:1–31, Jesus used imperative verbs when instructing his disciples in their ministry of the message and works, strengthening the emphasis on Jesus's authority on the earth.

21. Gibbs says, "Matthew has already proclaimed an unbreakable connection between Jesus bringing to his people salvation from their sins (1:21) and his ministry as the in-breaking of the reign of God through preaching, teaching, *and healing*

of Man's healing ministry and ultimately his role in "saving his people from their sins" (1:21) is illustrated through the healing of paralytic in 9:1-8. Through the Son of Man's authority, he physically healed the man's paralysis and forgave him for his sins (9:2, 6).

In Matt 9:9-13, Jesus's authority to forgive sins is implied when Jesus chose Matthew, a tax collector, to join his disciples. Matthew's positive response to Jesus's request to follow him is indicated through his obedience to the request (9:9) and in sharing a meal with Jesus, his disciples, and other tax collectors and sinners (9:10). When the Pharisees criticized Jesus for eating with tax collectors and sinners, Jesus appealed to the need to demonstrate mercy (9:12-13). He desired (θέλω) to be merciful toward those who were in need of both physical and spiritual restoration because mercy manifests God's will on earth. Jesus the Son of Man mediated to humans—Matthew, the other tax collectors, and sinners present, his ministry of forgiveness of sins which would restore a proper relationship between them and God the Father. The Son of Man mercifully extended his love and grace to all people, especially those with sinful lifestyles. In his ministry, physical healing was a manifestation of his desire to love others by forgiving them of their sins and enabling them to participate in the kingdom of the heavens (9:13). Therefore, he was fulfilling the answer to his own prayer when asking that his Father's will be done on earth as it already was in heaven (6:13).

Matthew 9:8b is debated among scholars. Many believe that the phrase "the one who gave authority to humans" (τὸν δόντα ἐξουσίαν τοιαύτην τοῖς ἀνθρώποις) refers to authority given by God to the disciples.[22] This argument is based on the dative plural construction τοῖς ἀνθρώποις. Scholars reference 16:19 and 18:18-20 to substantiate this position by emphasizing Jesus's giving authority "to bind and loose on earth" to Peter and the other disciples to forgive others in the church when they sin. However, other scholars believe 9:8b refers back to Jesus since it appears more tenable from the immediate context.[23] The dative plural τοῖς ἀνθρώποις more likely refers back to Jesus because he is the only one from the immediate context (9:2, 6; also in regards to teaching, 7:29) who possessed the authority to heal and forgive sins. In

---

(4:23-24)" (*Matthew 1:1—11:1*, 426). Gundry asserts that Jesus's healings are illustrations of Jesus's redemptive work, visible pledges of his taking away sin (*Use of the Old Testament*, 230-31). See also Meier, *Law and History*, 69.

22. Davies and Allison, *Matthew*, 2:95-96; Gundry, *Matthew*, 165; Carter, *Matthew and the Margins*, 217; Hagner, *Matthew*, 1:234; Luz, *Matthew 8-20*, 28-29; Turner, *Matthew*, 249; Schweizer, *Good News*, 224.

23. France, *Matthew*, 348; Blomberg, *Matthew*, 154; Hauerwas, *Matthew*, 99-100; Wright, *Jesus and the Victory*, 272-73, 434; Keener, *Gospel of Matthew*, 290-91; Morris, *Gospel*, 217-18; Osborne, *Matthew*, 329.

addition, the crowds who glorified God when Jesus manifested his authority would have seen him as a human gifted by God to do miracles. The crowds were filled with awe as they witnessed God's power manifested through Jesus. Matthew makes several references to God giving Jesus the authority and power to fulfill his work on earth.[24] From the context of 9:1–8, it appears untenable for the crowds to glorify God for giving such authority to the disciples when only Jesus healed the paralytic and demonstrated the authority to forgive sins. In 9:8, the crowds worshiped God because of his authoritative power resident in Jesus the Son of Man. God the Father sanctioned the Son of Man with the authority to forgive sins. Therefore, the ability to heal illustrated the Son of Man's divine authority to offer forgiveness to sinners and caused the crowds to stand in awe of God and worship him for giving his authority and power to Jesus. Similarly, Jesus would mediate God's authority and power given to him to his disciples so they could be empowered in their ministry (e.g., 10:2). The Son of Man's ministry of forgiveness of sins would bring glory to God when people received salvation (i.e., his grace and mercy), and when he was fulfilling God's will for his earthly ministry climaxing in his death and resurrection (cf. 16:21; 26:24, 26–28, 54, 56). Similarly, the Son of Man mediates to his disciples that it would be necessary to follow God's will in their future ministry by forgiving others of their sins, and preaching a message of forgiveness and salvation made possible through Jesus's death and resurrection (10:7, 27; 24:14; 28:18–20).

The dative plural construction of τοῖς ἀνθρώποις in 9:8b is not easily understood. However, the crowds had a limited understanding of Jesus; they did not view him as divine but only as human. By classifying Jesus with human beings, the crowds left him open to the scribes's charge of blasphemy in v. 3[25] and saw him only as a prophet (21:46), a God-ordained teacher (7:28–29; 22:33), as one empowered by God to heal and cast out demons (9:32–33; 12:22–23; 14:13–14), or the promised Messiah (12:22–23)[26] but not as God himself. Therefore, Matthew might be highlighting the crowd's limited understanding of Jesus's identity, which is more clearly revealed to his disciples later in the Gospel after his resurrection

---

24. See Matt 3:12–17, 23–25; 7:29; 8:3, 8–9, 13, 14–17, 26–27, 28–34; 9:6–8, 22–26, 29–34; 12:6–13, 15–22; 14:18–21, 27–36; 15:21–38; 17:18–19; 19:1–2; 20:29–34; 21:14–16, 18–19; 28:16–20.

25. Simonetti, *Matthew 1–13*, 175n14.

26. In 12:22–23, the crowds wondered whether Jesus was the "Son of David." In 21:9, the crowds declared Jesus as the Son of David, the royal Messiah. In the Gospel tradition, the *Son of David* is used at times as a christological title, pointing to Jesus as the royal Messiah in the line of David. See Bauer, "Son of David," 766, 769. See also Matt 1:1; 9:27; 20:30; 21:9; 22:41–45.

(cf. 10:23;16:28; and 28:18–20). God the Father gave the Jesus the Son of Man authority to forgive sins on earth, which relates directly to his calling to save his people from their sins (1:21) through his upcoming suffering and death (20:17–19, 28). Even though 9:8b refers to Jesus and not his disciples, it is implied that the ministry of forgiveness of sins will be extended to his disciples in their present and future ministry (cf. 18:21–35; 28:18–20), and will be central in their future proclamation of the effects of Jesus's death and resurrection (i.e., the grace of a restored relationship with God the Father). Therefore, Jesus the Son of Man is the mediator of God's will for his present and future disciples.

God's will was mediated through the Son of Man in relationship with the faith of those who brought the paralytic for healing (and possibly the paralytic himself), and in Jesus's authority, which healed the paralytic through his spoken word (see 8:5–10, 13). Jesus taught the disciples, crowds, and the scribes that faith in Jesus's works is necessary to manifest God's will on earth. Jesus mediated God's will by revealing through his miraculous work and teaching that genuine disciples must have faith if they are to accomplish God's will. The ones who brought the paralytic (and possibly the paralytic himself) demonstrated the kind of faith that enabled Jesus the Son of Man to use his authority to heal the paralytic and forgive him for his sins. The Son of Man's mission to "save his people from their sins" (1:21) through his preaching of repentance (4:17) and in his upcoming suffering and death (e.g., 16:21; 20:28; 26:28) accentuates his mercy and grace towards humanity, and mediates the kind of ministry he called his present and future disciples to practice (e.g., 18:21–35; 5:43–48; 28:18–20). Once the paralytic got up, picked up his stretcher, and went home, he was completely restored.

2.4. God's Will to Genuine Disciples: Faithfulness in Following after Jesus the Son of Man (Matthew 10:16–23)

2.4.1. *Textual Orientation*

Jesus saw the need to commission his disciples to join him in his ministry (9:36–38; 10:1–2). He gave them the authority to exorcise unclean spirits and heal the sick (10:1). Then, he sent them out into Israelite cities and towns to minister, yet in time they also ministered among the Gentiles (10:5–18). Throughout chapter 10, Jesus instructed his apostles how to engage their culture in ministry and described the inevitable oppression and persecution that would occur as a consequence of obeying his instructions (10:16–31).

The last part of the chapter focuses on Jesus's insistence on fidelity to himself and the ministry to which he called them (10:32–40).

2.4.2. Synoptic Comparison: Matthew 10:16–23; Mark 13:9–13; and Luke 21:12–19

Matthew 10:16–23 has some similarity to Mark 13:9–13 and Luke 21:12–19; however, the author of Matthew has a different agenda. Mark and Luke have an eschatological focus (i.e., Jesus's instructions are for the future ministry of the disciples in preparation for the eschaton). Mark and Luke focus on the signs of the eschaton and the call to faithfulness in preparation for the future coming of the Son of Man. Matthew 10:1–42 focuses on genuine discipleship—what is necessary to fulfill God's will on earth in the disciples's present and future ministry.[27] Only Matthew records the Son of Man reference in 10:23. Mark 13:9–13 and Luke 21:12–19 emphasize the future results of discipleship, while Matt 10 emphasizes the present requirements of discipleship, which will have ramifications in the near future. These present ministry requirements are located in other contexts in Mark and Luke. Even when a future-oriented outlook is in view in 10:16–23 (note the future indicative verbs) an eschatological future regarding the eschaton is not considered. Rather, the focus is on the disciples's ministry in the near future after Jesus's death and resurrection when the disciples will receive further instructions relating to their universal commission to all the nations (28:18–20). When Matthew refers to Jesus's parousia, descriptions of Jesus's exaltation are accentuated: "glory," "coming with his angels," and "on the clouds of heaven" (13:36–43; 16:27; 19:28; 24:30–31, 44; 25:31). Matthew's eschatological discourse is reserved to chapter 24, where Jesus teaches about the events prior to his return and his parousia at the end of the age. However, all of these eschatological cues are absent in 10:23.

2.4.3. Exegesis

The warning of persecution in 10:16–23 is intended to encourage the disciples's faithfulness to God's will through their reliance on the "Spirit of their Father" as a witness before both Jews and Gentiles (10:18–20). The promised

---

27. Hare correctly states that Matthew provides a different meaning to Mark 13:9–13. Mark focuses on the persecution of Christians during the period of messianic woes during the eschaton. However, Matthew de-eschatologized this passage by emphasizing that Christian persecution is a "normal concomitant of the Church's mission." See Hare, *Theme of Jewish Persecution*, 99–100.

THE SON OF MAN'S MEDIATORIAL SIGNIFICANCE ON EARTH   53

reward of salvation for endurance to the end (10:21–22) encouraged the disciples to obey God's will, as Jesus adhered to his Father's will (10:24–25). In 10:23, Jesus told his disciples that they would not minister in all the cities of Israel before the Son of Man returned. The encouragement to endure in their appointed ministry (10:22) makes sense in light of 10:23. Faithfulness in obeying God's will was more important than the inevitable persecution and possible death the disciples would face (10:16–22, 26–31, 38–39). Jesus commanded his disciples to endure in God's will onto death. After Jesus's death and resurrection (10:23), he will come back and give his disciples further instructions on their ministry to all the nations (cf. 28:18–20).[28]

Scholars debate the meaning of 10:23. Many interpret Jesus's coming eschatologically, referring to his parousia, because, in their estimation, the author of Matthew relied on Mark 13:9–13 and Luke 21:12–19 since these accounts focus on Jesus's eschaton.[29] Others interpret Jesus's coming non-eschatologically. Jesus will come again sometime within the disciples's lifetime before the parousia. Scholars have argued five different views regarding a non-eschatological interpretation to Jesus's coming in 10:23: (1) It refers to the Jewish and Gentile apostolic mission occurring concurrently until the end of the world;[30] (2) it refers to Jesus's presence returning to the disciples during his lifetime;[31] (3) it refers to Jesus's return after his resurrection when a new era of the church/discipleship is inaugurated;[32] (4) it refers to the coming of the Spirit at Pentecost (cf. Acts 1:8);[33] and (5) it refers to the judgment on Jerusalem and the destruction

---

28. Foster provides a compelling argument for 10:23, emphasizing the continuation of evangelizing mission to the Jews until the return of the Son of Man. However, since the ministry to the Jews was a relative failure due to their rejection of the message (cf. 10:5–22), Matthew advocates a new way forward—evangelizing primarily to the Gentiles. The responsibility to share the message with the Jews is still valid but takes only a subordinate position in comparison to sharing the message with the Gentiles who are open to the message. See Foster, *Community*, 223–27.

29. See Turner, *Matthew*, 277; Carter, *Matthew and the Margins*, 239; Gnilka, *Matthäusevangelium*, 1:379; Harrington, *Matthew*, 145, 148; Bonnard, *L'Évangile*, 149; Davies and Allison, *Matthew*, 2:190; Keener, *Gospel of Matthew*, 324–25, Osborne, *Matthew*, 391; Weaver, *Matthew's Missionary Discourse*, 100.

30. Luz, *Matthew 8–20*, 91, 93–94; Schweizer, *Good News*, 243–44; Morris, *Gospel*, 258 (emphasis also on the exaltation of the Messiah in his passion and resurrection); Gundry, *Matthew*, 194–95; Gaechter, *Kunst im Matthäus*, 41–42.

31. Schweitzer, *Quest*, 327–33.

32. France, *Matthew*, 396–98; Meier, *Vision of Matthew*, 74, 74n48; Sabourin, "Son of Man," 9–10; Albright and Mann, *Matthew*, 125; Tasker, *St. Matthew*, 108; Mounce, *Matthew*, 96.

33. Calvin, *Harmony of the Evangelists*, 1:458.

of the temple in AD 70.³⁴ After his resurrection, Jesus will return to his disciples and will inaugurate a new era of the church/discipleship (option 3), as the Jewish and Gentile mission expands to the ends of the earth until Jesus's parousia. Jesus will be given all authority by his Father in heaven and, after his resurrection, will commission his disciples to continue his mission by taking their ministry to all the nations (cf. 28:18–20) through his power and authority unto the end of the age.³⁵

Matthew's eschatological cues regarding the Son of Man's future coming (i.e., "glory," "coming with angels," and "on the clouds of heaven") are absent in 10:23. In addition, Matthew reserves the future eschatological return of Jesus the Son of Man for Matt 24. Therefore, the context in chapter 10 and broader book context suggest that one should interpret 10:23 non-eschatologically. A comparison between Jesus's and the disciples's ministries in chapter 10 is essential for understanding these important instructions given to Jesus's disciples (especially emphasized in 10:24–25). In chapters 4, 8, and 9, Jesus's preaching and healing ministry is synonymous with that of the appointed ministry of his disciples in chapter 10. The persecution of the disciples in 10:11–15 (by the Jews) and 10:16–23 (by Jews and Gentiles; note also 5:10–12) is inevitable for any follower of Jesus who is committed to following Jesus in obeying God's will (10:32–40). In addition, in 10:38–39 the disciples are called to "take up their crosses and follow him" even onto death. In 16:13–28, Jesus the Son of Man explicitly connected the disciples's inevitable persecution with his own suffering and death.³⁶ Eung Chun Park helpfully connects the inevitable persecution of Jesus's disciples in 10:16–33 with Jesus's passion predictions by discussing the three verbs mentioned in this section for suffering and persecution, namely, παραδιδόναι, διώκειν, and ἀποκτείνειν. Park notes an implicit echo of these three dangers—παραδιδόναι, διώκειν, and ἀποκτείνειν—in the three passion predictions of

---

34. Hagner, *Matthew*, 1:280; Lenski, *Interpretation*, 405–6; Lagrange, *Évangile*, 205; Benoit, *L'Évangile*, 79; Feuillet, "Origines," 192–98; Gibbs, *Matthew 1:1—11:1*, 521–22. For a helpful understanding of the history of interpretation of Matt 10:23, see Künzi, *Naherwartungslogion*. See also Luz, *Matthew 8–20*, 92–94; Sabourin, "Son of Man," 5–11.

35. I will discuss Matt 28:18–20 in greater detail in chapter 3. Paul Hertig argues that the Gospel of Matthew keeps "two extremes in dialectical tension throughout his Gospel." The Gospel does not reject evangelizing to Jew or Gentile but embraces both "within a framework of separate epochs in time" (Hertig, *Matthew's Narrative*, 102). Relating to Matt 28:18–20, he states, "Clearly the death and resurrection of Jesus inaugurated a new age of mission" (111).

36. I will discuss Matt 16:13–28 in chapter 3. David R. Bauer highlights the strong comparison between Jesus and his disciples's future persecutions as they remain faithful to their respective ministries (*Structure*, 59–60).

Jesus (16:21–23; 17:22–23; 20:17–19) and as presented in the passion narrative: παραδιδόναι (27:2, 26), παθεῖν (27:27–31), and ἀποκτείνειν (27:33–37, 45–54). The only difference is in the use of διώκειν instead of παθεῖν in 10:23. According to Park, a parallel exists between Jesus's suffering and death and that of his disciples, emphasizing the solidarity between Jesus and his disciples.[37] Similarly to Jesus, suffering and persecution is inevitable for disciples who follow God's will on earth.

A significant parallel exists between 10:16–23 and 24:9–14. The following terms and phrases are found only in these passages: (1) παραδώσουσιν (10:17; 24:9);[38] (2) ἔσεσθε μισούμενον ὑπο πάντων ... διὰ τὸ ὄνομά μου (10:22; 24:9); and (3) ὁ δὲ ὑπομείνας εἰς τέλος οὗτος σωτήσεται (10:22; 24:13). This comparison between chapters 10 and 24 has led some scholars to argue that 10:23 refers to the Son of Man's parousia.[39] Others believe 10:16–23 refers to the present and/or near future ministry of the disciples.[40] The contexts of chapters 10 and 24 are different. The future indicated in 10:16–23 refers to the period after Jesus's resurrection as the disciples will continue the ministry of Jesus (28:18–20). Before Jesus's eschatological return, the disciples will face persecution (and death) by both religious and political leaders, especially as they spread the gospel among the Gentiles. Persecution, suffering, and death will occur among family members, and hostility and hatred toward the disciples will increase. The call to endurance is for both the near future, between the Son of Man's resurrection and the eschaton (10:22), and immediately prior to the eschaton (24:13). The gospel will be preached in some of the cities of Israel after the Son of Man's resurrection (10:23) but will reach throughout the entire world to all the nations (28:18–20) before the Son of Man's parousia (24:13–14). In addition, in 10:16–23, no mention of false prophecy or false christs exists, nor of wars or rumor of wars. All of these future events are described in the more distant future of 24:9–14. Therefore, the similarities between chapters 10 and 24 do not indicate the

---

37. Park, *Mission Discourse*, 127. William L. Kynes also notes how Jesus's suffering and death is echoed through the inevitable persecution of the disciples in Matt 10, calling the chapter an "implicit Passion prediction" (*Christology of Solidarity*, 81–82).

38. Παραδώσουσιν is also found in the third passion prediction of Jesus in 20:19. As discussed, this verb emphasizes the comparison between Jesus's and the disciples's fates.

39. Davies and Allison, *Matthew*, 2:181–82, 187; Carter, *Matthew and the Margins*, 238–39; Harrington, *Matthew*, 145–48.

40. France, *Matthew*, 394–95, 904–7; Hagner, *Matthew*, 1:275–76, 278–80; Hare, *Matthew*, 113–15; *Theme of Jewish Persecution*, 97–109; Morris, *Gospel*, 254–58; Schweizer, *Good News*, 244–45; Park, *Mission Discourse*, 132–38; Gibbs, *Matthew 1:1—11:1*, 518–20; Evans, *Matthew*, 223–24; Albright and Mann, *Matthew*, 124–25; Mounce, *Matthew*, 93–95.

same future time is being envisioned: one is a near future (10:23; 28:18–20) and the other is the eschaton (24:9–14).

The parallel ministries of Jesus the Son of Man and his apostles emphasize God the Father's grace and mercy to others. The apostles were called to go to the lost sheep of Israel and preach that the kingdom of the heavens was near (9:35–38; 10:6–7) and to testify of the good news before governors and kings (10:18–20, 23). The apostles's preaching ministry parallels Jesus and John the Baptist who proclaimed a message of repentance for the forgiveness of sins (3:2, 6; 4:15–17). The purpose of their ministry was to urge people to repent of their sins and have a restored relationship with God the Father. Like Jesus and John the Baptist, the apostles's commitment to such a ministry would result in suffering and possible death from preaching the gospel message (10:21–22, 28, 38–39). Similarly, the Son of Man's upcoming suffering and death would offer the most complete expression of God the Father's grace and mercy, as it would ransom people from their sins (i.e., provide forgiveness for human sin) and restore a relationship with the Father in the heavens (cf. 1:21; 20:28; 26:28). Jesus the Son of Man is the mediator of God the Father's grace and mercy to human beings through his message of repentance and his sacrificial suffering and death. He is also the mediator of God's will on earth—calling his apostles to share his ministry of preaching the message of repentance and the forgiveness of sins to others.

The disciples will accomplish God's will on earth if they faithfully adhere to the instructions of Jesus as given in chapter 10. These instructions are grounded in the Gospel's important theological motif of discipleship. The strong comparison between the disciples's mission with Jesus's ministry emphasizes that Jesus mediates God's will on earth for his disciples. As the disciples follow Jesus's example and ministry objectives, they will accomplish God's will in reaching the Jews and Gentiles throughout his world. Without Jesus's revelation mediated through his instructions and example, the disciples would not be able to fulfill God's will for their appointed ministry. The apostles and Jesus (John the Baptist) have a similar ministry—proclaiming a message of repentance for the forgiveness of sins because the kingdom of the heavens is near. God the Father's grace and mercy is emphasized through this message of repentance and forgiveness. In addition, the Son of Man's upcoming suffering and death culminates the message of forgiveness of sins through offering himself as a ransom for the many and, consequently, restoring one's relationship with God. The Son of Man mediates God the Father's grace and mercy through his sacrificial death and mediates God's will to the apostles—their ministry will include preaching the message of repentance for the forgiveness of sins. The Son of Man will appear to his disciples again on earth after his death and resurrection to give them further instructions about their future ministry. The disciples will not have traveled throughout the Jewish cities before this reunion with Jesus (10:23; see also 28:18–20).[41]

2.5. God's Will to Genuine Disciples: The Revelation, Call, and Response of God's Salvific Plan (Matthew 11:11–19)

2.5.1. Textual Orientation

In Matt 11, Jesus spoke to the crowds and the disciples about John the Baptist. He compared his ministry with that of John the Baptist and specifically emphasized Jewish rejection of their ministries. Jesus claimed that if the Gentiles had the knowledge the Jews did, they would have repented of their sins. The Jews would persecute the disciples and Jesus's followers as they obeyed Jesus's instructions on being his genuine disciples. However, Jesus encouraged those who would be persecuted by calling them to continue following him.

2.5.2. Synoptic Comparison: Matthew 11:1–19 and Luke 7:18–35; 10:13–15, 21–22

The discussion of the ministries of John the Baptist and Jesus in Matt 11:1–19 is almost identical with Luke 7:18–35 and absent in Mark. The difference between Matthew and Luke is best understood through the surrounding context, which emphasizes the different agendas of each Gospel writer. Matthew 10 stresses the persecution that Jesus's disciples would experience as they continued Jesus's ministry to other Jewish cities. Those who rejected the disciples's ministry essentially rejected Jesus. Throughout this chapter, Jesus the Son of Man encouraged his disciples to endure the persecution and suffering in order to experience the salvation promised to those who

---

41. I have already made the connection between Matt 1:21 and the Son of Man. The connection between Matt 28:18–20 and Jesus as the Son of Man is accentuated in his "authority in heaven and on the earth." In 9:1–9, Jesus the Son of Man has authority on earth to forgive sins and the authoritative power to heal. The crowds feared him and glorified God because of his authority. In addition, in 8:18–27, the Son of Man demonstrated his self-relinquishment of a secured residence by taking his genuine disciples with him on the boat. When a great storm threatened the lives of the disciples, they called upon the Son of Man (i.e., the Lord) for help. Once he rebuked the winds and lake, they were amazed and recognized his authority over God's creation. Finally, later in 16:28, Jesus told his disciples that they would not die until they see the Son of Man coming with his kingdom, which I will argue in chapter 3, referring to the events after his resurrection (cf. 28:1–10, 16–20).

chose to follow and remain loyal to him (10:21–23). The theme of persecution and suffering in Matt 11 surfaces in the note that John the Baptist was in prison while Jesus and the disciples engaged in itinerant ministry (i.e., preaching, teaching, and performing miracles). Throughout Matt 11, the emphasis on the Jewish leaders and people rejecting Jesus and his disciples's ministry is continued from chapter 10, highlighting the strong contrast between those who reject and accept Jesus's itinerant ministry. However, in Luke the focus is on Jesus's healing miracles—the healing of the centurion's slave (7:1–10) and the raising of the widow's dead son (7:11–17), along with the attention given to Jesus's miraculous works (7:21–22), with no mention of the persecution of Jesus or his disciples. The point of comparison between Matthew and Luke is the response of rejection to Jesus's ministry from the Jewish people. However, much more space is given to this important issue in Matt 11 than in Luke 7.[42]

Luke 10:21–22 includes the material in Matt 11:25–27 but not 11:28–30. However, Luke 10:21–22 is part of Jesus's missionary discourse in chapter 10, whereas in Matthew, missionary instructions are given in the preceding chapter (Matt 10). While Matt 11 continues Jesus's missionary discourse from chapter 10, the emphasis in chapter 11 is persecution in light of the ministries of Jesus and John the Baptist. Luke 10:21–22 serves as Jesus's response to the seventy-two disciples who were excited over having authority over demons. Instead of rejoicing over their power over demons, Jesus taught them to celebrate over their salvation (10:17–21). Jesus then praised his Father for the message of salvation he revealed to them and their acceptance of the good news (10:21–22). The unique contribution of Matt 11:28–30 provides a different agenda and focus from what is recorded in Luke 7:24–35. Jesus's compassion for the persecution the disciples would face by the Jews is accentuated. It emphasizes the fuller, more complete understanding of God's will mediated through Jesus the Son of Man's message and deeds. The disciples would find rest for their souls as a result of their acceptance of Jesus's revealed message of salvation. Luke does not mention Jesus's role as mediator of the revelation of rest for one's soul in this new era of salvation history. In addition, Luke 10:13–15 includes the woes to the Jewish cities in Jesus's missionary discourse to the seventy-two, particularizing his general claim of rejection to their message in 10:10–11. However in Matthew, the condemnation of Jewish cities immediately follows the Jewish (and their religious leaders) rejection of the Son of Man and John the Baptist (11:18–24), and is part of Jesus's missional instructions in chapter 10. Both Luke and Matthew

---

42. This theme of response to (and especially rejection of) Jesus the Son of Man's ministry is important to Matthew and is carried over into chapter 12.

mention the contrast between the unbelieving Jewish cities and Gentile cities that would have believed in Jesus's message.

2.5.3. Exegesis

Matthew 11:1–19 is a literary unit connected by an *inclusio*—opening with the "works of Christ"(ἔργα τοῦ Χριστοῦ) in 11:2 and ending with the statement "wisdom is justified by her works" (ἐδικαιώθη ἡ σοφία ἀπὸ τῶν ἔργων αὐτῆς) in 11:19. These works include Jesus's deeds (i.e., miracles) and message (i.e., preaching, teaching, and evangelism; 11:4–5; see also 10:7–15, 27). The *inclusio* connects Jesus as the Christ with Jesus as the Son of Man. In other words, Jesus the Son of Man is the Christ spoken about in 11:2 who does the ministry (i.e., miracles, preaching) on earth. The works of Christ spoken about in 11:5 are associated with the marginalized of society (i.e., the blind, crippled, lepers, deaf, and poor) and, similarly in 11:19, the Son of Man's works include a relationship of hospitality and friendship with the tax collectors and sinners who were hated and ostracized by society. The inclusion implies that part of Jesus's ministry is to associate with tax collectors and sinners, so they might hear and respond. One cannot dismiss this intentional connection by disassociating Jesus the Christ from Jesus the Son of Man. Therefore, as ὁ Χριστὸς, the Son of Man is the Messiah, the Anointed One who was empowered by the Holy Spirit as the Son of God (cf. 2:4, 15; 3:16–17), and uses his authoritative power to call all humanity to hear and respond to his message and works—especially in his ministry to forgive the repentant of their sins (11:20–24).

The theme of persecution in chapter 10 continues in chapter 11 and is particularly accentuated through the rejection of John the Baptist (11:2, 18) and Jesus the Son of Man (11:19). The Jewish people and leaders, crowds, and Gentiles were given the choice either to accept or reject John the Baptist and Jesus's ministry, and the common response was rejection. A strong indication of rejecting Jesus's ministry is found in 11:12. This highly disputed passage has resulted in two different interpretations of this verse by interpreting βιάζεται either in the middle-intransitive voice or in the passive voice. If taken in the middle–intransitive voice, it indicates that the kingdom of the heavens is being accepted and a great emergence of believers would enter into the kingdom of heavens and receive salvation. Since John the Baptist, the kingdom of the heavens is breaking in irresistibly, and the people (the followers of Jesus) seize it eagerly.[43] If taken in the passive voice, it would

---

43. Verseput, *Rejection*, 97–99; Harnack, *Zwei Worte Jesu*, 942–57; Keener, *Gospel of Matthew*, 339–40; Merklein, *Gottesherrschaft*, 81–83. According to Merklein, βιασταί

indicate one of two things. First, the hearers of the word inflict violence on the kingdom of God; it is violently coveted or accepted. People overcome all obstacles that separate them from the kingdom of God. This position ignores the negative connotations of βιάζομαι/ βιαστής (passive tense–positive voice).[44] Second, the kingdom of the heavens suffers violence; violent people take possession of (i.e., try to harm) it. Scholars think violence might occur by the Zealots and/or the opponents of Jesus and John the Baptist (e.g., Satan, Herod Antipas, the Jewish leadership). Since John the Baptist, violence has been done to the kingdom of the heavens; it is being rejected through a great emergence of persecution in regard to Jesus's ministry and, consequently, his disciples (i.e., deeds and message [passive tense–negative voice]).[45] The problem with interpreting βιάζεται in the middle–intransitive or passive tense–positive voice is that it ignores the statement "violent people seize it" (βιασταὶ ἁπάζουσιν αὐτήν), which immediately follows βιάζεται, a negative phrase emphasizing *violent people*.[46] Interpreting βιάζεται in the passive tense–negative voice is the best way to read this verse based on the context of Matt 10–12 and the Gospel as a whole. The Pharisees, scribes, and the Jewish people predominantly rejected Jesus the Son of Man's ministry, eventually leading to his suffering and death (Matt 26:1–2). In 11:6, Jesus pronounced a blessing on those who accepted his ministry and refused to "take offense at me" (σκανδαλισθῇ ἐν ἐμοί). The verb σκανδαλίζομαι is commonly used in Matthew (seventeen times),[47] and in all instances it is used negatively. Σκανδαλίζομαι is used in three basic ways: (1) relating to people

---

are "people who are determined for anything" (*Gottesherrschaft*, 82–83).

44. Schweitzer, *Quest*, 218–19, 326; Schniewind, *Evangelium nach Matthäus*, 2:144–45; Weiss, *Proclamation*, 70–71.

45. Schweizer, *Good News*, 262; Cameron, *Violence and the Kingdom*, 181, 235–38, 242, 244–46, 251–53; Schrenck, "βιάζομαι, βιαστής," 609–14; Baur, *Kritische*, 615–16; Catchpole, "Doing Violence," 58–61; Davies and Allison, *Matthew*, 2:256; Turner, *Matthew*, 294–95; Luz, *Matthew 8–20*, 141–42. For the discussion, see Luz, *Matthew 8–20*, 140–42; Barnett, "Biastai," 65–70.

46. Nolland argues that βιάζομαι/βιαστής are contrasting ideas. βιάζομαι is best translated in the middle voice, emphasizing the preaching of the kingdom of God through the power and authority of John the Baptist and Jesus (and Jesus's assault on illness, disability, and death). In contrast, βιαστής relates to the violent people (i.e., the governing authorities) who have imprisoned John and in their growing opposition that Jesus's ministry provokes (e.g., Matt 10) (Nolland, *Matthew*, 457–58). Nolland's position is plausible. However, from chapters 9–12 (14:1–12), the primary response is rejection and opposition to John and Jesus's works and message predominantly by the religious leaders. Such growing opposition led to their common fate, suffering and death. John and Jesus fulfilled God's will through their commitment to their itinerant ministries in light of rejection and persecution.

47. Matt 5:29–30; 11:6; 13:21, 41; 16:23; 17:27; 18:6–9; 24:10; 26:31–33.

who reject Jesus's message and way of life (i.e., 16:23; 26:31, 33), (2) indicating people who cause others to sin or reject Jesus (i.e., 13:41; 17:27; 18:6–7), and (3) specifying people who sin (i.e., 5:28–30; 13:21; 18:8–9; 24:10). Each use emphasizes a rejection of Jesus's ministry or a desire to cause other people to dismiss him. In Matthew, rejection relates to persecution that is violently opposed to the kingdom of the heavens and to the works and message of John the Baptist and Jesus. The danger of rejecting Jesus's works and message throughout chapter 11 (esp. 11:20–30) and the placement of Jesus the Christ the Son of Man and John the Baptist in 11:1–19 is intentional.

In 11:1–11, Matthew mentions that God divinely appointed both Jesus (11:1–6; 3:13–17; 4:11b–17) and John the Baptist (11:7–11) to itinerant ministry. By referring to Jesus as Christ (Χριστός), Matthew is identifying Jesus the Son of Man as the Anointed One, Messiah of God. By highlighting the prophecy of Mal 3:1 and 4:5, Matthew stresses that John the Baptist was greater than all prophets because he was sent by God himself ("I myself send" [ἐγὼ ἀποστέλλω]; 11:10a) to "prepare the way" for Jesus the Christ (11:10b) and was divinely sanctioned as "the Elijah, the one who is to come" (11:14). Standing in contrast with Jesus and John the Baptist are those who rejected them (11:16–19). By rejecting John the Baptist and Jesus, they rejected God and his will. As divinely appointed ministers, John the Baptist and Jesus were aligned with God's will. With regard to 11:16–19, scholars have presented three different interpretations of the identity of "this generation." First, this generation is compared not with a group of children but with all people. People are not agreeing—some want to play a wedding, some a funeral.[48] Second, this generation is compared with the children calling out: They wanted to give orders, have authority, and be in control. John the Baptist and Jesus refused to play by their rules, which do not fit this new day of salvation.[49] Third, along with the majority of scholars, a better understanding of this generation is to identify them as those who rejected John the Baptist and Jesus.[50] The parable of 11:16–17 envisions these children as sitting and refusing to dance or mourn when Jesus's and John the Baptist's messages and works were revealed. When Jesus displayed

---

48. Mussner, "Der nicht erkannte Kairos," 599–613; Hoffmann, *Studien zur Theologie*, 226.

49. Linton, "Children's Game," 177; Jeremias, *Parables of Jesus*, 161–62; Cotter, "Parable of the Children," 295–304; Keener, *Gospel of Matthew*, 341; Carson, *Matthew*, 2:270; Gibbs, *Matthew 11:2—20:34*, 577–78.

50. Zeller, "Bildlogik des Gleichnisses," 252–57; Meier, *Matthew*, 123–24; Turner, *Matthew*, 296; Morris, *Gospel*, 284–86; Hill, *Matthew*, 201–2; Harrington, *Matthew*, 161; Gundry, *Matthew*, 212; Carter, *Matthew and the Margins*, 254–55; Luz, *Matthew 8–20*, 148–49; Nolland, *Matthew*, 462–63; Osborne, *Matthew*, 426; Evans, *Matthew*, 240–41; France, *Matthew*, 434.

or preached the message of joyful hope (e.g., salvation through repentance and the forgiveness of sins), this generation refused to join in and accept it (e.g., Jewish cities; 11:20–21). When John the Baptist preached his message of judgment on the sinful and unrepentant, this generation ignored the warnings and refused to repent of their sin and change their ways (3:1–12). John the Baptist's preaching caused this generation to say he had a demon (a strong form of rejection). As the Son of Man, Jesus's desire was to embrace all people, especially sinners, which caused this generation to reject and condemn his actions by calling him a sinner (a strong form of rejection; 9:9–13). John the Baptist's and Jesus's ministries caused John the Baptist's imprisonment and subsequent death (14:1–12) and Jesus's rejection and eventual suffering and death (e.g., 12:1–14).[51] However, by faithfully fulfilling their ministries, John the Baptist and Jesus demonstrated their complete submission to God's will. Matthew 11:16–19 can be compared with 7:21–27. Since John the Baptist and Jesus were committed to their divinely appointed ministries, they represented those who "do the will of [the] Father in the heavens" (7:21, 24–25). However, those who rejected John the Baptist's and Jesus's ministries (e.g., the religious leaders; cf. 23:28) can be compared to those who say, "Lord, Lord," but prove by their dismissal of God's ministers that they did not follow the will of the Father (7:22–23, 26–27). Jesus the Son of Man's role is as the mediator of God's will on earth. Jesus's embracing of tax collectors and sinners as his friends (also 9:9–13) in spite of the rejection he endured demonstrated his desire to live in complete submission to the Father's will. Accepting sinners as recipients of the gospel message is what necessitates the disciples's mission (Matt 10).

The role of Jesus as mediator of God's will is stressed in 11:19–30. In 11:19–24, Jesus mediates God's will primarily through his works (ἔργων). Through his message and works, he revealed to those who were willing to "hear and see" (11:4, 15, 22–24) true "wisdom that is justified" (ἐδικαιώθη ἡ σοφία). Jesus's works were displayed in two ways. First, Jesus was a friend to tax collectors and sinners (11:19). In 9:9–13, Jesus accepted an invitation by Matthew the tax collector to associate with his friends, fellow tax collectors, and sinners. The Pharisees criticized Jesus's actions, which, ironically, led him to teach the Pharisees and the disciples the meaning of Hos 6:6: "I desire mercy and not sacrifice." The verb θέλω in Hos 6:6 LXX could be interpreted "I will" instead of "I desire." God's will is manifested through deeds of mercy. Jesus the Son of Man's ministry to tax collectors

---

51. My interpretation of 11:16–19 is advocated by Turner (*Matthew*, 296–97). Luz would also agree with my view since he focuses on the contrasting response of the parable and how that relates to John the Baptist and Jesus the Son of Man (Luz, *Matthew 8–20*, 147–48).

and sinners is one way he mediated God's will both to his disciples, and to Jewish and Gentile peoples.[52] In 11:19, Jesus declared his desire to minister and befriend tax collectors and sinners was grounded in God's will and, therefore, was the wisdom which justified his works. Jesus's reference to teaching wisdom is reiterated by the same imperative verb, learn (μάθετε), used in 9:13 and 11:29. Both texts highlight Jesus's authoritative desire to teach God's will on earth, so that the misguided teaching and praxis of the Pharisees would be replaced by the wisdom Jesus offered.[53] In addition, Jesus performed miracles (δυνάμεις) to lead people to repentance (11:20–24). Jesus criticized the Jewish cities that rejected his works and refused to repent of their sins. Through his miracles, Jesus mediated God's will for people by providing opportunity for them to witness his works and repent of their sins. The Jewish cities of Chorazin, Bethsaida, and Capernaum are examples of those who saw Jesus's miraculous deeds yet refused to repent of their sins. However, the wicked Gentile cities of Tyre, Sidon, and Sodom would have repented (μετενόησαν) of their sins and would have remained (ἔμεινεν) faithful to Jesus if given the same opportunity as the Jews. In contrast, the Jewish cities rejected Jesus's miraculous works and in the future will be judged with greater severity than the wicked Gentile cities. In Matt 11, tax collectors, sinners, and wicked Gentile cities are representative of those who would accept Jesus and are contrasted with the scribes, Pharisees (cf. 9:3–4, 11–12, 14), and Jewish cities that rejected Jesus (11:20–24). The emphasis on Gentile reception of Jesus and his ministry is prominent (e.g., 8:5–13; 12:41–42; 15:21–28).

The Son of Man's acceptance of the marginalized in 11:5, 19 (and Gentiles in 11:21) highlights his desire to extend God's grace and mercy to them. He fulfilled God's will by preaching the good news of grace and mercy to sinners (9:13 [1:21; 4:17]). His deep concern that people repent of their sins and receive salvation is accentuated in 11:21 and in his concern to give the burdened rest for their souls in 11:28–30. It is ironic that the Son of Man (i.e., Son of Humanity) is accused by the religious leaders of being a "human" (ἄνθρωπος) who ministered to sinners, when the purpose of his association with humanity was to lead people to repent of their sins and have a restored relationship with God (11:19, 21–24). The Son of Man mediates God's will to his disciples in two ways. First, the message of repentance must be shared with sinners so that they may have an opportunity to

---

52. The emphasis on θέλω in Hos 6:6 will be discussed in my exegesis of Matt 12:6–8. In both contexts, θέλω suggests that works of mercy are grounded in God's will.

53. This same form of μάθετε occurs in 24:32, where Jesus taught about the nearness of the eschaton through his parable of the fig tree (cf. Mark 13:28). Luke does not include this conjugation of μάθετε.

receive his grace and mercy, and second, for them to associate with sinners (i.e., embracing the ostracized of society) so sinners might repent of their sins and receive salvation.

In 11:11, John the Baptist is contrasted with the little ones (μικρότερος) in the kingdom of the heavens. These little ones are considered greater than John the Baptist.[54] In chapter 11, the little ones are grouped alongside the infants (νηπίοις) (11:25). John the Baptist and these little ones/infants received divine revelation, but the more complete revelation of God's will was mediated through Jesus and given only to these little ones/infants. The only way to know the Father and, consequently, his will is through Jesus the Son of Man (11:25-27).[55] The identity of the little ones is disputed. Three interpretations have been argued. First, Jesus, in reference to his humility, or being younger than John, or as being John's disciple, was specifically referring to himself.[56] Second, the term refers to anyone in the coming kingdom of heaven. A contrast exists between the present state of the greatest with the future state of the least in the coming kingdom.[57] Third, the term refers to anyone now in the kingdom of heaven. John led his followers up to the verge of the new order initiated by Jesus, but he could not enter.[58] Matthew 11:11 includes John the Baptist in the new era of salvation where the fullness of revelation is given to the little ones. Anyone who accepts Jesus's ministry in the present and/or the future is included among the little ones (i.e., disciples). The little ones receiving Jesus's ministry is substantiated in 18:1-14.

---

54. Matthew 18:1-9 emphasizes the μικρότερος in greater detail. The "greatest in the kingdom of heaven" is compared to a child (παδίον)/children (παιδία). The one who "will humble" (ταπεινώσαι) him/herself like a child will be considered the greatest in the kingdom of heaven. According to 18:5, those who accept children are similarly accepting Jesus.

55. Jesus as the Son of Man is specifically connected to "wisdom" in 11:19. As Son of Man, Jesus's wisdom is demonstrated in his actions (11:2-6, 19) and through the revelation he received from the Father (11:25-30). In addition, "the son" (ὁ υἱός) is only referred to as the Son of Man in chapter 11 (i.e., 11:19, 27). Also, the Son of Man is connected to God as *his/my* Father in 16:27 and 25:32-34a.

56. Cullmann, *Christology*, 32; Suggs, *Wisdom*, 46-48; Vermes, *Jesus the Jew*, 32-33; Hoffmann, *Logienquelle*, 220-24.

57. Allen, *St. Matthew*, 115-16; McNeile, *Gospel according to St. Matthew*, 154; Verseput, *Rejection*, 88-90; Davies and Allison, *Matthew*, 2:251-52; Hagner, *Matthew*, 1:306. Keener surmises that this view does not exclude John in the coming kingdom: "Jesus' division of time into eras hardly means that John would be excluded from the future kingdom; those before the kingdom nevertheless would participate in it (8:11)" (*Gospel of Matthew*, 338-39).

58. This view is the most popular position among modern commentators. See, e.g., Manson, *Sayings of Jesus*, 70; Wellhausen, *Einleitung*, 134-35; Meier, *Matthew*, 122-23; Morris, *Gospel*, 280-81; France, *Matthew*, 428-29; Nolland, *Matthew*, 456-57.

Jesus warned against anyone who causes these little ones to fall (σκανδαλίσῃ) as a result of their trust in and acceptance of Jesus (cf. 11:6; 18:6-7) or who might look down on them (18:10). Jesus stressed that God's will is for none of these little ones to perish.[59] Jesus the Son of Man mediates his Father's will by presenting these little ones positively, in order to urge sinners to accept his grace and mercy as well (e.g., 11:19, 21, 23).

In 11:25-27, the infants are contrasted with the wise and intelligent. The identity of these two groups of people as understood from the context of chapter 11 is clear: the little ones (and infants) were those who accepted Jesus's ministry (e.g., present and future disciples of Jesus; cf. 4:18-25; 5:1, 20; 7:21; 8:18-23; 9:9-13, 37-38; 10:1-42; 13:16-17),[60] while the wise and intelligent are those (e.g., Pharisees, scribes, teachers of the law, and at least some of the crowds; cf. 5:17-20; 6:1-8, 16-18; 7:24-29; 9:3-8, 10-13, 32-34; 13:1-2, 10-15) who refused to accept Jesus's ministry because it did not fit within their prescribed paradigm accentuated in the law and teachings of the elders. In addition, they are described as those whose teaching and lifestyle

---

59. Immediate context may support the inclusion of Matt 18:11: ἦλθεν γὰρ ὁ υἱὸς τοῦ ἀνθρώπου σῶσαι τὸ ἀπολωλός, since minor support is given through Western and Byzantine documents. However, the Alexandrian, Egyptian, and Antiochian witnesses document a less probable inclusion. Metzger, *Greek New Testament*, 36: "There can be little doubt that the words ἦλθεν γὰρ ὁ υἱὸς τοῦ ἀνθρώπου (ζητῆσαι καὶ) σῶσαι τὸ ἀπολωλός are spurious here, being absent from the earliest witnesses representing several textual types (Alexandrian, Egyptian, Antiochian), and manifestly borrowed by copyists from Lk 19:10. The reason for the interpolation was apparently to provide a connection between ver. 10 and verses 12-14." The transcriptional evidence also makes this verse suspect. The scribe may have intentionally attempted to harmonize 18:11 with Luke 19:10 since Luke 19:10 could fit into the context of 18:10-14 well (i.e., the lost sheep motif). In addition, a scribe could have added 18:11 as a general statement for 18:12-13 (i.e., the lost sheep motif being an example to illustrate 18:11). If added, 18:11 works well with 18:14 since saving one of the little ones would be complementary with the Father's will that none of the little ones perish. This internal evidence against 18:11 is described in Metzger, *New Testament*, 197-99. Other evidence for adding 18:11 relate to themes already present in the Gospel of Matthew, that is, (1) Jesus's call to offer mercy to sinners (9:13; 11:19); (2) Jesus's call to minister to the lost sheep of Israel in the missionary discourse (10:5-15); (3) the description of Jesus's purpose in mission to "save his people from their sins" (1:21); and (4) the theme of μικρότερος/νηπίοις in Matt 11 (i.e., vv. 11, 25), and the immediate context of 18:1-9 where παιδία/μικρῶν are described. See also Aland and Aland, *New Testament*, 296. This evidence makes it hard to account for how or why this verse would be eliminated from the original text, yet, if it were not original, this internal evidence would give easy account for its addition, given the scribal familiarity with the Gospel of Matthew and the NT canon. For these reasons, I have chosen not to include this Son of Man reference in my discussion.

60. This view is also argued by Weren where he identifies νηπίοις as Jesus's disciples. He states, "*Nepioi* also has a figurative sense in Matt 11:25. Children are recipients of God's revelation. Jesus is referring to his disciples and contrasting them with the wise and understanding" ("Children in Matthew," 55).

might cause people to fall from their faith (cf. 23:1-2, 13-15). The lack of acceptance of Jesus's ministry causes these things (ταῦτα; i.e., revelation of God's will) to be hidden from the wise and intelligent. However, those who have accepted Jesus's ministry were able to have these things revealed to them.[61] In 11:27, a more complete revelation of the new era of salvation is discussed in greater detail (note the repetition of ἀποκαλύπτω in vv. 25, 27). Without a fuller revelation of God's plan of salvation, no one can understand his will.[62] Therefore, Jesus the Son of Man is the only mediator between God the Father and the little ones/infants. Without Jesus's mediation, saving knowledge of the Father is not possible.[63] In 11:19, Jesus the Son of Man's wisdom is exemplified by what is displayed and proclaimed through his ministry. Tax collectors and sinners are representative of those who hear and see (see also 11:4-5, 13-15, 20-24) Jesus's message and deeds and accept them; they are part of these little ones/infants who will become Jesus's followers. In 11:27, Jesus's wisdom (cf. 11:19) is clearly particularized. The revelation of this new era of salvation will be given to those who accept Jesus's ministry—God the Father's will of his salvific plan given to Jesus, which is greater than John the Baptist's incomplete message (11:11).

---

61. The verb ἀποκαλύπτω is only found in one other place in Matthew, 16:17, where Peter was blessed by Jesus for correctly identifying him as "the Christ, the Son of the living God." Peter's response is credited as divine revelation since the Father in the heavens is the one who revealed Jesus's identity to him.

62. The Father's plan of salvation will be revealed in greater detail later in Matthew, where Jesus the Son of Man discussed his upcoming suffering and death (cf. 12:40; 16:4, 21; 17:9, 22; 20:17-19; 21:37-43; 26:1-2, 12, 24-29, 45-46). See chapter 3.

63. Hagner concurs with my argument that 11:27 highlights Jesus as the mediator of God's will to humanity (i.e., the little ones/infants). Hagner says, "The point is that Jesus thus has a unique role as the mediator of the knowledge of God to humankind. This role is directly linked with the person of Jesus, his identity as the unique representative of God. . . . Jesus is the unique agent of the Father—the one fully known by the Father alone. He is the sole mediator simultaneously of the knowledge of the Father and of his salvation purposes, for the Father and his will are fully known to Jesus" (*Matthew 1-13*, 320).

Matt 11 points to the climactic invitation of Jesus in 11:28–30.[64] Jesus

64. Five main scholarly views on 11:28–30 have been asserted: First, Davis, Suggs, and Deutsch each argues that Matt 11:25–30 is influenced by Wisdom Christology. This source-critical argument emphasizes that Sir 6:24–31; 51 and the Dead Sea Scrolls are the sources behind "sophia" in 11:25–30 due to the parallels between them. Jesus is the "Teacher of Righteousness" and/or "Wisdom Incarnate," revealing "knowledge," the secrets of the prophets (i.e., the Torah), to those who are willing to accept these eschatological teachings. This Wisdom Christology points to the Gnostic speculations about wisdom (Davies, "Knowledge," 113–39; Suggs, *Wisdom*, 80, 90–92, 95–97, 100–102, 106–8; Deutsch, *Hidden Wisdom*, 104–7, 115–18, 131–35). Second, Allison and Viviano argue that the source background for Matt 11:25–30 can be found in Exod 33:12–19 and Num 12:3, 6–8, in which the outstanding qualities of Moses are paralleled in Jesus. The comparison between these OT texts regarding Moses and the description of Jesus in 11:25–30 is intentional. The reciprocal knowledge (intimate relationship) between Moses and God/Jesus and God is comparably exclusive. In both contexts, God knows Moses/Jesus before they know God, emphasizing God's initiative in the relationship. Both Moses and Jesus are considered "meek" (LXX—πραΰς). Numbers 12:3 states that Moses was very meek, more than all people on the face of the earth. When Jesus spoke of being meek in 11:29, he was claiming for himself this outstanding quality of Moses (Allison, "Two Notes," 477–85; Viviano, "Revelation in Stages," 95–101). Third, Charette finds the sources and meaning of Matt 11:28–30 in light of OT prophetic expectations. Jesus is presented as announcing to the nations that the time of release from captivity and the return to rest has arrived. From Matthew's perspective, the restoration of the nation begins only with Jesus's ministry. Individuals either reject the invitation of rest, resulting in captivity, or accept the invitation of rest, resulting in the hope of salvation from captivity. By "taking up Jesus's yoke," individuals choose to obey the Torah as interpreted by Jesus in contrast to the yoke (teaching/opposition) of the Pharisees (Charette, "Proclaim Liberty," 290–97). Fourth, Bacchiocchi and Verseput find the source and meaning of Matt 11:28–30 as the fulfillment of the messianic rest typified by the OT Sabbath. The Sabbath weekly rest epitomized the future peace and rest to be established by the Messiah as eschatological hope. Jesus fulfilled this hope through his ministry by providing the need for truth and assurance of salvation. Recipients of this rest choose Jesus's yoke by having a genuine dedication to Jesus as the true interpreter and fulfiller of the law and the prophets and by being devoted to the law. Matthew 12:1–14 heightens and broadens this fulfillment by interpreting Sabbath keeping as utilizing the Sabbath day to celebrate and experience the messianic redemption rest by showing "mercy" and "doing good" to those in need (Bacchiocchi, "Matthew 11:28–30," 289–316; Verseput, *Rejection*, 139–87). Fifth, Hunter, Shaw, and Betz argue their case primarily from the immediate and broader book context of Matthew. They do not support the source-critical issues or OT echoes. They focus upon the relational emphasis between Jesus and the Father, which is initiated and sustained by the Father and complemented and fulfilled by Jesus's own filial response of obedience and love. Jesus stands in sharp contrast to the Pharisees and scribes. Jesus's teaching (interpretation of the Torah) provides a "mild yoke and easy burden" (11:30), while the teaching of the Pharisees "loads people with burdens hard to bear" (23:4). Unlike the Pharisees and scribes, Jesus's teaching presumes "justice, mercy, and faithfulness" (23:23). Since the Son knew the Father, only Jesus was uniquely qualified to mediate the relationship of Father/Son to his disciples (and the childlike/infant/humble who accept his invitation of rest). The eschatological reward of rest is a gift for the present and future life as well (Hunter, "Matt 11:25–30," 241–49; Betz, "Logion," 10–24; Shaw, *Discernment*, 208–41).

offered anyone (Jew and Gentile[65]) the opportunity to repent and accept his message and works, receiving the "rest for their souls" (ἀνάπαυσιν ταῖς ψυχαῖς ὑμῶν). Just as Jesus is the mediator between his Father and those who accept his ministry, so he is the only mediator who can give promised rest. Matthew 11:28–29 connects to 11:19 where tax collectors and sinners

---

Matt 11:25–30 must be interpreted based on immediate and broader book context. Therefore, I find Davis's, Suggs's, and Deutsch's emphasis on Jesus being wisdom incarnate based on the background in Hellenistic-Gnostic thought untenable. Except for the expression ἐδικαιώθη ἡ σοφία ἀπο τῶν ἔργων αὐτῆς in 11:19, I do not see any connection with a wisdom Christology from context. Wisdom is associated with Jesus mediating God's will through his message and works, not his identity. Even though Allison and Viviano present a more tenable case based on context from OT references to Moses, the immediate context of Matt 10–12 does not support a Moses typology. Rather, the context focuses on Jesus's message and works, the responses to them, either acceptance or rejection, and the present and future salvific hope that is given to those who accept him. Charette has presented an interesting argument from the vast OT prophetic expectations he utilizes. One can see the contrast of a captivity/rescuing theme in Matt 11:28–30. However, Charette does not connect his argument securely enough to the immediate and broader book context of Matthew itself. In addition, his captivity/rescuing theme is not evident in the Gospel as a whole. Like Charette, Biachiocchi and Verseput do not tie their emphasis of the OT Sabbath fulfilled in Jesus's messianic rest to the Gospel as a whole. Outside of 11:25—12:14, this theme is difficult to see from context. Hunter, Betz, and Shaw point out the main emphasis in 11:25–30 because they have based their views on the immediate and broader books contexts. The contrast between the reception of Jesus's teaching among the wise and intelligent and the infants is obvious within 11:1–19 and Matt 10–12. The contrast between the teaching of the Pharisees (e.g., teachers of the law, scribes) and Jesus is evident in 11:28–30 and Matt 9–12. The fuller revelation offered by Jesus's message of salvation is emphasized throughout Matt 9–12 and brought to a climax in 11:28–30. The fuller revelation can only be mediated through Jesus. The eschatological reward is given to those who accept Jesus's fuller revelation of God's will (i.e., salvation) mediated to them through Jesus the Son of Man (11:19).

Lang argues that the background for Matt 11:25–30 lies in the wisdom writings, especially Sir 51, OT contexts, and, in light of other passages, within the Gospel itself, since they are not in conflict with each other. Lang's position partly fits with each of the five interpretive views above. However, as I mentioned above, he does not adequately demonstrate how these three backgrounds work together within the immediate or broader book contexts of Matthew's Gospel. My contention is that the wisdom writings and OT references are not clear in the immediate context or in the Gospel as a whole. He is correct, however, in claiming that the contrast between the "heavy laden and burdened" and "easy yoke" in 11:28–30 refers to the teaching of the Pharisees versus the message and works of Jesus and as an invitation to be part of the intimate relationship between Jesus and the Father in heaven. See his *Jesus and the Sabbath*, 154–61.

65. Throughout Matthew, Jesus's itinerant ministry is directed to both Jewish and Gentile people (cf. 4:12–25; 8:5–13; 9:35–38; 10:1–15, 16–42; 11:20–24; 12:15–21, 38–42; 15:21–39; 28:16–20). In the immediate context of 11:20–24, Jesus's inclusive ministry is strongly implied from the contrast between Jewish and Gentile cities rejecting or accepting Jesus's deeds of power. In addition, in 11:28 the subject is general (i.e., πάντες), suggesting both Jewish and Gentile persons are included in the promised rest.

are blessed because they are justified through belief in Jesus's message and deeds. Jesus stated that those with the faith and willingness to repent and return to him would be placed alongside those who do the will of the Father (21:31–32).

Jesus also commanded these little ones/infants to learn from him. The verb μανθάνω is in the imperative, emphasizing the importance of learning from Jesus (cf. 9:13). This same construction is found with the verb αἴρω earlier in 11:29, commanding these ones to take up his yoke. Many scholars believe that the weariness and burdens these little ones/infants bear relate to the teachings of the Pharisees, scribes, and teachers of the law, since they had over 613 commandments to obey.[66] This view is likely since the Pharisees, scribes, and teachers of the law are so often criticized for their misguided, incomplete teaching, which kept people from accepting Jesus's message and works (cf. 3:7–9; 9:1–13, 27–35; 12:1–14, 23–37; 15:1–20; 18:1–6; 19:1–12; 21:23–32; 23:1–15), especially with the emphasis on the scribes's/Pharisees's teaching as "heavy loads which are hard to bear" in 23:1–4. However, in addition to this criticism, one can also understand the weariness and burdens the little ones/infants bear within the context of my previous discussion of 11:11, 25–27. The little ones/infants learn from Jesus the more complete revelation of God and his will, which belongs to the new era of salvation history mediated through Jesus. In my estimation, both perspectives are in view: (1) Jesus offered the correct teaching through his message and deeds in contrast to the misguided, incomplete teaching of the scribes, Pharisees, and teachers of the law, and (2) Jesus referred to a complete understanding mediated through his message and deeds (especially in his relationship with tax collectors and sinners; 11:19). The Son of Man is the mediator of God's revelation of his salvific will to all people. The contrast in 11:25–30 between Jesus's teaching according to God's will and the religious leaders's misguided, incomplete views is directly connected to one's understanding of Jesus the Son of Man's role as Lord of the Sabbath in 12:1–8.

Matthew 11:1–19 is connected by an *inclusio* between the "works of Christ" (11:2) and "wisdom is justified by her works" (11:19). The *inclusio*

---

66. This argument is emphasized in Hagner, *Matthew*, 1:323. Hagner concurs that, in 11:29, Jesus is the mediator of the more complete revelation through his works and message. He states, "The invitation to come to Jesus is an invitation to discipleship, that is, to follow him and his teaching. . . . He invites them to follow his own teaching as the definitive interpretation of the law (see on 5:17–20). . . . Jesus similarly calls to a discipleship of obedience to Torah, but, as always in Matthew, the Torah as mediated through his teaching. The cognate verb μαθητεύειν occurs in 28:19 together with the emphasis on keeping true to the teaching of Jesus" (324). This verb connects 11:25–30 with 28:18–20 by emphasizing teaching Jesus's message of salvation to future disciples. Cf. Janzen, "Yoke," 256–68.

identifies Jesus as the Christ and the Son of Man. The works referred to include his miracles and his message (evangelism, preaching, and teaching) to the marginalized, and his friendship to tax collectors and sinners who were ostracized by society (11:5, 19). The persecution of Jesus's messengers in chapter 10 is continued in chapter 11, and is particularly emphasized through the rejection of John the Baptist's ministry (11:2, 18) and Jesus the Son of Man (11:19) and, consequently, his present and future disciples. The religious leaders's rejection of Jesus the Son of Man eventually led to his suffering and death (26:1–2). Jesus and John the Baptist were God's divinely appointed ministers and, therefore, to reject them is to reject God and his will. By faithfully fulfilling their ministry amidst rejection, John the Baptist and Jesus demonstrated complete submission to God's will. In 11:19–30, Jesus the Son of Man mediated God's will both to his disciples and to Jewish and Gentile peoples, by providing the opportunity for them to witness his works (i.e., miracles) and repent of their sins. The Jewish cities and the religious leaders rejected Jesus's works (and message) and refused to repent, while the Gentile cities would have accepted his works (and message) and repented of their sins (e.g., tax collectors and sinners [11:19; 21:31–32]). The little ones/infants are greater than John the Baptist because they received a more complete revelation of God's will mediated through Jesus. Only through the Son of Man can the Father be known and, consequently, his salvific will (11:25–27). Since the little ones/infants accept and receive Jesus and his ministry, the more complete revelation of the new era of salvation can be mediated to them through the Son of Man. In 11:28–30, the "rest" Jesus promises his little ones/infants are the present and future benefits they will receive from their salvation (i.e., the revelation of the Father in 11:27). The tax collectors and sinners are representative of the little ones/infants who receive salvation (21:31–32). Jesus the Son of Man is the mediator of God's salvific will to all people who will repent of their sins and accept him and his ministry.

2.6. God's Will to Genuine Disciples: Mercy Redefines the Sabbath Law (Matthew 12:1–8)

2.6.1. Textual Orientation

Jesus's disciples went through the grain fields, picking grain and eating it. The Pharisees witnessed their behavior and accused them of breaking the Sabbath law. Jesus challenged the Pharisees's view on the Sabbath law by stating the Son of Man is Lord of the Sabbath. Therefore, the Sabbath law must be interpreted through Jesus. In the Son of Man's estimation, mercy redefines the Sabbath law by making it prominent and enforceable.

2.6.2. Synoptic Comparison: Matthew 12:1–8; Mark 2:23–28; and Luke 6:1–5

The controversy over Sabbath regulations is recorded in Mark 2:23—3:6 and in Luke 6:1–11. However, once again, the agendas of the Synoptic Gospels are different. Only Matthew accentuates human need. Jesus's disciples picked wheat on the Sabbath because they were hungry and wanted to eat something (v. 1). Initially, Jesus the Son of Man refuted the criticism of the Pharisees with three opposing arguments: (1) King David's violation of temple regulations, (2) the priests's violation of Sabbath regulations by exercising priestly work on the Sabbath, and (3) Jesus the Son of Man's being Lord of the Sabbath. Jesus dismissed King David's violation of the temple regulations because, like his disciples, David and his men were hungry. Even though only the priests were to eat the bread of presentation (cf. Exod 25:40; Lev 24:5–9), Jesus justified King David's actions based on the law of mercy. From Jesus's standpoint, mercy (i.e., relieving human need, such as being hungry) takes precedence over the Sabbath regulations. Unlike Mark 2:23–28 and Luke 6:1–5, only in Matt 12:5 did Jesus mention that the priests violated the Sabbath regulations on work. However, Jesus justified their actions by saying the priests were considered innocent even though they worked on the Sabbath. Similarly, the Pharisees should not condemn Jesus's disciples for eating (i.e., working) on the Sabbath day because they were hungry, since they were innocent as well.[67] In addition, only Matthew mentions that something or someone *greater* (μεῖζόν) than the temple is here (12:6), stressing Jesus's authority over the temple and the teaching regarding Sabbath law. Matthew 12:1–8 emphasizes the need to offer mercy to those in need. This emphasis on mercy is further accentuated by Jesus's reference to Hos 6:6, "I desire mercy and not sacrifice," which is not included in Mark and Luke. Only Matthew uses this reference in 12:7 and earlier in 9:13.

---

67. Robert Banks is helpful here: "It is the authority of Jesus which is paramount... conceived in personal terms. Just as the priests could 'profane' the sabbath in service of the Temple yet remain innocent, so could Jesus' disciples in the service of the one who was greater than the Temple (v. 7b). Thus as in vv. 3ff. it is a question of authority rather than legality as such which is at stake" (*Jesus and the Law*, 116–17).

2.6.3. Exegesis

Jesus the Son of Man justified his authority to redefine mercy over Sabbath law based on three christological statements in 12:6-8: (1) "Something greater [μεῖζόν] than the temple is here," (2) "I desire mercy [ἔλεος θέλω] and not sacrifice," and (3) "for the Son of Man is Lord of the Sabbath" (κύριος γάρ ἐστιν τοῦ σαββάτου ὁ υἱὸς τοῦ ἀνθρώπου). These statements are important to consider in turn.

Scholars debate how to interpret the neuter μεῖζόν. The first option is to interpret it christologically, emphasizing that the "something greater" refers to Jesus[68] and/or to Jesus's divine, authoritative presence (cf. Matt 1:20-23).[69] France believes it refers to Jesus's functional role on earth as mediator between God and humankind,[70] and Carter believes it refers to Jesus as God's agent who manifests God's presence and to his functional role.[71] The second is to interpret it non-christologically, emphasizing either that the "something greater" refers to the "kingdom of God,"[72] to "the acts of mercy as God's will,"[73] to "the love commandment,"[74] to "the ministry of Jesus and the disciples and the reality of the dawning kingdom,"[75] or to "the community of Jesus."[76] The neuter μεῖζόν as a christological statement is best supported from the context. In 12:1-14, Jesus placed himself authoritatively over the Pharisees through his interpretation of the Sabbath regulations. The emphasis is on Jesus the Son of Man's authoritative role as mediator, which makes his teaching "greater than the temple" and, therefore, the fulfillment of the temple and its priestly regulations.[77] Jesus mediates God's will for mercy towards

---

68. Davies and Allison, *Matthew*, 2:314; Banks, *Jesus and the Law*, 117; Guelich, *Not to Annul*, 51-54; Meier, *Matthew*, 129-30; Nolland, *Matthew*, 483-85; Thielman, *Law*, 64-66; Yang, *Jesus and the Sabbath*, 180-81; Lybaek, *New and Old*, 160-62; Barth, "Matthew's Understanding," 82; Gurtner, "Matthew's Theology," 135-36.

69. Harrington, *Matthew*, 177; Keener, *Gospel of Matthew*, 356-57; Morris, *Gospel*, 303 (and in the mercy at work in Jesus); Hagner, *Matthew*, 1:330; Turner, *Matthew*, 310-11, esp. 310n6.

70. France, *Matthew*, 460-61.

71. Carter, *Matthew and the Margins*, 266.

72. Manson, *Sayings of Jesus*, 187; Schweizer, *Good News*, 278; Hicks, "Sabbath Controversy," 86-87, 89-90.

73. Luz, *Matthew 8-20*, 181-82; Edin, "Learning What Righteousness Means," 357.

74. Sigal, *Halakhah of Jesus*, 161.

75. Hagner, *Matthew*, 1:330.

76. Harrington, *Matthew*, 172; Hill, *Matthew*, 211.

77. France is correct when stating about Matt 12:6 (cf. 12:41-42): "It is the authority of Jesus himself which is immediately at issue, but not so much Jesus in his own person as in his role, as now (in comparison with priest, prophet, and king in the OT) the *true*

human beings. As the mediator of God's revealed will, Jesus is greater than the temple and its regulations as indicated in the law.

Matthew uses the reference to Hos 6:6, "I desire mercy and not sacrifice," in 12:7 and earlier in 9:13. In 9:13, the theme of mercy is emphasized through Jesus's willingness to call sinners rather than the righteous. In relationship to 11:19 and 11:28–30, the sinners and tax collectors were most receptive to Jesus's ministry and, therefore, were examples of those who come to Jesus to receive his rest (cf. 20:31–32). The Son of Man's desire to associate with sinners and tax collectors so they would repent of their sins (cf. 11:20–24) and receive his rest demonstrated his love and mercy, and his declaration that as "Lord of the Sabbath" his command for mercy redefines the Sabbath regulations regarding work in 12:8, connect to the purpose of Jesus's mission on earth to "save his people from their sins" in 1:21. In 12:1–8, Jesus the Son of Man's teachings on mercy are grounded in God's will (θέλω; 12:7). Therefore, Jesus justified the disciples's need to satisfy their hunger and criticized the Pharisees for condemning the innocent. According to Jesus, mercy towards other people redefines the Sabbath regulations regarding work. People are more important than the Sabbath regulations. Jesus's mercy is intimately connected to God's will in 12:7, since mercy towards human beings must come before temple and priestly regulations. Jesus the Son of Man's (and his disciples's) mission on earth was to demonstrate the kingdom of the heavens through his (their) works of mercy, which would "fulfill all righteousness" (3:15) and "exceed the righteousness of the Pharisees" (5:20; cf. 3:12–17; 4:19, 23–25; 5:17–20; 8–9; 10:5–17; 11:1–6). Therefore, Jesus's attitude towards the law was to fulfill it and redefine the meaning of Sabbath law through his teaching: God wills mercy not sacrifice.

Jesus's statement that "the Son of Man is Lord of the Sabbath" (12:8) has great christological significance in light of 11:25. In 11:25, Jesus called his Father "Lord" of heaven and earth. After Jesus's resurrection, the Father will give the exalted Jesus all authority in heaven and earth (28:18). By calling his Father "Lord" in 11:25 and himself "Lord" in 12:8, he was implying that the Son of Man has divine identity—he shares the title "Lord" with God the Father. Therefore, as in 11:26–27, what the Father wills (i.e., grace and mercy towards humanity), so the Son of Man wills as Lord of the Sabbath. The Son of Man mediates the divine will to his disciples—revealing and demonstrating mercy and grace towards others is essential in following God's will.

---

mediator between God and his people, such role is something new" (*Matthew*, 460–61 [emphasis mine]).

Significant scholarly debate exists over Jesus's attitude towards the law. The view almost universally rejected among scholars is that Jesus summarily abrogated the law.[78] However, several other options have been suggested. Only the main positions will be highlighted: First, Jesus's teaching was an exposition of the Mosaic commands and requirements, bringing new demands upon the law, but not abrogating it;[79] second, Jesus's teaching penetrated behind the letter of the law to its inner moral and spiritual principles;[80] third, Jesus abrogated the ritual commands only;[81] fourth, Jesus is the last and greatest expositor of the law of God, upholding the moral law, applying it to his life and teaching and teaching the original intent of the law;[82] fifth, Jesus radicalized the law, intensifying and moving beyond the demands of the law having been carried out due to Jesus's immediate awareness of God's will[83] and/or demand of love,[84] resulting in abrogation of some commands;[85] sixth, Jesus's teaching was a new messianic law, which replaced the Mosaic law;[86] and seventh, Jesus's teaching fulfilled the law in the sense that the law pointed forward to his teaching. His demands are above and apart from the law. Thus, the law's continuing validity exists only in and through him.[87]

From the context, Jesus's attitude toward the Sabbath law was to fulfill it according to God's will (cf. 9:13; 11:19; 12:7). God's desire (or will; θέλω) is for Jesus and his disciples to offer works of mercy to people as their

---

78. See Moo, "Jesus and Authority," 4.

79. McArthur, *Understanding the Sermon*, 44–57; Kevan, *Grace of Law*, 155–59; Reicke, *Zehn Worte*, 53–69; Derrett, *Law*, xxvi, 378–84.

80. Harnack, "Jesus," 227–36.

81. Manson, "Jesus, Paul, and the Law," 125–41; Schnackenburg, *Moral Teaching*, 59–65.

82. Bahnsen, "Reformed Approach," 102–15; Ridderbos, *Coming of the Kingdom*, 285–329.

83. Kümmel, "Traditionsgedanke," 26–35; Bornkamm, "End-Expectation," 15–51; Bornkamm, *Jesus of Nazareth*, 96–117 (also the demand of love/mercy); Schnackenburg, *Jesus in the Gospels*, 114–23; Westerholm, *Scribal Authority*, 78–112; Verseput, *Rejection*, 168–73.

84. Gutbrod, "νόμος," 1063; Barth, "Matthew's Understanding," 58–164; Loader, *Jesus' Attitude*, 137–272; Dunn, *Jesus, Paul, and the Law*, 10–29.

85. Bultmann, *Theology*, 1:11–22.

86. Davies, *Setting*, 93–108, 447–50; Sanders, *Jesus and Judaism*, 251–52, 255, 267–69; Allison, "Torah, Urzeit, Endzeit," 187, 193.

87. Banks, *Jesus and the Law*, 209–35; Meier, *Law*, 87–88, 168–70; Knight, *Law and Grace*, 85–89, 104–9; Wenham, *Lord's View*, 23–32; Guelich, *Not to Annul*, 227–28, 243–46, 262–68; Dienes, "Not the Law," 53–84; Moo, "Jesus and Authority," 3–49; Carson, "Jesus and the Sabbath," 77–80; Jeremias, *New Testament Theology*, 205–7; Bird, "Jesus as Law-Breaker," 3–26.

service to God. Jesus the Son of Man is the mediator of God's will to the disciples (and consequently, the general populace and the religious leaders). However, Jesus's works offended the Pharisees because they extended beyond their authority, did not fit their interpretation of the law, and did not submit to their traditions (cf. 11:6). The Pharisees's criticism is what caused Jesus to condemn them for lacking the weightier matters of the law: justice, mercy, and faith (23:23). In 11:16–19, the Pharisees are representative of those who rejected Jesus's works and message and condemned him for his association with tax collectors and sinners. Therefore, they stood in opposition to God's will, since acts of mercy towards others are directly connected with God's will as this is mediated through the ministry of Jesus (also 20:26–27; 25:34–40). Unlike the disciples, the Pharisees do not belong to the kingdom of the heavens because they were separate from Jesus's kin—that is, from those who "do the will of his Father in the heavens" (12:50). Jesus's teaching on mercy continued in his healing of the man with a withered hand (12:9–14).[88] The Pharisees tried to find reason to accuse Jesus by seeing if he would heal on the Sabbath. Jesus responded by using the hermeneutic rule, *qal wahomer*—a how-much-more argument (e.g., how-much-more valuable is a human being than a sheep).[89] If the Pharisees would rescue their sheep if it fell on the Sabbath, how much more willing should they be to demonstrate mercy to others in need. Jesus justified healing the man with the withered hand on the Sabbath by claiming that God's will mediated through Jesus the Son of Man must be practiced; merciful acts redefine the meaning behind the Sabbath.[90] The emphasis placed on

88. Matthew 12:9–14 must be included in the discussion of 12:1–8, even though Jesus is not referred to as the Son of Man. The healing of the man with a withered hand illustrates Jesus's desire to obey God's will (12:7) by mercifully providing for a human need. Jesus the Son of Man demonstrated that God's will is greater than the Sabbath regulations. As the mediator of God's will, Jesus solidified (through demonstration) what he taught in 12:1–8, namely, that mercy is more important to God than the Sabbath law.

89. Matthew 12:11–12 is not mentioned in Mark and Luke; it is unique to Matthew. The illustrations are used to emphasize the importance of mercy over Sabbath regulations and the concern of demonstrating mercy/love to others (cf. 22:37–40). This focus on mercy strengthens the contrast between the Pharisees's "weary and heavy laden" teaching versus Jesus's "easy and light yoke" of mercy and love (cf. 11:28–30).

90. Harrington mentions that the problem posed here is that Jesus was intentionally breaking a rabbinic rule in Yoma 8:6: "A case of risk of loss of life supersedes the Sabbath (law)." The case of a withered hand was considered a long-term, nonthreatening condition; therefore, Jesus broke the rabbinic tradition. However, in 12:5–7, Jesus obeyed the Torah and placed "eating on the Sabbath" within the confines of the Jewish law, since priests were allowed to work on the Sabbath (Lev 24:8; Num 28:9–20) (Harrington, *Matthew*, 172–73). Harrington's comments are helpful. However, 12:6–7 is more concerned with demonstrating that God's will mediated through Jesus the Son of

the term *human* (ἄνθρωπος) in vv. 11–12, demonstrates that acts of mercy towards humanity are much more important than Sabbath law. The Son of Man is Lord of the Sabbath—he is the mediator of God's grace and mercy to humanity by caring for their needs and consequently, mediates the importance of mercy for the disciples who are called to extend the Son of Man's ministry of mercy to others who are in need of grace and salvation (cf. 22:39). The Son of Man's mission of mercy will culminate in his death—his blood shed for the forgiveness of sins (26:28). As stated above, Jesus's healing ministry prefigures his suffering and death.

Matthew 12:14 is the first place in the Gospel where the Pharisees intended to destroy him (αὐτὸν ἀπολέσωσιν). The Pharisees were likely angry because Jesus was placing his authority over them, especially by claiming that "he is greater than the temple," and that God's will characterized through acts of mercy is the real meaning behind the Sabbath (12:6–7). The intent to destroy Jesus the Son of Man meant the intent to kill; 12:14 is the first instance where Jesus the Son of Man's premeditated death is discussed in the Gospel.[91]

The claim, "The Son of Man is Lord of the Sabbath," corresponds to Jesus's previous claims—"something greater than the temple is here" and "I desire mercy not sacrifice" (12:6–8). These claims emphasize that Jesus's authority is greater than the Pharisees's interpretation of God's will for the Sabbath.[92] Jesus the Son of Man shares his Father's identity as "Lord," and, therefore, mediates God's will of grace and mercy to his disciples so they will extend it to others. Jesus defines the Sabbath as what is acceptable according to God's will: acts of mercy toward those in need. Jesus functions as the mediator of God's will on earth. Jesus's ministry of mercy towards human beings defines for his disciples what God's will is and how it is to be practiced.

Man redefines the true intention of the Sabbath (i.e., acts of mercy).

91. Matthew uses the verb ἀπόλυμι also in 27:20, where the chief priests and elders were trying to convince the crowds to release Barabbas and to crucify ("destroy") Jesus.

92. Regarding the statement, "The Son of Man is Lord of the Sabbath," Banks says, "Matthew clearly regards this final saying as both the goal and the ground of the various christological assertions that have preceded it. The Son of man . . . authorizes the kind of behavior that is legitimate on the sabbath. In his account, then, the emphasis throughout is placed upon the personal authority of Jesus. . . . what is acceptable or unacceptable in the way of conduct upon it is defined in relation to an altogether new reference point, i.e., Christ's estimation of the situation. . . . it leads to a consideration of his own authority, and of the response that is appropriate to it, rather than to reflection on the status of the Law" (*Jesus and the Law*, 120–21, 123). Banks's statement is a good summary. However, his view is connected to 12:6–8, which emphasizes Jesus the Son of Man's role as mediator of God's will. Jesus's authority is grounded in his faithful obedience to God's will during his earthly ministry.

2.7. God's Will to Genuine Disciples: The Need of Spirit-Empowered Ministry (12:22–32)

2.7.1. Textual Orientation

Jesus healed the demon-possessed man who was both blind and mute. The healing amazed all, but the Pharisees stated that the source of the healing came through Beelzebul, the prince of demons. Jesus claimed that he was able to perform the exorcism by the Spirit of God and charged the Pharisees with blaspheming against the Holy Spirit. To speak against the Son of Man is forgivable; however, to blaspheme against the Holy Spirit is unforgivable.

2.7.2. Synoptic Comparison: Matthew 12:22–32; Mark 3:20–30; and Luke 11:14–23

Mark does not mention the Holy Spirit as the source of Jesus's ministry to cast out demons (cf. Mark 3:22–27). With the ministry of the Holy Spirit being so prevalent in Luke-Acts, Luke's use of the "finger of God" (δακτύλῳ θεοῦ) rather than the Holy Spirit as the agency of Jesus's ministry is surprising. Only Matthew explicitly emphasizes the Holy Spirit's role in Jesus's ministry of exorcizing demons. Mark 3:28 mentions that all sins of the "sons of humans" (τοῖς υἱοῖς τῶν ἀνθρώπων; plural) will be forgiven, and does not include the Son of Man. However, in Matt 12:31–32, Jesus only highlights that the every sin and blasphemy of "humans" (τοῖς ἀνθρώποις) will be forgiven, and reserves the title Son of Man (τοῦ υἱοῦ τοῦ ἀνθρώπου; singular) only to Jesus. Luke's account does not highlight the issue of forgiveness and does not include the Son of Man.

Unlike Mark and Luke, Matthew stresses the unforgivable judgment for blaspheming the Holy Spirit in both the present, ἐν τούτῳ τῷ αἰῶνι (in this age), and the future, ἐν τῷ μέλλοντι (in the one coming). Only Mark mentions that the judgment is an eternal sin (3:29–30). Luke does not mention the blasphemy of the Holy Spirit or refer to the Son of Man, nor does he include any judgment associated with it (11:17–26). Only Matthew sees the unforgivable sin as having both present and future consequences.

2.7.3. Exegesis

The textual units in Matt 12 appear to be separated by an introductory phrase or term indicating time (i.e., ἐν ἐκείνῳ τῷ καιρῷ [12:1], τότε [12:22; 12:38]). Therefore, 12:22–37 is part of the same textual unit. Matthew

12:22–29 stresses the contrast between Jesus and the Pharisees in relationship to the source of the Son of Man's authority. The Pharisees claimed Jesus's power came from Satan, which, in Jesus's estimation, was impossible (12:22–29). The Pharisees were against Jesus and committed the unforgivable sin by rejecting the Holy Spirit as the source of Jesus the Son of Man's ministry (12:30–32). In 12:34, Jesus characterized the Pharisees as offspring of vipers (γεννήματα ἐχιδνῶν)[93] due to the internal dispositions of their hearts which were evil (i.e., περισσεύματος τῆς καρδίας; 12:34) that led to their blasphemous speech (i.e., their evil and careless words; 12:35–36), and, therefore, they will be condemned both now and on the day of judgment (12:35–37; cf. 3:10, 12; 7:15–20, 23).

Scholars have debated 12:31–32. Two options have been proposed. First, the present blasphemy of the Son of Man and the future blasphemy of the Holy Spirit contrasts two different periods: the time of the earthly ministry of Jesus the Son of Man (pre-Easter sayings) and the time of the post-Easter Spirit. The blasphemous speech against Jesus is forgivable, but what is said against his messengers who are anointed with the Spirit is unforgivable.[94] Second, the blasphemy of the Holy Spirit is a rejection of the source of Jesus's earthly ministry—that is, condemning the work of the Holy Spirit in and through Jesus is unforgivable.[95]

From the surrounding context in 12:15–32, Matthew is not contrasting two different periods—earthly Jesus versus post-Easter Spirit. The blasphemy is against the power and authority of the Holy Spirit working in and through Jesus the Son of Man. Therefore, to speak against Jesus's work of demon exorcism is the same as blaspheming against the Spirit of God (or the Holy Spirit) working in and through Jesus. Matthew 12:28–32 stresses the authority and power behind Jesus's deeds, namely, the Spirit of God,

---

93. γεννήματα ἐχιδνῶν is used in Matthew to characterize the Sadducees and the Pharisees by John the Baptist (3:7) and Jesus (12:34; 23:33). This reference emphasizes the condemnation of these religious leaders for their hypocrisy and opposition to Jesus's mission and the kingdom of the heavens. Such a description is not found in Mark and only in a parallel account of John the Baptist's condemnation in Luke 3:7.

94. Tödt, *Son of Man*, 119–20; Bornkamm, "End-Expectation," 34; Bornkamm, *Jesus of Nazareth*, 212n1; Edwards, *Sign of Jonah*, 102; Scroggs, "Exaltation of the Spirit," 359–73; Hahn, *Titles of Jesus*, 98; Schweizer, *Good News*, 285, 287–88; Gundry, *Matthew*, 237–38.

95. Osborne, *Matthew*, 477; Hagner, *Matthew*, 1:347–48; Meier, *Matthew*, 135; Overman, *Church and Community*, 183; Carter, *Matthew and the Margins*, 274–75; Morris, *Gospel*, 318–19; Harrington, *Matthew*, 184–85; Nolland, *Matthew*, 505–6; Turner, *Matthew*, 323; Luz, *Matthew 8–20*, 209; Plummer, *Exegetical Commentary*, 178–79; Barrett, *Holy Spirit*, 103–5; Swete, *Holy Spirit*, 115–18; Donaldson, "Blasphemy against the Spirit," 170–71; Yates, *Spirit and the Kingdom*, 77–78, 85–94; Dunn, *Jesus and the Spirit*, 46–53; Combs, "Blasphemy," 92–95; Verseput, *Rejection*, 239–41.

the Holy Spirit (πνεύματι θεοῦ, τοῦ πνεύματος τοῦ ἁγίου). In 12:18, the Holy Spirit is emphasized as the source of Jesus's ministry, when Isa 42:1–4 is used to highlight Jesus's divinely sanctioned ministry. God's Spirit is put on Jesus (θήσω τὸ πνεῦμά μου ἐπ' αὐτόν), empowering him to proclaim judgment to the nations. Matthew 12:18 is reminiscent of Jesus's baptism where God anointed Jesus with the Holy Spirit (3:16–17), and of Jesus's being led by the Spirit into the wilderness to be tempted by Satan (4:1–11). Only in 3:16–17 and in 12:32 is the Holy Spirit emphasized as the source of empowerment in Jesus's ministry. God the Father called Jesus *his* Son when he received the Spirit at his baptism. In this context, the Son of Man is anointed with the Spirit. These verses imply that Jesus the Son of Man and Jesus the Son of God share the same Father. In other words, Jesus the Son of Man is also the Son of God who is anointed with the Spirit of God. The Holy Spirit was the agent through whom Jesus accomplished his ministry. The advent of God's kingdom is accentuated through the Holy Spirit's empowerment of Jesus. In Matthew, Jesus is dependent on the Holy Spirit to cast out demons and heal people (12:28).[96] In 10:8, Jesus granted authority to his disciples so they could extend his ministry of casting out demons. Matthew 10:20 implies that the Father's Spirit will empower the disciples in their itinerant ministry just as the Spirit empowered Jesus in his mission.

The conflict between Jesus and the Pharisees is paralleled with the opposition between the kingdom of the heavens and the kingdom of Satan. No middle ground is offered. The Pharisees align themselves with Satan's kingdom through their rejection of Jesus, the Spirit of God within him, and his divinely sanctioned mission.[97] A similar episode occurs in 9:32–34. In both

---

96. Meier states, "Since the Holy Spirit is the source of repentance and forgiveness, to blaspheme the Holy Spirit and to reject his clear operations within one's range of experience is to close oneself off from all hope of salvation" (Meier, *Matthew*, 135). Osborne says, "The key is the Spirit as the active force of God in this world. To slander God or Jesus is one thing, but to slander his work in this world through the Spirit is another. Since the Holy Spirit is the instrument through which God's eschatological salvation has entered the world, blaspheming that divine tool of salvation cannot be forgiven" (Osborne, *Matthew*, 477). Carter surmises, "The Spirit is the power at work in Jesus which accomplishes his liberating work of saving from sin and establishing God's empire (12:18, 25, 28). To blaspheme against the Spirit is to refuse to recognize God's eschatological, liberating work under way in Jesus (cf. 11:2–6). Speaking against the Spirit . . . suggests a constant refusal to see God's Spirit empowering Jesus. This is not forgivable because it is a sustained rejection of God's work" (Carter, *Matthew and the Margins*, 274–75).

97. Lammé argues that the blasphemy of the Holy Spirit is a sin which is specific to false teachers (e.g., the Pharisees's rejection of Jesus's person and work). Since the Pharisees rejected Christ and his work (i.e., the gospel) and taught others to reject it as well they committed blasphemy against the Spirit. He states, "The blasphemy of the Holy Spirit is, therefore, a public rejection of the Spirit's testimony about the person and work

contexts, Jesus healed a demon-possessed man. The difference in 9:32–34 is that the demon-possessed man was mute, not both blind and mute as the man in 12:22–23. In both contexts, the demon-possessed men were healed as the demons are exorcised. Jesus's authority to heal and cast out demons amazed the crowds, yet the Pharisees accused Jesus of casting out the demons through the authority and power of the ruler of demons (ἄρχοντι τῶν δαιμονίων; Beelzebub in 12:24). Only in Matthew do these parallel episodes of demonic healing occur. These accounts of demonic healing emphasize Jesus's authority and power in contrast to the Pharisees's rejection through aligning Jesus's power to the "ruler of demons."

In 12:18, 28, the emphasis on the Holy Spirit's agency in Jesus's earthly ministry solidifies the meaning of 12:31–32—the blasphemy of the Holy Spirit. In 12:31–32, the contrast between the Holy Spirit and Jesus the Son of Man does not minimize the person of Jesus and exalt the Holy Spirit. The emphasis is solely on the Holy Spirit's role in Jesus's earthly ministry. When the Pharisees spoke against Jesus's ability to expel demons as the work of Beelzebub (Satan), they blasphemed God who gave the Holy Spirit to Jesus so he could accomplish his ministry (e.g., expel demons). The Holy Spirit also empowered Jesus the Son of Man in his mission to forgive sins and restore humanity's relationship with God through his suffering and death. In 12:31, humans (ἀνθρώποις) will be forgiven every sin (πᾶσα ἁμαρτία) and blasphemy. In 12:32, whoever speaks a word against the Son of Man (i.e., Son of Humanity) will be forgiven. Jesus the Son of Man was anointed by the Spirit to preach salvation through the forgiveness of sins (4:19) and to ransom people from their sins (1:21; 20:28; 26:28). The Son of Man's desire to forgive humanity of their sins was an integral part of his ministry climaxing in his suffering and death. Since the Holy Spirit empowered Jesus ministry, no forgiveness is available to those who reject the work of the Spirit in the Son of Man and in the disciples's future ministry when they continue his ministry by proclaiming the message of the forgiveness of sins (12:32; cf. 24:14; 28:18–28). The Son of Man is the mediator of God's will for his disciples specifically in their ministry of preaching the forgiveness of sins through his suffering and death.

The Pharisees opposed God when they rejected Jesus, since his works were accomplished through the Holy Spirit (12:30). Darrel L. Bock's monograph, *Blasphemy and Exaltation in Judaism*, provides the socio religious background: The Pharisees would probably have seen Jesus's statements regarding demon exorcism as (1) putting himself too close to God and (2) claiming total

---

of the Son of God, by teachers, for the purpose of leading others astray from Christ as offered to us in the gospel" ("Blasphemy," 40–41, 42). Lammé's view is plausible but may be limited by restricting the sin of blasphemy to the religious leaders (teachers) alone.

THE SON OF MAN'S MEDIATORIAL SIGNIFICANCE ON EARTH 81

independent authority over the nation's highest religious authorities who, in their mind, were appointed by God as the religious establishment of Judaism. Both claims would have been offensive to the Pharisees.[98] Ironically, Jesus was indicating that the source of his authority and power came through God's empowering Spirit, enabling his earthly ministry.

Matthew emphasizes that the consequence of blaspheming the Holy Spirit is judgment both in this age and in the one coming. Attributing the Son of Man's works to Satan rather than to the Holy Spirit is blasphemy; similarly, when people speak against the disciples's ministry, that will also be empowered by the Holy Spirit (cf. 28:18–20), that too will constitute blasphemy. Throughout chapter 12, and especially during Jesus's demon exorcism, the disciples (and crowds) have been the witnesses to this miracle (cf. 12:1, 15). Jesus's exorcism through the Spirit's power and his teaching regarding blasphemy mediate the need of the Holy Spirit for the disciples's post-Easter ministry. Blasphemy will have both present and future consequences: in the present, the sin will be unforgiven; in the future, it will result in the loss of one's salvation (e.g., 12:36–37). Jesus's warning to the Pharisees and crowds about blaspheming the Spirit was meant to stress that Jesus the Son of Man is the mediator between God and humanity, since the Spirit was the agency of his earthly ministry. By accepting Jesus's ministry, people were accepting the source, namely, the Spirit of God (3:16–17; 12:18, 28) who provides the forgiveness of sins and salvation to them. In 7:22–23, 12:27, and 16:21–23, the ability to cast out demons is no guarantee of the acceptance of God's will in Jesus's ministry. Aligning with Jesus's mission requires total submission to (agreement with and obedience to) God's will mediated through Jesus the Son of Man. In 16:21–23, when Peter spoke against God's will for Jesus's upcoming suffering and death, Jesus rebuked Satan's influence in him and commanded him to submit to his authority—"Get behind me, Satan; you are a stumbling block to me, for you are not thinking the things of God but the things of humans" (16:23).[99] One's complete acceptance of Jesus the Son of Man's mission is necessary in aligning with the Spirit's work in him. To reject any part of Jesus's mission comes dangerously close to blaspheming the Holy Spirit, the source of Jesus's power and authority. A commitment to align oneself with Jesus's mission is characteristic of a true family member of Jesus, since, consequently, a person is "doing the will of my Father the one in the heavens" (12:46–50). To emulate Jesus's ministry, a complete submission to the Holy Spirit as the source of the disciples's ministry is mandatory. Similar to Jesus, the ability to fulfill their earthly ministry requires the

---

98. Bock, *Blasphemy and Exaltation*, 231–32.
99. I will discuss Jesus's rebuke of Peter (16:21–23) in chapter 3.

source of Holy Spirit as their power and authority, which is only possible as he is mediated to them through Jesus the Son of Man.

The Pharisees claimed Jesus's power to exorcise demons came from Satan. They were against Jesus's ministry and committed the unforgiveable sin by rejecting the Holy Spirit as the source of the Son of Man's ministry (12:22–32). Rejecting the Holy Spirit's work in and through Jesus's ministry is blasphemy. The Pharisees's condemnation of Jesus, the Spirit's work within him, and his divinely sanctioned ministry, aligned themselves with Satan and his kingdom. Through the Son of Man's ministry of forgiving sins climaxed in his suffering and death, he was able to forgive humanity of their sins. Similarly, his disciples will extend this message of forgiveness in their future ministry (24:14). The blasphemy of the Holy Spirit will lead to judgment both in this age (during the Son of Man's ministry) and in the age to come (when the Holy Spirit empowers Jesus's disciples's ministry [cf. 28:18–20]). Like Jesus, a complete submission to the Holy Spirit as the source of the disciples's future ministry is mandatory in fulfilling God's will. The Son of Man's dependence on the Holy Spirit as the agent of his ministry and his teaching regarding blasphemy, mediate the need of the Holy Spirit for the disciples's post-Easter ministry.

2.8. God's Will to Genuine Disciples: Imitating Jesus's Self-Sacrificial Ministry (Matthew 12:38–42)

2.8.1. Textual Orientation

The scribes and the Pharisees wanted to see a sign from Jesus the Son of Man. Jesus stated that only the sign of Jonah would be given to them—a reference to the Son of Man being in the heart of the earth for three days and nights. Jesus then highlighted Gentile peoples (i.e., the people of Ninevah and the Queen of the South) as representatives of those who accepted Jesus's ministry. He contrasted them with members of this generation (e.g., the scribes and Pharisees) as representatives of those who rejected Jesus's ministry.

2.8.2. Synoptic Comparison: Matthew 12:38–42 and Luke 11:29–32[100]

In 12:38–39, the scribes and Pharisees approached Jesus and asked to see a sign. Jesus identified them as representatives of those who are part of an

---

100. In Mark 8:11–12, the Pharisees asked Jesus for a sign from heaven and Jesus

evil and adulterous generation who seeks signs. In Luke 11:29, the crowds appear as representatives of an evil generation (also 11:14–15, calling Jesus Beelzebul). Only Matthew combines the scribes and Pharisees with an evil and adulterous generation and, unlike Luke, includes *adulterous* (μοιχαλίς) as a description of them.

Luke 11:29b–30 provides no description of the sign of Jonah. Only Matthew indicates that the sign of Jonah is connected to Jesus being in the "heart of the earth three days and three nights" (12:40). Scholars have argued that the use of future verb ἔσται relates to the parousia in Luke 11:30. However, the description of the sign of Jonah in Matt 12:40 does not connect ἔσται with the future parousia but with the near-future death and resurrection of Jesus the Son of Man.

2.8.3. *Exegesis*

An *inclusio* exists in 12:38–39 and 12:45 that keeps the section of 12:38–45 as a structural unit. Jesus identified the Pharisees and scribes as evil and adulterous. The emphasis placed on *evil* directly connects this section with 12:22–37. Only Matthew includes the phrase "evil and adulterous generation" (γενεὰ πονηρὰ καὶ μοιχαλίς; 12:39; 16:4). Jesus used this phrase to identify the character of the scribes and Pharisees—those opposed to God's will in Jesus the Son of Man's ministry.[101] The Pharisees were supposed to be the religious leaders of God, but they proved their unfaithfulness to him in their opposition to Jesus's ministry, which, throughout Matt 9–12, mediated God's will on earth. Their rejection of Jesus's ministry (e.g., 12:22–32) led him to identify them as representatives of an evil and adulterous generation. The Pharisees requested to see a sign from Jesus the Son of Man; however, they have already rejected the signs of his kingdom works (miracles) and message (cf. 9:1–8, 32–34; 12:14, 22–32). Therefore, as 16:1 mentions, the Pharisees were testing (πειράζοντες) Jesus. Such rejection aligned the Pharisees with the kingdom of Satan by doing what

---

responded by saying that this generation will not be given a sign. I did not include it in the Synoptic Comparison because Mark's account of this "sign" does not specifically relate to the "sign of Jonah" as in the Gospels of Matthew and Luke.

101. In Matt 17:17, a similar structure, "faithless and depraved generation" (γενεὰ ἄπιστος καὶ διεστραμμένη), is used to describe those who do not have faith to cast out demons. The lack of faith relates to Jesus's insistence that the kingdom of God is greater than the kingdom of Satan. Jesus demonstrated the power of the kingdom of God by healing the demon-possessed boy. Faith in the authority and power of Jesus the Son of Man (and the Holy Spirit in him) is necessary for genuine discipleship, that is, for one who is aligned with God's kingdom.

Satan did in 4:1–10. In 4:1, 3, 7, the same verb, πειράζω (to test, to tempt), is used as the motivation behind Satan's evil work in trying to persuade Jesus to forfeit God's mission. In 19:3, 22:18, and 22:35, the verb πειράζω is an action of tempting or testing by Satan, the Pharisees, or the Pharisees and Sadducees. Therefore, πειράζω aligns the Pharisees and Sadducees with the kingdom of Satan, not with the kingdom of God.

In 12:39 and 16:4, Jesus stated that the only sign he would give the Pharisees, scribes, and Sadducees is the sign of Jonah. The meaning of the sign of Jonah in 12:39 (16:4) has been debated. Scholars have argued four main positions. First, the sign of Jonah refers to Jesus's preaching of repentance, which has been rejected mostly by the religious leaders. In 12:41–42, Jesus stated that the Ninevites accepted Jonah's preaching, and the Queen of Sheba received Solomon's wisdom, emphasizing Gentile receptivity in contrast with the Jewish leaders's rejection.[102] Second, the sign of Jonah refers to the coming of Jesus the Son of Man in judgment at the parousia. The main impetus behind this interpretation is the strength of the future indicative, 3rd person, singular ἔσται in Luke 11:30, indicating the future eschaton and not Jesus's present earthly ministry.[103] H. E. Tödt argues that this view is strengthened by Matt 24:30, which speaks of the future parousia of Jesus the Son of Man.[104] Third, the sign of Jonah refers to the resurrection of Jesus. Jonah 1:17–2:10 and Matt 12:40 are compared to emphasize deliverance from death. Jonah's burial in the sea monster can be compared with Jesus's death and burial in the tomb. Most scholars support this view.[105] Fourth, the sign of Jonah refers to the resurrected Son of Man's public return from the dead. After Jesus the Son of Man rises from the dead, he will make a public return prior to his exaltation. During this time, he will commission his disciples to extend his warning of judgment and peoples's need to repent by continuing with Jesus the Son of Man's ministry, which he taught and demonstrated before them.[106]

---

102. Harnack, *Sprüche und Reden Jesu*, 20–21; Manson, *Sayings of Jesus*, 89–91; Kümmel, *Promise and Fulfillment*, 68–69; Hammerton-Kelly, *Pre-Existence*, 33–35; Hagner, *Matthew*, 1:354; Keener, *Gospel of Matthew*, 367; Nolland, *Matthew*, 511–12 (specifically a preacher of judgment to "this generation" for their rejection).

103. Bultmann, *History*, 124; Tödt, *Son of Man*, 52–54, 211–14; Higgins, *Jesus*, 138–40; Rengstorf, "σημεῖον," 200–261; Klostermann, *Das Matthäusevangelium*, 112.

104. Tödt, *Son of Man*, 53.

105. Jeremias, "Ἰωνᾶς," 406–10; Barrett, *Holy Spirit*, 90; France, *Jesus and the Old Testament*, 44; Chow, *Sign of Jonah*, 64–67; Wright, *Resurrection*, 432–33; Beasley-Murray, *Jesus*, 256–57; Davies and Allison, *Matthew*, 2:355–56; Luz, *Matthew 8–20*, 217–18; Gundry, *Matthew*, 244–45; Hare, *Matthew*, 143; Meier, *Matthew*, 138; Morris, *Gospel*, 325–26; Harrington, *Matthew*, 188–90; France, *Matthew*, 490–92; Schweizer, *Good News*, 293; Turner, *Matthew*, 326; Osborne, *Matthew*, 486.

106. Edwards, *Sign of Jonah*, 47–58, 83–87; Vögtle, "Der Spruch vom Jonaszeichen,"

Joel Edmund Anderson believes that the sign of Jonah is a prediction of both Jesus's future death and resurrection, and the preaching of repentance with positive reception by the Gentiles.[107] A few scholars have argued three other views, which are worth mentioning but have little textual support in Matthew. Fifth, the sign of Jonah is a misunderstanding of the original sign of the dove, emphasizing Jesus's role as a messenger of God declaring redemption to the world.[108] Sixth, the sign of Jonah is a reference to John the Baptist and his preaching of repentance.[109] Seventh, the sign of Jonah is an allusion to the destruction of Jerusalem in AD 70.[110]

The first view argued by scholars relates the sign of Jonah to Jesus's preaching of repentance. As mentioned, this view takes into account Matt 12:41–42, with examples of the positive reception of Jesus's message among the Gentile people (i.e., the positive reception of Jesus's works among Gentile cities in 11:20–24). The problem is that this position dismisses the Gospel's unique contribution in 12:40, which compares Jonah's descent into the sea monster for three days and three nights and subsequent deliverance with Jesus the Son of Man's death, burial, and resurrection. Some argue that Jesus was not in the tomb for three days and three nights. This statement is true: Jesus was not buried for three nights, but Ulrich Luz provides a clear explanation for this position: (1) In Jewish thought three days was a symbolic number—"God leaves the righteous no longer than three days in distress" (*Yalqut* on Josh 2:16 par. 12 in Str-B 1.647; cf. Gen 42:17–18; Exod 19:11, 16; Hos 6:2), and (2) the Jewish day begins at "sunset so that with part of Friday, the Sabbath, and the night from the Sabbath to Sunday, one arrives at three 'days.'" In addition, "'day and night' is a common Hebrew expression for a calendar day, since יום primarily meant daylight time in contrast to the night (cf. e.g., Gen 7:4; 1 Sam 30:12–13)."[111] Therefore if one seriously considers these unique features in 12:40, the argument that the sign of Jonah refers to Jesus's preaching of repentance seems untenable. Anderson's position does accentuate the importance of 12:40 relating to Jesus's death, burial, and resurrection along with the preaching of repentance. His view is plausible but does not account for Jesus's public return after his resurrection which is also part of the sign of Jonah.

127–34; Verseput, *Rejection*, 261–65.

107. Anderson, "Jonah," 175–76, 182.

108. Howton, "Sign of Jonah," 288–304.

109. Michael, "Sign of John," 146–59; Wink, *John the Baptist*, 22, 23n2.

110. Schmitt, "Das Zeichen des Jona," 123–29; Swetnam, "Some Signs of Jonah," 74–79.

111. Luz, *Matthew 8–20*, 217, 218n42.

The second argument relates to the future indicative ἔσται in Luke 11:30. Due to the Lukan account (11:29–32), the sign of Jonah in 12:38–42 refers to the parousia. Three problems exist with this view. First, even if the sign of Jonah in Luke 11:29–32 does refer to the parousia of Jesus the Son of Man, the meaning of Matt 12:40 does not necessarily warrant the same future view of the sign of Jonah. Luke 11 does not mention Jesus's parousia or his role in the future. The context of the chapter relates to Jesus's earthly ministry. Second, the entire context of Matt 12 refers to Jesus's earthly ministry. The future role of Jesus at the parousia is not mentioned in this chapter. Rather, Jesus demonstrates through his words and deeds ministry that is consistent with God's will. Third, 12:40 is not considered with its particular reference to the sign of Jonah in 12:38–39. The unique Matthean contribution accentuates the meaning of the sign of Jonah with Jesus's death, burial, and resurrection.

The final three possibilities find little support among the majority of scholars. Only 3:16 mentions a dove in the Gospel, and this is the Spirit of God descending on Jesus at the beginning of his earthly ministry. Matthew 8–12 describes the words and deeds of Jesus the Son of Man, which demonstrate God's will on earth. The context of Matt 8–12 does not support an interpretation of the sign of Jonah as referring to the destruction of Jerusalem; the focus is on Jesus's earthly ministry. Finally, the view that the sign of Jonah refers to John the Baptist's ministry may have some textual support. Matthew does intentionally compare Jesus's ministry with that of John the Baptist (cf. 3:1–2; 4:17; 11:7–19). However, in Matt 12, Jesus is not compared to John the Baptist; the chapter only discusses Jesus's earthly ministry.

In 12:39–40, Jesus the Son of Man described the meaning of the sign of Jonah. From the context, the sign of Jonah refers to the resurrection of Jesus and his public return after his resurrection (relating to Jonah 1:17—2:10). Jesus the Son of Man's death and resurrection is compared with Jonah's burial in the sea monster and subsequent deliverance. Jonah's disobedience to God's will brought divine judgment: The Lord appointed a fish to swallow him, and for three days and nights he was in the fish's belly. Jonah felt separated from God while in the fish and repented of his sins, reclaiming his loyalty to God (Jonah 2:3–8). Jonah willingly chose to sacrifice for God, believing only God could save him (Jonah 2:9), and was delivered from the fish to continue his mission to the Ninevites (Jonah 2:10). Similarly, Jesus the Son of Man received divine judgment and punishment for the sins of the world through his suffering and death on a cross, was buried, and was resurrected (cf. 16:21; 17:22–23; 20:17–19; 26:2). Matthew 12:39–40 provides the first direct mention of the Son of Man's suffering, death, and resurrection. Just as Jonah fulfilled God's will by going to Ninevah to preach a message of judgment in order that the Ninevites would repent of their sins, turn to God, and be saved from destruction (Jonah 1:1; 3:1–10; 4:11), so the Son of Man fulfilled God's will through his sacrificial death and resurrection. Jonah knew God's character and will—to demonstrate mercy and compassion to the Ninevites (Jonah 4:2). Through the Son of Man's suffering, death, and resurrection, God would display his mercy and compassion to sinners. Jesus's death and resurrection mediated to his disciples specifically and the religious leaders/crowds generally, that God the Father is merciful and compassionate. His will on earth is that sinners would repent of their sins, receive forgiveness through the Son of Man's sacrificial death and resurrection, and be saved from their separation from God (cf. 6:10). After his resurrection, Jesus commissioned his disciples to emulate his ministry of word and deed (cf. Matt 28:18–20). Similar to Jesus, the disciples will be required to deny themselves through relinquishing people and possessions, and suffer opposition, persecution, and possible death in their faithful obedience to Jesus's commission (i.e., God's will) (cf. 8:18–22; 10:16–39; 11:18–24; 12:30–33; 16:21–26). A main way the disciples will fulfill God's will on earth is to preach about God's mercy and grace through the Son of Man's sacrificial death. Forgiveness for the sinner is available to those who repent of their sins and turn to God for salvation. The Son of Man is the mediator of God's will to his disciples.

Jesus condemned those who opposed and rejected his ministry. The Pharisees, scribes, Sadducees, and all others have rejected and opposed God's kingdom through their unwillingness to repent of their sins and listen to the Father's wisdom revealed through Jesus. The Gentile city of Ninevah and the Gentile Queen of the South will stand up and condemn this generation because they have not rejected and opposed God's kingdom but heeded his warnings to repent and embrace his wisdom (12:41–42). The polarity between rejecting the kingdom of God and accepting his kingdom is vast; no middle ground is possible (cf. 12:30). In comparison with 11:20–27, the emphasis of Jewish people rejecting Jesus (e.g., religious leaders; Chorazin; Bethsaida; Capernaum), and the Gentile people accepting Jesus (e.g., tax collectors and sinners [11:19]; Tyre; Sidon; Sodom) accentuates the missional concern to make disciples of all nations (both Jews[112] and Gentiles; πάντα τὰ ἔθνη; 28:18–20). Therefore, God's will is for all people to accept Jesus's ministry (works and message), repent of their sins, and experience the fullness of God's salvific plan mediated through Jesus's death and resurrection

112. Jesus's words in 23:37–39 substantiated his desire for the Jewish mission. Jesus stated that even though he longed for the Jews (and religious leaders) to accept him and become his children, they were not willing and, consequently, rejected him and all the prophets (God's messengers) sent before him.

(e.g., the forgiveness of their sins). The universal scope of Jesus's invitation is important to Matthean theology (cf. 11:28–30; 24:14).

In 12:41–42, the repetitive phrase "behold, something much greater ... is here" (ἰδοὺ πλεῖον ... ὧδε) is reminiscent of 12:6 and functions in the same way. The sign of Jonah in 12:40–41 stresses that Jesus the Son of Man's works and message are far greater than Jonah's preaching and Solomon's wisdom. Jesus the Son of Man's teaching, preaching, and wisdom reveal the fullness of God's will to his people as the mediator of God's will on earth. Jesus the Son of Man's sacrificial death and resurrection accomplished the ultimate salvific will of God for all humanity.

In contrast to the Pharisees and this evil generation who opposed Jesus the Son of Man's works and message (cf. 12:38–39a, 43–45), Jesus's true family are his faithful disciples who learn and practice how to follow Jesus and align themselves with the kingdom of God (12:46–50). They accept Jesus the Son of Man by emulating his obedience: to "do the will of my Father, the one in the heavens" (cf. 7:21). Jesus the Son of Man is the mediator of God's will on earth for his disciples, and they prove their allegiance by continuing to follow Jesus as he fulfilled his Father's will.

The Pharisees requested to see a sign from Jesus the Son of Man, even though they had already rejected the signs of his kingdom works (miracles) and message. The only sign Jesus would give them is the sign of Jonah, namely, his resurrection from the dead and his public return after his resurrection (12:40; 28). Just as Jonah fulfilled God's will by preaching judgment to the Ninevites which led to the repentance of their sins (Jonah 3), so the Son of Man fulfilled God's will through his sacrificial death and resurrection. After his resurrection, Jesus commissioned his disciples to emulate his ministry (28:18–20). Like Jesus, the disciples would suffer opposition, persecution, and possible death in their faithful obedience to God's will (10:16–39; 16:21–26). Jesus the Son of Man's sacrificial death in fulfillment of God's will mediates the kind of self-sacrificial ministry which will be required of his disciples. In addition, the disciples will preach the message of repentance for the forgiveness of sins (as Jesus did, 4:19), and will proclaim that the Son of Man's sacrificial death occurred so that humanity could be forgiven of their sins and restored in their relationship with God. Gentile people will stand up and condemn the Jewish cities and religious leaders for their rejection and opposition to God's kingdom (e.g., 11:20–27). Jesus's ministry is greater than Jonah's preaching and Solomon's wisdom, because, through his ministry, he revealed the Son of Man's sacrificial death and resurrection which accomplished God's ultimate salvific will for humanity (e.g., the forgiveness of their sins). God's will is for all people (Jews and Gentiles) to accept Jesus's ministry (works and message) and experience the fullness of his grace—his salvific plan mediated through Jesus's sacrificial death and resurrection.

3. Conclusion

The focus of this chapter has been on the earthly ministry of Jesus the Son of Man in chapters 8–12. I have argued that the Son of Man logia in these chapters reveal that Jesus mediates God's will on earth to his genuine disciples. Jesus's faithful disciples are "doing the will of my Father the one in the heavens" (emphasized by the *inclusio*, namely, 7:21 and 12:50). They have accepted Jesus's earthly ministry and are committed to follow him by emulating his ministry in their present (9:35–10:42) and their future mission (28:18–20). Jesus mediates God's will by revealing what is required of a genuine disciple.

First, genuine disciples understand the necessity of obeying Jesus the Son of Man through their willingness to relinquish all earthly attachments (i.e., self-denial of family, status, position, and geographical location) to follow Jesus as Lord. Releasing oneself from earthly attachments is the essence of self-denial and a genuine follower of Jesus the Son of Man (8:18–22). In 8:20, the Son of Man offered grace by inviting the scribe and disciple to a life of self-renunciation. His upcoming suffering and death will accentuate his desire to relinquish his life for the sake of others. Similarly, the disciples will follow the Son of Man through their willingness to sacrifice their lives if necessary. God's will is revealed through the Son of Man's mediatorial role of self-abasement.

Second, genuine disciples consider the importance of having faith (πίστις). God's will was mediated through Jesus's positive reaction to the faith of his disciples. Healing and forgiveness of sins are manifestations of God's will on earth demonstrated through the authoritative work of Jesus the Son of Man. The Son of Man would bring glory to God by restoring the relationship between God the Father and this paralytic (all humanity) through his sacrificial death—the means of forgiveness of humanity's sin. Jesus's healing ministry prefigures his suffering and death. Similarly, forgiving the sins of others would be an integral part of the disciples's future mission (e.g., 18:21–35). The Son of Man is mediator of God's will to his disciples by emphasizing the importance of forgiving others, which will be culminated in his own death and resurrection. Jesus the Son of Man also mediated that faith is a mandatory characteristic for those who want to follow God's will (9:1–9).

Third, genuine disciples follow Jesus the Son of Man's own example and instructions, which mediate for them the fulfillment of God's will in their present and future ministry. Jesus the Son of Man's example and teaching reveal to his disciples how to know and practice God's will on earth. When the disciples go to the lost sheep of Israel and governors and kings with the good news of salvation through the forgiveness of sins, they will exemplify Jesus's own ministry of preaching repentance to others (4:19). Both Jesus and his disciples urge others to repent of their sins so they can have a restored relationship with God the Father. Like his own upcoming suffering and death which is the most complete expression of God's grace and mercy, Jesus emphasized to his disciples the necessity of faithfully doing God's will even when facing the consequences of their loyalty (i.e., persecution, opposition, and possibly death). Sometime after this death and resurrection, Jesus will return to his disciples and give them further instructions on their ministry both to Jewish and Gentile people (28:18–20). As with Jesus, suffering and persecution are inevitable results of following the Father's will on earth (10:16–23). The Son of Man is the mediator of God's will (i.e., his grace and mercy) to his disciples through his emphasis on extending his ministry by their sharing of the message of forgiveness with others offered through his sacrificial death.

Fourth, true disciples demonstrate their acceptance of Jesus by learning from him the full revelation of God's will and being willing to embrace all people as recipients of God's salvation. The contrast between accepting and rejecting God's will is mediated though Jesus and is located throughout Matt 8–12, and particularly in chapter 11. Those who reject Jesus the Son of Man and John the Baptist as God's divinely appointed ministers are, consequently, rejecting God and his will. Jesus and John the Baptist faithfully aligned themselves with God's will. Jesus the Son of Man mediated God's will on earth by embracing tax collectors and sinners as his friends, in spite of the rejection he received from others (cf. 9:9–13; esp. 9:13, quoting Hos 6:6, "I desire [will; θέλω] mercy not sacrifice"). Through his miracles (δυνάμεις), Jesus mediated God's will by providing the opportunity for people to see his works and repent of their sins, which was more characteristic for Gentiles, especially tax collectors and sinners in 21:31–32. Only Jesus can mediate God's will to the little ones and infants (μικρότερος and νηπίοις; μικρῶν in 18:1–14), the more complete revelation of God's will (i.e., his salvific purposes; his promised rest in 11:28–30; 11:11–19). Consequently, the Son of Man mediated God's will to his disciples in two ways: (1) by urging that the message of repentance be shared with sinners, so they will have the opportunity to repent and receive God's grace and mercy, and (2) for them to embrace the ostracized of society (i.e., the sinners, tax collectors) so they might repent of their sins and receive salvation—a restored relationship with God the Father (e.g., 11:25-28).

Fifth, Jesus the Son of Man mediated God's will by revealing the need for mercy toward others. Jesus's deeds of mercy were grounded in God's will. His mercy towards other people redefined the Sabbath regulations regarding work. Jesus the Son of Man's (and his disciples) mission on earth involved demonstrating (revealing) the kingdom of the heavens through his (their) works of mercy. When Jesus the Son of Man revealed himself as the "Lord" of the Sabbath (12:8), he emphasized his divine identity since, earlier in 11:25, he called God the Father "Lord" of heaven and earth. As the Lord of the Sabbath, the Son of Man is mediator of God's grace and mercy to humanity by caring for their needs and, consequently, mediating the importance of mercy to his disciples who are called to extend his ministry to others who are in need of God's grace and mercy (cf. 22:39). The Son of Man's mission of mercy will culminate in his upcoming death—his blood shed for the forgiveness of sins of humanity (26:28). Humanity and their needs are more valuable than the law, as seen through the story of Jesus's healing of the man with the withered hand in 12:9-14 (12:1-8), where the value of humanity is accentuated and viewed as an example of God's grace and mercy.

Sixth, Jesus the Son of Man mediated God's will through the agency of the divinely sanctioned Spirit within him, which empowered him to accomplish God's will. The religious leaders spoke against Jesus the Son of Man's works and message and, consequently, were unable to receive forgiveness of their sins because they were blaspheming the Holy Spirit at work in Jesus. To attribute Jesus's works such as demon exorcism to Satan was to blaspheme against the Spirit, since the Spirit empowered Jesus to accomplish his works. Similarly, Jesus will give the Holy Spirit to his disciples to enable them to fulfill God's will through their works and message in their future ministry (cf. 10:8, 20; 28:19-20). In contrast to the religious leaders, genuine disciples accept Jesus the Son of Man's earthly ministry and, consequently, accept the agency of the Spirit in him. These genuine disciples are able to receive forgiveness of sins and salvation (12:22-32). The emphasis on forgiveness in 12:31-32 highlights the Holy Spirit's empowerment of the Son of Man's ministry of preaching the message of repentance for the forgiveness of humanity's sins, and restoring their relationship with God through offering his life as a ransom in his upcoming suffering and death. Similarly, in their future ministry, the Spirit-empowered disciples will preach the message of repentance and forgiveness of sins available through the Son of Man's death and resurrection. The Son of Man's own mission of forgiving humanity's sin mediates the importance of preaching this message of forgiveness to humanity in their future ministry.

Finally, Jesus the Son of Man mediated the salvific purposes of God's will through his climactic deeds emphasized in 12:40. The sign of Jonah refers to the death, burial, and resurrection of Jesus and his public return to his disciples after his resurrection. During this public return, Jesus will commission his genuine disciples to emulate his ministry subsequent to his exaltation (cf. 28:18–20). Jesus mediated God's will to his genuine disciples by revealing his future death, burial, and resurrection. In addition, Jesus revealed the kind of ministry that fulfills God's will to his genuine disciples: like Jesus, they will suffer persecution, opposition, and death. God's will is for all people to accept Jesus's ministry and to experience the fullness of God's salvific plan mediated through Jesus's death and resurrection. Jonah knew God's character and will—to demonstrate mercy and compassion on the Ninevites. Through the Son of Man's suffering and death, God would perfectly display his mercy and compassion to sinners. God's will on earth was for sinners to repent of their sins and receive forgiveness through the Son of Man's death and resurrection, restoring his Father's relationship with humanity (cf. 6:10). Similarly, the disciples will be required to deny themselves and suffer opposition, persecution, and possible death in their obedience to Jesus's commission (i.e., God's will) (e.g., 10:16–39; 16:21–26). The Son of Man's suffering and death which makes God's mercy available to humanity, mediates the kind of self-sacrificial ministry expected of the disciples in their mission to share the message of God's grace with others. The evil generation will miss out on the fullness of God's will mediated through Jesus, but genuine disciples (and sinners like tax collectors) will accept God's wisdom and salvation revealed and displayed through Jesus (12:38–45).

Chapter 3

The Son of Man's Mediatorial Significance in His Passion

Fulfilling God's Will through Obedience

1. Introduction

IN CHAPTER 2, I demonstrated that Jesus the Son of Man mediates God's will to his genuine disciples during his earthly ministry. In this chapter, I will show ways that Jesus the Son of Man mediates how to fulfill God's will through obedience to his Father in the passion material. Through his teaching and example, Jesus commanded his disciples to obey God's will in order to fulfill God's will for their lives. The theme of fulfilling God's will through obedience finds its climax in the passion material where Jesus the Son of Man is mentioned. Therefore, I will analyze each of the Son of Man sayings (i.e., Matt 16:13,[1] 27–28; [the passion predictions, 16:21; 17:22–23; 20:17–19; 26:2[2]]; 17:9, 12; 20:28; 26:24, 45) within their co-texts and, through immediate and broader-book contexts, emphasize the ways Jesus (and consequently the disciples) obeys God's will.

Mark and Luke do not center their theological perspective of the passion narratives around Jesus the Son of Man's obedience to God's will with the same intentionality as Matthew. Therefore, Matthew's contribution to the understanding of Jesus as the Son of Man is different from and, in many ways, unique when compared with what is found in Mark and Luke. I will demonstrate Matthew's different theological understanding of Jesus as Son of Man by comparing the Synoptic Gospels. Finally, I will conclude by highlighting Matthew's theological perspective on Jesus the Son of Man's fulfillment of God's will through his unrelenting obedience to God in the passion

---

1. I will demonstrate that structurally Matthew 16:13 belongs with the first passion prediction in 16:21.

2. Matthew 26:2 is Matthew's unique contribution and is considered the Gospel's fourth passion prediction.

narratives, and what implications unrelenting obedience would have had for the genuine disciples's present and future ministry.

2. The Son of Man as Mediator of Fulfilling God's Will through Obedience

2.1. God's Will Obeyed: Jesus the Son of Man's Fidelity to God's Revealed Confession (Matthew 16:13–28)

2.1.1. Textual Orientation

Jesus asked his disciples, "Who do humans say the Son of Man is?" (16:13). The disciples named John the Baptist, Elijah, Jeremiah, or one of the prophets. Jesus probed them further: "But who do you say I am?" (16:15). At this point, Peter, the disciples's representative, answered, "You are the Christ, the Son of the living God" (16:16). Jesus pronounced a blessing on Peter and stated that his (i.e., my) Father the one in the heavens revealed this confession to him. According to the Father, Jesus the Son of Man is the Christ and God's Son. In light of Peter's correct response, Jesus promised to give them authority in the church and commanded them not to tell anyone that he is the Christ. Jesus proceeded to predict that he must go to Jerusalem to suffer, be killed, and be raised on the third day. Peter rebuked Jesus's teaching and rejected his prediction of suffering and death as part of God's will. In contrast, Jesus rejected Peter's rebuke as coming from Satan and told his disciples that suffering and death are part of genuine discipleship. Finally, Jesus spoke of his near-future return as Son of Man sometime during the disciples's lifetime, and about his future return as the Son of Man in order to warn and encourage the disciples to fidelity to his teachings and God's will.

2.1.2. Synoptic Comparison: Matthew 16:13–28; Mark 8:27—9:1; and Luke 9:18–27

Unlike Mark and Luke, Matthew does not include the saying about the Son of Man in the first passion prediction. Instead, the saying occurs earlier in the form of a question: "Who do humans say the Son of Man is?" (16:13), connecting the question regarding the Son of Man with Peter's actual confession: "You are the Christ, the Son of the living God" (16:16). Mark and Luke mention Peter's confession regarding Jesus as the Christ (Luke: "Christ of God" [9:20]), but does not mention, as Matthew does, that he is "the Son of the living God" (16:16b).

Matthew 16:17–20 is not found in Mark or Luke; it is unique to his Gospel. Only Matthew mentions that Jesus's Father, the one in the heavens, revealed the confession to Peter. Matthew intentionally binds Peter's confession together with predictions of the disciples's authority in the church (i.e., the rock on which Jesus builds the church, the claim that the gates of hell will not overcome it, and the keys of the kingdom of the heavens to bind and loose on the earth). In addition, only Matthew includes Jesus commanding his disciples not to reveal that he is the Christ.

The harsh dialog between Peter and Jesus in 16:22–23 is found in Mark but not in Luke. Matthew's account is much harsher and more descriptive than Mark's. For example, Peter's response in Matthew totally denies God's will in his statement: "May [God] be gracious to you, Lord; this will never happen to you" (16:22). In Mark's account, Peter just rebuked Jesus. In Matt 16:23, Jesus's response to Peter is harsher: "You are a stumbling block (σκάνδαλον) to me," once again emphasizing Peter's resistance to God's will. In Mark, Jesus told Satan to get behind him but does not state Peter is a "stumbling block" as Matthew does, instead Jesus immediately accused Peter of thinking like humans not God.

The teaching about denying oneself, taking up one's cross, and following Jesus in 16:24–26 is directed only to the disciples in Matthew. In Mark, it is directed to the disciples and the crowd, and in Luke it is directed to everyone. Matthew's account indicates how intimately the material in 16:13–28 is connected as a private episode between Jesus and his disciples regarding their present and future ministry.

In 16:27–28, Jesus predicted the future and near-present coming of the Son of Man. Mark and Luke include the material in Matt 16:27 but do not mention that the Son of Man will reward each one according to his or her actions. Mark and Luke include Matt 16:28, but do not mention the coming of the Son of Man with his kingdom. Mark states the kingdom of God has come in power (Mark 9:1) and Luke notes the viewing of the kingdom of God (Luke 9:27). Only Matthew mentions that the near-present coming of the Son of Man will occur sometime during the disciples's lifetime.

2.1.3. *Exegesis*

Matthew 16:13–28 is divided into two separate sections: 16:13–20 and 16:21–28. Matthew 16:13–20 is bound together through theme and structure. Thematically, the focus is on Peter's divinely inspired confession that Jesus is "the Christ, the Son of the living God" (16:16). The whole dialog between Jesus and Peter and the predictions concerning the church by Jesus are surrounded by the theme of the confession. Structurally, the title "the Christ" (ὁ Χριστός) binds 16:13–16 with 16:17–20, since Peter's confession ends with the identity of the Son of Man: "the Christ, the Son of the living God" (16:16); and the predictions concerning the church end with Jesus telling the disciples not to reveal that he is "the Christ" (ὁ Χριστός; 16:20). Matthew 16:13–20 provides a fuller understanding of Jesus the Son of Man's identity through the Father's revelation to Peter: He is the Christ, the Son of the living God. This confession reveals the holistic nature of Jesus's identity and emphasizes his authority. In other words, he is the divine-human—the heavenly Messiah and God the Father's Son, who came to earth as the Son of Man to fulfill God's salvific plan which will be highlighted in 16:21. In 11:2, 19, this same connection between the Son of Man and Christ appears. The works of the Christ are identified as the works of the Son of Man (cf. ἔργα τοῦ Χριστοῦ in 11:2; ἔργων in 11:19)—both relate to his ministry of mercy for the marginalized who he identified himself with and provided hospitality to. In 11:25–30, the Father's revelation was given to Jesus and his disciples since the Father's will for them was to know the things hidden from others. Peter's confession in 16:16 was revealed only in the presence of Jesus and the disciples, accentuating that the Father's will was for the disciples to understand the fuller revelation of Jesus the Son of Man's identity. The holistic revelation of Jesus's identity stresses the inadequacy of human understanding of the Son of Man: Jesus is more than a prophet he is "the Christ, the Son of the living God."[3] Earlier, in 1:21–23, divine inspiration was given to Joseph in

---

3. A similar construction is found in the high priest's questioning of Jesus and his response in 26:63–64. During his trial before Caiaphas, Caiaphas adjured him by the living God to confirm that he was the "Christ, the Son of God." Jesus gave further clarification to Caiaphas's question by stating that he is also the Son of Man who Caiaphas will see sitting at the right hand of power and coming on the clouds of heaven. In 16:21–23, God gave further clarification to Jesus's identity by stating that the Son of Man is also "the Christ, the Son of the living God" (v. 23). Both instances combine Jesus as the Son of Man, the Christ, and the Son of God. In Matthew, the title "Lord" (κύριε/κύριος) is used for the Son of Man and/or the Son of God. First, Matthew's account of Jesus and the disciples on a boat when a storm occurred (8:23–27; 14:22–33). In 8:23–27, Jesus referred to himself as the Son of Man who relinquished habitation and called others to follow his example. The disciple called him "Lord." In 8:27–28, the disciples called Jesus "Lord" when worried about the storm and Jesus calmed it. In 14:22–33, the disciples were again in a boat when a storm arose. Jesus came to them and Peter called him "Lord," asking to come to him on the lake and to be saved when drowning. Jesus stepped in the boat, the winds ceased, and the disciples stated that Jesus is the Son of God. Jesus the Son of Man is referred to as "Lord" just as the Son of God is testified by Peter as "Lord." Peter also called Jesus "Lord" when God revealed him as his Son during the transfiguration (17:1–8). Second, Jesus declared that "the Son of Man is Lord of the Sabbath," and, therefore, can redefine it according to mercy (12:6–8). Matthew's Gospel has examples of Jesus's merciful healing of marginalized individuals who called

a dream and the nature of Jesus's mission was revealed: "He will save his people from their sins.... He will be named Immanuel... God with us." In other words, Jesus the Son of Man is identified as the presence of God in human form. Jesus's identity as the God-human emphasizes that his mission to "save his people from their sins" is intimately connected to God's will. The divine revelation in 1:21 is particularized in 16:21 (and in subsequent passion predictions and at the Last Supper: 17:22-23; 20:17-19, 28; 26:27-28). The Father's revelation of Jesus's identity is more important and completely accurate, since God's word is greater than human teaching (alluded to by Jesus in 16:17). Earlier in 16:11b-12, Jesus warned about human teaching, specifically the teaching of the Pharisees and Sadducees.

Immediately after Peter's divinely inspired revelation of Jesus the Son of Man, Jesus blessed Peter due to his correct confession and began to reveal the ramifications this confession will have for the church.[4] Jesus

---

him "Lord" (e.g., 8:1-13; 15:22-28; 17:14-20; 20:29-34 [preceding the healing of the blind men, Jesus the Son of Man stated his mission is to serve others and give his life for them in 20:28]). Third, Jesus the Son of Man will come as judge to reward those who, like him, mercifully care for others (especially the marginalized). In judgment, these faithful disciples call him "Lord." He will also punish those who call him "Lord" but do not demonstrate it by serving others (e.g., 24:42-51; 25:31-46 [also 16:27]). Finally, as stated above, Jesus is the Christ, the Son of Man who intimately cares for and associates himself with the marginalized (11:2-6, 19 [also 9:9-13]).

4. Different scholarly perspectives exist regarding the significance of the name Πέτρος and the phrase ἐπὶ ταύτῃ τῇ πέτρᾳ in this cotext. The debate concerns to what "this rock" refers. The positions are as follows. First, the rock refers to Peter. Matthew 16:18 includes a play on the Greek words Πέτρος and πέτρα, indicating that Jesus was speaking about Peter as the rock on which the church is built. The Aramaic equivalent seems to identify Peter since the same term is used: "You are *Kepha* and upon this *kepha*." In this manner, Peter was being rewarded by Jesus for his correct confession and was elevated as head of the church (Cullmann, *Peter*, 212-17; Hagner, *Matthew*, 2:470-71; France, *Matthew*, 620-21; Meier, *Matthew*, 181-82; Morris, *Gospel*, 423-24; Turner, *Matthew*, 404; Nolland, *Matthew*, 669-70, 672; Davies and Allison, *Matthew*, 2:623-27; Nau, *Peter in Matthew*, 52; Brown et al., *Peter*, 92-93; Robinson, "Peter and His Successors," 85, 90-91). Second, the rock refers to Jesus Christ. Peter's confession revealed who Jesus the Son of Man is—the Christ, the Son of God; therefore, Jesus is the one on whom the church is built. He alone is the head of the church. (Derrett, "Thou Art the Stone," 276-85. Derrett uses Isa 54:11-12 to argue that, with Christ, the disciples are also the stones of the church). Third, this rock refers to Peter's confession. Since the masculine singular of Πέτρος differs from the dative feminine singular ταύτῃ τῇ πέτρᾳ, this rock cannot refer to Peter. Instead, the church is to be built on the revelation of the Father's word: Jesus the Son of Man is the Christ, the Son of the living God. The πέτρα is the content of Peter's insight (Caragounis, *Peter and the Rock*, 106-7, 113; Carter, *Matthew and the Margins*, 334; Evans, *Matthew*, 314 [and Peter's leadership]). Fourth, this rock refers to Jesus's preaching and teaching (i.e., the law of Christ. Matthew's Jesus will build only on the firm bedrock of his law; cf. 5:19-20; 7:24-27; 28:19). Since Jesus is the Christ, the Son of the living God, his preaching and teaching

promised to give Peter the keys of the kingdom of the heavens[5] in their future ministry and gave orders to the disciples not to reveal that he is the Christ (16:17–20).

The second section of 16:13–28 comprises vv. 21–28. The holistic understanding of Jesus the Son of Man's identity revealed to Peter (16:13–20) is connected with 16:21–28 by the sharp contrast between Peter's divinely inspired confession and subsequent blessing, with his rebuke of Jesus's passion prediction in 16:21 and Jesus's declaration of him as Satan or a "stumbling block" (σκάνδαλον). The authoritative teaching given to the disciples in 16:19 includes the suffering, death, and resurrection of Jesus the Son of Man. The context moves from divine revelation of Jesus's identity (16:13–20) to his upcoming fulfillment of God's will through obedient suffering and death (16:21–26) and the subsequent rewards that will follow their fidelity to God's

---

has ultimate authority for the church (Gundry, *Matthew*, 334; Overman, *Church and Community*, 241). Although an important debate, this discussion is not pertinent to my discussion of the Son of Man passages in the passion literature in Matthew.

5. Matthew 16:19 also raises considerable discussion among scholars. Diverse positions relate the identification of the keys of the kingdom of the heavens and the meaning of to bind and to loose. The following have been argued. First, the keys of the kingdom refer to the bestowing of teaching authority to the disciples (Albright and Mann, *Matthew*, 197–98; Nolland, *Matthew*, 677; Bornkamm, "End-Expectation," 45–47; France, *Matthew*, 625–26; Luz, *Matthew 8–20*, 365; Carter, *Matthew and the Margins*, 336; Morris, *Gospel*, 426–27; Hagner, *Matthew*, 2:472–73; Schweizer, *Good News*, 343–44; Marcus, "Gates of Hades," 449–55). Some scholars believe this authority was only given to Peter (Streeter, *Primitive Church*, 63; Davies and Allison, *Matthew*, 2:639; Hare, *Matthew*, 191–92 [given to the disciples/congregational leaders/local congregation after Peter's death]; Shaw, *Discernment*, 257–58). Second, the keys of the kingdom refer to the judgments regarding people's responses to the preaching of the kingdom. A person's present response determines their destiny at last judgment (Beasley-Murray, *Jesus*, 181–84; Schweitzer, *Quest*, 371). Third, the keys of the kingdom refer to the authority given to forgive or not to forgive sins (in light of 18:18; Cullmann, *Peter*, 210–12 [the authority is given primarily to Peter but shared with the disciples]; Bornkamm, "End-Expectation," 45–46, 48–49 [Bornkamm also appears to include teaching authority as well]; Jeremias, *New Testament Theology*, 238). Fourth, the keys of the kingdom refer to the teaching authority Jesus granted to Peter (16:19) and to others (18:18), so stress should not be on Peter's uniqueness (Kingsbury, "Figure of Peter," 73, 74–76, 80–82). Fifth, the keys of the kingdom refer to the authority to release or enforce an excommunication from the community (context of 18:15–20; Büchsel, "δέω (λύω)," 60–61). Sixth, the keys of the kingdom distinguish the church from the kingdom of heaven. It presupposes that heaven and earth are not yet unified under God's will (Allen, "On This Rock," 60–62). Seventh, the keys of the kingdom emphasize that decisions made on earth follow decisions already made in heaven (emphasis on the perfect tenses of λύω and δέω; Albright and Mann, *Matthew*, 197; Gundry, *Matthew*, 335). Eighth, the keys of the kingdom give the divine power and authority to bind and loose, in other words, to exorcise demons (cf. Rev 1:18; 20; Hiers, "'Binding' and 'Loosing,'" 235–50). Although an important debate, this discussion is not pertinent to my discussion of the Son of Man passages in the passion literature in Matthew.

will (16:27). In Matthew, the theme of obedience to God's will is particularly prominent in the passion predictions of Jesus the Son of Man,[6] in the teachings to the disciples in light of these predictions, and in the accounts of the Last Supper and Gethsemane in chapter 26.

The first passion prediction in Matt 16:21 reveals Jesus's desire to teach his disciples about his upcoming suffering, death, and resurrection (i.e., ἀπὸ τότε ἤρξατο ὁ Ἰησοῦς). The verb δεικνύειν is only used here in Matthew. The rest of the NT and LXX do not record δεικνύειν in the present infinitive form. The verb appears to have both a revelatory ("to explain" or "make known") and a demonstrative meaning ("to prove" or "to show"). These two meanings indicate that Jesus the Son of Man will be expounding the revelation of God's will for his ministry (and subsequently for the disciples) and will demonstrate to them the ways of his suffering (e.g., 17:22–23; 20:17–19; 26). The upcoming suffering (πολλὰ παθεῖν) in Jerusalem is directly connected to God's will. The δεῖ construction emphasizes the divine passive: "it is necessary" in God's plan for him to go and suffer many things, to be killed, and to be raised on the third day (16:21). In other words, it is God's will for his grace and mercy for humanity's sinful condition to be demonstrated

---

6. The authenticity of and source-critical concerns of the Son of Man passion predictions have generated much interest among scholarship. The following positions have been proposed. First, the Son of Man passion predictions are historically inauthentic and are a confession of the post-Easter church. They are *vaticinia ex eventu* (Wrede, *Messiasgeheimnis*, 111–18; Lohse, *History*, 12–13; Lohse, *Märtyrer und Gottesknect*, 111–18; Bultmann, *Theology*, 29–32, 82–86; Strecker, "Passion and Resurrection," 421–42; Higgins, *Jesus*, 30–36). Second, the Son of Man passion predictions are historically authentic and find their source in Jesus himself. Some scholars have different ways of viewing what influenced these predictions in Jesus's thinking: (a) Ps 118:22: stone metaphor—Jesus is the keystone/capstone. Along with this metaphor is the emphasis on "acceptance" versus "rejection" of the keystone (Tödt, *Son of Man*, 161–75, 201; Fuller, *Foundations*, 152–53; Jeremias, *Eucharistic Words*, 259–60 [Jeremias sees Ps 118:22 as a prophecy of Jesus's death and resurrection]). (b) The predictions are to be viewed in light of the Ebed Yahweh motif in Isa 52:13—53:12 (Taylor, *Jesus and His Sacrifice*, 88–105; Senior, *Passion of Jesus*, 31–33, 166–68; Jeremias, *New Testament Theology*, 286–92, 295–99; Otto, *Kingdom of God*, 250–55; Lindars, *Jesus Son of Man*, 64–69, 78, 81–84; Moo, *Old Testament*, 86–112 [Moo includes Ps 118:22 as having limited influence]). (c) The predictions find their influence in a martyr-motif signaled by the use of παραδίδωμι, with the context of the *passio iusti* concept (Schwiezer, *Erniedrigung und Erhöhung*, 24, 38, 43–48, 51–52). (d) The predictions find their influence in the motif of the *passio iusti*: vindication following suffering and death (cf. e.g., Ps 22; 31; 41; 69; Wis 2; 5). The resurrection is proleptically anticipated—the path of glory leads to suffering and death (Pesch, "Passion des Menschensohnes," 166–95; Wright, *Jesus and the Victory*, 574–91; Beasley-Murray, *Jesus*, 237–47; Bayer, *Jesus' Predictions*, 237–42). (e) The predictions find their influence in Dan 7 (esp. 7:14) and possibly Enoch (Hooker, *Son of Man*, 108–9, 113, 139–42; Schaberg, "Daniel 7–12," 208–22). Although important on their own terms, issues surrounding originality and source criticism are not pertinent to my discussion of the passion predictions in Matthew.

through the Son of Man's (i.e., Son of Humanity's) suffering and death—he will mediate God's love to humanity through his broken body and spilled blood for the forgiveness of sins (26:26–28). Although Jesus voluntarily accepted suffering, it was grounded in his obedience to the divine will. Therefore, Jesus the Son of Man mediates through his upcoming fulfillment of God's will the centrality of obedience to God's will to his disciples. Peter's rejection of Jesus's passion prediction is similar to the way the elders, chief priests, and scribes caused Jesus to suffer and planned his death. That is, both Peter and the religious leaders rejected God's will. Jesus called Peter a "stumbling block" (σκάνδαλον) and stated that he was "not thinking the things of God but the things of humans" (οὐ φρονεῖς τὰ τοῦ θεοῦ ἀλλὰ τὰ τῶν ἀνθρώπων; 16:23). Peter's rejection of Jesus's upcoming suffering and death proves that he did not have God's will in mind. Therefore, in light of his rejection, Peter was compared with Satan and commanded to submit to the divine will (ὕπαγε ὀπίσω μου, Σατανᾶ).[7]

Jesus's subsequent teaching in 16:24–26 aligns his disciples with the upcoming suffering and death of Jesus the Son of Man. In other words, Jesus's willing obedience to fulfill God's will through suffering and death in 16:21 is mirrored by what Jesus called his disciples to do in 16:24–26. The comparative pattern is emphasized: Jesus's suffering and death would lead to his vindication and the future award of resurrection (16:21). The disciples's willingness (θέλει in 16:24) to follow Jesus the Son of Man in suffering required them to "take up his cross and follow him" (ἀράτω τὸν σταυρὸν αὐτοῦ καὶ ἀκολουθείτω μοι), which would lead to their vindication and future reward (see 16:25–27). This teaching is reminiscent of 10:37–40, where Jesus taught his disciples that fidelity to him over family members might lead to death. This-worldly, temporary possessions and human relationships must always be secondary; saving the soul on account of Christ (and God's will) must be primary, even if it requires subsequent suffering and/or death. Through his teaching and upcoming passion, Jesus the Son of Man mediated the meaning of fulfilling God's will through obedience with absolute fidelity.[8] Matthew 16:27 names the primary reward for fidelity to God's will. Jesus the Son of Man will come in the glory of his Father and his angels at the parousia and reward (ἀποδώσει) each one according to his or her practice (πρᾶξιν). The reference to μέλλω at the beginning of v. 27 would usually indicate an event

---

7. The rebuke of Peter is reminiscent of Jesus's rebuke of Satan in Matt 4:1–11. Jesus's command to Peter in 16:23 is the same as what Jesus said to Satan in 4:10: ὕπαγε, Σατανᾶ. Satan obeyed Jesus and left him in 4:11 because his attempts to prevent Jesus from following God's will failed. Through his rebuke, Peter acted like Satan, tempting Jesus to abandon the divine will.

8. Jesus's teaching in 16:24–26 is illustrated later in 19:16–21.

THE SON OF MAN'S MEDIATORIAL SIGNIFICANCE IN HIS PASSION   101

in the near future (cf. 17:22); however, the eschatological language of the Father's glory and his angels coming with Jesus indicates that the reference is to the second coming of Jesus the Son of Man (cf. 24:30–31; 25:31—references to the last judgment). The Son of Man's identity is accentuated in 16:27. When Jesus stated he will come in the glory of *his* Father (πατρὸς αὐτοῦ) in v. 27, he connected *his* Father with *my* Father (πατήρ μου) in v. 17, when stating Peter's confession was of divine origin. Therefore, Matthew indicates that Jesus the Son of Man is Jesus the Son of God since both emphasize the possessive pronoun in both verses.

Matthew 16:28 is reminiscent of the *crux interpretum* in 10:23. The phrase ἐρχόμενον ἐν τῇ βασιλείᾳ αὐτοῦ in 16:28 has caused scholarly debate. As with 10:23, the concern surrounds whether Jesus's coming in his kingdom relates to the parousia or to an event during Jesus's lifetime. The positions are as follows. First, the "coming" refers to the Second Advent—the parousia of Jesus the Son of Man. Scholars connect 16:27-28 as referring to the same event.[9] Second, the "coming" refers to the transfiguration. Jesus promises a proleptic vision of his glory in the present, namely, the transfiguration.[10] Third, the "coming" refers to Jesus's resurrection (cf. 28:18-20); Jesus's kingly rule begins at the resurrection.[11] Fourth, the "coming" refers to the post-Easter outpouring of the Spirit.[12] Fifth, the "coming" refers to a fulfillment in the early triumph of Christianity (the church expands in the world).[13] Sixth, the "coming" refers to the destruction of Jerusalem in AD 70.[14] Seventh, the "coming" refers to Jesus's agony

---

9. Gnilka, *Matthäusevangelium*, 2:86, 89–90; Luz, *Matthew 8–20*, 386–87; Carter, *Matthew and the Margins*, 346; Gundry, *Matthew*, 341–42; Schweizer, *Good News*, 347; Beasley-Murray, *Jesus*, 192–93; Higgins, *Jesus*, 105–7; Nolland, *Matthew*, 693–96 (also argues for a possible connection between 16:28 and 20:21, indicating a preliminary fulfillment of 16:28 in "the royal rule of Jesus which is in a proleptic manner visible at the cross" [695]).

10. Keener, *Gospel of Matthew*, 436–38; Evans, *Matthew*, 319; Witherington, *Matthew*, 323; Blomberg, *Matthew*, 261; France, *Matthew*, 640–41 (who also refers to Jesus's resurrection and 28:18–20); Osborne, *Matthew*, 639; Harrington, *Matthew*, 249; Turner, *Matthew*, 413; Chilton, *God in Strength*, 264–70. Chilton identifies those who will not taste death with immortals (e.g., angels, Elijah, Moses, Jeremiah, Ezra, and Enoch). God's revelation on behalf of his people is a reality. Jesus is promising the kingdom in power, and immortals are sureties of this promise.

11. Meier, *Matthew*, 188; Lindars, *Jesus Son of Man*, 118–20; Davies and Allison, *Matthew*, 2:679 (who also refer to the parousia); Carson, *Matthew*, 2:382; Morris, *Gospel*, 434–35 (who also refers to parousia); Albright and Mann, *Matthew*, 201.

12. Glasson, *Second Advent*, 196–97; McNeile, *Gospel according to St. Matthew*, 248.

13. Hill, *Matthew*, 265–66.

14. Brown, "Matthean Apocalypse," 3, 8–10, 12, 14; Hagner, *Matthew*, 2:486–87; Gaechter, *Kunst im Matthäus*, 30–32; Wright, *Jesus and the Victory*, 338, 470.

in Gethsemane as the paradoxical timeframe of fulfillment when "the Son of Man is coming with his reign" (16:28).[15]

The context of Matt 16:21–28 does not give evidence of Jesus's coming occurring at the parousia in 16:28. As stated previously, v. 27 relates specifically to the eschaton as the future reward for practices and/or works (πρᾶξιν) throughout life. The prediction of death and/or martyrdom for the disciples in 16:24–26 leads to vindication after their death when Jesus the Son of Man comes again. The eschatological language in the phrases "in the glory of his Father" and "his angels with him" (v. 27) is typical for Matthew when speaking about the parousia. However, none of these eschatological cues is present in v. 28. The next time the disciples will see the Son of Man coming with his kingdom is after his resurrection (cf. 28:18–20), which makes sense in the context of 16:21–28. After Jesus fulfilled God's will through his suffering and death, he was vindicated through his resurrection. The emphasis on the vindication of Jesus (and his disciples in 16:27) makes sense in light of 16:28. When the disciples saw the vindicated Son of Man after his resurrection, they were encouraged and challenged to continue his ministry to death (28:18–20) and, in faithful obedience to God, they fulfilled God's will in their future ministry and would be rewarded for their fidelity to God's will at the parousia of the Son of Man. As Jesus faithfully fulfilled God's will through obedient suffering and death, he was vindicated in his resurrection and his disciples witnessed it (16:21, 28; 28:1–20).[16] As the disciples faithfully fulfilled God's will through obedient suffering and death (16:24–26), they would be vindicated when Jesus comes again at the parousia (16:27) and now receive hope of such future vindication as they witness Jesus's vindication after his resurrection (16:28).

Matthew gives no indication of a post-Easter outpouring of the Spirit, the destruction of Jerusalem in AD 70, or Jesus's agony in Gethsemane in the context of 16:13–28, nor does the author connect Matt 16 with 17:1–8. The only possible cue to the transfiguration might be the people's declaration that Jesus was a prophet (16:14; i.e., Elijah) in contrast to Peter's confession of Jesus as the Christ, the Son of the living God (16:16). However, the focus of 16:13–20 is on Peter's confession given through divine revelation so as to emphasize the importance of correct teaching in the church. In addition, the context of 16:21–28 regards future suffering and vindication, themes absent

---

15. Gibbs, *Matthew 11:2—20:34*, 847–48.

16. Eubanks correctly states, "An important and neglected implication of verses 21–28 taken as a whole is that Jesus' resurrection is the repayment he will receive from his Father for obediently submitting to rejection and death (26:39, 42)" (*Wages of Cross-Bearing*, 139).

from 17:1–8. Since the emphasis is on vindication after suffering and death, therefore, 16:28 does not refer to the transfiguration.

The divine revelation given to Peter regarding Jesus the Son of Man's identity is to be taught in the future church, along with the other teachings Jesus shared with the disciples throughout his ministry (16:13–20; 28:19–20). The climax of Jesus's ministry is revealed through the prediction of his suffering, death, and future vindication (his resurrection), which is the fulfillment of God's will (emphasized by the divine passive, δεῖ) for his ministry (16:21). Similarly, the disciples would also be subject to suffering and death on account of Jesus's name (16:24–26). However, the disciples were encouraged to persevere through their eyewitness to Jesus's vindication (i.e., resurrection; 16:28) and to continue his ministry to receive vindication ("[he] will receive recompense," ἀποδώσει) based on their actions, which fulfilled God's will for their ministry. Only Jesus the Son of Man was called to accomplish the divine "must" (δεῖ) which would mediate God's grace to humanity, since his death was the means through which the forgiveness of sins and a restored relationship with the Father in the heavens could be achieved. The disciples will mediate the meaning and message of Jesus's death to others—namely, the need to repent of sin and accept God's gift of salvation.

Jesus's Father the one in the heavens revealed to Peter a more holistic understanding of Jesus the Son of Man's identity: he is the Christ, the Son of the living God. He is the divine-human who came to earth as the Son of Man to fulfill God's salvific plan which will be highlighted in 16:21. Through the Son of Man's willing obedience to his mission, he fulfilled God's will for his ministry. The Son of Man mediates God's love and mercy to humanity through his suffering and death for the forgiveness of sins. Those who oppose Jesus's mission align themselves with Satan who tempted Jesus to disobey God's will (cf. 4:1–11) and, consequently, they do not fulfill God's will. Genuine disciples willingly submit to suffering and death for the sake of Jesus. Martyrdom is a real possibility for those who follow Jesus. After Jesus's resurrection, the disciples were to continue teaching the holistic revelation of Jesus's identity and mission. Faithfulness to God's will leads to vindication. The Son of Man received his vindication at his resurrection (16:21). The disciples will receive vindication in the future parousia of the Son of Man. Therefore, Jesus the Son of Man's willing obedience to fulfill God's will for his teaching ministry and followed by his suffering and death, mediates for his disciples the necessity of obeying God's will by revealing his teaching to others and submitting to future suffering and death on account of his name.

2.2. God's Will Obeyed: Jesus the Son of Man and John the Baptist as Examples of Genuine Discipleship (Matthew 17:9–13, 22–23)

2.2.1. Textual Orientation

Following the transfiguration, Jesus led Peter, James, and John, down from the mountain. He commanded them not to reveal what they saw on the mountain until the Son of Man was resurrected. The disciples questioned Jesus about the scribal teaching of Elijah, and Jesus responded by identifying Elijah as John the Baptist. Jesus compared his ministry as Son of Man with John the Baptist; both would suffer death. Jesus predicted for a second time that he, the Son of Man, would be betrayed, killed, and resurrected on the third day. The first Son of Man reference relates to Jesus's resurrection, the second to his suffering, and the third includes both Jesus's upcoming suffering and resurrection. Suffering is described through betrayal and death in the second passion prediction of the Son of Man.

2.2.2. Synoptic Comparison: Matthew 17:9–13, 22–23; Mark 9:9–13, 30–32; Luke 9:43b–45

Jesus's command not to reveal his transfiguration until after the Son of Man's resurrection and the discussion of the coming of Elijah is found in Matt 17:9–13 and Mark 9:9–13 but is absent in Luke. Although Matthew and Mark are similar in their accounts, they have some important differences. Mark's account emphasizes the disciples's lack of understanding by questioning among them what it meant for the dead to rise (9:9). However, in Matthew, after making the statement about revealing the vision after the Son of Man's resurrection, he moves immediately into the disciples's questions regarding the scribal teaching about Elijah.

Matthew 17:12–13 emphasizes the scribes's lack of recognition of Elijah who already came in the person of John the Baptist. In addition, Matthew specifically compares the upcoming suffering of the Son of Man with the suffering and death of John the Baptist. Finally, Matthew contrasts the scribes's lack of comprehension of the revelation that Elijah is John the Baptist in v. 12 with the disciples's understanding that Jesus was referring to John the Baptist as Elijah in v. 13. The emphasis on understanding the connection between Elijah and John the Baptist is not prevalent in Mark; it is only minimally implied in Mark 9:13.

Matthew 17:22–23 is almost identical to Mark 9:30–32. Both indicate that Jesus spoke his second passion prediction to the disciples in

Galilee. Both emphasize that Jesus was to be betrayed into the hands of humans, be killed by them, and then be resurrected the third day. Matthew emphasizes this passion announcement as a near-coming prediction with his use of μέλλει in 17:22. In other words, it will happen according to God's will. However, Mark does not indicate the near-coming nature of this prediction as Matthew does. Luke is different from both Matthew and Mark. Luke 9:44 mentions that the Son of Man is about to be delivered into the hands of humans but does not include his upcoming death and resurrection in the passion prediction. However, like Matthew, Luke also uses μέλλει to highlight the near-coming nature of this deliverance. Finally, after the passion prediction, Matthew indicates that the disciples grieved greatly when they heard the news (17:23b). However, Mark and Luke mention nothing about the disciples's emotional reaction. Rather, they both emphasize that the disciples did not understand the word spoken to them by Jesus (Mark 9:32; Luke 9:45).

2.2.3. *Exegesis*

Matthew stresses the authoritative word of Jesus. In 16:20 and 17:9, Jesus commanded the disciples to reveal neither that he is Jesus the Christ nor the vision they saw on the mountain. However, the disciples were permitted to disclose the vision once the Son of Man was resurrected from the dead (cf. 28:19–20). Matthew 17:9 is connected to 16:16 and 17:5. All three verses emphasize the message of the vision (i.e., God's revelation, first to Peter in 16:16 and then to the disciples in 17:5), namely, Jesus is the Son of God. In 17:5, however, this revelation is combined with a direct command from God: "Listen to him" (ἀκούετε). The disciples were commanded to listen to the teaching of Jesus so they could teach it to others in their future ministry (28:19–20), and they and future disciples would fulfill God's will through obedience (7:21–29). Matthew 17:5 is reminiscent of 3:16–17 at Jesus's baptism before he began his public ministry. In both contexts, God states, "this is my beloved Son in whom I am well pleased" (οὗτός ἐστιν ὁ υἱός μου ὁ ἀγαπητὸς ἐν ᾧ εὐδόκημα). The divinely inspired revelation of Jesus as God's Son (3:17; 16:16; 17:5) emphasizes Jesus's authority and anointing of the Spirit to carry out God's will. In 3:16–17, God himself empowered Jesus through his Spirit. God spoke from heaven, declaring both Jesus's identity as his Son and his pleasure with him. The authority given to Jesus through God enabled him to fulfill God's will revealed in 16:21; 17:12, 22–23 (cf. 1:21), which, essentially, is what is meant by Jesus's fulfilling all righteousness (πληρῶσαι πᾶσαν δικαιοσύνην; 3:15). In 5:17, Jesus did not come to abolish the law and the prophets but to fulfill them (ἀλλά πληρῶσαι). During Jesus's arrest, he stated clearly that his upcoming suffering and death was in fulfillment (πληρωθῶσιν) of the scriptures and the prophets (26:54, 56). These verses connect Jesus the Son of Man's identity as Son of God with his obedience as the Spirit-anointed Christ who fulfilled God's will. As the disciples heed Jesus's words and example, they would fulfill God's will in their future ministry. Similarly, Jesus told his disciples in 5:6, 10–12 that they would be blessed if they hungered and thirsted for righteousness (δικαιοσύνην) and if they were persecuted because of righteousness (ἕνεκεν δικαιοσύνης). Such opposition included reproach, persecution, and being spoken of in evil ways because of Jesus. An attitude of rejoicing and gladness ought to be included in times of persecution because of their reward (i.e., vindication; cf. 16:24–27) in the kingdom of the heavens. Similarly, the prophets before them endured persecution (e.g., 23:34). Finally, 17:9 stresses the Son of Man's vindication (i.e., his being raised from the dead, as in 16:22, 28; 17:23). The duty to share the vision in 17:1–8 after Jesus's resurrection proves that Jesus wanted his vindication at the forefront of their minds. Just as Jesus was vindicated as reward for his obedience in fulfilling God's will, so the disciples will be vindicated for their willingness to fulfill God's will (as in 16:24–27).

Matthew 17:10–13 emphasizes Jesus's re-clarification of the scribal tradition regarding the second coming of Elijah and his respective function. Earlier, in 16:12, Jesus warned the disciples about scribal teaching. The authoritative teaching of Jesus is to be heeded (cf. 17:5) above that of the scribal traditions. Jesus responded, "Elijah is indeed coming and will restore [ἀποκαταστήσει] all things" (17:11). The meaning of the future tense has generated scholarly attention. The following views have been proposed. First, it may simply reflect the form of the scriptural quotation in Mal 4:5–6.[17] Second, it may reflect scribal expectation, not Jesus's own: Elijah is to come and accomplish the Messiah's preparatory work of repentance and renewal; thus, Elijah is the forerunner of the Messiah.[18] Third, it is to be taken literally and Elijah will return before the parousia (cf.

---

17. Luz, *Matthew 8–20*, 400. Luz sees a similar use of the future tense in 17:11 with 1:23; 12:18–21. He notes, "Since the 'restoration' in light found in later rabbinic expectations included, among other things, the restoration of the purity of Israel, of peace, of the proclamation of the true halakah, and the preaching of repentance (Str-B 4.792–97), one could well combine the Baptist's activity with it" (*Matthew 8–20*, 400n47). See France, *Matthew*, 653–54; Meier, *Matthew*, 191–92; Morris, *Gospel*, 442–43; Nolland, *Matthew*, 707–8; Davies and Allison, *Matthew*, 2:714–15; Hare, *Matthew*, 200–201; Harrington, *Matthew*, 254, 256.

18. Hagner, *Matthew*, 2:499; Carter, *Matthew and the Margins*, 352.

perhaps, Rev 11:3–6).[19] Fourth, it is to be taken rhetorically, to be fulfilled in John the Baptist.[20] Sixth, it affirms that restoration has already begun in the advent of John the Baptist, just as the kingdom of God has already appeared in the ministry of Jesus, with restoration visible only to the eyes of faith and awaiting its consummation at the eschaton.[21] Seventh, it does not refer to John the Baptist but to Jesus, the messenger sent by God to prepare for the day of the Lord.[22]

The context of 17:10–13 identifies Elijah with John the Baptist. Justin Taylor's belief that 17:11 refers to Jesus, based on the notion that Mark 9:11–13 predates Matt 17:10–13, does not give due consideration to the context of the Matthean text. Taylor's view is refuted by 17:13 with the disciples's understanding that Jesus was speaking about John the Baptist, not himself. Gundry and Blomberg's view that the text may refer to an actual reappearance of Elijah before the parousia is untenable from context. First, the context is not focused on the parousia. Rather, it focuses on revealing the identity and function of Elijah (vis-à-vis John the Baptist), comparing him with the future ministry of Jesus. Second, 17:13 identifies Elijah as John the Baptist. Therefore, the future tense is taken rhetorically as being fulfilled in John the Baptist. In 17:12, Jesus contrasted (λέγω δὲ ὑμῖν ὅτι) the original scribal tradition regarding Elijah and its understanding with his revelation that Elijah is John the Baptist (see also 11:13–14). Jesus used the same wording in the Sermon on the Mount in Matt 5, λέλω δὲ ὑμῖν ὅτι, when he provided a more complete understanding of the OT law as taught by the scribes (cf. 5:17–20). In the same way, Jesus provided his disciples a more complete understanding of the identity and function of Elijah, and then compared his ministry with that of John the Baptist (vis-à-vis, Elijah). The comparison between Jesus and John the Baptist is indicated in 17:12. Jesus stated that John had already come and they did with him as they wished; that is, they killed him (14:1–12). Similarly, Jesus the Son of Man "is about to suffer by them" (μέλλει πάσχειν ὑπ' αὐτῶν; 17:12b). Matthew 17:12–13 is connected to both passion predictions—the first in 16:21, the second in 17:22–23. In 16:21, the Son of Man said that he would go to Jerusalem and "suffer many things" from the elders, chief priests, and scribes, and be killed. In 17:22–23, part of the Son of Man's suffering included being "betrayed into the hands of humans," and they would kill

19. Gundry, *Matthew*, 347; Blomberg, *Matthew*, 266.

20. Osborne, *Matthew*, 649; Schweizer, *Good News*, 351; Wink, *John the Baptist*, 15–16, 30–33; Allison, "Elijah Must Come First," 256–58; Jeremias, "Ηλ(ε)ίας," 936–38; Davies and Allison, *Matthew*, 2:715–17; Taylor, *Jesus and his Sacrifice*, 94.

21. Boring, "Gospel of Matthew," 8:364–65.

22. Taylor, "Coming of Elijah," 107–19.

him. John the Baptist and Jesus share in a common outcome to their ministries: they were killed. The comparison of Jesus and John is grounded in their common mission; they preached a message of repentance (cf. 3:1-2, 7-11; 4:17). In addition, the religious establishment rejected John and the Son of Man for their message and deeds (11:18-19). However, the reason John the Baptist and Jesus the Son of Man ministered in these ways, suffered, and inevitably were killed is because they obediently fulfilled God's will for their ministries. Jesus as Son of Man mediated to his disciples the costliness of obediently fulfilling God's will (similarly in 16:24-28). Martyrdom is a real possibility for those who follow God's will.

The second passion prediction in 17:22-23 reveals one of the many things the Son of Man suffered (16:21), namely, that he was about "to be handed over [betrayed] into the hands of humans" (παραδίδοσθαι εἰς χεῖρας ἀνθρώπων). Παραδίδωμι functions in both a passive and active sense in this passage. In the first passion prediction (16:21), Jesus mentioned that "it is necessary" (δεῖ) for him to suffer many things by the elders, chief priests, and the scribes. The divine passive indicates that the handing over of Jesus was part of God's will. Similarly, 17:22 indicates that the Son of Man "is about to" or "must" (μέλλει) be betrayed into the hands of humans." In Gethsemane Jesus submitted to God's will for his suffering and death (26:39, 42) immediately before he was handed over to suffering and death (26:45b-56). In 10:4, Matthew introduces Judas the Iscariot as the "the one betraying him" (ὁ . . . παραδοὺς αὐτόν). The use of παραδίδωμι connects 10:4 to 17:22. Judas, along with the religious leaders, "handed over" ("betrayed") Jesus to suffering and death (see also 26:14-16, 20-25, 45-50).[23] The mention of the Son of Man's being betrayed "into human hands" (εἰς χεῖρας ἀνθρώπων; 17:22) also directly connects to Judas, the soldiers, and the religious leaders as the ones who inevitably led Jesus to his suffering and death (see 26:45-50; "into the hands of sinners" [εἰς χεῖρας ἁμαρτωλῶν], 26:45).[24] There is irony in 17:22. The purpose for the suffering and death of the Son of Man (i.e., Son of Humanity) was to restore

---

23. For a helpful discussion on the uses of παραδίδωμι in the passion of Jesus the Son of Man, see Perrin, "Use of (Para)didonai," 94-103. Perrin highlights the active, passive, and active/reflexive uses of the verb.

24. Davies and Allison state that παραδίδωμι refers not primarily to Judas but points rather to God. They take the verb as a divine passive. In chapter 26, Judas, the Roman soldiers, chief priests, and elders were only the means to accomplish God's will. God was the one who delivered Jesus over into the hands of humans (*Matthew*, 2:734). Davies and Allison are correct in their understanding of the divine passive of παραδίδωμι; however, in Matthew, Judas (and the religious leaders) was actively involved in making this decision (emphasized especially in 26:2-5, 14-16, 24-25, 45-50, where they took deliberate actions against Jesus). Both the active and passive use of παραδίδωμι are in view.

humanity's relationship with God the Father through the forgiveness of sins (26:28), even though his demise would occur because of human betrayal, and humanity would cause his suffering and death. The Son of Man mediates God's grace to humanity, even to the sinners who are responsible for his death. In addition, Jesus's willingness to submit to being handed over to suffering and death in order to fulfill God's will mediated for his disciples the importance of fulfilling God's will obediently.

In 17:23, Matthew indicates that the disciples "grieved greatly" (ἐλυπήθησαν σφόδρα) when they heard about the Son of Man's upcoming betrayal and death. The disciples's response to this passion prediction implies they understood at some level that Jesus would endure such rejection. In 26:22, the disciples also grieved greatly when Jesus revealed that one of them would betray him. When the lord forgave a slave and pardoned him of his loan, his fellow slaves grieved greatly when they heard that the slave imprisoned and beat another slave who owed him one hundred denarii (18:23–35). Herod grieved when he realized he was bound to his oath and had to kill John the Baptist in prison (14:1–12). In Matthew such grief is associated with the betrayal or suffering and death that others endured. Rejection of Jesus and his ministry is contrary to the call Jesus gave his disciples to costly self-denial and genuine followership (cf. 8:18–22; 10:16–25, 32–39; 16:20–24). Therefore, the disciples began to realize that Jesus's betrayal and death was inevitable, and they possibly associated Jesus's suffering and death with the costly self-denial that would be required of genuine disciples. The Son of Man's willing obedience of costly self-denial in order to fulfill God's will mediated for his disciples the importance of fulfilling God's will obediently in their future ministry.

Jesus commanded his disciples to reveal neither that he is the Christ nor the vision on the mountain. Jesus's transfiguration was to be revealed after the Son of Man's resurrection (17:9; cf. 28:18–20). The disciples will need to obey Jesus's words (teaching) and follow his example, so as to fulfill God's will in their future ministry. In 17:10–13, Jesus re-clarified the scribal teaching on Elijah's second coming by identifying Elijah with John the Baptist. Jesus compared his ministry to John the Baptist so his disciples would have a more complete understanding of the identity and function of Elijah—both John the Baptist and Jesus the Son of Man would be killed (14:1–12; 17:12b, 22–23). John the Baptist and Jesus the Son of Man had common ministries—they preached a message of repentance, were rejected by the religious establishment (11:18–19), and both suffered and were inevitably killed, because they faithfully obeyed God's will for their ministries. Jesus the Son of Man mediated to his disciples the costliness of obediently following God's will (similarly 16:24–28). In 17:22–23, Jesus taught his disciples about his upcoming suffering, death, and resurrection. The Son of Man's upcoming passion would help the disciples to recognize that suffering and vindication is the fate for those who genuinely follow God's will (cf. 10:16–39). Jesus would be handed over for suffering and death according to God's will (16:21). Jesus the Son of Man's suffering and death would mediate God's grace to humanity, ironically, even to those who would hand him over to death (cf. 17:22; 26:45). Jesus's willingness to submit to suffering and death mediated for his disciples the importance of fulfilling God's will with complete obedience (cf. 26:39, 42). Like the Son of Man, the disciples will also be required to ensure costly self-sacrifice to obey God and fulfill his will for their ministry.

2.3. God's Will Obeyed: Jesus the Son of Man as the Sacrificial Servant of All People (Matthew 20:17–28)

2.3.1. Textual Orientation

As Jesus and his disciples drew closer to Jerusalem, he spoke to them privately about his upcoming passion. Jesus the Son of Man would be handed over to the religious leaders to be condemned to death, and the Gentiles would physically carry out his suffering and death. Jesus reminded his disciples of his vindication: he would be raised from the dead. The mother of the sons of Zebedee requested that Jesus allow her sons to sit on his right and left in his kingdom. Jesus stated that this honor is given only by his Father but predicted that they, along with him, would suffer and die. Jesus taught his disciples that genuine discipleship is uninterested in position or status; rather, its focus is on being a servant to others. Jesus the Son of Man will exemplify such servanthood by giving his life as a ransom for the many.

2.3.2. Synoptic Comparison: Matthew 20:17–28; Mark 10:32–45; and Luke 18:31–34

All three synoptic Gospels recount the third passion prediction similarly. Mark and Matthew are the closest. All three indicate that Jesus and his disciples were going up to Jerusalem. However, only Matthew mentions that Jesus was going up to Jerusalem (20:17) before stating that Jesus and his disciples were going up to Jerusalem (20:18). Both Matthew and Mark state that the Son of Man would be handed over to the chief priests and the scribes who would condemn him to death. Only Luke, however, notes that Jesus and the disciples were going up to Jerusalem. Luke mentions that the Son of Man's passion would fulfill all the writings of the prophets. Unlike Matthew and Luke, Mark states that the ones following Jesus were astounded and afraid. All three Gospels credit the Gentiles with physically causing the suffering and death of Jesus. However, only Mark and Luke mention that they would spit on Jesus and kill him. All three Gospels record that Jesus would be handed over to the Gentiles and be mocked and whipped by them. However, only Matthew states that they would crucify Jesus; the form of death is not mentioned in the other Gospels. Matthew records that Jesus would be raised, while Mark and Luke state that he would rise again.

Only Matthew and Mark record the story of the sons of Zebedee. In Matthew's account, the mother of the sons of Zebedee approached Jesus with the request that her sons might sit on the right and the left of Jesus in his kingdom. However, in Mark, the sons of Zebedee approached Jesus themselves. Only Matthew mentions that his Father had already prepared the kingdom positions on either side of Jesus. For the rest of the account, Matthew follows Mark very closely.

Matthew includes a story that compares the kingdom of the heavens to a lord who hires workers for his vineyards (20:1–16). Mark and Luke do not include this story. The story is significant because Matthew connects it to 20:17–28 by highlighting the theme of the first and the last, minimizing the issue surrounding status and greatness. This issue is highlighted more in Matthew than in Mark, especially since 20:1–16 immediately precedes the third passion prediction and the request regarding the two sons of Zebedee.

2.3.3. *Exegesis*

Matthew 20:1–16 provides an important theological context for the rest of the chapter. The kingdom of the heavens is likened to a master who invited individuals to work in his vineyard. The issue surrounding the master's generosity in offering people work, is that every person received the same wage. The amount of time worked was not the owner's concern; rather, treating the workers with equality was what was important to him. The giving nature of the owner was based on his will (θέλημα) (20:14–15). The character of the owner (i.e., "I myself am good" [ἐγὼ ἀγαθός εἰμι; 20:15)]) was determined by his compassionate action—he made the last ones equal with the first. Matthew ends the story with a striking statement that links this story with 20:17–28: "the last ones will be first and the first ones last" (ἔσονται οἱ ἔσχατοι πρῶτοι καὶ οἱ πρῶτοι ἔσχατοι; 20:16). In the kingdom of the heavens, every person is equal; however, some will criticize God's goodness (i.e., reject his character; cf. 20:10–12) and his deeds (compassion and love; i.e., God's will;

cf. 20:14–15), and others will receive his goodness (and mercy) and gratefully accept his deeds (i.e., God's will; cf. 6:10). Before 20:1–16, the statement "the first will be last and the last first" (ἔσονται πρῶτοι ἔσχατοι καὶ ἔσχατοι πρῶτοι) is recorded in 19:30. The context of 19:30 is Jesus's promised reward to his disciples who leave everything and everyone and follow him. The disciples who have sacrificially relinquished everything temporary will receive eternal life (19:29; see also 16:24–27); they are identified as the first; the ones who choose to obey God's will revealed through Jesus's teachings and actions.

These contextual connections with 20:1–16 enable a proper understanding of 20:17–28. Matthew 20:17–19 is the most detailed of all of Matthew's passion predictions. The emphasis is on the persecution and suffering of Jesus the Son of Man. Jesus is indirectly compared to the last ones who become first (19:30; 20:16). Those who criticize Jesus's ministry rejected him. He was handed over to the chief priests and the scribes, and they condemned him to death (17:18). Like the last ones, he was willing to give up his life—along with everything and everyone—to follow God's will. Jesus completely obeyed his Father's instructions. He was handed over to the Gentiles in order to be mocked, whipped, and crucified (17:19). However, like the last ones, Jesus experienced the Father's goodness. He was vindicated from suffering and death by being raised from the dead after he completed his Father's will.

Matthew 20:17–19 emphasizes the universality of Jesus's rejection; both the Jews (religious leaders) who condemned him to death and the Gentiles (Roman soldiers [cf. 27:26–50]) who mocked, whipped, and crucified him were responsible for Jesus's suffering and death. Like Mark and Luke, Matthew gives a more complete description of Jesus's suffering and death in the third passion prediction than in the first (16:21) and second (17:22–23). Mark and Matthew mention that Jesus would be handed over (παραδοθήσεται) to the chief priests and the scribes. Matthew 10:4 states that Judas Iscariot was the one betraying him (i.e., handing him over; παραδοὺς αὐτόν; see also 26:14–16, 23–25, 47–50). Only Matthew reveals the manner of Jesus's death—the Gentiles "to crucify" (σταυπῶσαι) him. The declaration of Jesus's upcoming crucifixion is also mentioned in Matthew's fourth passion prediction in 26:2. Once again Matthew states that Jesus's suffering and death would take place in Jerusalem (16:21; 20:17). Matthew includes the verb ἀναβαίνω twice within 20:17–18. In v. 17, he uses the present active participle, ἀναβαίνων, to emphasize that Jesus was determined to go to Jerusalem. The participle is important as it highlights Jesus's determined willingness to fulfill the Father's will obediently (note the divine passive δεῖ in 16:21). Matthew then records Jesus's desire for his disciples to join him in his mission through the present active plural form of ἀναβαίνομεν in v.

18. Matthew may be using this verb to keep the theme of discipleship at the forefront of Jesus's mission. In other words, just as God called Jesus to go up to Jerusalem to be crucified (serving others by giving himself as a ransom for many [20:28]), so genuine disciples would follow Jesus up to Jerusalem to witness his resolve to endure the costly sacrifice he would undergo to fulfill God's will obediently. Similarly, the disciples in their future ministry must be willing to endure sacrificially (especially in service to others [20:26–27]) to fulfill God's will (cf. 16:24–25).

The request of the mother of the sons of Zebedee—regarding who would sit to the right and left of Jesus in his kingdom—contrasts status and position with servanthood and lowliness (20:20–28). Essentially, this mother was requesting the best and most status-worthy positions in Jesus's kingdom, positions that would put her sons in first place among the disciples and exalt them above all others in Jesus's kingdom. The immediate response of the sons of Zebedee that they were able to drink the cup that Jesus would drink highlights their agreement with their mother's request. Ironically, the positions of "right" (δεξιῶν) and "left" (εὐωνύμων) of Jesus are connected with Jesus's suffering on the cross in 27:38. Matthew mentions that two thieves were crucified with him "one on the right and one on the left" (εἷς ἐκ δεξιῶν καὶ εἷς ἐξ εὐωνύμων). In Matthew, the places beside Jesus are on crosses, not in the kingdom John, James, their mother, or the other disciples envision. This connection is pertinent in light of the following discussion surrounding drinking the cup (20:22–23). Genuine disciples align themselves with Jesus's mission, including suffering and death according to God's will.

Jesus's response to the mother's request is important. He emphasized the importance of self-relinquishing sacrifice: "Are you able to drink the cup which I myself am about (ἐγὼ μέλλω) to drink?" (20:22b). The sons of Zebedee stated they were able, and Jesus affirmed that they would drink his cup (20:23a). Instead of status and position, Jesus was concerned with obediently following God's will. In Matthew, ποτήριον is used only in 20:22–23, at Jesus's Last Supper with his disciples (26:27–28), and his prayer at Gethsemane (26:39). The drinking of the cup refers to Jesus's voluntary death in obedience to God's will.

The cup is the symbol Jesus used for the shedding of his blood in the Last Supper narrative: the blood of the covenant for the many for the forgiveness of sins (26:27–28). The blood of the covenant refers back to the "covenant of blood" instituted to recall the Israelites's deliverance from Egypt. Moses told the Israelites to kill a lamb and spread its blood on their doorframes so the angel of death would pass over their homes. The Israelites obeyed Moses's command and, consequently, Pharaoh allowed Moses and Israel to flee Egypt (cf. Exod 12:21–27; 24:7–8). Jesus's willingness to succumb to self-sacrificial death fulfills the suffering Servant predicted by Isaiah in 52:13—53:11, who died for the forgiveness of sins of the many according to God's will (e.g., Isa 53:10-12 LXX).[25]

25. See also Jeremias, *Eucharistic Words*, 225–31; Senior, *Passion of Jesus*, 67–69; Keener, *Gospel of Matthew*, 631; Harrington, *Matthew*, 368; Meier, *Matthew*, 318–20; Davies and Allison, *Matthew*, 3:472–75; Cooke, "Synoptic Presentation," 21–23, 32–24; Edanad, "Institution of the Eucharist," 329–32; Lohse, *Märtyrer und Gottesknecht*, 124–29; Watts, *Isaiah's New Exodus*, 351–61; Higgins, *Lord's Supper*, 32. Other options have been proposed. First, scholars have argued for an eschatological "new covenant" replacing the historical "old covenant," based on the background from Exod 24:8 and Jer 31:31–34 (Fuller, "Double Origin," 60–69; Heil, *Death and Resurrection*, 36–38; Morris, *Gospel*, 660–61; Osborne, *Matthew*, 968; Turner, *Matthew*, 625; Luz, *Matthew 21-28*, 380–81; Marshall, *Last Supper*, 91–93, 100; Patsch, *Abendmahl*, 84–87). Second, Ham argues that the cup metaphor recounts the "new covenant" idea of Jer 31:31–34 and the self-sacrificial death for the many imagery in Isa 53:11–12. The emphasis is forward-looking and stands in contrast to the historical recollection of Exod 24:8 (Ham, "Last Supper in Matthew," 60–69). Third, McKnight argues that the cup metaphor is a memorial of God's liberation of Israel from Egypt, an act of both deliverance and judgment (Exod 24:8-11). Jesus's death is not an atoning or forgiving death; rather, it protects from God's judgment of human sin which finds its clearest expression in Jesus's warnings about Jerusalem's destruction. God has appointed Jesus's death to be the vicarious and protecting sacrifice, the means of escape from God's imminent judgment against Jerusalem and its corrupt leadership (embodied in the temple) (McKnight, *Jesus and His Death*, 281–339). Fourth, Hooker argues that the necessity of Jesus's suffering and death are integral to the concept of the Son of Man. Daniel 7 is the best background as it emphasizes the triumph of the human figure that brings comfort to those undergoing suffering for their faith. To individuals now faced with suffering, the Son of Man gives a promise: the righteous who are left will be given kingdom and glory. The promise of Mark 14:25 emphasizes the kingdom of God that God has "covenanted" to Jesus will be shared with his disciples as they eat and drink at the table of Jesus in the future, sitting on twelve thrones and judging Israel. Through his obedient death, Jesus stands in the mediating position between his Father, who has covenanted the kingdom to him, and his disciples, in whom he covenants a share in that kingdom (Hooker, *Son of Man*, 142–47). Fifth, Green argues that the supper words are an open unmistakably obvious prediction of Jesus's death. Numerous OT motifs and language stand behind the prediction of Jesus's death, including those having to do with covenant (Exod 24:8; Jer 31:31–34), the Servant of Isaiah (Isa 53), martyrdom, atonement, and the forgiveness of sins (Green, *Death of Jesus*, 193–96, 242–43).

The problem with associating Matthew's cup words with Jer 31:31–34 is the absence of "new" (καινῆς; Luke 22:20) with the term covenant. Green has pointed to the Dead Sea Scrolls, indicating that "covenant" and "new covenant" are virtually interchangeable (Green, *Death of Jesus*, 194). However, Green's argument does not consider why Matthew (and Mark) would not include καινῆς in Jesus's cup words. Especially in light of the context surrounding Matthew 20:28 (and Mark 10:45), the idea of Jesus's self-sacrificial death as a servant seems more probable. McKnight's view disregards the context of Matt 26 (and 20:28), which mentions nothing about Jerusalem's destruction or Jesus's death protecting from God's judgment. The emphasis is on Jesus's willing self-sacrificial death for the many for the forgiveness of sins (26:28 [also 1:21]). In contrast to McKnight's argument, Jesus's death is presented as atoning/forgiving rather than

As Jesus prayed in Gethsemane, he asked his Father whether this cup could pass from him, but stated, "Not as I myself will (ἐγώ θέλω) but as you [will]" (26:39). Later Jesus asked his Father once again if he could avoid death and stated, "Let your will be done" (γενηθήτω τὸ θέλημά σου; 26:42). The emphasis on Jesus's death in these passages connects Jesus's response of drinking his cup with his prediction of suffering and death in 20:17–19 (and indirectly the other passion predictions: 16:21; 17:22–23; 26:2). In addition, Jesus's death contrasts sharply with the request from the mother of the sons of Zebedee. Instead of status and position, Jesus focused on the culmination of his mission, namely, death. Jesus's death highlights the importance of obeying God's will. The passion predictions all emphasize the necessity of Jesus obeying God's will through his acceptance of his near-coming death. Through Jesus's obedience to God's will, he sought first the kingdom of God and his righteousness (6:33). In a similar way, the sons of Zebedee would be killed in the future as they continued to follow God's will and remain faithful to their mission (cf. 28:19–20).

Jesus rejected the request of the mother of the sons of Zebedee. Only Jesus's Father can give the positions of sitting at the right and left of Jesus in his kingdom and the rewards of the kingdom of the heavens; only he has ultimate authority.[26] The other disciples were angry with the two brothers after hearing the request. However, Jesus diffused their anger by teaching them how to be "great" (μέγας) (20:26) and "first" (πρῶτος) (20:27) in his kingdom. Jesus contrasted the Gentile view of greatness with his view of greatness: obeying God's will (20:25–28). The rulers of the Gentiles considered greatness as having authority over other people; status and position were valued. However, in 20:26–27, Jesus stated that true honor is given to those who are "servant[s]" (διάκονος) and "slave[s]" (δοῦλος) for

---

protecting. Finally, Hooker's notion that the meaning of the cup words is found in the title Son of Man (interpreted from Dan 7) and the promise of the kingdom (cf. Mark 14:25) minimizes the self-sacrificial role of the Son of Man indicated in Matt 20:28; 26:24–28. Matthew's context concerning Jesus's death as modeling servanthood and the means of forgiveness of sins points more readily to Isa 53 than to Dan 7.

26. Matthew 20:20–23 implies an important identity marker for Jesus the Son of Man. The mother's request is that her sons would sit at the right and left of Jesus in *his* kingdom (v. 21). Then, Jesus spoke about his upcoming suffering and death in v. 22 which is directly related to the fate of the Son of Man in 20:17–19, 28. Finally, Jesus mentioned that such positions are given/prepared only by *his Father* in v. 23. It appears from this context that the Father and the Son of Man share the same kingdom and that the Son of Man is the Father's Son, especially since *Son of Man* is the overarching title of Jesus in this context. In addition, the positions of sitting on the right and left of Jesus seem to be connected to suffering and death—the voluntary obedience of giving one's life for the sake of following God's will (also 16:21–27).

others. In Jesus the Son of Man's kingdom, being great and first is defined through practicing servanthood.

Jesus warned his disciples that they were not to emulate the works of the scribes and Pharisees (23:3). Jesus's followers are not to act so to be seen by others, desire to sit at places of honor, or be called "Rabbi" (23:5-8). Rather, they are to look to the Father in the heavens as their Father and the Christ as their teacher (23:8-10). As in 20:26-27, Jesus stated, "And the greatest of you will be your servant. But whoever will lift himself up will be humbled and whoever will humble himself will be lifted up" (23:11-12). In Jesus the Son of Man's kingdom those who practice a life of service for others will be lifted up, not those who vie for position and status.[27] In 18:1-5, Jesus compared the greatest in his kingdom to children and challenged his disciples to become like children. In light of 23:11-12, where the greatest and humble are servants, practicing servanthood is necessary for changing and being like a child (18:2-4). Therefore, humility, servanthood, and childlikeness are distinguishing characteristics of genuine disciples.

The strength of Jesus's teaching is found in the strong comparison between Jesus's disciples and himself in 20:28. This verse is one of the most essential statements about the Son of Man's mission in Matthew: "Just as the Son of Man did not come to be served but to serve and to give his life as a ransom for many." The emphasis on the verb διακονέω in 20:28 connects it with 20:26, as Jesus called his disciples to understand that greatness is demonstrated through servanthood.[28] Jesus's specific manifestation of his service is tied to his sacrificial death for the many for the forgiveness of sins (26:28 [also 1:21]). The description of Jesus's sacrificial death is tied to the previous passion predictions in 16:21; 17:22-23; and 20:17-19. The term λύτρον[29] is

---

27. Paschal explains Jesus's revolutionary concept well: "The call to service in love overshadows normal human desires for rank and preference and calls individuals to lay all these aside for the sake of Christ and the needs of others.... Jesus intended the community of faith to be radically distinct from the world in this regard. Indeed, selfless service and concern for the weak and powerless would prove to be the distinguishing mark of the Christian community and the most tangible and attractive witness to its character and faith" ("Service," 750).

28. Davies and Allison state: "Jesus refers to the Son of Man in whom word and deed are one, the true king whose one aim is to benefit his subjects (cf. Philo, *Vit. Mos.* 1.51, of Moses). He himself, destined to have authority in heaven and earth, is the outstanding example of the first who made himself last" (*Matthew*, 3:94).

29. The source-critical issue concerning λύτρον in Matt 20:28 (Mark 10:45) has attracted a range of scholarly views. Scholars argue that the primary source is from: (1) Isa 53:10-12 (Hampel, *Menschensohn und historischer Jesus*, 316-25; Lohse, *Märtyrer und Gottesknecht*, 118-22; Kertelge, "Menschensohn," 231-39; Davies and Allison, *Matthew*, 3:95-100; Jeremias, *New Testament Theology*, 286-94; France, "Servant," 26-52); (2) Dan 7 (specifically 7:14) (Barrett, "Background of Mark 10:45," 1-15; Hooker, *Son*

used in the NT only here in Matt 20:28 and Mark 10:45. However, whereas the passion predictions emphasize the more passive nature of Jesus's death, Matt 20:28 stresses Jesus actively demonstrating servanthood by giving his life as a ransom for many (offering his life of his own accord; διακονῆσαι and δοῦναι are both active infinitives). With the use of πολλῶν in 20:28, Matthew is preparing for the narrative of the Last Supper where Jesus stated that the cup represents the shedding of his blood for the forgiveness of "many" (πολλῶν; 26:28). Therefore, Jesus's death is the ransom (cf. Isa 53:10, 12) and through the shedding of his blood he will forgive the sins of many. Forgiveness is the result of the ransom that Jesus's death mediates for the many who will be pardoned from their sins.[30] The Son of Man mediates God's mercy and grace to sinful humanity. As a "servant" and "slave," the Son of Man's death as a ransom emphasizes his mission to forgive the sins of humanity so they can receive salvation—a restored relationship with God the Father in the heavens. The opportunity to seek forgiveness for their sins enables humanity to receive eternal salvation because of Jesus's death on the cross.

The meaning of *ransom* (λύτρον) has been understood differently by McKnight and Hooker. McKnight believes λύτρον means that Jesus's life was a kind of payment to a hostage power (Exod 21:30 LXX; Sir 29:15; 1 Macc 2:50). Hostage powers are sin (Mark 1:5, 15), Satan and his destructive cohorts (3:27), and the fearful self (8:34—9:1). Jesus is the savior who pays the price to rescue his followers from hostile powers, not a substitution for their sin.[31] Hooker believes λύτρον should be interpreted in light of the LXX in the technical sense of "purchase money" not as a sacrificial term. The idea relates to a payment that is equivalent of what is redeemed; i.e., the work Yahweh accomplishes for his people—the redemption from exile (looking back at the Israelite bondage of Egypt) and the deliverance from sin (looking forward to the return as a second Exodus). The Son of Man is the instrument of God's

---

of Man, 142–47); (3) Isa 43:1–7 (Grimm, *Weil Ich dich liebe*, 236–38); or (4) the Last Supper narrative (Matt 26:26–28 [Mark 14:22–24]) (Büchsel, "λύτρον," 342–44). This thesis focuses on how Matt 20:28 is understood within the text of Matthew itself, so the background of 20:28 is an unnecessary discussion.

30. See Jeremias, *New Testament Theology*, 288–93; France, *Matthew*, 761–63; Carter, *Matthew and the Margins*, 405–6; Turner, *Matthew*, 488–89; Watts, *Isaiah's New Exodus*, 272, 279–81; Ham, "Last Supper," 60–61; Taylor, *Jesus and His Sacrifice*, 100–105, 127; Higgins, *Jesus*, 36–50; Senior, *Passion of Jesus*, 166–68; Kertelge, "Dienende," 226, 231–34; Beasley-Murray, *Jesus*, 280–83. In his commentary on Matt 20:28, Beasley-Murray states, "It is in the concept of the service of the Son of Man, the mediator of the kingdom of God, that the unity of the ministry and self-offering of Jesus is perceived. And it is because the Son of Man is the mediator of divine sovereignty that his service spans the present and the future of the kingdom of God" (*Jesus*, 283).

31. McKnight, *Jesus and His Death*, 357–59.

purpose as the deliverer from the nation's sin through his willingness to give his life. The emphasis is on death and deliverance, not sin and suffering. The Son of Man is not a "servant" but a "deliverer"—the result and not the method of action is what is important.[32] McKnight and Hooker are correct in seeing λύτρον as a kind of payment on behalf of others. However, neither adequately considers the context surrounding 20:28. In Matthew, there is no indication that Jesus is rescuing people from hostile powers nor delivering them through his sacrificial death. In 20:17–28, Jesus taught his disciples the importance of servanthood over vying for positions of prominence. Jesus the Son of Man mediates the importance of servanthood through his sacrificial death on the cross, which is further emphasized by his statement of "drinking the cup" in 20:22. The "drinking of the cup" metaphor prepares for the Last Supper narrative in 26:26–28, indicating that his cup represents his upcoming sacrificial death for the forgiveness of sins.

The comparison between Jesus's servant role through his sacrificial death and his teaching on serving others emphasizes how Jesus's act of servanthood mediates the kind of self-sacrificing servanthood expected of genuine disciples.[33] Jesus's kingdom is about serving others even onto death, not vying for positions of prominence and exaltation. The first ones and the great ones are those who elevate others through acts of servanthood. Such merciful action towards others is the kind of worship God wills (12:7). Mercy is the essence of Jesus's mission as he came to call those who were sinners and not the righteous (9:13). The disciples's willingness to take up their cross and give up their lives on account of Jesus and his kingdom will be rewarded as their vindication at the eschaton (16:24–27). Jesus's willingness to take up his cross and give up his life on account of his Father led to his vindication when he was resurrected from the dead (16:21; 17:22–23; 20:17–19). The Son of Man's willingness to fulfill God's will through obedient self-sacrificial death[34] mediates for his disciples how to fulfill God's will, through obedient self-sacrificial suffering and death for his kingdom and for others. In addition, the Son of Man mediates God's grace and mercy to

---

32. Hooker, *Jesus and the Servant*, 76–79.

33. Meier states, "The true Son proves his sonship by always submitting to the Father's will instead of grasping at glory (cf. 4:1–11); his disciples, the true sons, must imitate the Son's humility and obedience.... Jesus first speaks of the servant, the person who freely puts himself at the disposition of others, and then radicalizes his statement with the image of the slave, the non-person who has no rights or existence of his own, who exists solely for others" (*Matthew*, 228).

34. In his study of Matt 20:28, Gerhardsson states, "Jesus' sacrifice of his life is presented as an act of obedience towards God, done on behalf of mankind. Jesus himself will, in conscious obedience, give his life for a ransom of many. Jesus gives his life in obedience to his heavenly Father's will" ("Sacrificial Service," 30).

THE SON OF MAN'S MEDIATORIAL SIGNIFICANCE IN HIS PASSION   119

sinful humanity through his sacrificial death, by forgiving the sins of humanity so they can receive eternal salvation—a restored relationship with God the Father in the heavens.

2.4. God's Will Obeyed: Jesus the Son of Man Accepts Rejection and Death (Matthew 26:1–5, 14–56)

2.4.1. Textual Orientation

Matthew 26 begins with Jesus's fourth passion prediction: the Son of Man is handed over to be crucified (v. 2). Immediately after the prediction, the religious leaders discussed how to trap Jesus so they might kill him after the Passover. In vv. 14–16, Judas Iscariot approached the religious leaders and agreed to betray Jesus for money. Judas and the religious leaders's opposition to Jesus is contrasted with a woman who poured expensive ointment on Jesus's head to prepare him for burial. Jesus's disciples criticized the woman for not selling the ointment and giving it to the poor; however, Jesus commended her for the act and stated she will be remembered wherever the good news is preached.

Jesus commanded his disciples to prepare the Passover meal and they obeyed him. At the meal he revealed to his disciples that one of them would betray him. Each disciple claimed he was not the betrayer. Jesus stated that the disciple who dipped his hand in the bowl with him would betray him. Jesus the Son of Man indicated once in 26:24 and twice in 26:54, 56 (during his arrest) that his death would fulfill the scriptures (i.e., God's will), but said that his betrayer should have never have been born. Unlike the other disciples who called Jesus "Lord," Judas called him "Rabbi," confirming that he was the betrayer. Jesus gave bread and wine for the disciples to eat with him. The bread symbolized his body and the contents of the cup his blood. Jesus told all his disciples to drink from the cup, because it symbolized the blood of the covenant shed for the many for the forgiveness of sins. Jesus explained that he would not drink of the cup until he drank it new with them in the Father's kingdom. Jesus predicted that all his disciples would be offended by him. Peter stated he would never deny him, but Jesus predicted that Peter would deny him three times.

After the supper, Jesus led his disciples into Gethsemane. Jesus told his disciples to stay awake and pray with him; however, instead of following his directions, his disciples slept. Jesus prayed three times that his Father would let this cup (i.e., his death) pass from him, yet in 26:39, 42, he stated his willingness to submit to God's will. Jesus knew that Judas, the religious leaders, and the large crowd with weapons came to arrest them. He told his disciples that the Son of Man was now going to be betrayed into the hands of sinners. During his arrest, Judas once again called Jesus "Rabbi," kissed him, and then the large crowd laid their hands on Jesus. Jesus called Judas a "Friend," and told him to arrest him. One of his disciples cut off the chief priest's servant's ear, but Jesus stopped the violence indicating that he could pray to the Father and have legions of angels to help him. However, in both vv. 54, 56, Jesus stated that his arrest was to fulfill the scriptures of the prophets.

The Son of Man is mentioned four times in 26:1–56. In each case, the title is associated with Jesus's betrayal and death in fulfillment of the scriptures (i.e., God's will).

2.4.2. Synoptic Comparison: Matthew 26:1–5, 14–35, 36–56; Mark 14:1–2, 10–31, 32–52; Luke 22:1–38, 39–53

Matthew's accounts of the Last Supper and Jesus's prayer at Gethsemane follow Mark closely. However, significant differences occur when comparing Matthew, Mark, and Luke. The differences between Matthew and Mark distinguish Matthew's theological concerns.

Matthew begins in 26:1–2 with a fourth passion prediction: the Son of Man being handed over for crucifixion. Immediately following the Son of Man's prediction of his imminent death, the religious leaders planned to trap, arrest, and kill Jesus. Mark and Luke do not highlight the Son of Man's predicted crucifixion, which minimizes Jesus's foreknowledge of his demise and the subsequent planning of his death by the religious leaders. Luke includes Judas in the religious leaders's plot by emphasizing that after Satan entered him, he went to see how he could betray Jesus (22:1–2).

All three Gospels narrate Judas's approach to the religious leaders in offering to betray Jesus to them. Matthew's tone emphasizes Judas's personal responsibility by asking for recompense if he handed Jesus over to them (i.e., "I will hand him over to you" [κἀγὼ ὑμῖν παραδώσω]; 26:15). Mark does not include Judas's request for a reward. Luke highlights that Judas agreed to the amount of money offered to him. Unlike Mark and Luke, Matthew records the exact amount of money offered Judas: thirty pieces of silver (26:15).

Matthew's account of the Last Supper has a different emphasis than Mark and Luke. First, Matthew highlights the disciples's obedience to Jesus's commands. In 26:18–19, Jesus told his disciples to go to the instructed location and prepare the Passover meal and they did as Jesus commanded them.[35] Unlike Mark and Luke, Matthew does not provide a detailed account of what the disciples did to prepare the Passover meal. Once Matthew indicates that the disciples obeyed Jesus's command, he records his account of the Last Supper.

Matthew's narration of the Last Supper is more attentive to the personal nature of Jesus's betrayal than Mark's and Luke's. Jesus immediately predicted that one of the disciples would betray him. In Matthew each disciple asked Jesus emphatically, "Surely I myself am [ἐγώ εἰμι] not the one, Lord?" (26:22). Judas asked Jesus emphatically as well, but did not call Jesus "Lord": "Surely I myself am not the one, Rabbi?" (26:25). Matthew also characterizes Judas as the one betraying him in 26:25, revealing the betrayer to whom Jesus referred in 26:23–24. Neither Mark nor Luke include the disciples's emphatic questions to Jesus, nor that Judas was the one betraying him. All three Gospels indicate that the Son of Man will die and mention the woe to the one who betrays him. However, only Mark and Matthew indicate that the Son of Man will go as "it has been written concerning him," and that "it would have been better" for the one who betrays him that he had not been born (Mark 14:21; Matt 26:24). Matthew records that Jesus commanded his disciples to take and eat the bread and drink from the cup, stating that the cup represents his blood being shed for many for the forgiveness of sins (26:26–28). Matthew's use of commanding language is not as apparent in Mark and is not indicated in Luke. Mark and Luke do not mention that the forgiveness of sins is the reason for Jesus shedding his blood. The Synoptic Gospels indicate that Jesus would not drink from the fruit of the vine until he drinks it new with them in his Father's kingdom. Luke also mentions that the disciples would eat in his memory (22:19). Matthew and Mark are close in Jesus's prediction of the disciples's denial of him (Matt 26:31–35; Mark 14:27–31). Luke only focuses on Peter's denial and does not indicate the other disciples's rejection (22:31–34).

The Gethsemane narrative is similar in Matthew and Mark but different in Luke. Matthew and Mark stress that Jesus commanded his disciples to keep awake and pray. Luke is concerned with the issue of temptation (i.e., the dual use of πειρασμός in 22:40, 46) and he mentions the angels strengthening Jesus while he prayed so fervently that he sweated blood (22:43–44). Matthew accentuates Jesus's posture of worship before his Father as he fell on his face praying (26:39), while Mark mentions Jesus falling on the ground

---

35. Matthew stresses Jesus's commands fourteen times in the Last Supper and the Gethsemane narratives through the use of the imperative (cf. 26:18, 19, 26 [two times], 27, 36, 38 [two times], 41 [two times], 45 [two times], 46, and 52). The emphasis on obedience to Jesus's instructions is more prominent in Matthew's account than Mark or Luke.

(14:35) and Luke notes that Jesus bent his knees in prayer (22:41). Matthew is more focused on Jesus's submission to his Father's will. First, Jesus's prayer was emphatic: "But not as I myself will (ἐγώ θέλω) but as you" (26:39), and, second, Jesus emphasized his submission twice, in 26:39 and in 26:43, when he prayed, "Let your will be done" (γενηθήτω τὸ θέλημά σου). Mark does include Jesus's emphatic plea but does not repeat Jesus's desire to submit to the Father's will. Luke includes neither of these emphases. Matthew and Mark finish the narrative with the Son of Man passage, stating that he was being betrayed into the hands of sinners and the time of betrayal had drawn near. Luke finishes with the warning of temptation and does not include these passages relating to betrayal.

The narrative of Jesus's arrest is similar in Matthew and Mark but different in Luke. As in 26:25, Matthew indicates Judas was the one who betrayed Jesus (26:48). This emphasis on Judas's being the betrayer appears more in Matthew than in Mark or Luke. Mark does not refer to Judas in this way at Jesus's arrest. Unlike Mark and Luke, when Judas approached Jesus to kiss him, Jesus called him "Friend" and gave him permission to betray him (26:50). Matthew's Jesus addressed the crowd of soldiers differently than Mark and Luke. In 26:53–54 Jesus stated, "Or do you think that I am not able to call upon my Father, and he will provide me now more than twelve legions of angels? How then may the scriptures be fulfilled that say this is necessary to happen?" Jesus's questions highlight his foreknowledge of God's will, his ability to be saved if he requested it, and his arrest and subsequent death. Mark and Luke do not emphasize Jesus's foreknowledge of God's will with the same intentionality. Mark and Matthew do include Jesus's statements on the soldiers's ability to arrest him in the temple if that had been prophesied in the scriptures. Only Matthew states that such divine help would not have fulfilled the scriptures. Matthew stresses that Jesus's arrest directly correlates with the fulfillment of God's will through the scriptures. Matthew ends the narrative by indicating that Jesus's disciples fled (26:56), while Mark is more generic, stating that everyone left him and fled (14:50). Unlike Matthew, Mark mentions a naked young man who fled and left his garment.

Luke's account of the arrest is different from Matthew and Mark in three ways. First, Luke includes a Son of Man statement when Jesus asked, "Judas, do you betray the Son of Man with a kiss?" (22:48). Second, a disciple cuts off the high priest's servant's ear, and Jesus touched the ear and healed the servant (22:51). Third, Luke darkens the arrest scene through Jesus's statement, "but this is the hour and authority of darkness" (22:53). Luke accentuates the contrast between Jesus's power and the power of darkness (i.e., Satan).

4.3.3. Exegesis

Matthew 26:2 is the Gospel's fourth passion prediction: the Son of Man is handed over to be crucified. The verb παραδίδωμι is repeated nine times in chapter 26 (vv. 15, 16, 21, 23, 24, 25, 45, 46, 48). Previously, Jesus the Son of Man predicted παραδίδωμι in the second and third passion predictions (17:22-23; 20:17-19). Therefore, chapter 26 fulfills the previous passion predictions, as his demise is planned, predicted during the Last Supper, submitted to through Jesus's prayer at Gethsemane, and culminated by his arrest and the events hereafter. Within the context of chapter 26, παραδίδωμι is connected specifically with Judas Iscariot. Matthew has already indicated that Judas would hand Jesus over (i.e., betray him) in 10:4, which leaves no doubt in Matthew that Judas is the prominent culprit of Jesus's demise. Matthew 26:2 serves as a general statement for the rest of the chapter. Chapter 26 develops specifically how the handing over of Jesus the Son of Man for crucifixion would happen.

Immediately after the passion prediction in 26:2, the religious leaders plan how they might arrest Jesus so they can kill him (26:3-5). Jesus the Son of Man is fully aware of what is going to happen; the context suggests Jesus's foreknowledge of his betrayal, arrest, and death (cf. 16:21; 17:22-23; 20:17-19). Between 26:1-5 and 26:14-16 is the narrative of a woman anointing Jesus's head with expensive ointment (26:6-13). This narrative stands in sharp contrast to the religious leaders's plan to kill Jesus and Judas's agreement to betray him. Instead of planning his demise, this woman worshiped Jesus by preparing his body for burial (26:12). Instead of agreeing to betray Jesus for thirty pieces of silver (26:15),[36] this woman sacrificed an expensive ointment from an alabaster flask to pour over Jesus's head (26:7).[37] The contrast between this woman and Judas accentuates the woman's selflessness and generosity with Judas's selfishness and desire for money. In light of Jesus's teaching on money in 6:24 and 6:33, this woman represents a genuine follower of Jesus while Judas represents a hypocrite. Judas is characterized as one who chooses worshiping mammon over God, while the woman as one who chooses to worship God and seek first the kingdom of the heavens. Jesus

---

36. Davies and Allison state that thirty pieces of silver would be the equivalent of about four months of minimum wage (*Matthew*, 3:452).

37. Keener mentions that people used expensive alabaster bottles to store the most costly ointments. Archaeologists have uncovered such long-necked flasks in first-century tombs near Jerusalem and suggest the frequent once-for-all expenditure of this expensive perfume at the death of loved ones. Mark 14:3 mentions that this balm was made of pure nard (a costly ointment imported from India or elsewhere in the east) (*Gospel of Matthew*, 618). According to Mark 14:5, the ointment could have been sold for more than three hundred denarii.

credited this woman with doing this act of love as a preparation for burying a loved one, and claimed that wherever the gospel is proclaimed her sacrificial love for him will be shared in memory of her (26:12–13).

Matthew stresses the contrast between this woman and Judas by immediately narrating Judas's request of money in payment for handing Jesus over to them. The statement, "one of the twelve," in 26:14 highlights Judas's hypocrisy; he was not a genuine follower of Jesus. Judas's choice to betray Jesus is indicated when he looked for an opportunity to hand Jesus over to the authorities (26:16). Judas's acquisition of silver appears to be a violation of Jesus's instructions to his disciples in 10:9: "Do not acquire gold or silver or copper in your belts." Judas's disobedience to these terms of discipleship implies that he was not a genuine disciple. In 28:11–15, the chief priests paid the soldiers a considerable amount of silver to report that Jesus's disciples stole his body. Both Judas and the soldiers accept the payment of silver from the chief priests, aligning them with those who were opposed to Jesus and his followers. The contrast between Judas and genuine disciples continues after Judas's agreement to betray Jesus. In 26:17–19, Matthew highlights the disciples's obedience to Jesus. After asking Jesus where he wanted them to prepare the Passover, Jesus commanded them to "go" (imperative: ὑπάγετε) into the city to find a certain person and make preparations with him. The disciples obeyed Jesus's command, which is characteristic of genuine disciples who fulfill God's will.

During the supper, Jesus predicted that one of disciples would betray him (26:20). Each disciple emphatically asked Jesus, "Surely I myself am not the one, Lord?" (26:22). In Matthew, genuine disciples called Jesus "Lord" (κύριος).[38] As seen previously, the name a disciple gave to Jesus reflected whether they were true followers of Jesus (cf. 8:18–23). In 26:25, Judas asked the same question but did not call Jesus "Lord": "Surely I myself am not the one, Rabbi (ῥαββι)?" By calling Jesus "Rabbi," Judas indicated that he was not a genuine follower of Jesus (also 26:49). Along with διδάσκαλε, ῥαββι is a name given to Jesus by those in opposition to him and/or his mission (e.g., Pharisees, scribes, and other religious leaders).[39] Jesus emphasized judgment on the one who betrayed him in 26:24: "Indeed the Son of Man is going just as it has been written concerning him, but woe to that man through

---

38. Κύριε is the name genuine disciples, followers of Jesus, and those who respond positively give to him in Matthew (see 8:2, 6, 8, 21, 25; 9:28; 13:27; 14:28, 30; 15:22, 25, 27; 16:22; 17:4, 15; 18:21; 20:30, 31, 33; 25:20, 22, 24, 37; 26:22). However, Jesus is called "κύριε, κύριε"/"κύριε" by those who hypocritically state Jesus as their "Lord" but do not live in a way characteristic of a genuine disciple. On judgment day, they will be rejected from the kingdom of the heavens (see 7:21–23; 25:11–13, 44–46).

39. See Matt 8:19; 12:38; 19:16; 22:16, 24, 36.

whom the Son of Man is betrayed. It would have been better for him if that man had not been born." The word *woe* (οὐαί) occurs eleven other times in Matthew,[40] and in all cases except 24:19 the word is used negatively in a condemning and judgmental tone. The cities of Chorazin and Bethsaida are judged for their lack of repentance (11:21). Whoever causes the little ones to fall away from faith are judged (and are described as those who should rather be killed than live; 18:6–7 [also 18:7–9]). In Matt 23, Jesus condemned the Pharisees for their hypocrisy, their opposition to Jesus and the prophets, and accused them of being responsible for killing the prophets. Jesus stated, "The one who has dipped his hand (χεῖρα) into the bowl will betray me" (26:23). Therefore, Judas was in alignment with those who are condemned and judged due to their opposition of Jesus. The emphasis on the "hand" of evil people is prominent in Matthew. In 17:22, Jesus predicted that he would be betrayed into human hands. Later in 26:45, Jesus stated that the Son of Man was being betrayed into the hands of sinners. Finally, in 26:50, after Judas kissed Jesus, the great crowd laid their hands on Jesus and arrested him. The implication is clear: Judas was grouped with the sinners who opposed Jesus and handed him over to death.[41] Matthew 26:24 highlights an important play on words. The Son of Man (i.e., Son of Humanity [ὁ υἱὸς τοῦ ἀνθρώπου]) is being betrayed by *that human* (ὁ ἄνθρωπος ἐκεῖνος [two times in verse]). In this verse, the Son of Man proclaimed judgment on the human sin of betrayal. Immediately after the mention of the sin of betrayal, 26:26–29 emphasize that the Son of Man's death makes the forgiveness of sins and provision of eternal life possible for those who seek to have their sins forgiven and receive salvation. However, in 26:45–56, Judas chose to carry through with his sinful behavior even though forgiveness of his sin was possible if he repented of his sin and sought forgiveness. Jesus the Son of Man mediates God's grace and mercy to humanity—the forgiveness of

---

40. See Matt 11:21 (two times); 18:7 (two times); 23:13, 15, 16, 23, 25, 27, 29; 24:19.

41. Klassen argues that God handed Jesus over to be crucified. Judas is presented more as an informer who hands Jesus over to the authorities in accordance to God's will for his life. Therefore, instead of viewing Judas in a negative light, he should be seen positively as one who aligned himself with God's will. He helped lead the authorities to Jesus so they could arrest and kill him, a demise that is in accordance to God's will for Jesus's life (*Judas*, 52–53, 66–70, 100–107). However, throughout the context of chapter 26 (also 10:4), Matthew indicates Judas's betrayal and choice to hand Jesus over to the authorities. Carey describes Judas's hypocrisy correctly, "While appearing to remain committed to Jesus' ministry, Judas joins the ranks of those who oppose Jesus's mission. In the Gospel narratives he serves as a foil to all who are faithful to Jesus—even when they do not understand fully. More than any other single character, perhaps, Judas is the antagonist of these stories, while Jesus is the clear protagonist" ("Judas Iscariot," 266).

sins is available to humans who repent of their sins, seek forgiveness, and receive eternal salvation, because of his obedient death.

As an adversary to Jesus and his mission, Judas clearly acted of his own accord and disobeyed God's will for a disciple, namely, to remain committed to Jesus. The contrast is clearly seen in 26:24.[42] Jesus the Son of Man was completely obedient to God's will for his mission and remained committed to God in fulfilling his will: "he is going as it has been written concerning him" (26:24). In Matthew 26, the emphasis on the Son of Man's obedience is prominent. In 26:24, 54, 56, Jesus stood as the one who fulfilled the prophets's message concerning God's will. Jesus was arrested and killed to give his life as a ransom for many (20:28). Jesus's obedience is also highlighted by Matthew's emphasis on time. Jesus knew "his time is near" (καιρός μου ἐγγύς ἐστιν; 26:18) and "the hour has drawn near" (ἤγγικεν ἡ ὥρα; 26:45 [also 26:46]), so he continued to move forward by celebrating the Passover with his disciples, going to Gethsemane to pray (declaring his willingness to submit to death), and telling his disciples to go with him to meet his betrayer and be arrested. Donald Senior helpfully states,

> Matthew's redactional emphasis on the foreknowledge of Jesus in regard to the events of the Passion and the filial obedience to the divine plan is crystallized in an expression consciousness of his "kairos" (or "hour" in some places) when the appointed moment of deliverance into the hands of sinners is to be accomplished and accepted.[43]

In 26:17–19, Jesus's willing obedience to the "kairos" and later to the words of scripture (26:24), can be compared with the disciples's obedience to Jesus's command to make preparations for the Passover meal.[44] The context of 26:17–19 ties the theme of obedience tightly together and is continually emphasized throughout chapter 26.

Matthew 26:17–19 highlights the disciples's obedience to Jesus's command to prepare the Passover meal. The disciples's obedience is implied as Jesus shared the bread and cup with them. In 26:26–27, Jesus commanded his disciples to *take* (λάβετε) and *eat* (φάγετε) the bread and then to *drink* (πίετε) from the cup. The command to drink from the cup is reminiscent

---

42. Heil emphasizes Judas's responsibility in rejecting Jesus: "Although Jesus' betrayal by one of the Twelve is embraced by God's salvific will, the betrayer, held fully and personally responsible, is to be greatly pitied for breaking his intimate bond with Jesus and betraying him" (*Death and Resurrection*, 33).

43. Senior, *Passion Narrative*, 49.

44. See Senior for a similar understanding of the theme of obedience. Senior, *Passion Narrative*, 62–65.

of Jesus's inquiry to the sons of Zebedee on whether they were able to drink from his cup (20:20–28). All the disciples received the call to sacrifice their lives for Jesus's sake and mission (cf. 10:16–39; 16:24–26; 26:27). Matthew appears to be connecting drinking the cup with willing self-sacrifice through these commands in 26:26–27.[45] Jesus stated that the cup represented his blood which was shed for many for the forgiveness of sins (26:28). Matthew uses the term *sins* (ἁμαρτιῶν) only in 26:28 and in 1:21, highlighting again the purpose of Jesus's mission—Jesus will save his people from their sins. The Son of Man voluntarily obeyed God's will by sacrificing his life for all humans so they could seek forgiveness for their sins and inherit eternal life. The Son of Man will celebrate God's mercy and grace, which was mediated through Jesus's sacrificial suffering and death, with his followers in the eternal kingdom.[46] Jesus's gift of the forgiveness of sins is accomplished through his self-sacrificial death (20:28), which was fulfilled by his arrest and crucifixion (cf. 26:2).[47] The Son of Man's resolve to fulfill the Father's will through his obedience to suffer and die mediates to his disciples the self-sacrificial mission outlined for their future ministry; they must be ready to obey the Father's will to suffer and die as well.

Matthew's narrative of Jesus's prayer in Gethsemane contrasts Jesus's obedience with the disciples's disobedience. Jesus's praxis of prayer mediated for his disciples the importance of obeying God's will. Jesus used command language throughout the narrative to accentuate the disciples's disobedience: "Sit here" (καθίσατε αὐτοῦ), "remain here" (μείνατε ὧδε), and

45. Heil makes the same observation: "The literal 'drinking' from 'the cup' that Jesus gives 'all' the disciples, then, indicates their sacramental participation in the suffering and death of Jesus through this new Passover meal and thus prepares them for their own future sufferings and deaths (10:16–25; 24:9–13)" (*Death and Resurrection*, 36).

46. In the context of 26:2, 24–29, the emphasis is on Jesus the Son of Man's voluntary suffering and death as prophesied in the scriptures in obedience to his Father's will. Jesus mentioned that his disciples would not partake of the cup again until they drank it anew with him in *his* Father's kingdom (v. 29). During his prayer at Gethsemane, he prayed that the Father would take the cup away from him but submitted to the Father's will. In his prayer, Jesus addressed the Father as *his* Father (vv. 39, 42). At the end of his prayer, Jesus stated that the Son of Man would be betrayed into the hands of sinners—in other words, arrested and then sentenced to death (vv. 45–46). Finally, during the arrest scene, Jesus stated that he could call on *his* Father to provide him with legions of angels but that would circumvent the divine will (δεῖ) in vv. 53–54. Matthew's connection between the Son of Man and suffering and death highlights his christological divine identity—the Son of Man is God's Son.

47. Matthew's use of "being shed" (ἐκχυννόμενον) in 26:28 connects Jesus's death with other prophets, wise men, and scribes who have been and will be condemned and crucified by the religious authorities (23:35 [23:29–39]). Matthew highlights that Jesus's death is aligned with other righteous and obedient followers of God who fulfilled God's will for their lives.

"watch"[48] with me (γρηγορεῖτε μετ' ἐμοῦ; 26:36–37). Additionally, 26:41 includes "watch" (γρηγορεῖτε) and "pray" (προσεύχεσθε). However, each time Jesus found the disciples sleeping (26:40, 43). Jesus used command language to stress his desire to follow God's will—to accept the cup of suffering and death. In 26:45 Jesus stated, "'Sleep' (καθεύδετε) from now on and 'rest' (ἀναπαύεσθε)." Finally in 26:46 Jesus told the disciples, "'Rise up' (ἐγείρεσθε); let us go." Jesus was in control over his arrest because he was completely invested in fulfilling his Father's will through obedient suffering and death. Jesus's obedience to his Father mediated for his disciples that obedience is the proper response in fulfilling God's will.

Matthew is concerned with Jesus's response to God's will. In 26:39 and 26:42, Jesus emphasized his willingness to submit to his Father's will, to drink the cup of suffering and death. The insistence on Jesus's voluntary obedience is highlighted especially in Jesus's emphatic prayer: "But not as I *myself* will (ἐγώ θέλω) but as you [will]" (v. 39). In both v. 39 and v. 42, Jesus asked if the cup might pass from him, yet as Jesus's response states in v. 42, "Let your will be done" (γενηθήτω τὸ θέλημά σου). Matthew parallels Jesus's prayer to his Father in Gethsemane with his prayer in 6:10, "Let your will be done [γενηθήτω τὸ θέλημά σου] on earth as it is in heaven." In Matthew, the ultimate proof of genuine discipleship and dedication to God is to submit completely to God's will (cf. 7:21; 12:50; 21:31–32).[49] Through the Gethsemane prayer, Jesus brought Matthew's theological thread to a climax: Jesus the Son of Man mediated for his disciples how to fulfill God's will through submission to his will; he is resolutely committed to drinking the cup of suffering and death for the many for the forgiveness of their sins (cf. 16:21; 17:22–23; 20:17–19; 26:2, 29).

Jesus's willingness to obey God's will in 26:39, 42 comes to fulfillment in 26:45b–46. Jesus the Son of Man knew the time had come for him to be betrayed into the hands of sinners. The Son of Man mediated for his disciples that a willingness to fulfill God's will must be expressed in active obedience—going to the place or people to be arrested in obedience to God's will. Judas is identified as the one who betrayed Jesus in 26:46 and 26:48. By combining παραδίδωμι in v. 45 with vv. 46 and 48, Judas is aligned with the hands of sinners. Jesus announced the arrival of his enemies, as Judas appeared with a great crowd armed with swords and clubs. Matthew highlights

---

48. Stanley describes one of the meanings of Jesus's command "to watch" as demanding unwavering obedience to Jesus. Therefore, the contrast between Jesus and his disciples accentuates Jesus's willing obedience to God's will and the disciples's failure of unwavering obedience to Jesus's commands (*Jesus in Gethsemane*, 179).

49. See Heil for a similar connection between discipleship and submitting to God's will (*Death and Resurrection*, 45).

Judas's betrayal of Jesus by contrasting the two descriptions of Judas: "one of the twelve" (also 26:14) with "the one betraying him" in vv. 47 and 48 (also 10:4; 26:46; 27:3). Judas demonstrated that he was not a genuine disciple, since he would not give up all possessions and life to follow Jesus (cf. 10:9; 16:24–26; 19:20–21, 27–30; 20:26; 26:7, 10, 12–13). Instead, he willingly betrayed Jesus by accepting thirty pieces of silver (26:14–16) and actively brought the great crowd to the place where they could arrest Jesus. Matthew highlights Judas's hypocrisy with his greeting to Jesus: "Χαῖρε, ῥαββί," καὶ κατεφίλησεν αὐτόν. Χαῖρε and κατεφίλησεν are both positive and affectionate terms; χαῖρε can be translated "rejoice, welcome, it is good to see you." Κατεφίλησεν can be translated "he kissed fervently." Therefore, these positive terms suggest that Judas was acting like a genuine disciple. However, by calling Jesus ῥαββί, Judas clearly placed himself outside the disciples's circle, since, in Matthew, genuine disciples call Jesus κύριος and enemies call him διδάσκαλε or ῥαββί. Even with Judas's hypocritical address, Jesus still called him "Friend" (ἑταῖρε). In Matthew, ἑταῖρε is only found three times (20:13; 22:12; 26:50), and in each case the term is an affectionate title given by someone who acted lovingly to a recipient. For example, in 26:50, Jesus accepted Judas into his disciples's circle where he revealed to him how to follow God's will. However, Judas willingly betrayed Jesus and chose to act contrary to a genuine disciple by betraying him.

After Jesus was arrested, someone tried to rescue Jesus by cutting off the ear of the servant of the high priest. Jesus responded negatively to the act of violence, commanding this person to sheath the sword. The four passion predictions (16:21; 17:22–23; 20:17–19; 26:2), the statement about obeying the scriptures (26:24a), and Jesus's statements of willing obedience (26:39, 42) all indicate that Jesus was ready to fulfill God's will for his life. However, even at his arrest, one of Jesus's followers still wanted to rescue him from God's will. This scene is reminiscent of Peter's rebuke of Jesus after the first passion prediction (16:21–23). Words and actions that are opposed to God's will for Jesus's life are of satanic origin (16:23; 4:1–11) and are not in alignment with God's thoughts (16:23). Jesus rebuked the violent actions that accompanied his arrest and made a statement found only in Matthew: "Do you not think I am not able to call upon my Father, and he will provide me with more than twelve legions of angels?" (26:53). However, Jesus resiliently focused on God's will by emphasizing that the scriptures of the prophets must be fulfilled (26:54, 56).[50] During the Last Supper, Jesus declared his

50. In regard to Jesus's arrest, Green states: "The most pervasive motif given expression in this pericope is the realization that Jesus' passion—and thus his arrest—was integral to God's plan. Because Jesus had already resolved to submit to the divine will, he now submits to his captors. Any attempts to resist arrest are therefore attempts to resist

dedication to God's will by fulfilling the scriptures that the Son of Man will die as it has been written concerning him (26:24). Both in Jesus's first passion prediction (16:21) and during his arrest (26:54), Jesus stated that "it is necessary" (δεῖ) for him to suffer and die. W. J. Bennett Jr. states, "Δεῖ and γέγραπται are synonymous but only in the sense that they are both circumlocutions for 'God wills it.'"[51] Jesus's insistence to obey God's will completely is stressed through the emphasis Matthew places on the scriptures being fulfilled. Throughout chapter 26, Matthew, more than any other Gospel,[52] emphasizes Jesus's willingness to fulfill God's will through obedience even unto death.[53] Similarly, a genuine disciple will fulfill God's will through obedience even unto death (16:21-26). Jesus the Son of Man fulfilled God's will through his obedient self-sacrificial suffering and death, which mediates the kind of obedient self-sacrificing ministry expected by genuine followers of Jesus in fulfilling of God's will for their lives.

Matthew 26:2 is Jesus's fourth passion prediction following 16:21; 17:22-23; and 20:17-19. Chapter 26 fulfills these passion predictions, as Jesus the Son of Man's demise is planned by the religious leaders and through the betrayal of Judas, predicted during the Last Supper, submitted to through Jesus's prayer at Gethsemane, and culminated by his arrest and events hereafter. Judas is the main culprit in Jesus's demise as he is the one who agreed to hand Jesus over to the religious leaders for thirty pieces of silver. Judas is contrasted with the woman who anointed Jesus's head with expensive oil and the disciples who followed Jesus's commands to prepare the Passover (26:3-19). In 26:20-25, Jesus predicted that one of his disciples would betray him. All the disciples, except for Judas, called Jesus "Lord" and vowed they would not betray him, while Judas called him "Rabbi," indicating he was not a genuine follower of Jesus and was his betrayer (also 26:49).

God's will and must be halted" (*Death of Jesus*, 270). In Matthew's arrest pericope, the submissiveness to God's will is more pervasive with the denial of angelic help (26:53) and the emphasis on fulfilling scripture (26:24, 54, 56).

51. Bennett, "Son of Man," 128.

52. Barbour reaches the following conclusions in his comparison of the Gethsemane narrative in the Synoptic Gospels: (1), Mark's narrative understands the suffering of Jesus as an anticipation of eschatological tribulation; (2) Luke's narrative emphasizes the role of Satan in the testing of Jesus; and (3) Matthew's narrative concentrates further on the figure of Jesus, whose determination to continue in the path of obedience carries him through the period of testing ("Gethsemane," 236-40). Barth also argues Matthew's emphasis on Jesus's voluntary acts of obedience in fulfilling God's will are more prominent than in the other Gospels ("Matthew's Understanding," 143-44).

53. Senior states: "A constant theme of Matthew's Passion narrative has been to emphasize Jesus' awareness of and obedience to his destiny as the suffering Messiah" (*Passion Narrative*, 112).

Jesus the Son of Man pronounced a "woe" on the one who would betray him. In other contexts in Matthew's Gospel, a "woe" is directed towards those who are condemned and judged due to their opposition of Jesus and his ministry (e.g., chapter 23). There is irony in 26:24–28, the Son of Man (i.e., Son of Humanity) is being betrayed by *that man* (i.e., Judas) emphasizing Judas's sin of betrayal. The Son of Man's death enabled the forgiveness of sins and eternal salvation, which Judas could have received but he chose to betray Jesus resulting in his arrest and death. The Son of Man mediates God's grace and mercy—his desire to forgive humanity of their sins which is possible through Jesus's death. Humans respond by genuinely repenting of their sins and seeking forgiveness. In 17:27 and 26:45, 50, Judas was grouped with sinners who opposed Jesus and handed him over to death. Judas aligned himself with the Pharisees and religious leaders who were enemies of Jesus and opposed his life and mission (e.g., his arrest, 26:47–50). In contrast, Jesus the Son of Man was completely obedient to God's will for his mission and remained committed to following God's will—as prophesied in the scriptures and the prophets (26:24, 54, 56). In Matt 26, the emphasis on Jesus's obedience is prominent. In contrast to his disciples who slept and would not keep awake at Gethsemane, Jesus committed himself wholeheartedly to submitting to God's will (26:36–46).

Jesus's genuine disciples continue to represent those who obeyed Jesus's commands by following his direction to eat the bread and drink from the cup (26:26–27). The cup represents self-sacrificial death, giving up one's life in obedience to God's will (cf. 20:20–28; 26:27–28). The emphasis placed on the cup and the shedding of Jesus's blood for the forgiveness of the sins of the many accentuated the ultimate purpose of the Son of Man's ministry, namely, saving his people from their sins through his self-sacrificial death (26:28; cf. 1:21; 16:21; 17:22–23; 20:17–19; 26:2). The Son of Man will celebrate in his eternal kingdom with those who have had their sins forgiven and received eternal life. The Son of Man mediates God's grace and mercy through his death which enables the forgiveness of sins. In 26:45b–46, the Son of Man knew his time had come for him to be betrayed into the hands of sinners. He mediated for his disciples that a willingness to fulfill God's will must be met with active obedience—going to the place or people to be arrested in obedience to God's will. At his arrest, Jesus rebuked the violent action that accompanied his arrest (26:51–52), and made the statement that he could ask his Father for twelve legions of angels to rescue him. However, in obedience to his Father's will revealed in the scriptures, he refused to oppose anything or anyone which might distract him from fulfilling God's will (16:21; 26:24, 54, 56). Jesus the Son of Man fulfilled God's will through his willing and obedient suffering and death, which mediates the kind of self-sacrificial ministry expected of Jesus's genuine disciples who are called to fulfill God's will for their lives.

3. Conclusion

Jesus the Son of Man mediated for Peter particularly, and his disciples generally, what they were to reveal to others in their future ministry. The revelation concerns the identity of the Son of Man; he is the Christ, the Son of the living God (16:13–16). He is the divine-human who came to earth as the Son of Man to fulfill God's salvific plan (16:21), which will mediate God's love and mercy to humanity through his suffering and death for the forgiveness of sins. Jesus commanded his disciples not to begin teaching about his identity until after his resurrection (16:20; 17:9). Jesus the Son of Man's willingness to fulfill God's will by obediently going to Jerusalem to suffer many things and be killed (16:21) mediated that is was necessary for genuine disciples to prove their fidelity to God's will by their willingness to suffer and die as they obediently revealed God's will to others (16:13–20, 24–26). In the near future, Jesus would be vindicated due to his fidelity to God's will through his resurrection (16:21, 28). Similarly, future reward is promised to genuine disciples when the Son of Man comes at the eschaton if they obediently practice God's will in their earthly ministries (16:27). Therefore, Jesus's vindication for his fidelity to God's will mediates for his disciples their future vindication for their fidelity to fulfilling God's will.

Jesus the Son of Man and John the Baptist shared a common fate because they both faithfully preached a message of repentance (cf. 3:1–2; 4:17) and were rejected by the religious authorities (cf. 11:18–19). Both suffered and died for their fidelity to fulfilling God's will (14:1–12; 16:21; 17:22–23). Through Jesus's willing obedience to the Father's will to preach a message of repentance and to suffer and die, he mediated for his disciples the kind of costly obedience needed for their future ministries, which would also include rejection, suffering, and death (10:16–28, 37–41; 16:24–26). In addition, the Son of Man's suffering and death would mediate God's grace to humanity, ironically, even to those who would hand him over to death (cf. 17:22; 26:45).

Jesus the Son of Man is the ultimate example of servanthood for his genuine disciples. As a servant, he placed himself among the "great" and "last ones" by self-sacrificially offering himself as a ransom for the many (20:26–28). Jesus fulfilled his Father's will by obediently going up to Jerusalem, being handed over to Jewish religious authorities to be condemned, and being handed over to the Gentiles to be mocked, whipped, and crucified for the sake of others (20:17–19). Instead of seeking prominence on earth, Jesus was vindicated through his resurrection and the establishment of his kingdom (20:19, 21). Jesus's fidelity to the fulfillment of God's will mediated for his disciples God's will for their future ministry: they were not to vie for positions of worldly greatness (20:20–25), but, like Jesus, were to offer themselves obediently and self-sacrificially as the "last ones" and "great." They would demonstrate such self-sacrifice by serving and be slaves to others even onto death (20:26–28), knowing they will receive their vindication in Jesus's kingdom in the future (cf. 16:27). As a "servant" and "slave," the Son of Man's death as a ransom (20:28) emphasizes his mission to forgive the sins of humanity so they could receive a restored relationship with God. The ability to seek forgiveness from their sins enables humanity to receive salvation because of Jesus's death on the cross (20:19).

The inevitable nearness of Jesus the Son of Man's demise is emphasized in Matthew's fourth passion prediction in 26:2. In chapter 26, Jesus the Son of Man mediated the character and fidelity required to fulfilling God's will, which needed to be emulated by genuine disciples. Matthew demonstrates such emulation through sharp contrasts between Judas and the other disciples and between Jesus and his twelve disciples.

First, Judas and the other disciples are contrasted in the following manner. Judas hypocritically is described in this chapter as "one of the twelve" (26:14, 47), but his actions prove that he was not a genuine disciple. Judas helped the religious leaders in their plot to kill Jesus in return for payment to betray him (26:3–5, 14–16). In contrast to being one of the twelve, he is described as the "one betraying him [Jesus]" (26:25, 46, 48), who led the crowd to Gethsemane to arrest him (26:46–50). The other disciples are characterized differently. A woman brought an alabaster flask of expensive ointment and poured it over Jesus's head to prepare him for burial (26:6–13). Instead of seeking payment to betray Jesus, she gave her resources away for Jesus. The disciples obediently followed Jesus's command by going to prepare the Passover (26:17–19). The other disciples did not betray Jesus but greatly grieved the thought of betraying him and called him "Lord," in contrast to Judas who, like Jesus's other enemies, called him "Rabbi" (or "Teacher"; 26:20–25, 49–50). Finally, Judas hypocritically ate and drank with Jesus and the disciples at the Last Supper; however, he had no intention of giving his life sacrificially for kingdom purposes, which was required by Jesus for genuine discipleship (26:26–28; cf. 10:4; 20:22–28).

Second, Jesus and his twelve disciples are contrasted in the following ways. Throughout chapter 26, Matthew strongly emphasizes Jesus the Son of Man's obedience in fulfilling God's will. In 26:24, 54–56, Jesus announced his death as necessary in fulfillment of the scriptures. Jesus willingly obeyed God's Word—by fulfilling the scriptures that predict Jesus's arrest, suffering, and death. Jesus's prayer in Gethsemane portrayed his commitment to obey God's will and acceptance of the cup of suffering and death (26:39, 42). Jesus allowed his blood to be shed as a sacrifice for the forgiveness of sins—his divine mission from the beginning of his earthly life (26:28; 1:21). Jesus obediently went to meet Judas who would betray him and deliver him into the hands of sinners (26:45–46). Once he was surrounded by the crowd, Jesus gave Judas permission to capture and arrest him (26:50). Finally, when one of the disciples cut off the ear of the servant of the high priest, Jesus told him to put the sword away. He could have called twelve legions of angels to help him, yet doing so would be in violation of the scriptures (i.e., God's will) (26:52–54).

In contrast to Jesus's willing obedience to God's will, the disciples failed to obey Jesus's commands at Gethsemane. He told them to "remain," "watch with him," and "pray," but the disciples disobeyed Jesus's instructions and fell asleep (26:27–45). In addition, once Jesus was arrested, all the disciples left him (26:56).

Jesus the Son of Man mediated for his disciples the message, character, and fidelity needed to fulfill God's will as required of genuine disciples. After Jesus's resurrection, his disciples were to reveal to others the identity of the Son of Man: he is the Christ, the Son of the living God. Disciples choose to fulfill God's will through obedience in a self-sacrificial manner (i.e., giving up possessions, rejection, suffering, and death) for God's kingdom. They obey Jesus's commands and call him "Lord." Like Jesus, disciples choose to obey God's will over their own by going to the people and places where God wants them to (even if it leads to their demise). A willingness to fulfill God's will requires obedience. Throughout chapter 26, Jesus mediated for his disciples the sacrificial ways necessary in obediently fulfilling God's will for their ministry and life.

In 26:24–29, the Son of Man's death mediates God's grace and mercy by enabling humans to receive forgiveness for their sins and inherit salvation. Judas could have received forgiveness and eternal salvation, but he chose to betray Jesus which resulted in arrest and death. The Son of Man will celebrate the gift of God's grace and mercy, mediated through Jesus's suffering and death, with his genuine disciples in the eternal kingdom.

Chapter 4

The Son of Man's Mediatorial Significance at His Parousia

Judgment, Vindication, and Reward for Fulfilling God's Will

1. Introduction

IN CHAPTER 3, I demonstrated that Jesus the Son of Man mediated how to fulfill God's will through obedience to his Father. Through his teaching and example, Jesus commanded his genuine disciples to obey God's will for their lives. Nowhere in Matthew is Jesus's obedience to the Father more clearly realized than in the passion predictions and narrative, providing the climax to Jesus's obedience to the Father's will. As Jesus's genuine disciples follow him in their ministry, they will also demonstrate fidelity to the Father through their faithful obedience to his will.

In this chapter, I will argue that as eschatological judge at his parousia, Jesus the Son of Man will mediate his promised vindication and reward to his faithful, obedient disciples who have followed his Father's will throughout their lives and ministry. Matthew stresses the theme of judgment through the sharp contrast between faithful, obedient genuine disciples, and unfaithful, disobedient disciples who refuse to follow the Father's will.[1] No other Gospel develops Jesus the Son of Man's role as eschatological judge as fully as Matthew does. In Matthew, of the thirty Son of Man passages in the Gospel, twelve relate to the Son of Man as judge at his parousia. However, in Mark, there are only three references mentioning the Son of Man at his

---

1. Throughout many of the Matthean texts studied in this chapter, the Pharisees and religious leaders demonstrated unfaithfulness and disobedience to the Father's will through their unwillingness to heed the Father's will in their positions in the Matthean cultural context. However, "unfaithful" and "disobedient" do not refer *only* to the Pharisees and religious leaders, but include *any person/disciple* who chooses not to adhere to the Father's will as was demonstrated though the ministry of Jesus.

parousia, and only seven in Luke (though four[2] are unique to Luke). Matthew's presentation of the Son of Man as judge at his parousia is especially poignant when he contrasts the faithful/obedient (and positive vindication/reward) with the unfaithful/disobedient (and punishment). I will demonstrate Matthew's unique contribution to Jesus the Son of Man's role as judge by analyzing the parable of the wheat and weeds in 13:24–30, 36–43; 16:27; and 19:28 within their immediate contexts, Matthew's (parousia discourse and judgment scene in 24:3—25:46), and, finally, 26:64 in its immediate context. I will include in my exegesis how Matthew's broader-book context contributes to his portrayal of Jesus as the judge at his parousia.

2. The Son of Man as Mediator of the Father's Judgment at His Parousia

2.1. The Parable of the Wheat and Weeds: Separating the Children of the Kingdom from the Children of the Evil One (Matthew 13:24–30, 36–43)

2.1.1. Textual Orientation

Jesus spoke in parables to the crowds but explained them only to his disciples (13:11–17). After sharing with his disciples the meaning of the parable of the sower, he then presented the parable of the wheat and weeds. As before, Jesus spoke the parable of the wheat and weeds to the crowd (13:24–30) but reserved the meaning of the parable to the disciples alone (13:36). Jesus revealed to his disciples the events characteristic of his role as judge at the Son of Man's parousia. The Son of Man is the sower of the children of the kingdom who are the good seed. Amidst the good seed are the children of the evil one (the weeds) who have been sowed among the seed by the devil. The harvest is the Son of Man's parousia. At that time, he will send his reapers out (his angels) to gather all that causes offense and those practicing lawlessness (children of the evil one) and will throw them in the furnace of fire, where there will be weeping and gnashing of teeth. The angels will gather the righteous ones (children of the kingdom) and they will shine in the Father's kingdom (13:37–43).

---

2. (1) Matt 13:37, 41; 16:27; 19:28; 24:27, 30 (two times), 37, 39, 44; 25:31; 26:64; (2) Mark 8:38; 13:26; 14:62; (3) Luke 9:26; 17:22, 24, 26, 30; 21:27; 22:69, plus those that are unique to Luke: 12:8, 40; 18:8; 21:36. Except for 12:8 and 18:8, these texts do not specifically relate to the Son of Man as judge at his parousia. Only 12:8 appears in a context that contrasts the faithful with the unfaithful. An essential element in the Matthean judgment scenes is the sharp contrast between those who are obedient and disobedient to the Father's will.

2.1.2. Synoptic Comparison

The parable of the wheat and weeds is unique to Matthew's Gospel. Mark and Luke do not record this parable, nor do they highlight the theme of separation between the faithful and unfaithful in their eschatological material on Jesus the Son of Man's parousia.[3]

2.1.3. Exegesis

Matthew 13:24-30 and 13:36-43 belong together as a unit, description followed by interpretation. Matthew 13:24-30 is the description of the parable without specific revelation regarding its meaning. There is a significant difference between 13:24-30 and 13:36-43; the master of the house (i.e., κύριος; 13:27) does not want the gathering (i.e., judgment) of the wheat and weeds to occur until the harvest. The master of the house commands his slaves to permit (ἄφετε) them to grow together (13:30) lest while gathering they might uproot (ἐκριζόω) the weeds with the wheat. The concern of the master of the house appears to be protecting the wheat from its being uprooted, while, at the same time, providing opportunity for the wheat to remain in the midst (ἀνὰ μέσον) of the weeds. The kindness and patience of the master of the house toward the weeds and protection for wheat is not recorded in 13:36-43. In Matt 10, Jesus sent his twelve apostles out to preach to both Jews and Gentiles (cf. 10:5-7, 18, 23) sharing that the kingdom of the heavens is near (10:7). They were to imitate John the Baptist and Jesus who preached about the need for people to repent of their sins because the kingdom of the heavens is near (3:2, 6; 4:17; cf. 4:18-21). In addition, the Son of Man's mission was to mediate God the Father's grace and mercy towards humanity by providing the means of the forgiveness of sins through his sacrificial suffering and death (cf. 16:21;

---

3. Some scholars suggest that Matthew was influenced by Mark 4:26-29 (the parable of scattered seed) when including the parable of the wheat and tares (e.g., Luz, *Matthew 8-20*, 253-54; Gundry, *Matthew*, 261-62; Manson, *Sayings of Jesus*, 192-93). I concur with other scholars who see little dependence on Mark at this juncture (e.g., France, *Matthew*, 524, 524n8; Hagner, *Matthew*, 1:382; Osborne, *Matthew*, 520; Morris, *Gospel*, 348; Kingsbury, *Parables of Jesus*, 64-65; Beasley-Murray, *Jesus*, 132; Jones, *Matthean Parables*, 311-19; Jeremias, *Parables of Jesus*, 81-85). Dodd states, "The parable of the Tares is peculiar to Matthew (xiii. 24-30), and is often supposed to be that evangelist's elaboration of the Marcan parable of the Seed Growing Secretly. This does not seem to me in the least probable. The Matthean parable stands on its own feet" (*Parables*, 147). However, if even Matthew was influenced by Mark, the contents of these parables are different, especially in light of the sharp contrast between the "children of the kingdom" and "children of the evil one" highlighted in the Matthean parable.

17:22–23; 20:17–19, 28; 26:2, 28). In Matthew's eschatological discourse, it is clear that "the good news of the kingdom is to be announced as a testimony to all the nations and *then* (τότε) the end will come" (24:14). The need to spread message of the kingdom to the world is emphasized in Jesus's instructions to his disciples in 28:18–20. Finally, in 9:13 and 12:7, the need for mercy is associated with the treatment of others—especially those who are sinners or those in need. Therefore, it is probable that Jesus emphasized the importance of the missionary task by ensuring that the wheat and weeds grow together until the eschatological harvest.[4] Protection for the wheat is also important to the master of the house. As 13:28, 38 indicate, the enemy is the devil himself who has sown children of the evil one among the children of the kingdom. In this *corpus mixum*, the evil ones might try to uproot the children of the Son of Man from the kingdom. Therefore, the Son of Man (master of the house) warns the children of the kingdom of the dangerous evil ones who exist among them.

Within the parable of 13:24–30, 36–43, a strong contrast exists between the Son of Man and the devil, and between the children of the evil one and the children of the kingdom. The characteristics of the children of the evil one are summarized by two terms evident in Matthew: τά σκάνδαλα ("offensive things") and τούς ποιοῦντος τὴν ἀνομίαν ("the ones practicing lawlessness"). In Matthew, τά σκάνδαλα refers to sinful actions or behaviors that cause others to sin or fall away (cf. 13:21; 18:6–9, 14). Individuals who are identified with the phrase τὴν ἀνομίαν are those who never knew the Lord because they refused to do the will of the Father in the heavens. The Lord commanded them to "depart" (ἀποχωρεῖτε) from him—they will not enter the kingdom of the heavens (7:21–23). In the following context violating the Father's will is associated with disobeying Jesus's words (7:26–27). In 23:1–3, 27–28, the Pharisees were described by Jesus as being full of hypocrisy and lawlessness (ἀνομίας).[5] They were considered unclean on the inside with every kind of impurity. Jesus

---

4. A similar understanding has been argued by Beasley-Murray, *Jesus*, 134; Kingsbury, *Parables of Jesus*, 74; Lambrecht, *Out of the Treasure*, 165; Jones, *Matthean Parables*, 341–42, 345; Marguerat, *Le jugement*, 439–40; Charette, *Theme of Recompense*, 145; Hare, *Matthew*, 155; Keener, *Gospel of Matthew*, 389.

5. Matthew uses the term hypocrites (ὑπόκριται) several times in his Gospel; he describes hypocrites as those who do their righteousness to be seen by others and who will not receive reward by the Father in the heavens (6:1–2, 5, 16). The term otherwise refers exclusively to the religious leaders—the Pharisees, Sadducees, and scribes. The two accusations Jesus assigned to the religious leaders as hypocrites are (1) they nullified (i.e., disobeyed) God's word by their tradition (15:6), and (2) their hearts were far from God (15:7). See 22:18; 23:13, 15, 23, 25, 27–29. True disciples of Jesus are to ensure their righteousness (i.e., obedience) exceeds that of the scribes and Pharisees if they want to enter the kingdom of the heavens (5:19–20).

cautioned genuine disciples not to do what they practice, because they do not practice what they teach (i.e., they are disobedient to the Father's will, revealed in the scriptures). In 23:15, Jesus described the Pharisees as children of hell, and in 23:31–34, as children of those who murdered the prophets, and who will follow their example by murdering, crucifying, and whipping prophets, the wise, and scribes. Within this condemnation, Jesus also implied that they would receive the judgment of hell (23:33). In 24:10–12, those who lead others into sin (σκανδαλισθήσονται) will betray and hate others; lawlessness (τὴν ἀνομίαν) will increase and the love of many will become cold. In these verses, conduct inconsistent with loving others is highlighted as a violation of God's will revealed in the command to love God and others (cf. 22:37–40).[6] However, Jesus the Son of Man was patient with the children of the evil one, giving them an opportunity to repent. Jesus stated this same desire for grace on behalf of the Pharisees and residents of Jerusalem when he stated: "Jerusalem, Jerusalem, the one killing the prophets and stoning the ones having been sent to her, how often I wanted (or willed; θέλω) to gather your children . . . and you were not willing (οὐκ ἠθελήσατε)" (23:37). Therefore, the children of the evil one are those who lead others into sinful actions, and demonstrate conduct which violates God's will as revealed in the scriptures.

The characteristics of the children of the kingdom stand in sharp contrast to the children of the evil one. They are sown as good seed in the world by the Son of Man and are described as "the righteous ones" (οἱ δίκαιοι) in 13:43. Matthew 7:21–23 clearly contrasts the lawless ones with those who are doing the will of the Father in the heavens; they alone will enter into the kingdom of the heavens. In 7:24–25, doing the Father's will is associated with those who obey Jesus's words as revealed in the scriptures. Looking back to the parable in 13:27–30, these children of the kingdom are compared with the slaves (οἱ δοῦλοι) of the master of the house (κύριος), that is, those who hear the commands of their Lord and obey them. Kingsbury states, "Broadly speaking, a slave in terms of the New Testament is one who possesses no personal autonomy and is totally subject to the will of another."[7] In 20:26–28, Jesus commanded his disciples to follow his example by being servants/slaves who were willing to sacrifice their lives for God's will as he was, by giving his life for a ransom for the many. In Matthew the οἱ δίκαιοι are characterized as: (1) Jesus himself, who fulfills all

---

6. For a helpful, thorough study of the term ἀνομία, see Davison, "Anomia," 617–35. Davison makes a strong case for understanding ἀνομία as a violation of God's will as revealed in the law. In relationship to Matt 13:41 he states, "In this brilliant apocalyptic imagery, *anomia* is used once again in a very general, nonspecific sense for those who act contrary to God's will" (630).

7. Kingsbury, *Parables of Jesus*, 68.

righteousness by being baptized by John the Baptist and having the Spirit of God descend on him, and who is considered the beloved Son in whom God is pleased (3:15–17);[8] (2) prophets, the wise, and scribes, who will be sent by Jesus himself, and whom the Pharisees will kill, crucify, and whip in the synagogues (like the righteous blood of Abel and Zechariah) (23:33–35); and (3) those who help/care for the needy (least ones [τῶν ἐλαχίστων]), with whom Jesus personally identifies (25:31–40, 45). Therefore, the children of the kingdom have a deep fidelity to God's will. They, like Jesus, are committed to sacrificing their lives for God's will; they are like the persecuted and martyred righteous prophets, wise people, and scribes sent by Jesus; and they are like those who care for and help the needy with whom Jesus identifies. Both Jesus and the children of the kingdom are committed to fulfilling God's will through their obedient actions.[9]

At the time of harvest (13:30), Jesus the Son of Man will tell his reapers (his angels; 13:39, 41) to gather together/collect (συλλέγω; 13:30, 40–41) the weeds and throw them into the furnace of fire; in that place there will be weeping and gnashing of teeth. In Matthew, fire (πυρός) is part of eschatological judgment referring to the judgment of hell (γέενναν) due to sinful actions (σκανδαλίζω) (cf. 5:29–30; 18:6–9). John the Baptist condemned the Pharisees and Sadducees to be thrown into the fire due to their unwillingness to produce good deeds worthy of repentance (3:7–10). In addition, the ones who will be uprooted in 15:13 are the Pharisees because they were not planted by Jesus's Father. In other words, the Pharisees are representative of the sons of the evil one. The judgment of separation in 15:13 and 13:29–30, 40–43 will be determined by the Son of Man alone, who will send his angels to remove the sons of the evil one from his kingdom. The phrase "weeping and gnashing of teeth" (ὁ κλαυθμὸς καὶ ὁ βρυγμὸς τῶν ὀδόντων) is also part of eschatological judgment, and refers to the judgment of being thrown out into the darkness (τό σκότος) due to rejecting Jesus (e.g., his word[s] and power) (8:10–12), not wearing the proper wedding garments (22:11–14), being a wicked slave and hypocrite unprepared for their master and one who engages in sinful actions (24:48–51), and being a wicked and lazy slave who did not invest the master's money and was unprepared for his return (25:24–30). Karl Heinrich Rengstorf states that the expression ὁ κλαυθμὸς καὶ ὁ βρυγμὸς τῶν ὀδόντων "simply denotes the despairing remorse which shakes their whole body."[10] Therefore, it appears that the judgment for the

---

8. Even though Jesus was not called δίκαιος in Matt 3:15–17, by fulfilling all righteousness, he is indirectly grouped with those who are the righteous ones.

9. Osborne concurs, "For Matthew, the 'righteous' are those who live their lives according to God's will (see on 3:15; 5:6)" (*Matthew*, 535).

10. Rengstorf, "βρύχω, βρυγμός," 642.

children of the evil one involves banishment to hell where they experience the agony of despairing remorse due to their past sinful lifestyle—which, in turn, separates them from the Father in the heavens. It is ironic that in 8:5-13 a Gentile centurion is contrasted with Israelites who were considered children of the kingdom. The centurion demonstrated great faith; however, children of the kingdom will be thrown into the extreme darkness due to their lack of faith. However, it is apparent that the children of the kingdom in 8:12 are different from the children of the kingdom in 13:38,[11] since Jesus the Son of Man commends them as being righteous ones who will shine like the sun in the Father's kingdom (13:43).[12] In other words, the children of the kingdom in 8:12 are most likely Israelites who are not true followers of Jesus (i.e., lack faith and are disobedient to the law). In contrast, the children of the kingdom in 13:38 are faithful followers of Jesus who obey the law (i.e., the commands of Jesus) and will inherit eschatological blessing as they are gathered for the kingdom of their Father in the heavens.

Throughout the parable of the wheat and weeds, Jesus the Son of Man is the judge who has complete authority over his angels and the fate of the children of the kingdom and children of the evil one. The devil has no control over what happens at the end of the age. The Son of Man will command his angels (reapers) to collect (συλλέξατε) (13:30, 41) the children of the kingdom and the children of the evil one, and he will determine their eschatological fate (13:30, 42-43). In 24:30-31, only the Son of Man comes on the clouds of heaven with power and great glory, and sends his angels to gather together the sons of the kingdom (i.e., "chosen ones" [τοὺς ἐκλεκτούς]) from one end of heaven to the other. The Son of Man is the "Lord" (κύριε; 13:27) who will only allow the sons of the kingdom into the kingdom of their Father (13:30, 41-43). In addition, the Son of Man's kingdom in 13:41 is the same as the Father's kingdom in 13:43. Both will only have the sons of the kingdom ("the righteous ones") as the residents in their kingdom. The Son of Man will purge all evil from his (i.e., his Father's) kingdom. Therefore, as judge, the Son of Man knows who the true children of the kingdom and the children of the evil are, and he mediates their eschatological fate based on whether they have faithfully fulfilled

---

11. Catchpole surmises, "The term 'sons of the kingdom' occurs nowhere in the New Testament except in Matt 8:12 and 13:38. The meaning in one case (Jews who will be excluded from God's kingdom) is quite different from the meaning of the other (genuine participants in the kingdom)" ("Parable of the Tares," 566).

12. See Hagner, who argues that the "sons of the kingdom" in 8:12 in large part reject the Messiah, in contrast to true "sons of the kingdom," that is, those who respond positively to the proclamation of Jesus (cf. 13:38; 5:45) (*Matthew 1-13*, 206; cf. France, *Matthew*, 318-19; Morris, *Gospel*, 195-96; Nolland, *Matthew*, 357).

the will of the Father in the heavens. Those who are faithful and obedient to God's will receive eschatological blessing and the evil children who are disobedient to God's will receive eschatological punishment, which leads to agonizing regret. The children of the kingdom are completely vindicated and rewarded for their commitment to God's will.[13]

The parable of the weeds and wheat provides an illustration of the fate of those who either obey or disobey the Father's will. God offers grace to the disobedient, allowing them to experience the faithful living of the "righteous ones" so they can turn from their wicked living and become part of the "righteous ones." The twelve apostles were told to preach a message of warning—the kingdom of the heavens is near (10:7). In this way, they imitate John and Baptist and Jesus who told people to repent of their sins for the kingdom of the heavens is near (3:2, 6; 4:17). In addition, the Son of Man's suffering and death mediates God's grace and mercy by providing the forgiveness of sins to the repentant, enabling them to become children of the kingdom. The children of the evil one are characterized by sinful behavior that leads others into sin, hypocritical actions, lawlessness that is demonstrated by a lack of love for others (especially in killing God's messengers), and a disregard for Jesus's words. However, the "righteous ones" continue obeying Jesus's words through their acts of loving others in servanthood, caring for the needy, and being God's messengers even in times of persecution (emulating Jesus's ministry). At the parousia, the Son of Man will be the mediator of eternal reward or punishment. He will assign the children of the evil one eternal torment for their evil actions, separating them from the Father's presence, while the children of the kingdom will experience future, eternal vindication and reward for their faithful adherence to the Father's will.

---

13. The Matthean structure from 13:36–50 is worth noting. After giving the interpretation of the parable of the wheat and weeds (13:36–43), the author records two distinct parables about the kingdom's worth (13:44–46), then records a parallel parable (the fish and the net) that parallels the wheat and weeds. The only major difference between the parables of wheat and weeds and the fish and the net is the emphasis on the master of the house's patience in 13:27–30. Both parables are a message of judgment on the gathering and separating of the righteous ones and evil ones. Between these parallel parables, 13:44–46 emphasizes choosing the kingdom of the heavens above everything else. This is another important characteristic of the righteous (οἱ δίκαιοι)—they relinquish everything in life to attain the kingdom of the heavens. Charette concurs with the role 13:44–46 plays in the Matthean structure of 13:36–50: "It is likely that Matthew has introduced these parables at this point in order to illustrate the behavior that is essential if one is to be numbered among the righteous and thus avoid the punishment of Gehenna. According to these succinct and forceful parables, the message of the kingdom is one which calls for absolute sacrifice and obedience" (*Theme of Recompense*, 147).

2.2. The Promised Eschatological Rewards for Following Jesus (Matthew 16:21–27; 19:16–30)

2.2.1. Textual Orientation

In Matthew 16:21–27, Jesus has given his first passion prediction in the Gospel. He will go to Jerusalem, suffer many things from the elders, chief priests, and scribes, will be killed, and will be raised on the third day. Peter took Jesus aside and rebuked him for his prediction. Jesus compared Peter's rebuke to that of Satan, since both Satan (cf. 4:1–11) and Peter were attempting to keep Jesus from fulfilling his Father's will. Jesus told his disciples that if they truly wanted to follow him, they must deny themselves, pick up their cross, and follow him. In other words, Jesus was asking his disciples to be willing to give the ultimate sacrifice for the kingdom, namely, death. Jesus the Son of Man promised that he will come in the glory of the Father with his angels and reward his faithful disciples for their actions (i.e., deeds that demonstrate a complete self-denial).

In Matthew 19:16–30, a young man approached Jesus asking, what he must do to inherit eternal life. At first, Jesus told him to obey the commandments listed in the Torah. The man claimed that he had followed all the commandments since he was young. Jesus told him that if he wanted to be perfect, he would need to sell his possessions, give them to the poor, and follow him—then, he would have treasure in the heavens. The young man refused to follow Jesus. The disciples inquired Jesus about how a rich man could be saved. Jesus told them only with him was it possible for someone to be saved. Peter asked what their reward will be for leaving everything and following him. Jesus told Peter in the new world when the Son of Man sits on his throne in glory, these twelve disciples will sit on twelve thrones judging the tribes of Israel. Jesus concluded by saying that anyone who leaves everything behind to follow him will receive abundant eschatological blessing and inherit eternal life.

2.2.2. Synoptic Comparison: Matthew 16:21–27; Mark 8:31–38; and Luke 9:21–26 // Matthew 19:16–30; Luke 18:18–30

2.2.2.1. MATTHEW 16:21–27; MARK 8:31–38; AND LUKE 9:21–26

In the Synoptic Gospels, Jesus predicted his suffering, death, and resurrection, spoke about the importance of self-denial and possible martyrdom, and concluded with an eschatological statement about his parousia. In Matthew and Mark, Peter rebuked Jesus for his passion prediction and was compared to Satan for attempting to entice him not to fulfill the Father's will. Only Matthew has Jesus speak about self-denial to the disciples alone. In Mark, the self-denial is spoken to both the disciples and the crowds (8:34). In Luke, a more general audience is assumed by his use of πάντες in 9:23. Only in Mark, did Jesus commend those who are willing to deny themselves and relinquish their life for his sake and the good news (τοῦ εὐαγγελίου) (8:35). In Mark and Luke, the eschatological statement about Jesus's parousia is based on his judging people who were ashamed of him and his words throughout their life. If people are ashamed of Jesus the Son of Man's words, he will be ashamed of them when he returns in his glory. Only Mark describes those who are ashamed of Jesus and his words as "this adulterous and sinful generation" (8:38). Matthew's emphasis, however, concerns recompense: if Jesus's disciples lived in self-denial and followed him, then at his parousia he will reward them according to their actions (16:24–27). In Matthew's eschatological statement about Jesus's parousia, the Son of Man would bring his angels with him (16:27). Mark and Luke describe the angels as holy angels, but Matthew calls them the Son of Man's angels. The most significant difference between the Synoptics is that Mark and Luke emphasize being ashamed of Jesus and his words, while Matthew is concerned with the promised reward for faithful disciples who deny themselves, pick up their cross, and follow Jesus the Son of Man.

2.2.2.2. Matthew 19:16–30 and Luke 18:18–30

Matthew records Jesus's discussion with a rich young man (19:20, 22), while Luke records his discussion with a certain ruler (18:18). Matthew and Luke closely parallel each other. Both recorded: (1) a request about attaining eternal life; (2) Jesus's response about keeping the commandments; (3) the rich young man/certain ruler's unwillingness to give to the poor and follow him for heavenly treasure; (4) the impossibility of rich people entering eternal life apart from Jesus's ability; and (5) Peter's inquiry regarding forsaking everything to follow Jesus. Only Matthew mentions: (1) if the rich young man wished to be perfect then he would sell his possessions (19:21); (2) the rich young man heard the word, yet chose to ignore it and go away from Jesus (19:22); and (3) the Son of Man's eschatological promise: in the new world the twelve would sit on thrones judging the twelve tribes of Israel, for the first will be last and the last first (19:28–30). Unlike Luke, Matthew is concerned about the Son of Man's eschatological reward for the disciples's self-denial of earthly things/rewards and their commitment to following Jesus. In Matthew, Jesus commended his disciples for giving up everything on behalf of his name (ἕνεκεν τοῦ ὀνάματός) (19:29). However in Luke, Jesus commended his disciples for giving up everything and following him on behalf of the kingdom of God (ἕνεκεν τῆς βασιλείας τοῦ θεοῦ) (18:29). Luke records the content of Matt 19:28 in a different context, the Last Supper shared between Jesus and his disciples. The disciples were arguing over who was the greatest among them. Jesus reminded them that servanthood was the ethic of the kingdom. He told them that since they remained with him throughout his temptations, he promised them two eschatological rewards: they would eat with him in the kingdom and sit on thrones judging the twelve tribes of Israel (Luke 22:24–30).

Matthew's unique theological emphasis on eschatological reward for faithful disciples is prominent in both 16:27 and 19:28–29, and partly informs his understanding of Jesus the Son of Man as judge at his parousia.

2.2.3. Exegesis

2.2.3.1. MATTHEW 16:21–27

The comparison between Jesus and his disciples in 16:21–26 provides the reason for the Son of Man's eschatological reward for faithful disciples at his parousia in 16:27. Jesus stated it was necessary (δεῖ) for him to go to Jerusalem, to suffer many things from the religious leaders, to be killed, and to be raised on the third day (16:21). The use of δεῖ accentuates Jesus's total commitment to obey God's will even though it would include suffering and death. The divine necessity accentuates Jesus's realization that to obey the Father's will for his life would mean he had to deny himself, pick up his cross, and follow his Father's mandate.[14] The vindication and reward for Jesus's total commitment to obey God's will would occur at his resurrection when he would be raised three days later and be eternally exalted (cf. 26:64). Therefore in 16:21, suffering and death would result in the promise of future vindication and reward. Peter's rebuke of Jesus's words in 16:22 was considered a means of stumbling (σκάνδαλον), since he adamantly questioned God's will and attempted to encourage Jesus to disobey his Father which would have been sin. Peter's words of stumbling led Jesus to compare him

---

14. Osborne surmises, "He is aware of his impending death in 9:15, hints at it in 10:38, and must know of the plot against his life in 12:14. But now he is explicit and explains that his movement to Jerusalem is a divine necessity ("must" [δεῖ]), the very will of God" (*Matthew*, 635).

with Satan. In 4:1–11, Satan attempted to lead Jesus into sin by tempting him in ways that adamantly questioned and would circumvent God's will. Peter's rebuke demonstrated that he was not thinking in a way consistent with the wisdom of God. Similarly, Jesus told his disciples that if one wishes/wills to come after (θέλει ὀπίσω μου ἐλθεῖν) him in following God's will, then they *must* deny (ἀπαρνησάσθω) themselves, *must* take up (ἀράτω) their cross, and *must continually* follow (ἀκολουθείτω) him.[15] Whoever is willing to lose their life on account of Jesus (ἕνεκεν ἐμοῦ)[16] will find life. Jesus was calling his disciples to emulate his ministry by faithfully obeying God's will for their life even if it meant suffering and death. In Matthew's account of the Sermon on the Mount, Jesus stated that those who were reproached and persecuted on behalf of him (ἕνεκεν ἐμοῦ) would receive eschatological blessing and reward (cf. 5:10–12; 10:16–22). In 10:37–39, Jesus told his disciples if they would put him above everyone else and pick up their cross and follow him they would be considered worthy of him and would be rewarded with eternal life (cf. 19:27–29). The relational commitment between Jesus and his genuine disciples is prominent in Matthew; fidelity and obedience to Jesus is essential in following God's will. Like Jesus, genuine disciples were willing to sacrifice their lives to follow the Father's will. In 16:27, when the Son of Man comes in the glory of his Father with his angels (his parousia), he will recompense (ἀποδώσει)[17] each person based on their actions (namely, denying themselves, sacrificing their life if necessary, and following him). Jesus would receive vindication through his resurrection for his suffering and sacrificial death. Similarly, genuine disciples will be promised the reward of eternal life at the Son of Man's parousia for their willingness to sacrifice their lives for the sake of Jesus (also 6:24, 33). In Matthew, the relational commitment between Jesus and his genuine disciples results in eschatological reward, as demonstrated in 16:24–27. At his parousia, the angels will

15. Davies and Allison concur, "The first two verbs in v. 24b—ἀπαρνησάσθω and ἀράτω—are aorist, the third—ἀκολουθείτω—present. This suggests that the decision to renounce the self and take up one's cross stands at the beginning of the disciple's journey and is to be followed by a continued determination to stick to the chosen path. One first picks up the cross and then one carries it, following the trail first walked by Jesus" (*Matthew*, 2:671).

16. Davies and Allison state, "ἕνεκεν ἐμοῦ . . . here means in effect that the disciple is Jesus' possession: believers act for the sake of Jesus in obedience to his will. The lord of the self has become another" (*Matthew*, 2:672).

17. ἀποδίδωμι occurs in Matt 6:4, 6, 18. In this context, Jesus taught that worship that is pleasing to the Father involves an attitude of humility—alms, prayer, and fasting, should not be done to be seen by people but as an expression of worship to God that will please the Father in the heavens. The emphasis is on God, not the one engaging in worship. Similarly, the Son of Man's promised reward to his faithful disciples pleases God the Father as he receives into the kingdom of the heavens those committed to his will.

accompany the Son of Man and will gather and separate the righteous ones from the evil ones (cf. 13:36–43; 24:31), and they will be present as he gives his faithful disciples their promised reward.

In the context of 16:21–27, Jesus the Son of Man will mediate promised reward to faithful disciples who, like him, are willing to give up their lives even onto death in obedience to God's will. Jesus's resurrection was the Father's promised vindication for his unwavering obedience, the reward for denying himself, talking up his cross, and continuing to follow his Father throughout his life. Similarly, when the Son of Man comes at his parousia he will mediate the Father's promised reward of eternal life for those who practice sacrificial self-denial and continue to follow Jesus throughout their lives. Eternal life is the genuine disciple's vindication for the suffering, persecution, and reproach they have experienced while fulfilling God's will.

2.2.3.2. MATTHEW 19:16–30

The story of the rich young man's unwillingness to relinquish all his possessions to the poor and follow Jesus (19:21–22) stands in contrast with the twelve disciples who have left everything, possessions and family, to follow Jesus (19:27–29). The rich young man's statement of Torah obedience in vv. 16–20 is nullified by his unwillingness to do the one thing that will make him complete (τέλειος) in his obedience to Jesus, namely, leave all possessions behind and follow Jesus. Partial obedience is insufficient for genuine followership; only total obedience will be accepted. The term τέλειος is used only in 5:48 and 19:21. In 5:48, Jesus taught that complete love was required towards all people, including one's enemies (i.e., those who mistreated them). Instead of seeking revenge, genuine disciples were commanded to love (ἀγαπᾶτε) and pray (προσεύχεσθε) for their persecutors (5:44). By acting with complete love, a genuine disciple would emulate their Father in the heavens (5:48). In 19:21, the emphasis on moral completeness is demonstrated through the following commands: *go!* (ὕπαγε), *sell!* (πώλησόν) your possessions, *give!* (δός) to the poor, and you will have treasure in the heavens ... come *follow!* (ἀκολούθει) me. Moral completeness in 19:21 would occur if the rich young man was willing to obey the commands (the word; τόν λόγον [19:22]) of Jesus. Therefore, the sense of τέλειος in 19:21 (and 5:48) is not perfection devoid of sin or inability, but moral completeness, involving actions that are expected by genuine disciples who obey and follow Jesus.[18]

---

18. In regard to τέλειος in 19:21, Davies and Allison state, "The rich man would be perfect if he exhibited whole-hearted obedience to Jesus Christ. This, then, is the point to be generalized: all are called to be perfect, by which is meant: all are called to obey

Jesus gave the rich man a choice to obey and follow Jesus's commands or ignore them: "if you wish/will" (εἰ θέλεις) (19:21). The rich man heard the word and disobeyed it because he had many possessions. He chose treasures on earth (temporal possessions) over treasures in the heavens (following Jesus and receiving eternal life [cf. 19:23–26]). Jesus promised an eschatological reward (i.e., eternal life [19:16]) for this young man if he chose to forfeit his earthly treasures, but he loved his possessions more (cf. 6:24). Jesus used the image of a camel going through the eye of a needle to emphasize that without God's help, it is impossible for a rich man to be saved and enter the kingdom of the heavens (19:23–25).[19] In 19:26, Jesus stated that only through God's power could a rich man be saved. In light of 19:21, God's power is manifested through people who are willing to give up all their temporal attachments to follow Jesus. In contrast to the rich young man, Peter stated that he and the other disciples had left everything to follow Jesus and asked what reward they would receive for their faithfulness (19:27). Jesus told Peter those who persevered in following him throughout their lifetime would be rewarded in the renewal or regeneration. Even though ἀκολουθήσαντές is an aorist participle, its connection to ἐν τῇ παλιγγενεσίᾳ implies that the disciples would continue following Jesus until the end of their life or until the parousia, whichever comes first. In 10:22b, Jesus stated that "the one who endures to the end will be saved." Therefore, salvation is for those who faithfully continue to persevere in following him until the end of their life. The term παλιγγενεσία has been debated. J. Duncan M. Derrett has argued that παλιγγενεσία refers to the general resurrection from the dead: "*Palingenesia* does not suggest *standing up* (as from the grave) but that *one has been caused to live again*—to which the non-disqualified may look forward, caused to live again, *in order to be judged*."[20] According to Derrett, eschatological reward will involve resurrection from death in order to be judged for one's faithful (or unfaithful) obedience to Jesus. However, most scholars do not concur with Derrett's view. They argue that παλιγγενεσία follows the thought-world of Jewish apocalyptic as the idea of the "new world." With this understanding, the disciples will receive their eschatological

---

the divine word that comes to them" (*Matthew*, 3:48).

19. Derrett, "Camel," 465–70, provides a helpful background: The camel was known for its devotion to bearing burdens, its uncertain temper, and its inability to manage rocky defiles or low headroom, especially when loaded. The "hole" (i.e., a needle) implies a cavern that a camel would not fit through unless it was unloaded. *Gāmal* means "to treat" for acts of benevolence, implying many kinds of treatment like payment, recompense, and requital. Those who unload benevolent acts (e.g., giving to the poor) for the sake of others work to make the poor and rich equal before God.

20. Derrett, "Palingenesia," 53. See also Luz, *Matthew 8–20*, 517.

THE SON OF MAN'S MEDIATORIAL SIGNIFICANCE AT HIS PAROUSIA   149

reward when Jesus establishes his renewed world after judgment has passed, evil has been destroyed, the unfaithful have been sent to eternal torment, and faithful followers have been given eternal life in his regenerated world.[21] In 19:28 and 25:31, the Son of Man sits on his throne of glory as judge at the eschaton to reward his faithful followers and to send the unfaithful to eternal punishment. In 19:29, faithful disciples who have sacrificed everything and everyone to follow Jesus will inherit eternal life. When the Son of Man comes as judge at his parousia, vindication and eschatological reward will be granted to his faithful followers (cf. 13:43; 16:27; 24:13, 30-31, 46-47; 25:19-23, 34, 46b). In 5:18 and 24:35, the renewal of the world involves the passing away of the present heaven and earth, but Jesus's words of promise will never pass away. Therefore, Derrett's argument that παλιγγενεσία refers to the resurrection of the dead for judgment does not fit the immediate context in 19:16-30, nor is his interpretation represented in the contexts of Matthew's eschatological Son of Man passages. Faithful disciples will be rewarded in the new creation when the Son of Man returns at his parousia and has already judged the faithful and evil ones.

In 19:28, Jesus promised his faithful disciples that they would "sit upon twelve thrones judging the twelve tribes of Israel," along with the eschatological reward of eternal life (19:29). Scholars have long debated over the meaning of the nature of the disciples's eschatological reward of judging (κρίνοντες). Two main views have been proposed. First, κρίνοντες means that the twelve disciples will share the role of judge with the Son of Man. At the eschaton, the disciples will participate with the Son of Man in judging his faithful followers and the unfaithful who will be condemned.[22] Second, κρίνοντες means that the twelve will rule (but not judge) with the Son of Man over the house of Israel in some kind of governmental, authoritative responsibility.[23] A few scholars are unsure which meaning of

21. Burnett, "Παλιγγενεσία in Matt 19:28," 60-72; Sim, Apocalyptic Eschatology, 112-14; Turner, Matthew, 475; Hagner, Matthew, 2:565; Nolland, Matthew, 798-80; Beasley-Murray, Jesus, 274-75; Charette, Theme of Recompense, 87-90, 113; Marguerat, Jugement, 463-64; Kümmel, Promise and Fulfillment, 47-48; Manson, Sayings of Jesus, 216-17; Depont, "Douze trônes," 364-68; Konradt, Israel, 259n479.

22. Luz, Matthew 8-20, 517; Derrett, "Palingenesia," 53-54; Reiser, Jesus and Judgment, 260-61; Harrington, Matthew, 278-29; France, Matthew, 744; Nolland, Matthew, 801; Sim, Apocalyptic Eschatology, 126-27; Bruner, Matthew, 2:312; Gnilka, Mattaüsevangelium, 2:171-72; Beasley-Murray, Jesus, 275; Kümmel, Promise and Fulfillment, 47-48; Charette, Theme of Recompense, 114-15; Manson, Sayings of Jesus, 217; Schweizer, Good News, 389; Osborne, Matthew, 722.

23. Davies and Allison, Matthew, 3:55-56; Burnett, "Παλιγγενεσία," 63-64; Keener, Gospel of Matthew, 478-79; Carter, Matthew and the Margins, 392-93; Gundry, Matthew, 393; Meier, Matthew, 223; Turner, Matthew, 475, 475n3; Weiss, Proclamation, 127, 129; Marcus, "Entering," 671-72; Marguerat, Jugement, 464-65; Lagrange,

κρίνειν is more tenable.[24] The meaning of κρίνειν[25] is not easily understood from the immediate context of 19:28. However, broader book evidence in Matthew suggests that "ruling" is a better interpretation than "judging." In the contexts where the Son of Man parousia passages are present, Jesus the Son of Man alone functions as the judge. In 13:40–43, only the Son of Man sends out his angels to gather the righteous ones and evil ones for judgment. In 16:27, only the Son of Man comes in the glory of the Father with his angels to reward faithful disciples for their actions. In 24:30–31 (as in 13:40–43), only the Son of Man comes on the clouds of heaven with power and great glory and sends out his angels to gather the chosen ones. In 25:31–32, 46, only the Son of Man comes in all his glory with the angels to sit on his throne of glory, and separates from all the nations the righteous to eternal life and the evil ones to eternal punishment. The disciples do not share the role of judge in any of these contexts. In 20:25–26, the disciples are told that greatness involves being servants and slaves to others rather than lording themselves over people as the Gentiles do.[26] Jesus stated that

---

Évangile, 382; Depont, "Douze trônes," 372–89; Bornkamm, Jesus of Nazareth, 209–10; Konradt, Israel, 260–63. Konradt helpfully argues for "ruling" based partly on etymology, "κρίνειν itself does not imply that the twelve disciples will 'convict' or 'condemn' the twelve tribes. . . . Had Matthew wanted to advocate a collective *condemnation* of Israel, he could have done so unambiguously with καταχρίνειν (cf. 12:41–42)" (*Israel*, 262).

24. Morris, Gospel, 496; Hare, Matthew, 229; Hagner, Matthew, 2:565.

25. The meaning of verb κρίνω incurs a philological issue. In the LXX, κρίνω is most frequently a translation of שׁפט which (in the OT) means both to "judge" and to "rule" (e.g., Exod 2:14; 1 Sam 8:20; 2 Sam 15:4, 6) (see Schneider, "κρίμα," 363). The question of ambiguity rests in whether the office of the ruler includes judging, or that of the judge includes ruling. The following can be understood from שׁפט. First, God as judge over the society in which he is God. He is the ruler of the tribe, the God of the tribal religion and their judge. Second, God is judge and is Lord over the tribe as its owner, and regulates the social relationships in the tribe. He has bound himself in a covenant with the tribe as their Lord and judge. Third, in his covenant with tribal members, he is their Lord and judge and, therefore, reveals his will and rests an obligation on his people. Fourth, with an emphasis on grace and mercy, God provides salvation to afflicted people and justice for those without rights (the helpless and needy). Yahweh demonstrates his gracious action through delivering his people, especially as it relates to saving his people from sins of judgment (e.g., Isa 30:18–19). Fifth, God's rule and judgment extends to the whole world (all nations, both Jew and Gentile) God's covenant of salvation is for every person (cf. Isa 42:1–4) (see Herntrich, "κρίνω," 923–33). In relationship to 19:28, the question related to the LXX usage is: will the twelve "judge" and "rule" over the twelve tribes of Israel? However, as noted in my exegesis, only Jesus the Son of Man judges his people/nations. Nowhere in Matthew do the disciples share this role with the Son of Man. Therefore, the LXX understanding of κρίνω does not pertain to its usage in 19:28.

26. Davies and Allison state, "In Mt 20:20–21 the mother of James and John asks Jesus to let them sit at his right hand and his left in the coming kingdom. The imagery is

only the Father would determine who would receive the honor of sitting on his right and left in his kingdom (20:23).

Matthew 19:29 serves as Jesus's second eschatological promise for the disciples's willingness to leave everything and follow him (cf. 19:27). The emphasis moves from relinquishing possessions (home, lands) to primarily family relationships (i.e., brothers, sisters, father, mother, or children), all on account of my name (ἕνεκεν τοῦ ὀνόματός μου). The term ἕνεκεν also occurs in 5:10–11; 10:18, 39; and 16:25. In all of these contexts, the emphasis is related to one's willingness to endure persecution and even death on Jesus's behalf. In 10:37–39, being worthy of Jesus required loving him above family members, and being willing to pick up one's cross and follow Jesus even to death (as in 16:24–26). Genuine disciples who faithfully place Jesus above possessions and natural family relationships represent Jesus's true family—those who "do the will of his Father the one in the heavens" (12:50). The Son of Man will vindicate and reward self-denying, genuine disciples at his parousia in ways beyond what they received on earth and will grant them eternal life (also 6:19–21, 24, 33). In 19:30, Jesus reminded his disciples that those who truly seek eternal life will choose to do the Father's will by sacrificing everything and everyone for the sake of Jesus. In 20:16, 26–28, the first ones (πρῶτος) are those who faithfully accomplish the Father's will by living a life of self-denial for the sake of following Jesus, and, consequently, follow his example, as the one who fulfilled God's will by serving others through giving up his life as a ransom for many. The Son of Man mediates the Father's promised vindication and reward at his parousia for those who have faithfully obeyed God's will.

Jesus the Son of Man promised that at his parousia he will vindicate and reward faithful disciples who obey the Father's will through their willingness to deny themselves of material possessions, family relationships, and their life in two ways: (1) in the new creation, he will have the twelve sit on twelve thrones ruling (governing, administrating) over Israel, and (2) he will recompense them beyond what they could receive on earth by granting them eternal life.

At his parousia, the Son of Man will mediate vindication and reward for faithful disciples who have emulated Jesus's life and are willing to die by denying themselves, picking up their crosses, and continually following him, and so prove their allegiance to obeying God's will. Unlike the rich young man, genuine disciples will relinquish property and family relationships to obey God's will and faithfully follow him. The twelve disciples

---

very close to 19:28. Yet 20:20–21 is naturally taken to be about governing, particularly in view of 20:25 ('the rulers and Gentiles lord it over them'). Is it not preferable to interpret 19:28 and 20:20–21 as referring to the same set of circumstances?" (*Matthew*, 3:56).

who have endured in faithful obedience to God's will, experience future vindication and reward in two ways: they will inherit eternal life and, after judgment when the renewed world is established, they will help rule the twelve tribes of Israel in some sort of authoritative, governing role in the kingdom of heaven.

2.3. The Events Surrounding the Parousia of Jesus the Son of Man: A Call for Endurance and Watchfulness in Light of a Disciple's Promised Coming Reward (Matthew 24:3–51)

2.3.1. Textual Orientation

In Matthew 23:1–36, Jesus spoke to the crowds and the disciples about the hypocritical actions of the scribes and the Pharisees, and warned them not to emulate them because they did not practice what they taught (v. 1). Throughout 23:2–36, Jesus spoke about the ways the scribes and Pharisees demonstrated their hypocrisy. As a climax to his speech, Jesus condemned the scribes, Pharisees, and residents of Jerusalem for killing and stoning the prophets sent to them, and for their unwillingness to accept Jesus. He promised judgment on the city of Jerusalem, namely, the destruction of Jerusalem's temple and the removal of his presence (23:37—24:2). Only at Jesus's parousia will Jerusalem bless Jesus and realize their past sinfulness and the consequences of rejecting him (23:39).

Jesus and his disciples sat alone on the Mount of Olives. His disciples asked when his parousia would take place, and what signs to expect at the close of the age (24:3). In 24:4–51, Jesus taught his disciples about the events preceding his parousia: the appearance of false christs, wars, famines and earthquakes, persecution, and lawlessness (24:4–12). He also encouraged those who followed him to endure to the end, and charged them with proclaiming the good news to all nations until the end (24:14). During the time before the end, Jesus's followers may see the rise of an abomination of desolation having stood in the holy place as prophesied by Daniel (24:15). When this occurs, Jesus warned his followers of future tribulations and the rise of more false christs and false prophets before the Son of Man's parousia. Jesus encouraged his disciples about his imminent second coming as the Son of Man, and exhorted his followers to be watchful and ready when he returns. Jesus told his disciples that no one knows when his parousia will occur but promised that his return would be inevitable and, at his parousia, he would send his angels to separate the chosen ones from the others (24:16–44). At the end of his discourse, Jesus told his disciples a parable of the faithful and wicked slave. In this parable, Jesus taught his disciples the difference between his chosen and evil ones. The chosen ones will be vindicated and rewarded because they will be doing what the Lord required them and will be ready for his return. However, those who are not ready when the Lord returns will be treating others poorly and living sinful lives, and will be assigned with the hypocrites who are suffering with weeping and gnashing of teeth (24:45–51).

2.3.2. Synoptic Comparison: Matthew 24:1–51; Mark 13:1–37; Luke 21:5–36; 17:20–36; 12:42–46

The previous contexts of Matt 24:1–2, Mark 13:1–2, and Luke 21:5–6 are very different. In Mark and Luke, Jesus commended a poor widow who gave all her money to the temple treasury, then described the coming destruction of the temple buildings. However in Matt 23:1–39, the author did not include the story of the poor widow, but emphasized Jesus's condemnation regarding the hypocritical behavior of the scribes and Pharisees. Jesus taught that the temple would be destroyed due to the scribes, Pharisees, and residents of Jerusalem stoning and killing the prophets and refusing to accept him. Jesus predicted that the residents of Jerusalem would accept him at his parousia (23:37–39). Mark does not record any of this previous material. In Luke 13:34–35, the author mentions Jerusalem's history of killing prophets and the sent ones, but as a response to Jesus learning that Herod wanted to kill him. Matthew 24:1–2, Mark 13:1–2, and Luke 21:5–6 have many parallels with one another in regards to Jesus's discussion of the destruction of the temple's buildings. In Matt 24:1–2 and Mark 13:1–2 Jesus changed locations by leaving the temple. In Mark, Jesus sat opposite from the temple with James, John, and Andrew. However in Matthew, Jesus sat with all his disciples alone on the Mount of Olives. Luke 21:5–6 does not include Jesus's change of location, but does mention that people were talking about the temple when Jesus spoke of its destruction.

Matthew 24:3 is different than Mark 13:3–4 and Luke 21:7. In Matthew, the disciples's question to Jesus was focused on their concern over the sign of Jesus's parousia at the end of the age. However, in both Mark and Luke's account, the emphasis on the sign is related to the previous discussion of the destruction of Jerusalem and the temple (Mark 13:3–4) or the time when the destruction will occur (Luke 21:7). Neither Mark nor Luke mentions the end of the age.

Matthew 24:8 and Mark 13:8 speak of false christs, wars, famines, and earthquakes as birth pains/agony (ἀρχή ὠδίνων) before the coming of the Son of Man, while Luke does not mention these events as birth pains/agony.

Matthew 24:9–10 mentions twice that people will deliver up (παραδώσουσιν) the followers of Jesus (like the disciples) to tribulations and death, and will hate them. However, unlike Matthew, Mark 13:9–12 and Luke 21:12–16 state once that the followers of Jesus will be delivered up, but highlight those to whom they will be handed over: the Sanhedrin, synagogues, governors, kings, and family members (Mark); and before synagogues, jails, kings, governors, and family members (Luke). Matthew reserves the discussion of whom the disciples's will be handed over to for persecution to his missionary discourse in 10:16–22, in which their response to such suffering will be a testimony to their persecutors and the Gentiles.

Matthew 24:10–12 is unique to the author's eschatological discourse. Part of Jesus's followers's persecution near the end will include many who will be led into sin (σκανδαλισθήσονται) and there will be an increase of lawlessness (τό πληθυνθῆναι τήν ἀνομίαν) resulting in a lack of love among many. This description of the disciples's persecution is not included in Mark or Luke's eschatological discourse.

In Matthew 24:14, the good news of the kingdom will be announced to the entire world as a testimony to the nations, and then the end will come. This missional statement is not included in Mark's or Luke's eschatological discourse.

Matthew 24:15, Mark 13:14, and Luke 21:20, record the abomination of desolation. Only Matthew states that the abomination of desolation is the one spoken about by the prophet Daniel, standing in the holy place. Luke is unique in mentioning that when Jerusalem was surrounded by armies, then the disciples would know the desolation has come near. Luke 21:21–22 connects Jerusalem's being surrounded with armies with a warning—during these days of vengeance, those inside the city were to flee from it and those in the fields should not enter them. Matthew and Mark do not mention the emergence of an army surrounding Jerusalem. Matthew and Mark state that during the abomination of desolation, followers of Jesus were to pray that the desolation would not occur in the winter (Matt 24:20; Mark 13:18). However, only Matthew mentions that they should also pray that it would not happen on the Sabbath. Luke does not include the instructions to pray that the desolation would not come during these situations. Luke 21:23b–24 is unique in predicting that Jerusalem would be trodden by Gentiles until the time of the Gentiles was fulfilled. Neither Mark nor Matthew records an attack by the Gentile people. Luke's eschatological discourse emphasizes the destruction of Jerusalem more than Mark or Matthew.

Matthew's eschatological discourse places greater emphasis on the return of Jesus the Son of Man than do Mark or Luke. In 24:27, the author states that the imminent return of the Son of Man (ἡ παρουσία τοῦ υἱοῦ τοῦ ἀνθρώπου) would be seen by all people. In 24:30, the author mentions the sign of the Son of Man (τό σημεῖον τοῦ υἱοῦ ἀνθρώπου) in heaven, which will cause grief among the tribes of the earth when they see the return of the Son of Man on the clouds of heaven with power and great glory. In 24:44, the author issues a warning that Christ's followers should be ready at any time because the Son of Man will come at an unexpected time. Mark's eschatological discourse only mentions that the disciples "will see the Son of Man coming on the clouds with great power" (13:26), which is similar to Matt 24:30. However, Mark does not include Matthew's other Son of Man sayings. Luke follows Mark 13:26 closely, but, similar to Matthew, includes the Son of Man will come "on a cloud with power and great glory" (21:27). However, unlike Matthew, Mark and Luke do not include the sign of the Son of Man and the grieving associated with his coming (24:30). Luke records the material of Matt 24:44 at Luke 12:40. However in Luke's account, the context including this Son of Man saying focuses on Jesus's teaching about abandoning temporal possessions and needs for the sake of waiting for the eternal reward (12:13–40). Matthew's eschatological discourse has less to do with temporal attachments and more on preparing for the Son of Man's return. Matthew is more concerned with emphasizing the coming of the parousia in his discourse than Mark and Luke.

Both Matthew 24:37–39 and Luke 17:26–27 compare the sinfulness and state of humanity at the time of Noah building the ark with what humans will be like prior to the return of the Son of Man. The emphasis on the condition of humanity at the time of Noah highlights the destruction of sinful humans who are not ready when the Son of Man comes. Matthew 24:37, 39 forms an *inclusio* around v. 38, strongly accentuating the state of human sinfulness when the Son of Man's parousia occurs. Mark does not record the Noah narrative in his eschatological discourse. Unlike Matthew, Luke does not place the Noah narrative within his eschatological discourse in chapter 21.

Matthew 24:45–51 and Luke 12:42–46 record the parable of the wise and wicked servant. Only Matthew includes this parable in his eschatological discourse. This parable emphasizes the need to be ready when the Son of Man comes again by comparing a wicked, sinful servant with a faithful, prepared servant. Only Matthew mentions the punishment of cutting the wicked servant in two, assigning him with the hypocrites, and putting him where there will be weeping and gnashing of teeth. The context of Luke's parable is related to abandoning temporal attachments and needs (Luke

12:13–40) and less on preparing for the eschaton. Unlike Matt 24:51, in Luke's account the wicked slave will be cut in pieces and put with the unbelievers (12:46), rather than placed with the hypocrites where there will be weeping and gnashing of teeth.

2.3.3. Exegesis

The structure of Matthew 24 has been understood differently by scholars. The debate concerns how 24:1–2 relates to the rest of the chapter. The following are the most common positions. First, Matthew 24 in its entirety is about the historical punishment and vindication in and through the destruction of Jerusalem and its temple.[27] Second, France argues that the majority of Matt 24 relates to the destruction of Jerusalem and its temple (24:1–35) and the rest of the chapter relates to the Son of Man's parousia (24:36–51).[28] Third, Matthew 24:1–2 connects to 24:3–51: the chapter relates to the destruction of Jerusalem (outlined in 24:1–28 [29–30]) and the Son of Man's imminent parousia (24:29 [30–31]–51).[29] Fourth, Meier argues that Matt 24 is a single prophecy with two fulfillments, referring simultaneously to both the destruction of Jerusalem and the future advent of the Son of Man (i.e., not separated by chronology).[30] Fifth, all of Matt 24 is purely eschatological with no historical connection to the destruction of Jerusalem.[31] Sixth, Matthew 24:1–2 relates to 23:37–39 as part of the judgment on the religious leaders's hypocrisy and martyrdom of prophets and scribes sent by God, namely, the destruction of Jerusalem and the temple in AD 70. After Jesus left the temple and moved with his disciples to the Mount of Olives, he began his eschatological discourse on the events preceding the end of the age and of Jesus the Son of Man's parousia (24:3–51).[32]

---

27. Wright, *Jesus and the Victory*, 320–25, 333–34, 339–67; Gaston, *No Stone on Another*, 483–86; Theophilos, *Abomination of Desolation*, 92–107, 152–53.

28. France, *Matthew*, 889–946; Wilson, *When Will These Things Happen?*, 133–35; Gibbs, *Jerusalem and Parousia*, 167–71; Kik, *Matthew Twenty-Four*, 9–15. Kik argues the Son of Man's parousia begins at 24:35.

29. Via, "Ethical Responsibility," 84–87; Brown, "Matthean Apocalypse," 2–7; Davies and Allison, *Matthew*, 3:333–57; Hagner, *Matthew*, 2:685–710; Osborne, *Matthew*, 864–96; Turner, *Matthew*, 568–93; Beasley-Murray, *Jesus*, 324–32; Beasley-Murray, *Last Days*, 377–434; Lambrecht, "Parousia Discourse," 319–29.

30. Meier, *Matthew*, 283.

31. Gnilka, *Matthäusevangelium*, 2:309–33; Hare, *Theme of Jewish Persecution*, 177–79; Hare, *Matthew*, 272–80; Harrington, *Matthew*, 331–41.

32. Agbanou, *Discours Eschatologique*, 39; Marguerat, *Jugement*, 372–73; Burnett, *Testament of Jesus-Sophia*, 18–24, 112–16, 152–65, 198–215; Carter, *Matthew and the Margins*, 468–69; Gundry, *Matthew*, 476–77; Schweizer, *Good News*, 448–50; Luz,

After Matthew's account of Jesus's triumphant entry into Jerusalem (21:1–11), his conflict with the religious leaders continues to escalate with opposition to him and his ministry, and with his parables relating to the rejection of the religious leaders towards his teaching and mission (21:12—22:45). In 23:1—24:2, Jesus taught on the future judgment of the scribes and Pharisees due to their hypocritical actions, pride, impurity, and rejection of God sent prophets, wise people, and scribes (i.e., righteous ones [τῶν δικαίων: 23:29, 35]). Due to the rejection of Jesus (and his messengers) by the religious leaders and residents of Jerusalem (23:37), judgment will fall on Jerusalem and the temple in AD 70 as a punishment for their continual opposition (23:37—24:2). Jesus's rejection of the religious leaders's sinful actions is accentuated by the repetition of "woe to you" (οὐαί ὑμῖν)[33] at the beginning of each statement of condemnation (23:13, 15, 16, 23, 25, 27, 29). The climax of the scribes and Pharisees's sinfulness is described in 23:33-37, when Jesus prophesied regarding their persecution and killing of God sent prophets, wise people, and scribes. The religious leaders's future judgment will be both temporal and eternal—the destruction of Jerusalem and the temple in 23:37-38; 24:1-2 (AD 70), and the judgment of hell (τῆς κρίσεως τῆς γεέννης) in 23:33. Jesus's climactic statement of judgment in 23:38—24:2 is contrasted with the grace and mercy previously offered many times to the residents of Jerusalem and the religious leaders in 23:37. Jesus claimed that it was his will ("I wanted": ἠθέλησα) to gather their children but they were not willing (ἠθελήσατε).[34] The residents of Jerusalem and the religious leaders rejected God's will, and, therefore, will reap the consequences of their rejection of Jesus and their opposition to God sent messengers. As Jesus left

---

Matthew 21-28, 178-85; Morris, *Gospel*, 594-96; Keener, *Gospel of Matthew*, 559-67; Wouters, *Willen*, 104-10; Tisera, *Universalism*, 242-44; Hahn, "Die Eschatologische Rede," 116-23; Pesch, "Eschatologie und Ethik," 223-28; Vadakumpadan, "Parousia Discourse," 36-38; Sim, *Apocalyptic Eschatology*, 99-109 (asserts that 24:6-7a indirectly refers to the Jewish war of AD 66-70; see 156-60).

33. In Matthew, the term οὐαί occurs in contexts referring to the rejection of Jesus's miracles (11:21), persons/world who caused other followers of Christ to fall away through sin (18:6-7), or in regard to Judas who betrayed Jesus and handed him over for crucifixion (26:24). Only in 24:19 is the term not used in this fashion. The repetition of οὐαί ὑμῖν in chapter 23 emphasizes the scribes and Pharisees as representatives of those who opposed Jesus's message and works. In each of these contexts, punishment is the result for such opposition and rejection.

34. Mercy and grace were previously offered by John the Baptist when he called the religious leaders to repent and produce fruit that exemplified such repentance (3:6-9), and by Jesus through his message of repentance (4:17) and miraculous, salvific works (8:1-14; 9:1-35; 11:1-24; 12:1-50). However, Jesus predicted that the religious leaders would be instrumental in his suffering and death (20:17-19), and, unlike the tax collectors and prostitutes, they refused to repent and enter the kingdom of God (21:28-33).

the temple, he reminded his disciples that in the future Jerusalem and its temple would be destroyed (24:1–2).

In 24:3, Jesus changed his location from the temple to sitting on the Mount of Olives. Mark's account focuses on Jesus and the disciples sitting opposite the temple (13:3), and throughout Luke's eschatological discourse, Jesus emphasizes Jerusalem's destruction to his disciples (21:5, 20, 24). In 24:3–51, Matthew does not mention the temple again, separating this temporal judgment from his eschatological discourse. In addition, Matthew highlights important eschatological cues that strongly emphasize his interest in the eschaton. For example, in 24:3, his disciples inquired about the sign of Jesus's parousia and the end of the age (τί σημεῖος τῆς παρουσίας καί συντελείας τοῦ αἰῶνος). Also, when the disciples asked about the timing of "these things" (ταῦτα), the author used "and" (καί) to connect their inquiry with Jesus's parousia at the end of the age. In 24:36–44, Jesus responded to the timing of "these things" as it relates to the parousia when he said that only the Father knows when the parousia will take place. One of the most prominent ways Jesus focused on the eschaton was through his emphasis on the Son of Man's parousia in his eschatological discourse (24:3, 27, 29–31, 36–39, 42, 44). Matthew mentions the Son of Man's parousia six times (24:27, 30 [two times], 37, 38, 44) in his eschatological discourse, while Mark mentions it only one time (13:26) and Luke only two times (21:27, 36).[35] Therefore, it is unlikely that Jesus was speaking about the destruction of Jerusalem and the temple in any part of 24:3–51. Scholars who argue for a historical interpretation in any part of 24:3–51 do not take into account Matthew's strong eschatological cues in the discourse and the absence of any discussion of the destruction of Jerusalem in this context. However, it is likely that 24:1–2 relates to the destruction of Jerusalem and its temple in AD 70, since it is part of the judgment on the residents of Jerusalem and especially the religious leaders whom Jesus condemned throughout chapter 23. In my estimation, it is probable that 24:1–2 connects to the preceding context of chapter 23, and that 24:3 begins a new discussion on the Son of Man's parousia that extends from 24:4—25:46.

Jesus began answering the disciples's question in 24:3 by discussing the eschatological events which will occur before the Son of Man's parousia in 24:4–28. In 24:4–6, 11, 24–26, Jesus warned the disciples about the emergence of false christs and false prophets who will try to deceive people, even followers of Jesus (the chosen ones: τούς ἐκλεκτούς; 24:22, 24, 31). In 7:15–20, Jesus previously warned the disciples about false prophets

---

35. Luke also mentions the coming of the Son of Man in 17:24, 26, and 30. However Luke 17:20–37 is not part of Luke's eschatological discourse recorded in 21:5–36.

THE SON OF MAN'S MEDIATORIAL SIGNIFICANCE AT HIS PAROUSIA 159

who might appear as genuine prophets but are actually like ravenous wolves who produce bad fruit (i.e., deeds). Jesus also warned his disciples of wolves who would persecute them (10:16–23). Therefore, false prophets and persecutors would oppose Jesus's mission and that of his disciples. This warning of false prophets is connected to those Jesus was referring to in 7:22. These individuals claim Jesus as Lord, state that they prophesy in Jesus's name, and do mighty works of healing and casting out demons. However, Jesus proclaimed that he never knew them and calls them people working lawlessness (οἱ ἐργαζόμενοι τὴν ἀνομίαν). In 23:27–28, Jesus spoke the same kind of rebuke to the scribes and Pharisees, individuals who might look clean on the outside but are unclean on the inside: filled with lawlessness, hypocrisy, and characterized by impurity. Like the false prophets and persecutors, the scribes and Pharisees are representative of those who opposed Jesus and his disciples and, consequently, refused to accept the will of the Father in the heavens.

In 24:7–8, Jesus mentioned the rise of wars between nations and kingdoms, and the frequency of famine and earthquakes. The emphasis on persecution, and death of Jesus's followers in 24:9–14 is reminiscent of Jesus's missionary instructions in 10:16–23 and also 11:12. In Matthew, the hatred, persecution and death of Jesus's followers is directly related to their loyal relationship to Jesus and his mission; they are those who do the will of the Father in the heavens (5:11; 10:17–18, 22a; 24:9; see also 7:21; 12:50). Another important characteristic of the events preceding the Son of Man's parousia is the increase of lawlessness (τό πληθυνθῆναι τὴν ἀνομίαν), which will result in many living with a lack of love (24:12).[36] Lawlessness is characteristic of the false prophets, scribes, and Pharisees, who were hypocrites and represented those who opposed Jesus and the disciples's mission and, consequently, the will of the Father in the heavens (7:23; 23:28). In 13:41, the Son of Man will judge and punish those who are practicing lawlessness and all offensive things (σκάνδαλα)[37] by throwing them in a furnace of fire where there will be weeping and gnashing of teeth. In contrast to such hatred, persecution, lawlessness, and death, Jesus's promised future salvation as the vindication and reward for those disciples who endure

36. In Matthew, love is directed toward loving God with one's whole being and loving one's neighbor as oneself (19:19; 22:37–40). Also, loving neighbors includes loving one's enemies. In this way, one will be perfect as the heavenly Father is perfect (5:43–48). Therefore, it appears that a lack of love would relate to disobeying God's will to love him and others, even one's enemies.

37. In Matthew, σκάνδαλον refers to sinful actions/deeds that are opposed to God's will or to leading others into sin (cf. 5:27–30; 18:6–9; 24:9). In Peter's case, σκάνδαλον refers to the sinful actions characterized by rejecting Jesus's mission (16:21–23) or being embarrassed of Jesus, which led to denying him (26:33–34).

to the end (10:22; 24:13). Endurance is related to the disciples's loyalty to Jesus and their obedience to the mission Jesus called his disciples to follow (10:1–40). The disciples were called to announce the good news of the kingdom particularly in the cities of Israel until after Jesus the Son of Man's resurrection (10:23). Future disciples will announce the good news throughout the entire world as a testimony to all nations until the Son of Man's parousia (24:14; 28:18–20). In Matthew, fulfilling God's will requires faithful proclamation of the good news by all his followers—John the Baptist (3:1–2), Jesus (4:17; 9:35), Jesus's present disciples (9:36—10:40), and Jesus's future disciples (24:14). Such faithful proclamation will usher in the Son of Man's parousia.[38] In 24:4–14, Jesus provided hope for future disciples who will go through perilous times characterized by false christs, false prophets, sinful living, and much persecution.[39] When the Son of Man comes, he will be the mediator of vindication and reward for his future disciples because they fulfilled God's will. He will grant them eternal life for their enduring loyalty to Jesus and their commitment to announce the good news throughout the world.

In 24:15–31 Jesus spoke to his disciples about the events that will immediately precede the Son of Man's parousia, and what will happen when he comes on the clouds of heaven. The revelation of the abomination of desolation (τό βδέλυγμα τῆς ἐρημώσεως)—the thing spoken through Daniel the prophet, which stood in the holy place (24:15), will immediately precede the Son of Man's parousia. Scholars have debated the following views on what the abomination of desolation refers to: (1) the Roman army (or generally, the Gentiles) destroying Jerusalem in AD 70 (as stated in Luke 21);[40] (2)

---

38. The Son of Man's return will be delayed until the good news of the kingdom is announced throughout the world as a testimony to all the nations (cf. 10:23; 24:14). The emphasis on "delay" indicates the grace and mercy contained in the Son of Man's eschatological role. The message of repentance and the forgiveness of sin through the Son of Man's death (e.g., 26:2, 26–28) must be shared so the world can hear the message of salvation, then the Son of Man will come as Lord at God's appointed time (24:42–44).

39. Gempf, in his article "Birth-Pangs" (130–34), mentions that these pains must run their course until completion. These pains (suffering) are a sequence of events that are repetitive throughout history. These waves of suffering are inescapable and will continue until the Messiah comes again. Such inevitability of repetitive suffering warns the disciple to be on guard—suffering will come and will continue until the end is finally revealed. In other words, a faithful disciple must be prepared to endure these birth-pains and is warned to remain steadfast in obeying God's will until the Son of Man returns.

40. Kik, *Matthew Twenty-Four*, 43–44; Reicke, "Synoptic Prophesies," 126–27, 131, 133; Wright, *Jesus and the Victory*, 350–52; Luz, *Matthew 21–28*, 195–96; Schweizer, *Good News*, 452; Keener, *Gospel of Matthew*, 576–77; Gaston, *No Stone on Another*, 28, 483–84; Wilson, *When Will These Things Happen?*, 139–43; Vadakumpadan, "Parousia Discourse," 96–98.

both the Roman armies and Antiochus Epiphanes in 167 BC, and as a shadow of the final opposition to Jerusalem and the church manifested by the antichrist (cf. 2 Thess 2:6-7);[41] (3) only to the Roman armies and Antiochus Epiphanes in 167 BC;[42] (4) Caligula's attempted profanation of the temple in AD 39-40[43] (5) the statue of Titus erected on the side of the desolated temple;[44] (6) the statues erected by Pilate (the image of the emperor) and Hadrian (the statue of Capitoline Jupiter);[45] (7) the desecrating atrocities of the Zealots during the seize of Jerusalem in AD 67-68;[46] (8) the abomination of Israel due to their sinful rejection of God, resulting in the desolation of Jerusalem and the temple by Roman armies in AD 70;[47] (9) only to the final opposition to Jerusalem and the church manifested by the antichrist (cf. 2 Thess 2:6-7);[48] and (10) the future desecration of the antichrist (cf. 2 Thess 2:4, 6-7), viewed through the various historical desolations of Jerusalem and the temple as a sequence of anticipatory fulfillments that lead up to the ultimate eschatological desolation of the antichrist.[49]

Matthew 24:4-51 does not support any of the historical interpretations scholars have argued in regards to 24:15. Luke 21:20-24 does appear to align with a historical reading and possibly Mark 13:1-4 supports some historical emphasis, but 24:3-51 is strongly eschatological and is not congruent with a historical reading. Turner's view might be plausible, since he argues that 24:15 relates to a future antichrist that will rise immediately prior to the Son of Man's parousia. Osborne and Meier argue that both the abomination by Antiochus Epiphanes in 167 BC and the future rise of the antichrist is in

41. Ford, *Abomination of Desolation*, 151-67; Wenham, *Rediscovery*, 176-86; Osborne, *Matthew*, 883; Meier, *Matthew*, 283-84.

42. France, *Matthew*, 911-13; Davies and Allison, *Matthew*, 3:345; Harrington, *Matthew*, 336, 339; Hagner, *Matthew*, 2:700; Beare, *Gospel*, 468; Agbanou, *Discours Eschatologique*, 86; Dodd, "Fall of Jerusalem," 53.

43. Manson, *Sayings of Jesus*, 329-30. This view is not represented by current Matthean scholars. Manson argues this view in relationship to Mark 13:14.

44. This view is not represented by current Matthean scholars.

45. This view is not represented by current Matthean scholars.

46. Stein, *Coming Son of Man*, 89-93; Morris, *Gospel*, 603.

47. Theophilos, *Abomination of Desolation*, 20-21, 120-26.

48. Rigaux, "Βδελυγμα της ερημωσεως," 675-83; Hare, *Matthew*, 278; Gundry, *Matthew*, 482; McNeile, *Gospel according to St. Matthew*, 348; Sim, *Apocalyptic Eschatology*, 100-103, 171-72; Gnilka, *Matthäusevangelium*, 2:322-23; Foerster, "βδελύσσομαι, βδέλυγμα, βδελυκτός," 600; Pesch, "Eschatologie und Ethik," 232; Burnett, *Testament of Jesus-Sophia*, 301-31. Burnett indicates the abomination refers to apostasy, the forsaking of God's law as interpreted by Jesus, during the time of the eschaton (*Testament of Jesus-Sophia*, 331).

49. Turner, *Matthew*, 577, 579-80.

view. In conjunction with the emphasis on prophecy by Daniel, it appears this view might have some credibility.[50] However, it is more plausible that Matthew was referring to Dan 12:11, since there are direct parallels between Dan 12:1–13 and Matt 24:15–41: (1) the description of judgment between the faithful (elect ones) and evil ones due to their deeds (Dan 12:2–3, 9–10; Matt 24:31, 38–51); (2) the mention of evil increasing and running back and forth during the latter days (Dan 12:4; Matt 24:12, 17–18); (3) the implication of persecution and the mystery regarding the time of the end of the age (Dan 12:5–9; Matt 24:9–10, 21, 32–36, 42–44); and (4) the emphasis on reward for those who endure and persevere to the end (Dan 12:12–13; Matt 24:13, 22, 31, 42–44, 46–47). Daniel 12 is an eschatological prophecy of the end time that fits much better with the events preceding the Son of Man's parousia in Matt 24:4–51. Matthew 24, 2 Thess 2:1–17 (esp. 2:1–6), and Dan 12 emphasize the importance of faithful endurance until the end, the judgment on evil and especially the antichrist, and the vindication for those who faithfully follow Jesus. Matthew 24:5, 11, 23–26 and 2 Thess 2:3, 9–10 both emphasize a warning regarding false messengers prior to the end. In addition, Matt 24:11 and 2 Thess 2:3, 7–8 both highlight the increase of lawlessness (τήν ἀνομίαν) and, in 2 Thess 2:3–4, "the man of lawlessness" (ὁ ἄνθρωπος τῆς ἀνομίας) who exemplifies the epitome of lawlessness by desecrating the holy place when he sits in the temple declaring himself to be God (see Matt 24:15). Therefore, Matt 24:15 is best understood as an eschatological event in which an antichrist figure rises up and commits the epitome of lawlessness by standing in the holy place and desecrating it thus causing an abomination of desolation. The Son of Man is the mediator of God the Father's promised vindication and reward for his future disciples who endure during persecution and the rise of lawlessness by remaining faithful to him. After the antichrist desolates the holy place, Jesus predicted continued persecution (θλῖψις μεγάλη; 24:21) of those faithful to him and continued deception among false prophets who claim Jesus has already returned (24:16–26). Jesus warned that during these perilous times, future disciples should not return to temporary attachments (24:17–19), avoid temporary pleasures (24:37–44), and focus on being ready when the Son of Man returns (cf. 6:19–21, 24, 33; 19:16–30).

50. Daniel 8:11–13; 9:27; and 11:31 most likely refer to the historical profanation of the temple by Antiochus IV Epiphanes in 167 BC. However, Antiochus's desecration might also be understood as a precursor event to the future prophetic eschatological event of the desecration of the antichrist at the end of the age. Therefore 8:11–13; 9:27; and 11:31, might relate to both events, especially since 12:1–13 clearly emphasizes a future eschatological prophecy of the rise of the antichrist at the end of time and his desecration of the temple. For a similar understanding, see Baldwin, *Daniel*, 168–69, 174–75, 177–78, 192, 199–210.

Matthew 24:20 mentions the inability to flee on the Sabbath, which has been understood differently by Matthean scholars. Three main positions have been argued. First, on the Sabbath gates will be shut and provisions unattainable.[51] Second, flight on the Sabbath will antagonize Jewish opponents and make Palestinian Christians immediately visible.[52] Third, some members of Matthew's community still observed the Sabbath;[53] and given Sabbath-related travel restrictions, they would have been hesitant and unprepared for a flight on the Sabbath.[54] In Matthew, the law has a prominent place and is viewed by Jesus positively (cf. 5:18-20; 23:3). Therefore, it is most probable that members in Matthew's community still observed the Sabbath in obedience to the law. To flee on the Sabbath might have caused a moral problem for some members, causing them to believe they were disobeying God's will. Only in 12:1-14 and 24:20 is the Sabbath mentioned. In 12:1-14, Jesus superseded the Sabbath law through his radical statement: "the Son of Man is Lord of the Sabbath" (12:8), emphasizing that acts of mercy and compassion towards others are more important that following the Sabbath law's moral requirements (12:6-7, 9-13; see also 9:9-13). Jesus came not to abolish the law but to fulfill it (5:18). Therefore, by placing acts of mercy and compassion over the Sabbath's legal restrictions, Jesus was fulfilling God's will by redefining what was permissible on the Sabbath. Similarly, future disciples were to disregard the Sabbath's legal restrictions of not traveling (24:20) in obedience to Jesus's command to leave all behind and focus on preparing for the Son of Man's parousia (24:16-18). Since Jesus is "Lord of the Sabbath" (12:8), future disciples were to obey Jesus the Son of Man's call to prepare for the eschaton—a call that superseded the legal restrictions concerning the Sabbath. As future disciples focus on preparing themselves (imperative: keep awake! [γρηγορεῖτε], 24:42) prior to the Son of Man's return, there will be the threat of great persecution (cf. 24:9-11) and deception by false prophets during those days which will be shortened for the sake of the chosen ones (τούς ἐκλεκτούς) (24:21-26).[55] Future disciples who

---

51. Gundry, *Matthew*, 483; Banks, *Jesus and the Law*, 102.

52. Stanton, "Pray That Your Flight," 17-30; Wilson, *When Will These Things Happen?*, 142-43.

53. Meier, *Matthew*, 284.

54. Gnilka, *Mattäusevangelium*, 2:323-24; Davis and Allison, *Matthew*, 3:349-50; Wong, "Matthean Understanding," 3-18; Harrington, *Matthew*, 337; Schweizer, *Good News*, 452; Luz, *Matthew 21-28*, 198; Osborne, *Matthew*, 885; Morris, *Gospel*, 605.

55. Davies and Allison correctly state that 24:21 is a generalizing summary of the future persecution experienced by the disciples who endure to the end: The phrase "great tribulation" is most likely taken from Dan 12:1, which mentions the great persecution

choose to obey God's will during difficult times of persecution and loss will be vindicated and rewarded by the Son of Man at his parousia. Jesus the Son of Man is the mediator of vindication and reward for faithful, enduring disciples.

In 24:27–35, Jesus spoke to his disciples about the imminent signs and event of his parousia as the Son of Man. In contrast to the false prophetic claims of the Son of Man's return, Jesus stated that no one will be able to deny the imminent eschatological signs that will precede the Son of Man's arrival on the clouds of heaven. The skies will display the Son of Man's imminent parousia: the sun will be darkened, the moon will not have light, the stars will fall from heaven, and the powers of the heavens will be shaken. These celestial changes in the skies will be as apparent as lightning that shines from the east as far as the west (24:27). While all humanity are watching the skies, Jesus stated, the sign (τό σημεῖον) of the Son of Man will appear in heaven (24:30). Matthean scholars have debated endlessly over the nature of the sign of the Son of Man. The following positions have been argued:[56] (1) the sign could be a great light (cf. Isa 60:1–5; Matt 24:27; Rev 21:23–25);[57] (2) the sign is cosmic signs in heaven, an echo of 24:27, 29;[58] (3) the sign refers to the glorious clouds that come with the Son of Man;[59] (4) the sign will be the destruction of Jerusalem, evidence that God has vindicated Jesus; it will show Jesus is exalted on high (cf. Matt 26:64);[60] (5) the sign (Heb. נס—"ensign"/banner) for the eschatological battle between good and evil,[61] or for the standard that will come with the Roman armies

---

directed towards future disciples, which will be incomparable to past persecution and will never be witnessed again (*Matthew*, 3:350). In my judgment, the connection to Dan 12:1 strengthens my argument that Matt 24:15 refers to a future antichrist. Also, future deliverance is promised both in Dan 12:1 and Matt 24:13, 22 for the chosen ones—vindication and promised reward for the great suffering they have endured due to their allegiance to Christ.

56. Patristic exegesis interpreted the "sign" as the cross that appeared in the sky with Jerusalem's destruction. "Now Christ's own true sign is the Cross; a sign of a luminous Cross shall go before the King" (Cyril of Jerusalem, *Catechetical Lectures* XV.22; see also Chrysostom and Origen). See Higgins, "Sign," 380–82; Gaston, *No Stone on Another*, 484–85. However, nothing in the text supports this view, nor do contemporary Matthean scholars argue in favor of it.

57. Waetjen, *Origin and Destiny*, 229.

58. Wenham, *Rediscovery*, 321–22; Overman, *Church and Community*, 335; Beare, *Gospel*, 471; Witherington, *Matthew*, 452.

59. Kim, *Signs of the Parousia*, 206–7, 272–78.

60. Gibbs, *Jerusalem and Parousia*, 199–201; Nel, "Sign," 6–7.

61. McNeile, *Gospel according to St. Matthew*, 352; Schweizer, *Good News*, 456; Gnilka, *Mattäusevangelium*, 2:330; Sim, *Apocalyptic Eschatology*, 104; Carter, *Matthew and the Margins*, 478; Harrington, *Matthew*, 338; Davies and Allison, *Matthew*,

for battle against Israel;[62] (6) the sign is the vindication of the Son of Man: he is in heaven sitting at the right hand of power (Matt 26:64);[63] (7) the sign is the Son of Man's majesty, glory, and kingly presence, which distinguishes him from the false christs/prophets (Matt 24:3, 24 [cf. 16:27; 25:31]);[64] (8) the sign is the Son of Man's parousia: it announces the end and ushers in the judgment;[65] (9) the sign is the Son of Man himself (i.e., the genitive τοῦ υἱοῦ ἀνθρώπου may be an appositive epexegetical genitive: the sign which is the Son of Man, or, more precisely, the Son of Man's coming);[66] (10) the meaning of the sign is not easily understood.[67]

In the Matthean passages that speak of the Son of Man's exaltation and parousia with his angels with power and great glory (16:27; 19:28; 24:30; and 25:31), the emphasis is only on the appearance of the Son of Man himself and his role in rewarding the faithful by sending out his angels to gather them into his kingdom. The mention of a sign apart from the Son of Man himself is nowhere found in these Matthean contexts or anywhere else in Matthew's Gospel. Therefore, the sign of the Son of Man (τό σημεῖος τοῦ υἱοῦ τοῦ ἀνθρώπου) should be taken as an appositive epexegetical genitive construction, explaining what the sign is: "The sign *that is* the Son of Man will appear in heaven." In light of Jesus's mention of the emergence of false prophets and false christs, all the tribes of the earth who followed these deceptive leaders would mourn when they realize that Jesus had not already returned but is now visible, coming on the clouds of heaven with power and great glory. Also, the tribes of the earth will mourn when they see the Son of Man's angels gathering together the chosen ones for their reward due to

---

3:359–61; Nolland, *Matthew*, 983n104; Glasson, "Ensign," 299–300; Draper, "Development," 1–21; Higgins, *Son of Man*, 118–19; Evans, *Matthew*, 410–11; Carson, *Matthew*, 2:505.

62. Theophilos, *Abomination of Desolation*, 134–37.

63. France, *Matthew*, 926.

64. Vadakumpadan, "Parousia Discourse," 157.

65. Burnett, *Testament of Jesus-Sophia*, 342–50.

66. Luz, *Matthew 21–28*, 202; Bruner, *Matthew*, 2:510; Keener, *Gospel of Matthew*, 585; Hare, *Matthew*, 279; Schnackenburg, *Matthew*, 244; Meier, *Matthew*, 287; Bonnard, *Saint Matthieu*, 352; Allen, *St. Matthew*, 258–59; Gundry, *Matthew*, 488; Lindars, *Son of Man*, 128–29; Geist, *Menschensohn und Gemeinde*, 223; Brown, "Matthean Apocalypse," 13; Pesch, "Eschatologie und Ethik," 229; Lambrecht, "Parousia Discourse," 324; Broer, "Redaktionsgeschichtliche," 231; Kirchhevel, "He That Cometh," 105–11; Caragounis, *Son of Man*, 207–9.

67. Morris, *Matthew*, 610; Hagner, *Matthew*, 2:713–14; Osborne, *Matthew*, 894 (but leans closest to the "ensign"/standard for the coming of the eschaton); Turner, *Matthew*, 582–83; Agbanou, *Discours Eschatologique*, 115; Rengstorf, "σημεῖον," 236–38; Theophilos, *Abomination of Desolation*, 157.

their faithful allegiance to Jesus the Son of Man (24:31). In 24:4–51 and the Gospel as a whole, there is no mention of an eschatological battle with an "ensign"/banner going before the Son of Man, nor is there any mention of the Son of Man's vindication manifested through the destruction of Jerusalem. The options of a "great light," celestial signs in the heavens, or the glorious clouds, as the sign of the Son of Man, are plausible but do not fit the context of other passages in the Gospel, which point to the Son of Man himself coming with his angels to vindicate and reward the faithful who endure to the end (10:22; 24:13). France's view that the sign refers to the vindication of the Son of Man manifested in the glorious splendor of his return (26:64) is attractive and more plausible than the other options mentioned. However in Matthew, the Son of Man's vindication is more prominent in his resurrection from the dead (cf. 16:21; 17:23; 20:19; 27:62–64; 28:1–20). Vadakumpadan's view that the sign is the Son of Man's glory, majesty, and kingly presence in contrast to the false prophets in 24:3–5 is possible and is close to France's argument. However, the suggestion that the sign relates to the contrast with the false prophets is too restrictive, and does not take into account the eschatological discourse as a whole. The focus of 24:3–51 is on the Son of Man himself as mediator of vindication and reward for his future, faithful disciples, not as a contrast with those who oppose him. The Son of Man's parousia does emphasize his glory, majesty, and kingly presence, but as an expression of his victory over the period of the antichrist and the antichrist himself. Such a victory brings to fulfillment the vindication and reward for genuine disciples (24:13, 22, 31, 42–44, 46–47). Burnett's notion that the sign is the parousia itself is unquestionable, but the focus is on the Son of Man himself; his glory, majesty, and presence, and his vindication and reward for his faithful followers. In 24:30–31, the emphasis is on the Son of Man's gathering of those faithful disciples for their vindication and reward. Unlike 10:16–23 and 24:9–13, where faithful disciples were warned of future persecution, in 24:30–31, they are vindicated after their suffering and death through the Son of Man's parousia. Similarly, Jesus the Son of Man was vindicated after his suffering and death through his resurrection. As all humanity witness the Son of Man's glorious parousia, they will recognize that only faithful disciples of Jesus will be gathered together for future reward. Therefore, the emphasis of 24:30–31 is on the Son of Man as mediator of the promised reward to those genuine disciples who have lived fulfilling God's will through their enduring faith and obedience.

In contrast to false prophets and false christs who try to deceive, Jesus's words will not pass away; they will prove truthful when the Son of Man returns with power and great glory (24:30–33).

False prophets (24:11, 24) false christs (24:5, 24), false disciples (24:48–51), the tribes of the earth (24:30), and many others (24:37–41) will not be prepared when the Son of Man comes. Jesus warned his future disciples to be ready since no one knows the day or the hour of the Son of Man's return, except the Father alone (24:36–44). Jesus spoke of the days of Noah before the flood as an illustration of unpreparedness. In Gen 6:1–13; 7:17–24, God's judgment was universal; humanity was characterized with great wickedness, as every inclination of the thoughts of their hearts was continually evil. Therefore, God decided to destroy all humanity except Noah and his family, only Noah found favor in God's sight. Noah and his family were prepared for the great flood, the rest of humanity perished in the flood. Jesus was teaching his disciples that, similarly, the Son of Man will come to judge all humanity: genuine disciples will be saved because they obeyed God's will (24:13), but the wicked will perish because they neglected to obey God's will (24:48–51).[68] The Son of Man will send his angels to gather the chosen ones who are ready and the others will be left for judgment (24:31, 36–51).[69] This part of Jesus's eschatological discourse is reminiscent of 13:40–43, 47–50, where the Son of Man will gather together both the faithful disciples and sinners and will judge them accordingly. In 24:42–44, Jesus strongly commanded his faithful disciples to "stay awake!" (γρηγορεῖτε) and "be ready!" (γίνεσθε ἕτοιμοι) since they do not know when the Son of Man will return. In 24:42, Jesus the Son of Man is identified as the disciples's "Lord" (ὁ κύριος ὑμῶν)—the one who is coming on an unknown day. The verb ἔρχομαι in this verse is connected with the Son of Man's coming in 24:30, 44. Therefore, as Lord, the Son of Man has authority over his disciples; he is the one they are to obey. Through their obedience, the disciples demonstrate that the Son of Man is their Lord—they have kept guard, stayed awake, and were ready for the Son of Man's parousia. Jesus further defined what he meant by staying awake and being ready through his analogy between a wise and faithful slave and a wicked slave (24:45–51). The wise slave is blessed because when the master returns he finds him "*continually* doing" (ποιοῦντα) his job of managing his household (24:46). The use of the verb "I am doing" (ποιέω) in 24:46 is reminiscent of the reward of eternal life given to genuine disciples who are doing the will of the Father

---

68. For a similar understanding, see Lövestam, *Spiritual Wakefulness*, 104–5.

69. The emphasis on being watchful and ready is illustrated further by the parable of the ten virgins (25:1–13) and the parable of the talents (25:14–30). Like 24:36–51, both parables illustrate the difference between those who are focused on being prepared when the Son of Man returns through practice of obeying the Father's will, and those who are focused on their own agendas (i.e., disobedient to the Father's will) and are not prepared when he returns.

in the heavens (7:21; 12:50). At judgment, what will matter is the genuine disciples's commitment to doing (obeying) the Father's will. Therefore, to stay awake and be ready is synonymous to a continuous practice of obeying God's will as revealed through Jesus. Faithful disciples who endure in their faithful allegiance to God and his will to the end (10:22; 24:13) will receive their future reward of inheriting a hundredfold and eternal salvation (24:47; 16:27; 19:29). Evald Lövestam concurs with this understanding: "The wakefulness and the preparedness, which are exhorted in Matt 24:42–44, accord with the faithful servant's mode of life, he who lets himself be determined by his lord's will and is directed on and prepared for his return."[70] The wicked slave's heart is contrasted with the faithful slave. He is characterized as a person who refuses to endure to the end, acts sinfully towards and with others, and is not prepared when the master returns at an unexpected hour. The wicked slave is representative of those who live by their own will and disobey their master's will. Instead of blessing, the wicked slave receives judgment: he will be cut into two and placed with the hypocrites, where there will be weeping and gnashing of teeth (24:48–51; 13:41–42; 25:30). The term "hypocrite" is assigned to the religious leaders (scribes and Pharisees) in Matt 23, and the place of weeping and gnashing of teeth is reserved for all offensive things and the ones who are practicing lawlessness (i.e., not loving others) (cf. 13:41; 24:10–12; the Pharisees, 23:28). Jesus compared the wicked slave with the scribes and Pharisees and those who live lawless lives, lead others into sin, and do not love others. Such behavior is incongruent with genuine disciples who are called to obey God's will by loving God entirely and loving others, even one's enemies (22:37–40; 5:43–48). Lövestam concurs: "The unfaithful servant, on the other hand, persuades himself that his lord is a long time coming, and neglects his orders and lives according to his own wishes. Characteristic of his situation is thus that he in his life and actions does not allow himself to be governed by his lord's will and is not prepared for his lord's return."[71] The Son of Man is the Lord (ὁ κύριος) who has authority over the fates of the faithful and unfaithful at his coming. He will judge them based on their behavior—whether they have lived a life of obedience or disobedience to his command to be on guard, ready, and watchful (see also 25:19–30). Throughout the eschatological discourse, Jesus emphasized that at the Son of Man's parousia he will be the mediator of vindication and promised reward only for those faithful disciples who obediently follow his Father's will.

---

70. Lövestam, *Spiritual Wakefulness*, 104.
71. Lövestam, *Spiritual Wakefulness*, 103.

The structure of Matthew's eschatological discourse determines how to interpret 24:3–51. In 23:37—24:2, the emphasis is on Jesus's judgment on the religious leaders due to their persecution and murder of God's faithful servants. Even though Jesus wanted their allegiance, the religious leaders and residents of Jerusalem rejected him and, consequently, God's will for their lives. The punishment for their rejection was the destruction of Jerusalem at its temple in AD 70. Jesus no longer spoke of the temple once on the Mount of Olives with his disciples. The rest of 24:3–51 is focused on events surrounding the end of the age and the Son of Man's parousia. In 24:4–14 (vv. 24–25), false christs and false prophets will attempt to deceive people by leading them into sin. Faithful disciples will experience persecution (cf. chapter 10) for remaining loyal to Jesus and obeying his will. As in 7:21–23, false prophets might claim to follow Jesus, but due to their lawless actions (i.e., lack of love for others) they prove their unconcern for obeying God's will. Even in times of persecution, faithful disciples will endure to the end and receive salvation as their future vindication and reward for obeying God's will. They will also be committed to preaching the good news after Jesus's resurrection (10:23) until the Son of Man's parousia (24:14). In 24:15–26, the antichrist will emerge and become the abomination of desolation as prophesied by Daniel. He will be opposed to Jesus and will persecute those who follow him. At that time, many people will choose temporal attachments over striving to endure to the end. Jesus warned his disciples that they should put his will first by abandoning temporal attachments, even if it means needing to flee on the Sabbath. As the Lord of the Sabbath (12:1–14), the Son of Man's will must come before legal requirements. As part of his promised future vindication and reward, Jesus promised his genuine disciples what the days before his (the Son of Man's) parousia would be cut short. In 24:27–35, Jesus promised celestial changes in the skies which will usher in his parousia. The sign of the Son of Man's parousia will be the Son of Man himself. He will come in the clouds with great power and glory with his angels and will have them gather his faithful ones (cf. 13:36–43). In contrast to the false prophets, Jesus's words will not pass away (24:35). In 24:36–44, Jesus taught his disciples that no one knows when the Son of Man's parousia will occur, so they must focus on being ready (and alert) when he returns. Faithful disciples prove their readiness by living in obedience to God's will. Like Noah before them, such readiness is demonstrated in being faithful and obedient to God's will, even when the rest of humanity are disobeying his will through their sinful lifestyle. In the parable of the slaves (24:45–51), the faithful slave demonstrated God's will by continually loving others, while the wicked slave was unprepared for his master's return by persecuting others and engaging in a sinful lifestyle. At his parousia, the Son of Man will mediate vindication and reward faithful disciples who are prepared for his return; however, the wicked who are unprepared will be assigned with the hypocrites (e.g., Pharisees and other religious leaders), where they will experience eternal torment and separation from God.

2.4. The Parousia: The Division of the Sheep and the Goats Based on Love for God and Neighbor (Matthew 25:31–46)

2.4.1. *Textual Orientation*

After Matthew's eschatological discourse in 24:3–51, the author illustrates the importance of preparing for and focusing on God's will until the Son of Man's return with the parables of the ten virgins (25:1–13) and of the talents (25:14–30). Then he describes the judgment scene at the Son of Man's parousia through a contrast between the sheep and the goats.[72] In this illustration, Jesus discussed the universal judgment when every person will be judged based on how they loved him (and his Father) and human beings who were needy. Jesus's faithful disciples followed the Father's will by producing deeds which demonstrated a deep love for others. The Son of Man will reward those faithful disciples who have loved him through their compassionate and merciful concern for others.

2.4.2. *Synoptic Comparison*

The judgment scene illustrating the sheep and goats has no parallels in Mark or Luke. Therefore, it is unique to the Gospel of Matthew.

2.4.3. *Exegesis*

The judgment scene begins with the Son of Man's parousia. As in 16:27, 19:28, and 24:30, 25:31 emphasizes the eschatological return of the Son of Man, specifically as it relates to reward (13:43; 16:27; 19:28; 24:31) and judgment (13:40–42; 24:30). The events preceding the Son of Man's parousia are over (24:4–29), and his promise of the imminent return has now occurred.

---

72. I concur with Davies and Allison: "Although reminiscent of the earlier parables of separation (13:24–30, 36–43, 47–50), this is not a parable but a 'word-picture' of the Last Judgment" (*Matthew*, 3:418). Hagner has noted that the future tense forms are typical of an apocalyptic revelation discourse, and not a parable (*Matthew 14–28*, 740). Contra Keener who refers to 25:31–46 as a parable throughout his discussion (*Gospel of Matthew*, 602).

THE SON OF MAN'S MEDIATORIAL SIGNIFICANCE AT HIS PAROUSIA   171

The Son of Man returns as mediator of promised reward to those faithful disciples who have obeyed God's will, and of judgment to those who have rejected him and disobeyed God's will. Matthew 25:31-46 is the climax of Matthew's eschatological discourse (24:4—25:46).

Jesus began by stating that all the nations (πάντα τά ἔθνη) will be gathered before the Son of Man for final judgment. The identity of the nations (τά ἔθνη) has been debated among scholars. The positions argued are: (1) they are all non-Jews;[73] (2) they are all non-Christians;[74] (3) they are all non-Jews who are non-Christians;[75] (4) they are all Christians;[76] (5) they are all humanity.[77] In Matthew's eschatological discourse (24:3—25:46), the phrase "all the nations" appears in 24:9 (πάντων τῶν ἐθνῶν), 24:14 (πᾶσιν τοῖς ἔθνεσιν), and 25:32 (πάντα τά ἔθνη). In each case the emphasis is on a non-descript universal group of people. In 24:9, all nations will hate genuine, faithful disciples because of their loyalty to Jesus. In 24:14, genuine, faithful disciples will announce the good news in the whole world as a testimony to all the nations and then the end will come. In 24:3-51, Jesus discussed with his disciples what would happen prior to the Son of Man's parousia. Then, as a climax to Jesus's eschatological discourse, Jesus taught his disciples on what grounds all nations will be judged (25:32). Matthew is connecting 24:14 and 25:32 with the Great Commission in 28:19. In 28:19, Jesus charged his disciples to make disciples of "all nations" (πάντα τά ἔθνη). Just prior to 28:19, Jesus told his disciples that he has been given all authority in heaven and on earth (ἐπί [τῆς] γῆς; 28:18), emphasizing a universal commission. The same construction for "all the nations" (πάντα τά ἔθνη) is used in both 25:32 and 29:18, highlighting a non-descript universal group of people. Finally, when the Son of Man returns, all of the tribes of the earth (πᾶσαι αἱ φυλαί

73. Keener, *Gospel of Matthew*, 603; Allen, *St. Matthew*, 265; Brandenburger, *Das Recht des Weltenrichters*, 112; Senior, *Matthew*, 284; Pond, "Sheep and the Goats," 296-97, 301; "Who Are 'The Least.'" 438, 443, 448.

74. Stanton, "Once More," 207-31; Ladd, "Parable," 191-99; Gray, *Least of My Brothers*, 358; Jones, *Matthean Parables*, 246; Manson, *Sayings of Jesus*, 250.

75. Hare, *Matthew*, 289; Harrington, *Matthew*, 358-59; Lambrecht, *Out of the Treasure*, 264-65, 271-72; Court, "Right and Left," 229; Cope, "Matthew XXV 31-46," 37.

76. Plummer, *Exegetical Commentary*, 350 (brothers: poor and needy/universal; 350-51); Maddox, "'Sheep' and the 'Goats,'" 25, 27.

77. Bornkamm, "End-Expectation," 23; Gnilka, *Mattäusevangelium*, 2:371; Davies and Allison, *Matthew*, 3:422-23; Carter, *Matthew and the Margins*, 493; Hagner, *Matthew*, 2:742; Luz, *Matthew 21-28*, 275; McNeile, *Gospel according to St. Matthew*, 368-69; Catchpole, "Poor on Earth," 389; Meier, "Nations or Gentiles," 99-100; Weber, "Image of Sheep," 676; Cranfield, "Christ's Brothers," 35-36; Heil, "Double Meaning," 5; Tisera, *Universalism*, 259; Sim, *Apocalyptic Eschatology*, 126, 232; Jones, *Matthean Parables*, 249; Marguerat, *Jugement*, 506; Agbanou, *Discours Eschatologique*, 183; Via, "Ethical Responsibility," 91; Walck, *Son of Man*, 207-8.

τῆς γῆς) will mourn when they see "the Son of Man coming on the clouds of heaven with power and great glory" (24:30). Note the emphasis on the universal judgment of the world in the days of Noah as an example of what the Son of Man's parousia will entail (24:37-39). The Matthean parousia scene highlights a universal picture of judgment, not one of a specific group of people. In light of this evidence, it is unlikely that Jesus was referring to a specific group of people (e.g., only Gentiles, only Christians, or generally non-Christians) in the judgment scene when he spoke of πάντα τά ἔθνη in 25:32. The Son of Man (i.e., Son of Humanity) comes back to judge all humanity based on their merciful works towards others.

The Son of Man will gather together and then separate the nations—as a shepherd separates the sheep from the goats—placing the sheep on his right and the goats on his left (25:32-33). Jesus called himself "the king" (ὁ βασιλεύς) in 25:34, identifying the Son of Man as the king in 25:31 and the positions of right (δεξιῶν) and left (εὐωνύμων) in 25:33. The title of "king" implies that the Son of Man has absolute authority over his subjects in terms of their eschatological fates. In v. 40, the Son of Man is also referred to as king. Though not specified, the Son of Man as king is implied in vv. 41, 45 as well. Therefore, the faithful are those who obeyed their king's mandate to love others through deeds of mercy. The unfaithful disregarded the king's command and treated others poorly. Both groups called Jesus the Son of Man "Lord" (vv. 37, 44), which may imply they recognized him as the king at his parousia. This reference to the positions of right and left is reminiscent of the request of the mother of the sons of Zebedee who wanted her sons to sit on Jesus's right and left in his kingdom. Jesus made it clear then that these positions were reserved by his Father (20:20-24). Then Jesus connected the mother's request with what really matters in his kingdom, namely, to be a servant (διάκονος) and a slave (δοῦλος) to others.[78] Becoming great and first in Jesus's kingdom depends on being humble servants and slaves to others (23:11-12). Jesus also compared his emphasis on servanthood with God's will for his life; to give his life as a ransom for the many (20:28; cf. 1:21; 26:26-28). Also, in the crucifixion scene, two thieves are placed at Jesus's right and left, emphasizing Jesus's identification as a lowly criminal before others, yet in reality, sacrificing his life as a servant according to God's will

---

78. Meier helpfully states, "Jesus first speaks of the servant, the person who freely puts himself at the disposition of others, and then radicalizes his statement with the image of a slave, the non-person who has no rights or existence of his own, who exists solely for others. Only this startling denial of self for the sake of others, and not power-politics, can effectively win mankind to the gospel" (*Matthew*, 228-29). Similarly, the righteous ones are concerned for providing for the desperate needs of people, serving Christ as they serve others.

(27:38). Therefore, exalted positions at the parousia will be given to those who have fulfilled God's will by being a servant and slave toward others, emulating the sacrificial servanthood of Jesus. In 22:44, Jesus is the Lord who will place his faithful followers at his right hand until all their enemies are under their feet. Also, in 26:64, Jesus stated before Caiaphas that he will sit at the right hand of the power when he comes on the clouds of heaven for judgment. As Son of Man, Jesus's parousia will be characterized by the power to judge the faithful, setting them on his right, and placing his enemies, namely, those on the left, under his (and his faithful followers) feet. Jesus is identified as the king (ὁ βασιλεύς) five other times in Matthew: first by the magi when they arrived in Jerusalem, inquiring the location of the king of the Jews (2:1–2); second at the triumphal entry, when it is prophesied that he is a humble king riding into Jerusalem on a donkey (21:5); third in the parable of the wedding banquet, when discovering a man without wedding garments, he, as king, judged him by sending him into the outer darkness where there is weeping and gnashing of teeth (22:11–13); fourth during Jesus's trial, when his enemies called him "king of the Jews" (27:11, 29, 37); and fifth at Jesus's crucifixion, the religious leaders mocked him as the king of Israel (27:41–42). In light of 25:34, 21:5, and 22:11–13, these texts are helpful in our understanding of the Son of Man's identification as king. Jesus's life exemplified that of a servant (20:28) and therefore, he will judge others based on their being a servant to others. As king at his parousia, Jesus will judge those unfaithful to God's will by separating them from the faithful, and placing them into the outer darkness where there is weeping and gnashing of teeth (25:46a).

In light of the material in 25:33–34, it is not surprising that the Son of Man will judge people based on whether they have been a servant to others. As seen from 20:26–28, Jesus mediated God's will to his disciples by teaching them the importance of servanthood as a summary of the ethics of God's kingdom, and by demonstrating its importance through his own sacrificial death (the culmination of God's will for his life). Therefore, faithful disciples will have been blessed (εὐλογημένοι)[79] by the Father[80] because

79. The term μακάριος occurs twelve other times in Matthew. In every case, "blessed" relates to faithful disciples who have a righteous character, understand God's revelation, produce deeds according to God's will, and are in complete allegiance to Jesus and his kingdom (5:3–11; 11:6; 16:17; 24:46 [the statement in the parable of the talents: "Well done, good and faithful slave . . . enter into the joy of your master" (25:21, 23) is similar to the blessing given to the faithful slave in 24:46]).

80. In v. 34, the Son of Man (the king) stated that *his* Father (τοῦ πατρός μου) would bless those on his right. This implies that the Son of Man is the Son of God. Note also the same connection between the Son of Man and *his* Father in 16:27. One could argue, therefore, that in other contexts in Matthew when Jesus spoke about *his* Father (i.e., τοῦ

of their selfless servanthood toward others; they will be rewarded by the Son of Man through inheriting the kingdom (25:34). The six deeds of servanthood: providing food and drink, being a friend to strangers, providing clothing, and visiting the sick and prisoners, all exemplify acts of selfless, humble, servanthood. In his life and ministry, Jesus taught and demonstrated both to his disciples and the religious leaders that acts of mercy to others were mandatory for those who practice God's will (cf. 5:7; 9:9–13 [also 11:19]; 12:1–13; 20:26–34; 23:23). Jesus quoted Hos 6:6 in 9:13 and 12:7: "I desire (will; θέλω) mercy and not sacrifice," to ensure that both his disciples and the Pharisees understood that God's will is grounded in having an attitude of mercy towards others. One specific way the Son of Man demonstrated an attitude of mercy was in his willingness to befriend tax collectors and sinners (9:11–13; 11:19). Therefore, it is not surprising that Jesus identified himself with the lives of needy human beings; to be merciful to the needy, is to be merciful to him. Jesus characterized the sheep as the righteous ones (οἱ δίκαιοι) who call their master "Lord" (κύριος), because they do God's will through their merciful attitudes and actions (25:37). In Matthew, the righteous ones (οἱ δίκαιοι) are those who receive eternal life because of their faithfulness to Jesus (cf. 13:43, 49; 23:29, 35 [implied in 5:10, 20; 6:33; 21:32]), and those who call Jesus "Lord" (κύριος) are in most cases either one of his disciples or are those committed to doing God's will (cf. 8:2–8, 25; 9:28; 14:28–30; 15:21–28; 17:4; 18:21; 20:29–34; 25:20–23; 26:22). Meier concurs: "The 'righteous' or 'just'; i.e., those who do God's will."[81] In Matthew, the way people prove their love for God is through loving others (22:37–40). Love includes one's neighbors and enemies, imitating the perfect love of the Father (5:43–48).

The identity of the recipients of such loving, merciful actions has been endlessly debated among Matthean scholars. The problem concerns who Jesus's brothers (τῶν ἀδελφῶς) and the least (τῶν ἐλαχίστων) are in 25:40, 45. The following positions have been argued: (1) they are all Christians/disciples;[82] (2) they are Jewish Christians;[83] (3) they are Christian mission-

---

πατρός μου) that he was speaking of himself as the Son of Man who is the Son of God (see 7:21; 10:32–33; 11:27; 12:50; 18:10, 19; 20:23; 26:29).

81. Meier, *Matthew*, 303.

82. Hagner, *Matthew*, 2:744–45; France, *Matthew*, 958, 964–65; Nolland, *Matthew*, 1032; Harrington, *Matthew*, 357–58; Manson, *Sayings of Jesus*, 251; Gibbs, *Jerusalem and Parousia*, 218; Gray, *Least of My Brothers*, 358; Catchpole, "Poor on Earth," 393; Via, "Ethical Responsibility," 91–92; Donahue, *Gospel in Parable*, 120; Heil, "Final Parables," 204–5; Charette, *Theme of Recompense*, 156–57; Getty-Sullivan, *Parables of the Kingdom*, 111–12; Walck, *Son of Man*, 214–15 (i.e., "the righteous").

83. Allen, *St. Matthew*, 265.

aries/leaders;[84] (4) they are Christians who are not missionaries/leaders;[85] and (5) they are everyone in need, whether Christian or not (a universalistic understanding).[86] In Matthew, the term *brother* (ἀδελφός) does not always designate a disciple of Jesus.[87] In 5:21–26, Jesus extended his judgment concerning disobeying the commandment against murder with the internal disposition of anger. The brother (ἀδελφός) is not specifically spoken of as a disciple or a Christian person.[88] The problem is allowing anger to control a person to the point where one curses the other—in other words, not treating them in a loving manner. Jesus instructed his disciples that God's will requires reconciling with a person one is angry with before going to the altar to worship God. Such reconciliation demonstrates one's love for God and is directly connected to loving one's neighbor (22:37–40). Hans Dieter Betz notes the connection between worshiping (loving) God and loving one's neighbor:

---

84. Cope, "Matthew XXV 31–46," 39–43; Lambrecht, *Out of the Treasure*, 265, 272; Gundry, *Matthew*, 514; Blomberg, *Matthew*, 378; Luz, *Matthew 21–28*, 280–83; Senior, *Matthew*, 283; Court, "Right and Left," 231; Sim, *Apocalyptic Eschatology*, 233; Pond, "Who Are 'the Least,'" 442–44; Jones, *Matthean Parables*, 249, 261; Marguerat, *Jugement*, 508–11; Zumstein, *Condition du Croyant*, 337–41; Stanton, "Matthew and Judaism," 279–80.

85. Maddox, "'Sheep' and the 'Goats,'" 21.

86. Meier, *Matthew*, 302–4; Gnilka, *Mattäusevangelium*, 2:375–77; Patte, *Matthew*, 349–50; Schweizer, *Good News*, 479–80; Hare, *Matthew*, 290–91; Davies and Allison, *Matthew*, 3:428–29; McNeile, *Gospel according to St. Matthew*, 370–71; Trilling, *St. Matthew*, 2:218–19; Agbanou, *Discours Eschatologique*, 191–95; Wenham, *Parables of Jesus*, 90–93; Pamment, "Son of Man," 126; Rowland, "Apocalyptic," 505–18; Heil, "Double Meaning," 9–13; Klein, "Least of the Brethren," 140–41; Cranfield, "Christ's Brothers," 33–37; Vadakumpadan, "Parousia Discourse," 321–23; Jeremias, *Parables of Jesus*, 207; Beasley-Murray, *Jesus*, 310–11; Kümmel, *Promise and Fulfillment*, 94–95.

87. The term τῶν ἐλαχίστων (25:40, 45) is considered a superlative of τῶν μικρῶν (10:42; 18:6–14), and it has been used as evidence to identify "brothers" as disciples or missionaries. Since ἀδελφός is not used in these contexts, the argument is weakened. Matthew 12:50 is more convincing evidence since ἀδελφός is used as a member of Jesus's family, that is, one of those who do the will of the Father in the heavens. However, I have provided significant evidence above (and will further below) in the Gospel as a whole for the universal meaning, supporting the notion that Jesus was speaking of "brothers" in a non-restrictive, universal sense. The emphasis is on the Matthean ethic of loving all neighbors as one's response to showing love for God (cf. 22:37–40; on loving others, see 5:43; 7:12; 19:19).

88. Davies and Allison state, "If the verse has to do with fellow believers in a Christian community (cf. 18:15–20), as it must if 'brother' means 'Christian brother,' it is a bit awkward for the evangelist to go on to mention the sanhedrin (5:22), the altar (5:23–24), and the prison (5:25–26): these are not peculiarly Christian things" (*Matthew*, 1:512–13).

> Offering a gift to God is an expression of love toward God; yet, according to the theology of the Sermon on the Mount, love of God and love of neighbor must go together. Going ahead with the sacrifice without reconciling with the brother would in effect separate love of God and love of the brother; it would contradict one of Jesus's central doctrines (see esp. Mark 12:30–31//Matt 22:37–40//Luke 10:27).[89]

Coming to terms with one's opponent quickly will prevent future conflict and encourage a peaceful relationship (5:25–26). Loving others is not reserved only for a specific group of people, but for all, even one's enemies, and thus imitating the Father's love for all (5:43–48). After Jesus taught his disciples the importance of being a servant and slave to others (20:26–28), he demonstrated servanthood before the disciples and crowds by healing two blind men. In contrast to the crowds who rebuked these blind men, Jesus was full of compassion and healed them, and they followed him (20:32–33). Jesus extended his merciful acts to all people, not to just to a particular group (cf. 4:23–25; 8:1–17; 9:1–35; 12:22; 15:21–39). Similarly, the righteous ones will extend their merciful, loving deeds to all the needy (25:34–40)—fulfilling the command to love their neighbors (22:39), and will be rewarded by shining as the sun in the Father's kingdom (13:43). Davies and Allison state convincingly, "the believer prepares for the *parousia* by living the imperative to love one's neighbors, especially the marginal. The chief moral imperative (7:12; 19:19; 22:39) is the law by which all are judged on the far side of history."[90] Also, Meier, "to be watchful means to be able to recognize the Son of Man in all those in need; to be ready means to be loving towards the Son of Man in these people; and to be faithful means to translate this love into active service, into concrete deeds of mercy."[91] Therefore, there is no exegetical reason to restrict God's mercy only to Christian believers or missionaries, when loving others with mercy has a universal application in many contexts in Matthew. The Son of Man will return at judgment to mediate the promised reward of eternal life (25:46) for those righteous ones who have faithfully obeyed God's will by practicing loving, merciful deeds towards others.

In contrast to the righteous ones, the ones on the Son of Man's left will be judged for their life-long rejection of those in need. Instead of mercy and compassion, they treated the marginalized who were represented in the Son of Man with a lack of love or concern. In 24:11, one of the characteristics of

---

89. Betz, *Sermon on the Mount*, 223.
90. Davies and Allison, *Matthew*, 3:432.
91. Meier, *Matthew*, 302.

people immediately preceding the parousia is an increase of lawlessness and the love of many becoming cold. Such a disposition is exemplified in those who have continuously rejected the needy among them. These individuals call the Son of Man "Lord" (κύριε) in 25:44, but their deeds do not demonstrate a lifestyle consistent with a follower of Jesus. In 7:21–23, those who call Jesus "Lord" will not enter the kingdom of heaven because they are not doing God's will. They might appear to follow Jesus, but their lives demonstrate that they never knew Jesus; they will be told to depart from his presence because they are the "ones working lawlessness" (οἱ ἐργαζόμενοι τὴν ἀνομίαν). Jesus stated that when the Son of Man comes, he will send his angels out to separate the righteous ones from all offensive things (σκάνδαλα) and the "ones practicing lawlessness" (τούς ποιοῦντας τὴν ἀνομίαν) (i.e., evil ones [πονηρούς] in 13:49), and throw them into a furnace of fire, where there will be weeping and gnashing of teeth (13:40–42, 49–50). In chapter 23, Jesus criticized the Pharisees and scribes because, even though they appeared to be righteous, their deeds are characterized by hypocrisy and lawlessness (23:27–38). In contrast to the faithful slave who was doing the master's will prior to the parousia, the wicked slave ignored the master's request and began beating his fellow slaves (i.e., ignoring the command to love others) and was not prepared when the master returned. In judgment, that wicked slave would be put with the hypocrites (e.g., the Pharisees and scribes) in the place where there is weeping and gnashing of teeth (24:45–51). Finally, in the parable of the ten virgins, five virgins called the bridegroom "Lord," but since they were unprepared when he returned, the bridegroom told them he did not know them (25:10–13). Since these individuals rejected God's will by refusing to provide compassion and mercy to the needy, the Son of Man will judge them by sending them away into eternal punishment (25:46).

At the parousia, the Son of Man will sit on his throne of glory and mediate the Father's promised reward of eternal life for those righteous ones committed to God's will by demonstrating their love for others in serving the needy in the world.

The Son of Man will judge all the nations—in other words, all humanity. As king, the Son of Man will place the "righteous" ones on his "right" because of their faithful love for others in need and their consistent practice of being a slave and servant to all people as Jesus was (especially in his sacrificial death—cf. 20:26–28). Faithful disciples obey God's will by being humble servants to those in need (23:11–12). The recipients of the loving actions of genuine disciples are Jesus's brothers, the least ones (25:40, 45). These recipients are anyone in need, both disciples and every other human on earth. There is no restriction concerning to whom a genuine disciple should demonstrate loving concern. In contrast, those on the Son of Man's "left" are those who have not faithfully obeyed God's will by demonstrating loving servanthood to people in need (cf. 22:37–40). They have ignored Jesus who is represented by the needy of the world, and will be separated from the Son of Man and sent to the eternal fire of hell as their eternal punishment (25:41, 46). Jesus the Son of Man will mediate the promised reward of eternal life to the "righteous ones," since they faithfully obeyed God's will in their love for others (25:34, 46).

2.5. The Son of Man's Judgment of Caiaphas at the Parousia: Vindication for All Faithful Disciples Who Follow God's Will (Matthew 26:63–66)

2.5.1. Textual Orientation

After the scene at Gethsemane, the soldiers who arrested Jesus brought him to Caiaphas the high priest. During this meeting, the scribes and the elders gathered together along with the chief priests and the Sanhedrin. After finding a few false witnesses, the religious leaders had them make false accusations against Jesus. Matthew highlights one of these accusations: "This one said, 'I am able to destroy God's temple and build it in three days'" (26:61). To Caiaphas's surprise, Jesus remained silent to these false claims. Caiaphas asked Jesus if he was the Christ, the Son of God. Jesus responded: "You said it, but I say to you, from now on, you will see the Son of Man sitting on the right hand of the power and coming on the clouds of heaven." (26:64). After Jesus's statement, Caiaphas tore his garments, accused Jesus of blasphemy, and, along with the other religious leaders, stated he deserved death.

2.5.2. Synoptic Comparison: Matthew 26:63–66; Mark 14:61–64; and Luke 22:54, 66–71

Mark and Matthew's account of the trial before Caiaphas are very similar. However, Mark does not mention the high priest's name, while Matthew discloses his name as Caiaphas (26:57). The high priest's question in Mark includes "the son of the blessed one" (ὁ υἱός τοῦ εὐλογητοῦ). In Matthew, Caiaphas charged Jesus to answer under oath to God if he is the Christ, the Son of God (26:63). In Mark, Jesus's answer to the high priest was a strong agreement: "I myself am" (ἐγώ εἰμι); he further expanded his answer with the term καί: "And you will see the Son of Man" (14:62). Jesus's answer to Caiaphas in Matthew is constructed as a need for further explanation: "You said it (σύ εἶπας), but I say to you (πλὴν λέγω ὑμῖν) from now on (ἀπ' ἄρτι) you will see the Son of Man" (26:64). Mark and Matthew indicate that the high priest identified Jesus's response as blasphemy. However, the sense in Matthew is more accusatory: "He has blasphemed" (ἐβλασφήμησεν), and Caiaphas stated the charge of blasphemy twice in 26:65 while Mark only mentions the charge once (14:64).

Luke's account of Jesus's trial is different from Mark and Matthew. Like Mark, Luke does not mention Caiaphas as the high priest. Unlike both Mark and Matthew, Luke states that a group of religious leaders (namely, elders, chief priests, and scribes) questioned Jesus in the house of the high priest before the council (22:66). Instead of calling Jesus the Son of God (Matt 26:63)/Blessed One (Mark 14:61), in Luke the religious leaders asked if Jesus is the Christ (22:67). Mark and Matthew record Jesus's response to the high priest as "you said it" (σύ εἶπας; Matt 26:64)// "I myself am" (ἐγώ εἰμι; Mark 14:61), but Luke includes a longer response: "If I tell you, you will not believe; and if I question you, you will not answer" (Luke 22:67-68). Like Matthew, part of Jesus's response in Luke begins with the phrase: "From now on," but instead of using Matthew's ἀπ' ἄρτι (26:64), Luke uses ἀπό τοῦ νῦν (22:69). Luke changes Jesus's prophetic statement by stating that "the Son of Man will be seated at the right of the power of God" (τῆς δυνάμεως τοῦ θεοῦ), while Matthew and Mark state: "of the power" (τῆς δυνάμεως) (Matt 26:64; Mark 14:62). Unlike Matthew and Mark, Luke does not mention the Son of Man coming on the clouds of heaven (22:69). Unlike Matthew and Mark, Luke includes an exchange between Jesus and the religious leaders: "All of them said, 'Are you, then, the Son of God?' He said to them, 'You say that I (myself: ἐγώ εἰμι)am'" (22:70). In Matt 26:65 and Mark 14:63-64, the high priest responded to Jesus's statement about the Son of Man with an accusation of blasphemy, but in Luke the religious leaders did not respond to Jesus's statement at all.

2.5.3. *Exegesis*

There is a similar structure between the accusations against Jesus and his response in both Jesus's trial before Caiaphas (26:61-64) and later before Pilate (27:11-14). In both cases we find similar elements: accusations were brought against Jesus, he remained silent amidst the accusations, questions about Jesus's identity (Caiaphas: "Are you Christ, the Son of the living God?" [26:63]; and Pilate: "Are you the king of the Jews?" [27:11]), and Jesus's response: "You said/are saying it." Even through the trial: led by Caiaphas and Pilate, Jesus appeared to be in control of the trial. Jesus did not attempt to defend himself before his accusers, or correct the high priest or governor's statements about Jesus identity; rather, he remained silent and added to what Caiaphas said about his identity in 26:64. It might appear that the statement "but I say to you" (πλήν λέγω ὑμῖν) contrasts with Caiaphas's statement that "Jesus is the Christ, the Son of the living God," but in other Matthean texts Jesus identified himself as the Son of God (e.g., 27:43). For example, Peter was blessed by Jesus for claiming through divine revelation that Jesus the Son of Man is "the Christ, the Son of the living God" (16:16-17, 20). Also, in 27:54, the centurion and guards watching over Jesus's crucifixion were afraid when they witnessed the way he died and stated: "Truly this man was God's Son." Therefore, it is improbable that Jesus would contradict Caiaphas's statement. Rather, Jesus made an addendum to Caiaphas's statement to clarify his identity more completely. In other words, Jesus the Son of Man is the Christ, the Son of God. This statement of his divinity accentuates his God-inspired mission—he will be killed but will rise again to save humanity from their sins by providing the forgiveness for their sins and will be vindicated from death through his resurrection. In addition, he will come again on the clouds of heaven to judge humanity based on their lifestyle and will assign them their eschatological fates. He will vindicate his faithful followers through the gift of eternal life (cf. 16:13-21; 20:17-19, 28; 26:28; 25:31-46).

Matthew 26:64 has been debated among scholars. The author of Matthew combines Ps 110:1 and Dan 7:13 in Jesus's response to Caiaphas and begins Jesus's prophetic statement with the phrase "from now on (ἀπ' ἄρτι) you will see (ὄψεσθε)." The debate concerns the time frame of Jesus's speech, namely, what future Jesus was referring to. Scholars have proposed the following. First, Jesus was speaking of his resurrection and exaltation up to the parousia (but not including the parousia). The emphasis is on the temporal relationship between the two participles "sitting" and "coming."[92] Second, Jesus was speaking of his parousia only. ἀπ' ἄρτι means in effect, "in the future."[93] Third, Jesus was speaking of his resurrection, exaltation, and his parousia—the two OT citations refer to two separate periods; Ps 110:1 refers to his resurrection and exaltation (time of Jesus's vindication), and Dan 7:13 refers to his parousia (time of Jesus's judgment).[94] In Mat-

---

92. France, *Matthew*, 1027-28; Hagner, *Matthew*, 2:800; Gibbs, *Jerusalem and Parousia*, 143-48; Giblin, "Theological Perspective," 652; Glasson, "Reply to Caiaphas (Mark xiv. 62)," 88-93; Hooker, *Son of Man*, 166-71; Wright, *Jesus and the Victory*, 524-28.

93. Morris, *Gospel*, 684-85; Keener, *Gospel of Matthew*, 650 (esp. 650n120); Luz, *Matthew 21-28*, 430 (esp. 430n43); Carson, *Matthew*, 2:555; Trilling, *St. Matthew*, 2:242-43; Hay, *Glory*, 68; Tödt, *Son of Man*, 36-40; Caragounis, *Son of Man*, 225; Casey, *Son of Man*, 180; Kümmel, *Promise and Fulfillment*, 50-51.

94. Carter, *Matthew and the Margins*, 518; Davies and Allison, *Matthew*, 3:530-32; Nolland, *Matthew*, 1131-32; Hare, *Matthew*, 308-9; Meier, *Matthew*, 332-33; Turner,

thew, the third option is the most plausible: Jesus was referring to both his resurrection (exaltation) and his parousia in 26:64. In Matthew, there is a strong emphasis on Jesus the Son of Man's resurrection as his vindication from death. Through his resurrection, the Father will place death—which is the ultimate enemy to be conquered—under Jesus's feet (cf. Ps 110:1). Three of the Son of Man passion predictions speak to the inevitability of Jesus's death in obedience to God's will and the vindication from death through his resurrection (16:21; 17:22; 20:17–19). The details of Jesus's resurrection also confirm his vindication from death and exaltation. First, the curtain in the temple was torn from top to bottom to indicate Jesus's victory over death and his provision of salvation for all (27:51). Second, the earthquake opened the tombs of dead saints and they were raised, and, after Jesus's resurrection, went into Jerusalem to appear to many (indicating the vindication of Jesus and his followers) (27:52–53). Third, the religious leaders were concerned that Jesus's statement about his resurrection might be true and wanted Jesus's grave sealed and guarded until the third day (27:62–66). Fourth, the guards at the tomb witnessed the appearance of the angel of the Lord coming down from heaven and rolling the stone away, which led to the chief priests realizing that Jesus was indeed resurrected (27:62–66). Fifth, the religious leaders tried to cover up the reality of Jesus's resurrection with lies (28:11–15). Sixth, Jesus's vindication included receiving all authority in heaven and on earth after his resurrection (28:18). Evidence from Matthew indicates how Jesus's resurrection provided vindication from his enemies (e.g., the religious leaders and death), anticipated vindication for his followers through their future resurrection, and resulted in his exaltation with authority over heaven and earth.

Matthew 16:27–28 merges Jesus's resurrection and parousia. In 16:27, the eschatological Son of Man will come in the glory of his Father with his angels and will reward faithful disciples for their self-denial, willingness to die, and commitment to following him (v. 27). Jesus also stated that some faithful followers will not die before they see the Son of Man coming in his kingdom (i.e., after his resurrection) (v. 28). Therefore, Jesus's vindication from death provided hope and promise for the disciples; they will be vindicated and rewarded at the Son of Man's parousia. Similarly, from now on the Son of Man will be sitting at the right hand of the power (after his resurrection he will be exalted), and all will see him coming on the clouds

Matthew, 640; Osborne, *Matthew*, 997–98; Gundry, *Matthew*, 545; Schweizer, *Good News*, 499; Sim, *Apocalyptic Eschatology*, 94–96; Bock, *Blasphemy and Exaltation*, 201–2; Jeremias, *New Testament Theology*, 273–74; Beasley-Murray, *Jesus*, 299–304; Juel, *Messiah and Temple*, 95; Feuillet, "Le Triomphe," 164–69; Brown, *Death of the Messiah*, 1:500–504.

of heaven. The future verb "see" (ὁράω), used in 24:30 and 26:64 relating to the Son of Man's parousia, indicates that all will see the Son of Man's return on the clouds of heaven. Note that he will come with (the) "power" ([τῆς] δυνάμεως) and glory at his parousia. The same power is implied in 24:30 and 26:64; the Father's power will accompany Jesus both in his exalted state and at his parousia. In 28:7, 10, the verb ὁράω is used to highlight Jesus's instruction of the disciples to go to Galilee on the mountain and see the resurrected Jesus (28:16–18). Matthew 19:28 promises faithful disciples a future reward for their willingness to give up everything for him. At the parousia when the Son of Man sits upon his throne of glory to judge the world, they will also sit on thrones ruling over the tribes of Israel. Jesus's emphasis on reward dominates his eschatological discourse about his parousia in 24:3—25:46. First, there are references of reward for Jesus's enduring, vigilant, followers who remain steadfast through persecution and tribulation (24:9–31) as they watch for the imminent parousia (24:27–31; 25:1–13). Second, there is reward for faithful followers who are committed to doing God's will on earth, especially in their treatment of their neighbors (24:45–47; 25:14–46; see also 7:21, 24–25; 13:43). Third, there is judgment and punishment for those who disobey God's will and treat others unjustly (24:11, 48–51; 25:26–30, 41–46a; see also 7:22–23, 26–27; 13:40–42). Matthew emphasizes Jesus's resurrection and exaltation (vindication from his enemies) and the Son of Man's parousia, where he will vindicate his faithful followers who have been committed to doing his will. Jesus's resurrection and exaltation provided hope and promise that his faithful followers will receive their vindication and reward at his imminent parousia. Jesus the Son of Man is the mediator of promised vindication and reward for his faithful followers who do his Father's will.

After Jesus's statement, Caiaphas tore his garments and accused Jesus of blasphemy. Since the religious leaders present heard Jesus's blasphemous statement, they concluded that he deserved death (26:65). The question remains: what is the nature of Jesus's blasphemy in 26:64? Scholars have argued three different positions.[95] First, Jesus was speaking and acting not only against God but his temple and his appointed leaders (based on Exod 22:28).[96] Second, Jesus was intruding into God's divine prerogatives, calling

---

95. Leviticus 24:16 condemns those who cursed and insulted God and demands stoning as a punishment; this reference is not supported in Matthew, and has very little support in scholarship.

96. France, *Matthew*, 1029; Wright, *Jesus and the Victory*, 526–28 (also in relationship to Jesus's words of exaltation: sitting at the right hand of God/on the clouds); Sanders, *Jesus and Judaism*, 296–306; Evans, "In What Sense 'Blasphemy,'" 222.

God's singularity (uniqueness) into question.⁹⁷ Third, Jesus was speaking against God and his temple/appointed leaders, intruding into God's divine prerogatives, and calling God's uniqueness into question (i.e., both 1 and 2).⁹⁸ Evidence in Matthew supports Bock's argument for option 3. In 26:61–62 and 27:40 the religious leaders and false witnesses accused Jesus of speaking against the temple. Jesus stated to the Pharisees that he was "greater than the temple" (12:6) and "Lord of the Sabbath" (12:8), which would have placed Jesus on a level equal to God and, in the Pharisees's estimation, nullified God's Sabbath requirement, leading them to plan to kill him (12:12–14). In 9:1–9, the scribes accused Jesus of blasphemy because he claimed to forgive sins, which, in their estimation, would be an insult God—the only one who can forgive sins. In 15:1–14, Jesus specifically spoke against the Pharisees and scribes, members of God's appointed leaders, by accusing them of nullifying God's word by their traditions and criticizing the genuineness of their relationship with God. Also in chapter 23, he urged the crowds and the disciples not to emulate the behavior and practices of the Pharisees and scribes, repeatedly called them hypocrites, and accused them of persecuting and killing God's righteous servants. From these examples, Caiaphas's charge of blasphemy coheres with evidence in Matthew that Jesus was speaking against God's temple and anointed leadership, and intruding into God's unique majestic prerogatives.

When Caiaphas asked Jesus if he was the "Son of the living God," he did not contradict Caiaphas but added to his statement when he spoke about the Son of Man's parousia. Jesus provided a more complete statement about his identity: Jesus the Son of Man is the Christ, the Son of God. His divinely appointed mission enabled humanity to receive salvation through his sacrificial death for the forgiveness of their sins. His resurrection brought the promise of his faithful followers being vindicated through the gift of eternal life. In addition, he would come again to judge humanity and assign them their eschatological fate. In 26:64, Jesus answered Caiaphas by revealing two periods of his future: first, Caiaphas (and the other religious leaders) would see him after his resurrection as he is exalted to the right hand of the power; second, the Son of Man would come on the clouds of heaven to judge the nations and gather his faithful followers. Jesus's vindication from his enemies,

---

97. Luz, *Matthew 21–28*, 432; Hagner, *Matthew*, 2:801; Carter, Matthew *and the Margins*, 518; Davies and Allison, *Matthew*, 3:533; Brown, *Death of the Messiah*, 1:523–26; Hooker, *Son of Man*, 173; Juel, *Messiah and Temple*, 103–6; Beyer, "βλασφημέω, βλασφημία, βλάσφημος," 1:623; O'Neill, "Charge of Blasphemy," 76–77; Catchpole, "Jesus' Answer to Caiaphas (Matt xxvi 64)," 221–26; Linton, "Trial of Jesus," 259–61; Powell, "Plot to Kill Jesus," 605–6.

98. Bock, *Blasphemy and Exaltation*, 203–9.

death, and the religious leaders, and his reward in his exaltation to the right hand of power, would mediate God's promised vindication and reward for his disciples who will be delivered from their enemies (including death) and rewarded for their commitment to obeying God's will. The Son of Man is the mediator of his disciples's promised vindication and eternal reward. Caiaphas charged Jesus with blasphemy because in his estimation Jesus spoke against God, his temple, and the role of the religious leaders; put himself on equal par with God; and stated his ability to invade God's divine prerogatives (that is, disrespecting his uniqueness). Such statements sealed Caiaphas's judgment of Jesus; he would be condemned to death.

3. Conclusion

Jesus the Son of Man mediates promised vindication and reward for faithful, obedient disciples who have demonstrated their fidelity to God's will.

Prior to the parousia (13:24-30), Jesus the Son of Man provided an opportunity for the children of the evil one to remain in the midst of the children of the kingdom. The disciples were to imitate John the Baptist and Jesus who preached the need for people to repent of their sins because the kingdom of heaven is near (10:7; 3:2, 6; 4:17). The Son of Man's mission was to mediate God the Father's grace and mercy towards humanity by providing the means of the forgiveness of sins through his sacrificial suffering and death (e.g., 20:17-19, 28; 26:2, 28). This good news was to be shared by the disciples in their future ministry to usher in the parousia (24:14; 28:18-20).

At his parousia, the Son of Man will separate the children of the evil one (i.e., the goats) from the children of the kingdom (i.e., the sheep). Those who continuously follow God's will prove their allegiance to Jesus and will inherit eternal life (13:43; 16:27; 19:29; 24:13, 31; 25:34, 46). The twelve disciples will get a further reward; they will sit on twelve thrones ruling over the twelve tribes of Israel in some authoritative, governmental role. However, those who neglect God's will and act in sinful, hypocritical, or unloving ways towards others, will be separated from the Son of Man and will go to eternal torment where there is weeping and gnashing of teeth (13:40-43; 24:50-51; 25:41, 46).

The "righteous ones" ("chosen ones," "sheep") are genuine disciples who have committed themselves to obeying God's will. They will be blessed with receiving vindication and reward by entering into the Son of Man's (i.e., king's) Father's kingdom (25:34); implying that the Son of Man is the Son of God (cf. 16:27; 26:63-64). They continually exhibit the following characteristics and actions that determine their allegiance to Jesus. First, they deny themselves of temporary possessions, pleasures, and family; they willingly die for the sake of Jesus (pick up their crosses); and they choose to follow him. Similarly to Jesus, they obey God's will through their willingness to serve God (by putting him first) unto death. They love God with their entire being (22:37-38; cf. 16:13-27; 19:27-30). Second, even though they are under intense persecution to fall away (false christs/false prophets, are subject to hatred, affliction, and imprisonment (24:3-26) (like the other "righteous ones" before them [23:34-35]), they remain faithful by continually obeying God's will (i.e., "keep watch") by preaching the good news to all nations (24:14) and enduring persecution until the day of their salvation (24:13). Third, they are committed to continually loving others in demonstrating mercy towards others (cf. 9:13; 12:7; 22:39-40). As faithful slaves, they demonstrate servanthood to others by providing for their needs, and emulating Jesus's ministry, who was committed to serving others and providing a ransom for many (20:26-28; 24:45-47; 25:35-40). Since the "righteous ones" fulfill God's will by putting him first and sacrificially loving others, the Son of Man will mediate to them the promised vindication and reward for their faithfulness.

The "children of the evil one" are the Pharisees, other religious leaders, residents of Jerusalem, false christs, false prophets, the lawless, and the hypocritical, who have no concern for obeying God's will. They might claim to be committed to God but their actions prove they have no interest in following him (7:21-23; 23 [esp. 23:2-3]; 24:4-5, 23-24). First, they lead other people into sin; cause others to stumble; persecute, arrest, and kill the followers of God/Jesus; and show a lack of love for many (13:41-42; 23:29-39; 24:9-12, 15-22). Second, they actively participate in sinful living and show a lack of mercy through their disregard for the needy (24:37-41, 48-49; 25:41-45). Third, they are focused on temporary possessions and attachments and disregard the call for self-denial to follow Jesus and obey God's will (19:16-29; 24:38, 49). Since the "children of the evil one" have continually rejected God and his will, the Son of Man will mediate to them the promised judgment of eternal separation and torment.

Matthew's eschatological discourse (24:3-51) concerns the events preceding the end of time and the imminent parousia of the Son of Man. Before the discourse, Jesus spoke about the judgment that will come upon the Pharisees, other religious leaders, and the residents of Jerusalem for their persecution and murder of God's prophets, wise ones, and scribes. This judgment is the destruction of Jerusalem and its temple in AD 70. The eschatological discourse concerns only the parousia of the Son of Man (24:3, 27, 30, 37, 39, 44). Immediately before the parousia, the antichrist will emerge (24:15) and great tribulation and persecution will affect the followers of Jesus. No one knows the timing of the parousia, but celestial signs will appear in the sky to demonstrate its imminence, and the Son of Man himself will appear as the "sign" of his parousia (24:27–30). When the Son of Man returns the tribes of the earth will mourn because they will realize their fate for rejecting God's will, as they see the Son of Man coming on the clouds of heaven with power and great glory (16:27; 24:30; 25:31). However, as for the faithful followers who have obeyed God's will, they will be gathered together and will receive eternal life (24:13, 31). Instead of concerning themselves with the timing of the parousia, they are to focus on being ready (by obeying God's will) knowing the Son of Man's parousia is imminent (24:42–44). The purpose of the eschatological discourse is to provide hope and promise of vindication over their enemies (including death) and reward of eternal life for these faithful disciples who will experience intense suffering until the Son of Man's parousia. At the Son of Man's parousia, he will mediate promised vindication and reward for those faithful followers who have lived continually obeying God's will through Jesus.

Jesus's promised vindication and reward from his Father occurred at his resurrection and exaltation (cf. 16:21). Caiaphas and all of Jesus's opponents will see his vindication in the near future (26:64a; cf. Ps 110:1). As Son of the living God, the Son of Man will come at his parousia and judge those who have not followed God's will (in other words, he will judge Caiaphas and the other religious leaders; 26:64b; cf. Dan 7:13). The Son of Man will be the mediator of judgment at his parousia for those who have refused to follow God's will. Caiaphas and the religious leaders condemned Jesus to death for blasphemy. In their estimation, he spoke against God and the temple/his appointed leaders, claimed he had the right to God's divine prerogatives, and called his uniqueness into question. In contrast, Jesus's promised vindication from death (enemies) and reward at the right hand of the power (exaltation) from his Father provides hope for his faithful followers of their own future vindication from death (enemies) and reward (eternal life [and as rulers of God's kingdom for the twelve; 19:28]) at the Son of Man's parousia. Jesus will be the mediator of promised vindication and reward for his faithful followers who have obeyed God's will.

Chapter 5

Conclusion: The Son of Man as Mediator in Matthew

1. A Brief Comparison between Matthew's Christological Titles

A COMPARISON BETWEEN THE Son of Man and other christological titles in Matthew will help summarize how distinct the title Son of Man is in light of the other titles given to Jesus in the Gospel.

The title *Son of God* is a name given to Jesus by God (3:17; 17:5 ["my Son" in 2:15] and revealed to Peter [16:16]). In Matthew, every other occurrence of this title is referred to by the devil (4:3, 6), demons (8:29), the disciples (14:33), Caiaphas and the religious leaders (26:63), people around Jesus's cross (27:40), the centurion after Jesus's death (27:54), and indirectly by Jesus himself (27:43). In 8:29, the demons in the demon-possessed men begged Jesus to cast them into pigs; emphasizing the Son of God's authority over demons. In 14:33, the disciples called Jesus the Son of God after he stilled the winds. The title *Son of God* describes how others—both human and non-human—identify Jesus. In contrast, the title *Son of Man* is strictly a self-reference of Jesus and is not mentioned in the crucifixion scene (chapter 27). However, it is indirectly connected to the storm scene in 8:23–27, when the Son of Man directed his disciples into the boat and was called *Lord* by his disciples (8:25). In this scene, he calmed the winds and the lake. In addition, I have argued that in Peter's confession (16:13–17) and in Caiaphas's question of identity (26:63), the title *Son of Man* is connected to the confession (highlighting his divinity): "You are the Christ, the Son of the living God" (16:13; 26:64). Therefore, there is some overlap between the titles *Son of God* and *Son of Man*.

The title *Messiah-Christ* identifies part of Jesus's identity in 16:13 and 26:63. The title is connected with the other titles *Son of God* and *Son of Man*. When John the Baptist inquired of the "works of Christ" in 11:2, Jesus responded by speaking about his works to the marginalized in society (11:5) which directly connects to the ministry of the Son of Man who associated with and befriended tax collectors and sinners (11:19). Jesus's ministry of healing is connected to both the titles *Christ* and *Son of Man* (11:5; 9:5–6). Jesus is called *(the) Christ* in Matthew's account of Jesus's genealogy and Jesus's birth narrative (1:16–18). In 2:4, King Herod asked the religious leaders and residents of Jerusalem where *the Christ* was to be born. In their inquiry of whose "son" Jesus was, the Pharisees answered their own question in stating that *Christ* was the *Son of David* (22:41–42). In Matthew's trial of Jesus and during his abuse prior to his crucifixion, the religious leaders abused and mocked Jesus while calling him *Christ* (26:68) and Pilate inquired whether the crowd wanted to release Jesus "the one being called *Christ*" (27:17, 22). Finally, when Jesus identified himself as the disciples's *Teacher*, he called himself *the Christ* (23:10). Unlike the title *(the) Christ*, *Son of Man* is not mentioned in the genealogy or birth narrative. Also, the title is not spoken as an identifying title of Jesus by other people. However, Jesus identified himself both as *Christ* and *the Son of Man*. In addition, in his ministry to the marginalized and sinners there is a connection between Jesus's role as *Christ* and *Son of Man*. Therefore there is some significant overlap between the titles *Christ* and *Son of Man*.

The title *Lord* occurs most frequently in the vocative in Matthew. Jewish, non-Jewish people in society, and Jesus's disciples addressed him as *Lord*,[1] most often when people wanted Jesus to fulfill a need, especially in regards to healing; highlighting his authority and power. In addition, when the Canaanite woman and blind men needed healing, they appealed to Jesus by connecting the two titles *Lord* and *Son of David* (15:22; 9:27–28; 20:30–31). In response to the Pharisees, Jesus stated that David prophetically referred to him (as the Christ) as *Lord* in 22:23–25. Jesus called himself *Lord* when he said he was the *Lord of the Harvest* (9:38), and told the disciples to refer to him as *Lord* if someone questioned them in getting a donkey and her colt for his triumphal procession (21:2–3). Finally, Jesus connected the titles *Lord* and *Son of Man* as a self-reference when he stated that the *Son of Man* was *Lord of the Sabbath* in 12:8 (emphasizing his authority over and re-definition of the Sabbath law), when he spoke about his parousia (24:42, 44), and following his parousia when he will come to judge the world (25:31, 37, 44). Therefore, there is some overlap between the titles *Lord* and *Son of Man*, but most references related to others addressing Jesus.

The title *King* is connected to the *Son of Man* in Matthew's unique judgment scene in 25:31–34, emphasizing his authority to mediate

---

1. See Matt 7:21 (25:11); 8:6, 8, 21, 25; 9:28; 13:27; 14:28, 30; 15:22, 25, 27; 16:22; 17:4, 15; 18:21; 20:33; 25:37, 44; 26:22.

humanity's eschatological fates. The only other times the title *King* is used is when Jesus is referred to as the *King of Israel* mockingly by the religious leaders (27:42); or as the *King of the Jews* by the governor Pilate when inquiring about Jesus's identity (27:11), mockingly by the Roman soldiers (27:29), as the inscription on Jesus's cross (27:37), and by the magi (2:2). Therefore, in the judgment scene there is an important overlap between the titles *King* and *Son of Man*.

The title *Son of David* has little connection with the *Son of Man* in Matthew. The title is used by those seeking healing from Jesus (9:27; 15:22; 20:30–31), by the crowds (12:22; 21:9), by children in response to Jesus healing blind men in the temple (21:15), or by the Pharisees when attempting to identify Jesus's identity (22:42). However, Jesus the *Son of David* and *Son of Man* participated in healing others (in regard to the Son of Man; 9:1–8). The author of Matthew emphasizes that only Jesus as the *Son of Man* has the authority and power to heal and forgive sins (9:6–7).

The title *Prophet* has no connection with the *Son of Man* in Matthew. The title is used once by Jesus when he called himself a dishonored prophet in his own hometown (13:54–57). The title is combined with the *Son of David* by the crowds during Jesus's triumphant entry (21:9–10). Finally, the religious leaders did not arrest Jesus because the crowd considered him a prophet (21:46).

The title *Teacher-Rabbi* has no connection with the *Son of Man* in Matthew. The title is used mostly by the religious leaders, their disciples, and once by the tax officials when referring to Jesus (8:19; 9:11; 12:38; 17:24; 22:16; 22:24, 36). The rich young ruler referred to Jesus as *Teacher* (19:16). Jesus referred to himself as the disciples's *Teacher* (23:8, 10 [connected with *the Christ*]; indirect reference, 10:24–25). Finally, Jesus instructed his disciples to address him as *the Teacher* when telling others where they are to make preparations for the Last Supper (26:18). The title *Rabbi* is used by Jesus when he told his disciples not to refer to themselves as *Rabbi* as the scribes and the Pharisees did (23:7, 8). Every other instance of the title *Rabbi* is used by Judas when referring to Jesus (26:25, 49), especially in contrast to other disciples who referred to him as *Lord* (26:22).

The final christological title referred to in Matthew is in 1:21–23. In these verses, Jesus's father Joseph was told by the angel of the Lord to call him *Jesus*—because he will save his people from their sins (1:21). In v. 23, the author of Matthew used Isa 7:14 LXX to state prophetically that Jesus is also entitled *Emmanuel*—meaning, "God with us," which is also indirectly referred to in 28:20. I have argued that the Son of Man's mission to forgive sins (9:2, 6) and the predictions of his sacrificial suffering and death (16:13,

21; 17:22–23; 20:17–19, 28; 26:2, 24, 28), connect the title *Son of Man* with the name *Jesus* in 1:21 and indirectly with *Emmanuel* in 1:23.

The function of the *Son of Man* in Matthew is very distinct in light of the other christological titles surveyed. First, only the Son of Man is described as denying himself of a home to pursue his itinerant ministry (8:20). Second, only the Son of Man has the authority to forgive sins on earth [manifested through healing] (9:6). Third, only the Son of Man is described as intimately associating with the marginalized (e.g., tax collectors/sinners) (9:9–13; 11:19). Fourth, only the Son of Man is described as Lord of the Sabbath—the authority to redefine the Sabbath according to mercy (12:8). Fifth, Jesus stated that there is forgiveness for those who blaspheme the Son of Man (but not the Spirit in him) (12:32). Sixth, Jesus only spoke of himself as the Son of Man when predicting his suffering and death (crucifixion) and his resurrection (12:40; 17:9, 12, 22–23; 20:18–19, 28; 26:2, 24, 45). Seventh, Jesus only spoke of himself as the Son of Man when referring to his exaltation after his resurrection when others will see him vindicated (10:23; 16:28; 26:64). Eighth, only the Son of Man will come on the clouds at the parousia to separate the righteous from the unrighteous (the prepared from the unprepared), rewarding those who have been faithful to Jesus (and punishing those who have not) (13:37–43; 16:27; 19:28–29; 24:27, 30–31, 37–41; 25:31; 26:64).

2. The Term *Mediator* in Relationship to Matthew's Son of Man

I have argued in this book that the function of the Son of Man in Matthew is as the mediator of God's will. I have used the term *mediator* as referring to the Son of Man's role as the go-between in the disciples's relationship with God the Father in two main ways. First, as the perfect God-human, the Son of Man represents God the Father before his disciples by revealing and demonstrating the Father's will for their present and future ministries. Second, the Son of Man represents the disciples/humanity before God by restoring their relationship with God the Father through his sacrificial suffering, death, and resurrection. As judge at his parousia, the Son of Man will represent God the Father by executing his eschatological vindication and reward to his enduring, faithful disciples who have followed God's will, while at the same time, separating them from sinners and who will be punished for rejecting God's will throughout their lives.

The *inclusio* in 7:21 and 12:50 is unique to Matthew's Gospel and emphasizes God the Father's will as being a central concern in Jesus the Son of Man's (and, consequently, the disciples's) earthly ministry. Seven Son of Man sayings are located within 7:21 and 12:50, indicating that Jesus's role as Son of Man should be seen in light of fulfilling God the Father's will, and teaching his disciples the ways they should fulfill God's will in their present and future ministries. Matthew 6:10 is unique in this Gospel and emphasizes the importance of seeking God the Father's will on earth as it is in heaven. Therefore, knowing and doing the Father's will on earth is essential in understanding the life of discipleship. Jesus the Son of Man is more than simply a "teacher," "prophet," or "exemplary figure" in the Gospel. He is the *Son of Humanity* ("human" in Hebrew, Aramaic, and Greek), who represents humanity to God as the God-human as indicated in 1:23 (i.e., Emmanuel, "God with us"). This God-human connection is made clear in 1:21, in which Jesus's mission is identified as the one that will save (forgive) his people from their sins. In the Gospel, the Son of Man's role is to have authority on earth to forgive sins (9:6), and it is predicted that he will suffer, die, and be resurrected from the dead as the scriptures foretold for the forgiveness of the sins of many (16:13, 21; 17:9, 12, 21–23; 20:17–19, 28 [26:28]; 26:2, 24, 45 [vv. 54, 56]). As the God-human, the Son of Man has been given the authority on earth to reveal to and demonstrate for his disciples how to fulfill God the Father's will on earth. In other words, the Son of Man is the *mediator* ("go-between") of God the Father's will to his disciples (and, consequently, all who accept and follow him). In the seven Son of Man statements between 7:21 and 12:50, Jesus revealed and demonstrated what was necessary in following God the Father's will. The culmination of Jesus the Son of Man's earthly ministry will be emphasized through the predictions of the Son of Man sacrificial suffering, death, and resurrection.

The Son of Man revealed to his disciples what following God the Father's will entails. First, like the Son of Man, itinerant ministry requires renunciation of family, home, possessions, and life (8:19–20; 10:9, 37–39; 16:24–27; 19:27–30). Jesus mediates God's will to his disciples: nothing or no one should prevent a disciple from giving up everything to follow God's will. In 8:18–22, the Son of Man's grace is offered through his invitation to follow him in an itinerant ministry of self-renunciation.

Second, Jesus used the positive example of those who brought a paralytic (and the paralytic himself) for healing, to teach his disciples that unrestricted faith is necessary in following God's will. The paralytic was healed due to faith—believing healing could come through Jesus. In addition, the Son of Man revealed that he has authority on earth to forgive sins (also 1:21; passion predictions [e.g., 20:19–20, 28; 26:28]), also highlighted in Jesus's message of repentance (4:17). Through his ministry of forgiving human sin, the Son of Man mediates a restored relationship now available between God the Father and humanity which is culminated in his death and resurrection. Through his earthly ministry, Jesus the Son of Man associated with people, especially the marginalized (e.g., tax collectors and sinners) (9:9–13; 11:19), calling them to repent of their sins and receive his forgiveness (e.g., 11:20–28). Similarly, the disciples were called to forgive others when they sinned against them by extending mercy in accordance to God the Father's will (e.g., 18:21–35; 5:43–46).

Third, in light of the Son of Man's commitment to self-renunciation to follow God's will in his itinerant ministry (cf. 8:20), so the disciples were called by Jesus to faithful obedience to God's will even when their itinerant ministry would lead to inevitable persecution and possible death (10:16–39). Jesus gave specific instructions throughout chapter 10 on the expectations of discipleship. The disciples were commanded to remain in God's will even onto death (10:21–23a, 28). After the Son of Man's death and resurrection, he would give further instructions for their ministry beyond the cities of Israel to all the nations (28:18–20). In 16:21–28, Jesus the Son of Man explicitly connected his own suffering, death, and resurrection, with the disciples's persecution, death, and vindication from death (also 5:10–12). In these contexts of persecution and death, the Son of Man mediates what faithfulness to God the Father's will entail in the disciples's present and future ministries, while encouraging them to persevere until their vindication from death and future reward. Jesus's ministry of preaching repentance for the forgiveness of sins (4:17) produced solidarity with his disciples in regards to their common ministries (10:7). However, unlike the disciples, only the Son of Man will give his life to forgive his people for their sins.

Fourth, in chapter 11, the Son of Man reiterated the threat of persecution for faithfulness to God the Father's will in one's itinerant ministry. In 11:5, 19, Jesus emphasized that the Son of Man's ministry involved embracing the marginalized in society, especially tax collectors and sinners, to lead them to repent and receive God's salvific will—a restored relationship between God and human beings through the forgiveness of their sins. Jesus the Son of Man mediated God's salvific will to his disciples and all people in his itinerant ministry by emphasizing their need to repent of their sins, accept his message and works, and choose to follow him (11:20–28). Only through Jesus the Son of Man is God's salvific will revealed to those who accept his rest for their weary souls (vv. 27–28 [also evident in the predictions of his passion; e.g., 20:17–20, 28]). Tax collectors and sinners are representative of those who accepted Jesus's ministry. In addition, the rejection Jesus the Son of Man (and John the Baptist) received for following God's will mediates to the disciples the rejection they will receive in their present and future ministry as they share the message of repentance and participate in deeds of mercy and grace.

Fifth, as Lord of the Sabbath, the Son of Man has the authority to redefine the Sabbath regulations. God the Father's will is that acts of mercy (and love) towards human beings in need fulfills the Sabbath law (cf. Hos 6:6; Matt 9:13; 12:7). Only the Son of Man specifically mediates God's will regarding demonstrating mercy and grace towards humanity (12:7-8). In 9:13, mercy is defined as a willingness to call sinners to repent of their sins and follow Jesus (e.g., 1:21; 9:2, 6-8) which meets their spiritual need. In 12:1-8, mercy is defined as being concerned for human physical needs (e.g., 25:34-40). From God the Father's perspective, people are more important than the law—which was manifested in Jesus's healing of the man with the withered hand (12:9-14), and will find its culmination in Jesus's suffering, death, and resurrection (e.g., 20:28; 26:28). Jesus's ministry of mercy towards humans defined for his disciples what God's will is and how it is to be practiced. The Son of Man mediated for his disciples the importance of the message and deeds of mercy to humanity and instructed them to extend his ministry of mercy to other people in need; especially in need of grace and salvation (cf. 22:39). Through engaging in a ministry of love and mercy towards others, the disciples would be doing the will of their Father in the heavens (12:50).

Sixth, the Holy Spirit was the agent through whom Jesus the Son of Man accomplished his ministry (12:22-32). The Holy Spirit's empowerment of Jesus's ministry accentuated that God's will was being done on earth. The Son of Man's desire to forgive humans of their sins was an integral part of his ministry which climaxed in his suffering and death on the cross (cf. 1:21; 4:19; 9:6; 20:17-20, 28). Since the Holy Spirit empowered the Son of Man in his ministry, no forgiveness would be available to those who rejected the work of the Spirit in Jesus. However, since Jesus is the Son of Man, every sin and blasphemy of humans can be forgiven through his ministry (12:31-32). Since God the Father's grace and mercy is mediated through the Son of Man, humans can receive forgiveness for their sins. Similarly, in their future ministry, when the disciples share the message of the forgiveness of sins which is available through the Jesus's death and resurrection (cf. 24:14; 28:18-20), humans will be invited to repent of their sins, receive forgiveness, and follow Jesus. In addition, similar to the Son of Man, the Holy Spirit's power and authority in the disciples will enable them to fulfill God's will for their earthly ministry. The Son of Man mediated to his disciples the need for the Holy Spirit in their future ministry, as they proclaimed the message of salvation and engaged in deeds of mercy in accordance with God the Father's will.

Seventh, the only sign that is given to humanity is the Son of Man's suffering, death, resurrection, and his public return after his resurrection (12:39–40). Within 7:21–12:50, 12:40 is the only direct reference to Jesus's passion and vindication. God the Father's will in Matthew is culminated in the climax of Jesus's ministry—his death and resurrection. God's mercy and compassion toward sinful humanity is located at the cross. The Son of Man's death and resurrection mediated to his disciples specifically and to the crowds/religious leaders generally, that God the Father's will on earth is for sinners to repent of their sins, receive his forgiveness, and be restored to a right relationship with him (cf. 1:21; 6:10). After his resurrection, Jesus would commission his disciples to emulate his ministry by preaching the message of repentance and forgiveness of sins available through his death and resurrection (cf. 28:18–20). God's will is that humanity would accept Jesus and the disciples's message of repentance as the citizens of Nineveh accepted the preaching of Jonah (12:41). The Son of Man mediated God's will to his disciples by highlighting his obedience to God the Father's ultimate plan for his ministry (12:40). Similarly, the disciples would prove their allegiance to God's will in their ministry through their obedience to his plan—even when obeying God would involve suffering and death (cf. 10:16–39; 16:21–26).

The predictions of the Son of Man's suffering, death, resurrection, and exaltation have a prominent place in the Gospel of Matthew. After 12:40, the predictions are recorded in 16:21, 28; 17:9, 12, 22–23; 20:17–19, 28; 26:2 (also 26:24 [vv. 54, 56], 45). The emphasis of Matthew's passion material stresses Jesus the Son of Man's active obedience to his Father's will. In 16:21–28, the divine will is accentuated by Jesus's statement that "it is necessary" (δεῖ; v. 21) for him to suffer, die, and be resurrected from the dead. Through the Son of Man's obedience to follow God's will of suffering and death, he mediates for his disciples that in their present and future ministry they might be required to prove their absolute fidelity to God by sacrificing their lives in obedience to his will (vv. 24–27) (also in 17:9–13, when Jesus compared his ministry with John the Baptist's ministry—both would suffer and die to fulfill God's will for their ministries). However, in vv. 21 and 27, Jesus compared his future vindication of resurrection and subsequent exaltation (also 16:28) with his disciples's promised vindication of resurrection from the dead and future reward at his parousia; both demonstrating their commitment to follow God's will for their ministry and lives.

In 20:17–20, 28, the disciples accompanied Jesus the Son of Man to Jerusalem where they would witness his enduring resolve to fulfill the culmination of God's will for Jesus's life; he would suffer by both Jews and Gentiles and be killed through crucifixion. Through the Son of Man's active obedience to God's will, he would mediate for his disciples that they might face the fate of suffering and death in obedience to God's will for their lives. The climax of the Son of Man's service to humanity would be to give his life as a ransom for the many (for the forgiveness of human sin; 26:28). Forgiveness of sin is the result of the Son of Man's death which was the ransom that pardoned humanity from their sin (which separates God from humanity). The fullest expression of God's grace and mercy would be mediated to humanity through the Son of Man's sacrificial death. Only through the Son of Man's death, could humanity be brought back into a restored relationship with God the Father, the one who is in the heavens. In addition, the true meaning of servanthood (mercy and grace) according to God's will was mediated to Jesus's disciples—being a "slave/servant" to humanity by giving up one's life for the sake of others is the fullest expression of what it means to love others (cf. 22:39). Instead of vying for selfish pursuits like status or position, God's will requires humility (e.g., 23:11–12); relinquishing worldly pursuits (and possessions) to serve humanity with acts of mercy and love (e.g., 25:34–40). As mentioned, God the Father's vindication for the Son of Man's sacrificial death would be his resurrection and exaltation, which mediated God's promised vindication of future reward at the Son of Man's parousia for their faithful obedience to his will (e.g., 16:27; 25:35–37).

The theological centerpiece of the Son of Man's active obedience to follow God's will is located in Matt 26. The ultimate danger of disobedience and betrayal is highlighted in the contrasting behavior and actions of: (1) Judas with the woman who anointed Jesus's feet (vv. 7–16), (2) the disciples's obedience to follow Jesus's instructions with Judas's disobedience and hypocritical characterization (vv. 14–27), and (3) Jesus the Son of Man's insistence to follow God's will according to the scriptures and prophets with the disciples disobedience in Gethsemane and Judas's betrayal during Jesus's arrest (vv. 36–56). However, throughout chapter 26, Jesus the Son of Man mediated to his disciples the importance of following God's will even onto suffering and death. Jesus went to the place and the people who he knew would arrest him so to obey God's will (26:2, 24, 39, 42, 45–46, 50, 53–54, 56). Similarly, in their future ministries, the disciples must be willing to suffer and die in following God's will (e.g., 16:24–27; 20:17–28). Jesus's prayer in Gethsemane accentuated his desire to see his Father's will to be done on earth as it is in heaven (26:42 [6:10]). In Matthew's Gospel, the ultimate proof of genuine discipleship is to submit completely to God the Father's will, the one who is in the heavens (i.e., 7:21; 12:50). In addition, the Son of Man mediated to his disciples that his suffering and death would produce a covenant between humanity and God the Father—his blood would be shed for many for the forgiveness of sins (vv. 2, 24, 26–28). As a result, humanity could have a restored relationship with God the Father, the one who is in the heavens. In their future ministry, the disciples would share this message of salvation with the world (24:14; 28:18–20).

The Son of Man passages relating to his parousia, emphasize the recompense given to genuine disciples at the eschaton for their faithful obedience to God's will. In 13:24–30, Jesus the Son of Man stated he wanted the weeds to remain in the midst of the wheat until the eschaton so they could be influenced by the wheat. Genuine disciples were sent out to preach the good news of God's grace and mercy to both Jews and Gentiles—announcing the good news to all the nations until the Son of Man's parousia (cf. 24:14; 28:18–20). Similarly to Jesus and John the Baptist, they were to announce the need for people to repent of their sins because the kingdom of the heavens was near (cf. 10:7; 3:2, 6; 4:17). The Son of Man's mission was to mediate God the Father's grace and mercy towards humanity through his sacrificial suffering and death which would provide the means to the forgiveness of their sins (e.g., 20:17–19, 28; 26:28). In addition, the Son of Man would warn the disciples that the evil ones might attempt to uproot the children of the kingdom from their dedication to God (13:29, 38–39). The righteous ones are those who do the will of their Father in the heavens through their obedience to Jesus's words revealed in the scriptures (e.g., 7:24–25); they alone will enter into the kingdom of their Father (e.g., 7:21–23; 13:43). The evil ones will be separated from them and will be thrown into hell (13:41; e.g., 23:3). Therefore, the Son of Man is the mediator of the righteous and evil ones's eschatological fate—those who are faithful and obedient to God's will revealed through the Son of Man will inherit the gift of eternal life (i.e., the Father's kingdom) (cf. 13:41–43). In 16:24–27 and 19:27–30, the Son of Man will come in his Father's glory with his angels and will reward faithful disciples for their deeds which demonstrate their obedience to God's will—they are willing to relinquish their life like the Son of Man (16:21, 24) and they are prepared to give up everything (e.g., possessions and family) to follow Jesus into itinerant ministry (19:27, 29). The Son of Man promised to mediate God the Father's vindication and reward to such faithful disciples who have obeyed God's will, by giving them the right to sit on twelve thrones to rule over the twelve tribes of Israel in the restored world and to inherit eternal life (16:26–27; 19:28–29).

In Matthew's eschatological discourse (chapter 24), Jesus promised vindication and reward to faithful disciples who endured in their commitment to him until the Son of Man's parousia. In 24:3–26, Jesus emphasized the importance of genuine disciples enduring through intense persecution and the rise of false prophets, false christs, and the antichrist, to the end so they can receive salvation for their faithful commitment to Jesus and for proclaiming the good news of the kingdom throughout the world. Many will experience the evil increase of lawlessness and lack of love towards others (24:12) and will have to be willing to relinquish everything of earthly value (24:16–21). Faithful disciples will prove their obedience to God's will through being ready and watchful for the Son of Man's imminent return (24:36–44). A main manifestation of a disciple's obedience to God's will, is their actions of love and mercy towards others (24:45–51; e.g., 9:13; 12:7–8; 11:19; 25:34–40). The unfaithful tribes of the earth will mourn when they see the Son of Man coming on the clouds of heaven with his angels. When he comes he will send out his angels to gather the faithful (24:27, 30–31) to inherit eternal life (24:13 [13:43]) and he will separate them from the sinful and unfaithful by assigning them to hell (24:51 [13:41–42]). At the Son of Man's parousia, he will mediate genuine disciples's vindication and reward by granting them the gift of eternal life for their faithful, enduring obedience to God's will. In Matthew's judgment scene (25:31–46), the Son of Man will come in his glory with all his angels and sit on his throne of glory. As king, the Son of Man will separate all of humanity based on their faithful obedience to God's will. Those who have lived by participating in deeds which demonstrate a love for others in the world, will be granted eternal life in the king's Father's kingdom (25:33–45). Those who loved others demonstrated their love for Jesus the Son of Man, since he identified himself with the needy in the world (25:40, 45; cf. 22:37–40). As judge, the Son of Man will mediate the eschatological fates of both the faithful disciples and the evil sinners on behalf of God the Father—obedient disciples who have fulfilled God's will inherit eternal life, while disobedient sinners will to away into eternal punishment (25:31–33, 46).

In Matt 26:63–64, Jesus the Son of Man's identity and role provided future hope for his genuine disciples. The Son of Man is the Christ, the Son of God. In addition to his divine identity, Jesus emphasized his role. After living in obedience to God's will which was culminated in his suffering and death on the cross, God the Father would vindicate and reward the Son of Man through his resurrection and exaltation—all would see him sitting at the right hand of the power. In addition, in the future, he would come upon the clouds of heaven to mediate God the Father's judgment on all humanity (cf. 24:30–31 [also 13:41–43; 25:31–46]). Similarly, the Son of Man would mediate the vindication and reward of his faithful disciples at his parousia. They would be vindicated from death and rewarded for their faithful obedience to God's will by receiving eternal life in their Father's kingdom and sitting on thrones ruling over the tribes of Israel (cf. 16:24–27; 19:28–29).

Based on the evidence presented in this study, the term *mediator* fits well into representing the function of the Son of Man in Matthew's Gospel.

3. Conclusion

3.1. Filling the Research Gap

The purpose of this monograph was to analyze all thirty occurrences of the Son of Man phrase in the Gospel of Matthew to determine the Son of Man's function in the entire corpus. Son of Man research has generally viewed the meaning of the Son of Man logia as (1) a designation of his incarnation (Neander; Wright), (2) an etymological/philological emphasis of the Aramaic term *bar nasha* (Lietzmann; Manson; Gaston; Vermes; Casey), (3) relating to his eschatological return (Schweitzer; Weiss), (4) a prototype of humanity (cf. Dan 7), or (5) a representation of the disciples's ministry (Moule; Campbell). The concern with these approaches is that they are either too specific, not taking into account the Son of Man's function in all contexts, or too exclusive, focusing on etymology/philology without accounting for the literary contexts in which Son of Man logia are found in Matthew's Gospel. Matthean research has limited the meaning of the Son of Man's function by focusing on the latter half of the Gospel, that is, on chapters 16–26 (Geist and Luz) or on the parousia in chapters 21–25 (Kingsbury; Schweitzer; Weiss). Meier focuses on the entire corpus of Matthew, but his work is too broad positing an overly wide continuum of meaning of the Son of Man's function. In other words, for Meier, the Son of Man designates various aspects of his ministry, which spread across his public ministry, passion and exaltation, rule of the world, and final judgment. Thus, Meier does not present a particular theological understanding of the Son of Man's role in Matthew. Pamment limits the Son of Man's function to a strictly representative figure whose work and destiny are emulated by his disciples. However, she does not develop the comparison between the Son of Man and the disciples, demonstrating the ways they are to continue the Son of Man's ministry into their own. Scholars have primarily studied the thirty Son of Man sayings based on source-critical concerns, namely, interest in what materials the author of Matthew might have used to develop his understanding of the Son of Man. Matthean scholars have tended to focus on the latter half of the Gospel (after 16:13) in developing the theological significance of the Son of Man, since the majority of the Son of Man logia are found there. Therefore, gaps exist in the theological study of the Matthean Son of Man, and they need to be filled. This book has attempted to fill those gaps by providing a consistent theological understanding of the Son of Man throughout Matthew's Gospel, namely *the function of the Son of Man as mediator of God's will to his disciples*. The Son of Man's role as mediator can be discovered in

Matthew's presentation of Jesus's earthly ministry, in his suffering, passion, resurrection, and exaltation, and in his future parousia.

The origin of the expression *Son of Man* has not been conclusively proven. In my estimation, Ps 8:4–6 is a plausible background for the life, death, resurrection, and exaltation of Jesus the Son of Man, while Dan 7:13–14 is possible for the Son of Man sayings which relate to his parousia. The meaning of the *Son of Man* idiom is endlessly debated. The terms אדם, נשא, and ἄνθρωπος, can all be translated *human*, indicating the *Son of Humanity*. Therefore, the Son of Man relates to Jesus's relationship to/with humanity and represents them before God the Father and God the Father to them. In this monograph I argue that in Matthew, the Son of Man (i.e., Son of Humanity) is the mediator of God's will to his disciples—those who choose to follow him. In addition, he is the mediator of God's grace and mercy to all humanity through his sacrificial death which provides the forgiveness of sins and a restored relationship with God the Father. Finally, he is the mediator of God the Father's promised vindication to genuine disciples when he comes as eschatological judge at his parousia.

The primary method I chose in analyzing the Son of Man logia in Matthew is new redaction criticism. Accordingly, in my thesis, the Son of Man's function as mediator is based on the theological interests of the author in Matthew's own account by beginning to highlight emphases through comparison with the Gospels of Mark and Luke, and then providing a literary-critical analysis of the Son of Man logion within Matthew's Gospel. Chapter 2 demonstrated the Son of Man's role as mediator by prophetically revealing God's will to his disciples during his earthly ministry (Matt 8–12). Chapter 3 showed the Son of Man's role as mediator by demonstrating God's will to his disciples through his resolve to offer himself as the priestly sacrifice through his suffering and death, and his subsequent resurrection and exaltation (16:13–28; 17:10–23; 20:17–28; 26). Chapter 4 concluded with the Son of Man's kingly role as the mediator of promised vindication and reward for genuine disciples at his parousia (13:24–30, 36–43; 16:13–27; 19:16–30; 24:3–51; 25:31–46; 26:63–66).

3.2. The Son of Man's Earthly Ministry: The Mediator of God's Revealed Will in Matthew

In chapter 2, I demonstrated that the Son of Man functioned as mediator by revealing God's will to his disciples during his earthly ministry. Jesus the Son of Man accomplished his role as mediator by teaching his disciples what behaviors and actions were necessary to be part of God the Father's family (i.e., children of the kingdom), identifying them based on their commitment to practicing God's will. Matthew structured the importance of his disciples doing God's will through an *inclusio* formed with 7:21 and 12:50. These verses are almost identical, highlighting kingdom people as those who do the will of the Father in the heavens. Matthew 8–12 includes the Son of Man logia related to Jesus's earthly ministry. Matthew 7:21 (also vv. 22–29) serves two purposes: (1) it is Jesus's concluding, climactic teaching on his Sermon on the Mount, and (2) it is the introduction to Jesus's earthly ministry in 8:1—12:50, since God's will is the central theme throughout Jesus's earthly ministry.

The Son of Man taught his disciples that it is necessary to relinquish temporal possessions and family members to follow God's will (8:18–22). Matthew's unique contribution to Jesus's teaching is seen primarily in his contrast between a scribe and one of his disciples (in Luke the individuals are unidentified [9:57, 59, 61]). Unlike Luke 9:57–62, Matthew forms an *inclusio* with the term *follow* (ἀκολουθέω in 8:19, 22), emphasizing the importance of the meaning of following Jesus and, consequently, the importance of obeying God's will. Since the scribe stated that he would follow Jesus, one might argue that he was a genuine disciple. However, in almost every place a scribe is mentioned in Matthew, a scribe was an enemy of Jesus who opposed him and his ministry (cf. 2:1–19; 5:19–20; 23 [esp. 23:6–7, 25–26]). The Son of Man mediated for his disciples the importance of following God's will through his homelessness (aspiring neither to status, possessions, nor family). Matthew 8:20 serves as an invitation to discipleship. To follow after the Son of Man in self-renunciation is to experience his grace—a divine opportunity to experience God's will as mediated through the Son of Man's praxis. The disciple called Jesus "Lord" in contrast to the scribe, probably emphasizing the disciple's willingness to relinquish his need to bury his father and follow Jesus. The disciples who followed Jesus into the boat in 8:23–27 also called him "Lord" (cf. 8:21, 25) when a great storm arose and they needed help. Therefore, the disciple in 8:21–22 was most likely among those who went with Jesus into the boat.[2] The call to relinquish temporal attachments is emphasized in Jesus's missionary discourse in 10:5–15, 37–39. The Son of Man is the mediator of God's will by teaching his disciples the necessity of relinquishing position, status, and family in following Jesus.

The Son of Man taught his disciples that faith in Jesus's authority is necessary in following God's will (9:1–8). Unlike Mark and Luke's accounts, in Matthew's presentation of the healing of the paralytic, the contrast between

---

2. The account of the disciples following Jesus into a boat is not included following Luke 9:57–62.

CONCLUSION: THE SON OF MAN AS MEDIATOR IN MATTHEW 201

the faith of those who brought the paralyzed man (and the paralyzed man himself) and the evil hearts of the scribes is important. The scribes charged Jesus with blasphemy because he claimed he had the authority to forgive sins (9:3, 5–6). This blasphemy was likely due to Jesus's claiming God's exclusive prerogative to forgive sins, thus challenging God's sole authority. The scribes's evil hearts related to their lack of faith in Jesus; in this way, they were among those opposed to Jesus and his ministry throughout Matthew (cf. 12:35, 38–45; 16:4; 15:8; 23:23). However, the faith of those who brought the paralyzed man (and the paralyzed man himself) led to Jesus's healing the man and forgiving his sins. Through his many miracles of healing in Matthew, Jesus mediated the view that faith is necessary for those who want to follow God's will. The necessity of faith is highlighted in Jesus's rebuke of his disciples for their lack of faith in him when threatened by a great storm (8:25–27). The connection between faith and healing is accentuated in chapters 8–9, which demonstrate his mercy for the sick who expressed faith in him (e.g., 8:5–13; 9:18–19, 23–26, 32–33). In 1:21–23, Jesus's mission to forgive and save his people from their sins was a manifestation of God's will and was highlighted through his preaching of repentance (like John the Baptist; 3:2, 6; 4:17). Since the culmination of the Son of Man's ministry was to suffer and die for humanity, physical healing and the forgiveness of sins are manifestations of the Son of Man's love and mercy for this paralytic. The Son of Man mediates his desire for a restored relationship between the paralytic (i.e., and all humanity) and God the Father through his sacrificial death; the means of forgiveness for human sin (cf. 20:28; 26:28). Therefore, the ministry of forgiving sins would need to be an integral part of the disciples's future ministry as well (e.g., 18:21–35). The paralytic's faith is demonstrated in his obedience to Jesus's command; he picked up his stretcher and went home (9:7). Jesus the Son of Man's mediatorial role in healing and forgiving sins is seen in the imperative verbs in 9:5–6, where he authoritatively commanded the paralytic to action. Since Jesus's authority is accentuated[3] in the healing episode, 9:8b refers back to Jesus as the only mediator of God's will. The Son of Man mediated the necessary response of faith (and obedience) in following God's will.

The Son of Man taught his disciples that faithful allegiance in following after Jesus and his call to itinerant ministry is necessary for following God's will (10:16–23). The purpose of the missionary discourse in Matt 10 is to encourage disciples to remain committed to God's will amidst inevitable persecution and possible death in their allegiance to God's will (cf.

---

3. Unlike Mark and Luke's accounts, Matthew emphasizes Jesus's authority twice in 9:6, 8.

10:16–22, 26–31, 38–39). Jesus encouraged his disciples to endure to the end (of their lives) so they could receive his promised reward of eternal life (10:21–22). Disciples who emulate Jesus's life and ministry are committed to doing his Father's will (10:24–25). Preaching of the nearness of the kingdom (10:7, 19, 27, 32) must continue throughout the cities of Israel before the Son of Man comes (10:23). Jesus and John the Baptist proclaimed a message of repentance for the forgiveness of sins (3:2, 6; 4:17), which is mirrored by the disciples (10:6–7). The purpose of their ministry was to urge people to repent of their sins, receive forgiveness, and have a restored relationship with God the Father. Like Jesus and John the Baptist, the apostles's commitment to such a ministry would result in suffering and possible death in preaching the gospel message (10:21–22). Sometime after his death and resurrection, Jesus will come back and give his disciples further instructions for their itinerant ministry both to Jews (10:6) and Gentiles (10:16–20; cf. 28:18–20). Jesus's instructions for preaching to the whole world are recorded in 24:14, which include eschatological cues of Jesus's parousia (cf. 24:3–51). Matthew's missionary discourse does not have the prominent eschatological emphasis on the parousia resident in Mark 13:9–13 and Luke 22:12–19. Therefore, unlike Mark and Luke, Matthew is concerned with the present and future ministry of the disciples after Jesus's resurrection and primarily reserves his discussion of Jesus's parousia for Matt 24. Solidarity between Jesus's ministry and his disciples is highlighted in the missionary discourse: (1) a preaching/healing ministry (4:17, 23–24; 9:36–38 [specific examples of Jesus's healing: 8:1–17, 28–34; 9:1–8, 18–34]; 10:1, 7–9), (2) persecution for following God's will (16:21; 17:22–23; 20:17–19; 10:11–15, 16–22 [cf. 5:10–12], 32–40), and (3) taking up one's cross and following Jesus (10:38–39; 16:21–28). Through the parallel ministries of Jesus and his disciples in chapter 10, Jesus mediated for his disciples the need for faithful, lifelong obedience to God's will, including an inclusive ministry both to Jews and Gentiles.

The Son of Man taught his disciples that continuing to follow Jesus by emulating his works of mercy and sharing his message of salvation amidst persecution is necessary in following God's will (11:11–19). Matthew 11:1–19 is almost identical with Luke 7:18–35. Their point of contrast relates to their surrounding contexts. Matthew emphasizes the persecution that Jesus's disciples would experience as they continued Jesus's ministry to other Jewish cities (10:14–40; 11:6, 11–12, 28–30). In 11:7–24, the persecution and rejection of the message of Jesus the Son of Man and John the Baptist are emphasized. Similarly, those who rejected Jesus and John the Baptist's mission represent those who will reject Jesus's disciples's ministry. However, Luke's account does not emphasize persecution or rejection of

CONCLUSION: THE SON OF MAN AS MEDIATOR IN MATTHEW   203

John the Baptist or Jesus's disciples's ministry. The surrounding context in Luke 7 is focused on Jesus's healing miracles and the rejection he received from the Jewish people.

The *inclusio* comprising 11:2, 19 serves two purposes: (1) It highlights Matthew's messianic association by connecting the Christ with the Son of Man, and (2) it emphasizes the works of the Son of Man according to God's will (i.e., miraculous deeds, preaching, teaching, and evangelism). Jesus associated with the marginalized, especially tax collectors and sinners, throughout his ministry, so they might hear and respond to his message. Throughout chapter 11, Matthew compared the ministry and rejection of Jesus the Son of Man with that of John the Baptist (cf. 11:2, 12, 18–19). In 11:12, the term βιάζεται carries a passive-negative sense, that is, the kingdom of heaven suffers violence (the rejection/persecution of John the Baptist [11:13–18; 14:1–12] and of Jesus the Son of Man [11:5–6, 16–17, 19; 26:1–5]). In contrast to rejection, God divinely appointed John the Baptist and Jesus the Christ to itinerant ministries (cf. 1:21–23; 3:1–17; 4:17). In 9:9–13, Jesus's ministry to tax collectors and sinners accentuated his interest in embracing the marginalized and complete submission to the will of God, who "desires mercy not sacrifice" (cf. 9:13; 12:7 [Hos 6:6]; the divine will is highlighted by θέλω). John the Baptist represented those who do the will of their Father in the heavens through their submissive obedience to God's will (cf. 7:21–27). Jesus the Son of Man is the mediator of God's will on earth, which is clearly demonstrated in his submission to God's itinerant ministry and his willingness to embrace and minister to the marginalized (that is, tax collectors and sinners). The Son of Man's acceptance of the marginalized in 11:5, 19 (and Gentiles in 11:21) highlights his desire to extend God's grace and mercy to them. His deep concern for people to repent of their sins and receive salvation is demonstrated in his preaching the good news and accentuated in 11:21, and in his desire to give the burdened rest for their souls in 11:28–30. Wicked Gentile cities and the marginalized (represented by children/little ones/infants in 11:11, 25–30 [cf. 18:1–14]) accepted the wisdom and miraculous deeds (the ἔργα [11:2, 19]) of the Christ, the Son of Man (11:22–24), but the Jewish cities and religious leaders/Pharisees persecuted and rejected the teaching and work of the Son of Man (11:16, 20–21, 25, 28–30; cf. 23:1–4, 23). The Pharisees represented those who cause the disciples/marginalized (other little ones/least important) to fall from their faith (18:6–7; 23:1–2, 10–15) through their faulty interpretation of the law and the teaching of the elders (11:28). However, Jesus the Son of Man provided wisdom that is an easy yoke and light burden that has the salvific power to bring rest to their souls (11:19, 29–30). Eschatological salvation and reward is reserved for those who accept Jesus's fuller revelation of God's will mediated through Jesus the Son of Man. Tax collectors and sinners represented those who accept his message, repent, and turn to Jesus (21:31–32), that is, the least important, little ones, and infants who embraced Jesus the Son of Man. As the disciples emulated Jesus the Son of Man's message and works (e.g., 10:5–15, 16–20, 23), they faithfully followed God's will for their present and future ministries. The Son of Man mediated God's will to his disciples by emphasizing the need to associate with sinners and the ostracized in society, and to share the message of repentance so they could have an opportunity to receive God's grace and mercy—namely, the forgiveness of their sins and salvation. In addition, the Son of Man mediated for his disciples the need to continue resolutely in their itinerant ministry, as he did, so to fulfill God's will fully for their lives and ministry.

The Son of Man taught his disciples that obeying Jesus's law of mercy toward the needy is necessary in following God's will. Matthew 12:1–8 is paralleled in Mark 2:23—3:6 and in Luke 6:1–11. Matthew's account is different due to its emphasis on human need. In Matthew, Jesus compared the need to accept the disciples eating on the Sabbath when hungry with the Pharisees actions, which broke the Sabbath law (12:1–5). In addition, only Matthew mentions that Jesus is greater than the temple (i.e., his redefinition of the law takes precedence over the Sabbath law) and quotes Hos 6:6 "I desire mercy and not sacrifice" (12:6–7). Jesus's insistence on showing mercy to the disciples is substantiated in Hos 6:6 that compassion triumphs over Sabbath regulations. Unlike Mark and Luke, Matthew accentuates mercy as more essential than the Sabbath law and highlights the need to love one's neighbor (22:39).

The Pharisees rebuked Jesus and his disciples for eating grain on the Sabbath. The Son of Man justified his authority to redefine the Sabbath law by placing mercy above the law through the following christological statements in 12:6–8: (1) The Son of Man is greater than the temple; (2) according to Hos 6:6, God "desires [wills (θέλω)] mercy over sacrifice"; and (3) the Son of Man is Lord of the Sabbath. The Son of Man is greater than the temple through his authoritative role as mediator—he mediated God's will of mercy towards human beings (cf. 9:9–13). Jesus's mission was to "save his people from their sins" (1:21), which is represented in his ministry to tax collectors and sinners (cf. 11:19) who accepted his message and inherited eternal life (11:25–30; 20:31–32). According to Jesus, mercy and compassion to people, manifested in Jesus's teaching (12:1–8) and in his healing of the crippled man in the temple (12:9–14), are more important than the law. Jesus's attitude toward the law was to fulfill it according to God's will, which he did by teaching his disciples to put others first by being their servant (perfectly fulfilled in Jesus's death; cf. 20:26–28). In contrast to God's will, the Pharisees opposed Jesus's redefinition of the law by plotting to kill Jesus, as seen in Matthew's first prediction of the Son of Man's premeditated death (12:12–14). Jesus's ministry defined for his disciples what God's will is and how it was to be practiced. Obeying God's will requires merciful actions toward others. Jesus the Son of Man is the mediator of God's revealed will to his disciples in his teaching and demonstrating that mercy towards others is a necessity for those committed to following God's will.

The Son of Man taught his disciples that just as the Holy Spirit's anointing was needed in his ministry, so his empowerment would be necessary in his disciples's future ministry if they were to fulfill God's will faithfully (12:22–32). Unlike Mark and Luke, Matthew explicitly mentions the Holy Spirit's role in empowering Jesus to exorcise demons (12:28). In Matthew, the writer connects the Pharisees's accusation of Jesus's ability to cast out demons through Beelzebub with the unforgiveable sin of blaspheming the Holy Spirit's work in Jesus's ministry (12:31–32). In Matthew, the emphasis on judgment is stronger than in Mark and Luke. The consequences for blaspheming the Holy Spirit are both for the present and the future (12:32), not just for the future (as in Mark 3:29–30). Luke bypasses the Spirit's work in Jesus's ministry and the judgment for blaspheming against the Spirit (cf. 11:14–23).

The Pharisees criticized Jesus's ministry of exorcism, stating that the source of his miraculous ability is Satan. However, Jesus revealed to the Pharisees that he exorcised demons through God's Spirit (12:22–28). The disciples and crowds witnessed Jesus's demon exorcism of a blind and mute man (12:1, 15, 23), which amazed the crowd and caused them to ask if he was the Son of David (12:23). Later in Matthew, the disciples were challenged after Jesus's resurrection to rely on the Holy Spirit in their respective ministries (28:18–20). Therefore, Jesus's teaching about the Holy Spirit would mediate to Jesus's disciples that God's will would necessitate the Holy Spirit's role in their future post-resurrection ministry. The Holy Spirit empowered Jesus the Son of Man in his mission to forgive sins and restore humanity's relationship with God through his suffering and death (cf. 1:21). No forgiveness is available to those who reject the work of the Holy Spirit in the Son of Man and, consequently, in the future ministry of the disciples when they continue his ministry by proclaiming the message of forgiveness of sins through his suffering and death (12:32; cf. 24:14). The Pharisees credited Jesus's miracle to demon possession (12:24). Jesus accused the Pharisees of committing the unforgiveable sin, blasphemy of the Holy Spirit (12:31–32). Criticizing and speaking against Jesus the Son of Man is forgivable, but speaking against the Holy Spirit, the source of Jesus's authoritative power, is unforgivable. Jesus's authoritative power came from God, who anointed Jesus with the Holy Spirit and divinely sanctioned his itinerant ministry (cf. 3:16–17; 4:1–17). The Pharisees's blasphemous speech aligned them with Satan in their rejection of the source of Jesus's power (i.e., the Holy Spirit) and, consequently, they rejected God himself (also 9:32–34). Their rejection of God's will for Jesus's ministry (and his anointing by the Spirit) is reminiscent of Peter's rebuke of Jesus in 16:21–23. Peter was influenced by Satan in his rejection of God's will in Jesus's ministry and, therefore, the Holy Spirit's work in aiding Jesus to accomplish God's plan. The Pharisees and Peter similarly emulated Satan's attempt to lead Jesus away from God's will for his ministry (cf. 4:1–11). In 12:18, 28, the Holy Spirit's presence and work in Jesus's ministry is spoken about and demonstrated, solidifying the Pharisees's blasphemous speech and bringing judgment upon them for committing the unforgiveable sin. Jesus the Son of Man was the meditator between God the Father and his disciples. Just as Jesus needed the Holy Spirit as the source of his ministry to fulfill God's will, so his disciples would need to rely on the Holy Spirit as the means to complete God's will (cf. 10:20; 28:18–20).

The Son of Man taught his disciples that imitating his self-sacrificial ministry even onto death would be necessary in following God's will (12:38–42). Luke 11:29–32 mentions that the crowds are representative of an evil generation, while Matthew's account specifically addresses the scribes and Pharisees as prime examples of an evil and adulterous generation (12:38–39). In addition, the comparison with the Jonah tradition (Jonah 1:17—2:10) and Jesus the Son of Man's suffering and death as the sign is emphasized in Matthew (12:39–40), while Luke only mentions the sign of Jonah without any description of the sign (11:30). Matthew's focus is on the Son of Man's death and resurrection, while Luke appears to have related the sign of Jonah to Jesus's parousia (future of ἔσται in 11:3).

The scribes and Pharisees's request for a sign caused Jesus to group them with "an evil and adulterous generation" (12:38–39). This emphasis on *evil generation* (γενεὰ πονηρά) connects this pericope together by an *inclusio* (12:38–39, 45). In 12:39 and 16:4, the Pharisees were representative of the "evil and adulterous generation" precisely because they were opposed to God's will in and through Jesus the Son of Man's ministry, which mediated God's will on earth throughout Matt 8–12 (cf. 9:1–8, 32–34; 12:14, 22–32). The evil nature of the Pharisees is accentuated in 16:1, when they are described as testing (πειράζω) Jesus. In Matthew, testing is an action of Satan, the Pharisees, or the Pharisees and Sadducees; in this way, these religious leaders are aligned with Satan's work and his kingdom (cf. 4:1, 3, 7; 19:3; 22:18, 35). The only sign given to the religious leaders will be the sign of Jonah, which is the resurrection of Jesus the Son of Man and his public return after his resurrection. Just as in Jonah 1:17—2:10, an emphasis on death and resurrection is identified as the sign of God's victorious redemption and vindication. The sign that will be apparent to the religious leaders is Jesus's resurrection. The judgment of Jonah is compared with the fate of Jesus the Son of Man. The Son of Man received God's judgment and punishment through suffering and death to "save his people from their sins" (1:21) and was buried and delivered from death (cf. Jonah 1:17—2:10). Just as Jonah fulfilled God's will by going to Nineveh to preach repentance (Jonah 3), so Jesus the Son of Man did through his sacrificial suffering, death, and resurrection. Similarly, the disciples would need to deny themselves by relinquishing all people and possessions and suffer opposition and persecution even onto death in order to obey Jesus's commission and fulfill God's will faithfully for their lives (cf. 8:18-22; 10:16-39; 11:18-24; 12:30-33; 16:21-26). Through the Son of Man's suffering, death, and resurrection, God's mercy and compassion to sinners would be displayed. Jesus's death and resurrection mediated to his disciples specifically and the religious leaders and crowds generally, that God the Father is merciful and compassionate. God's will on earth is that sinners would repent of their sins, receive forgiveness through the Son of Man's sacrificial death, and be saved from their separation from God. A main way the disciples will fulfill God's will in their future ministry is to proclaim this gospel message to others. As in 11:20-27, Gentiles (Gentile cities, Queen of Sheba) will condemn this evil generation (represented by Pharisees and Sadducees) because they accepted Jesus's message of salvation, while the evil generation (cf. 11:20-21) refused to repent and accept Jesus's message of salvation. Jesus's message is greater than the preaching of Jonah and the wisdom of Solomon. God's will is for all people (Jews and Gentiles) to accept God's salvific plan mediated through Jesus the Son of Man. Jesus the Son of Man mediated for his disciples the necessity of self-sacrifice even unto death to fulfill God's will faithfully for their lives.

3.3. The Son of Man's Passion and Death: The Mediator of Demonstrated Obedience to God's Will in Matthew

In chapter 3, I demonstrated that the Son of Man functioned as the mediator by fulfilling God's will through revealing and exemplifying his committed obedience to self-sacrificial suffering and death. Similarly, the disciples would learn the importance of obedience in following God's will.

The Son of Man demonstrated his fidelity to God's revelation of his fate to suffer and die and told his disciples such renunciation of life was necessary in following God's will (16:13-28). Matthew 16:13-20 provides a more complete messianic understanding by connecting Jesus the Son of Man with the Petrine confession of Jesus being "the Christ, the Son of the living God" (16:13, 16; cf. 11:2, 19). Mark 8:27—9:1 and Luke 9:18–27 do not mention Jesus as the Son of the Living God, nor that the Father revealed the confession to Peter. Jesus's divinely sanctioned mission in 1:21 is particularized in 16:21 and in the subsequent passion predictions in 17:22–23 and 20:17–19 (also 26:27–28). Peter's divinely revealed confession in 16:16 is contrasted with his rejection of Jesus's mission to suffer and die in 16:21, which led Jesus to rebuke Peter's response of rejection as inspired by Satan (cf. 16:22–23).[4] In 16:21, Jesus claimed he would suffer many things, be killed, and raised on the third day. In the subsequent passion predictions, Jesus revealed in greater detail what such suffering would involve (17:22–23; 20:17–19). The use of δεῖ in 16:21 emphasizes God's will for Jesus to suffer, die, and be resurrected. In other words, it is God's will for his grace and mercy for humanity's sinful condition to be demonstrated through the Son of Man's suffering and death, which will mediate God's love to humanity through his broken body and spilled blood for the forgiveness of sins (26:26–28). Only the Son of Man was called to offer his life as a means for the forgiveness of sins and to restore humanity's relationship with God the Father. The disciples will be called to share the meaning and message of Jesus's death with humanity. Jesus would need voluntarily to obey God's mission for his life. Jesus the Son of Man mediated to his disciples the importance of obeying God's will through his unwavering loyalty to God's future plan for his life, culminating in his suffering and death. Similarly, Jesus revealed to his disciples that faithful disciples[5] must also demonstrate their fidelity to God's will through their willingness to deny themselves voluntarily, take up their crosses, and follow him, accepting the fate of suffering and death (16:24). Jesus demonstrated his obedience to God's will through his suffering and death and will mediate for his present and future disciples that suffering and death will be necessary in yielding to God's will for their lives. The future reward of eternal life will be given to faithful disciples who, like Jesus, chose suffering and death over attachment to their present lives (16:25–27). At his parousia, the Son of Man will vindicate and reward faithful disciples with eternal life (16:27). Jesus's future recompense was meant to encourage Jesus's disciples to voluntary self-sacrificial renunciation in faithful obedience to God's will.[6] Through the Son of Man's

---

4. The harsh dialog between Jesus and Peter in 16:22–23 is more descriptive and accusatory in the Matthean account than in Mark. For example, Jesus called Peter a *stumbling block* (σκάνδαλον), indicating Peter's resistance to God's will.

5. Unlike the Mark and Lukan accounts, the instructions on self-denial in Matt 16:24–26 is directed only to Jesus's disciples.

6. Only the Matthean account mentions the disciples's reward of eternal life for

willingness to suffer and die, he mediated for his disciples the importance of obeying God's mission of self-denial, even of one's life, according to God's will. Only Matthew's account mentions that next time the disciples would see the Son of Man coming with his kingdom it would be after his victorious resurrection (16:28), when he would instruct and challenge his disciples to continue his itinerant ministry (cf. 28:18–20).

The Son of Man demonstrated the costliness of obediently following God's will so his disciples would understand the importance of voluntary self-surrender (17:10–13, 22–23). Jesus the Son of Man commanded his disciples to withhold his divine identity as the Son of God until after his resurrection (17:5; cf. 28:18–20). Earlier in 3:16–17, Jesus was similarly revealed as God's Son, whose authority and Spirit's anointing would enable him to fulfill all righteousness (3:15) by completing God's will revealed previously in 1:21. Later in 26:54, 56, Jesus's suffering and death would demonstrate his obedience to God's word—the fulfillment of the scriptures and the prophets. In 17:5, God commanded the disciples to listen to Jesus so they would also fulfill God's will for their future ministry, specifically in pursuing righteousness (i.e., God's will) even in times of persecution (5:6, 10–12). Enduring persecution in obedience to God's will should result in an attitude of rejoicing and gladness as the disciples have hope in their future vindication and reward (cf. 16:24–27). The Son of Man's vindication and reward, manifested in his resurrection and exaltation for his obedience to God's will, would mediate for his disciples their future vindication and reward of release from suffering and persecution and receiving eternal life. Jesus identified Elijah with John the Baptist in 17:10–13 (also 11:14). He compared his ministry with John the Baptist's since they preached repentance, received rejection from the religious leaders, and faced subsequent death (cf. 3:1–2, 7–11; 11:16–18; 14:1–12 [for John]; 4:17; 11:19; 16:21; 17:22–23 [for Jesus]). Both Jesus and John the Baptist would suffer and die as they obediently fulfilled God's will for their ministries. In 17:10–13, the comparison between Jesus and John the Baptist and the identification of Elijah with John the Baptist, are not mentioned in Luke and only implied in Mark 9:13. Through the Son of Man's voluntary obedience to suffer and die according to God's will, he mediated for his disciples the costly sacrifice of life, which is probable when committed to following God's will (16:24–28). Matthew 17:22–23 particularizes the previous passion prediction in 16:21. In 17:22, the verb *betray* (παραδίδωμαι) functions in both a passive and active sense. First, suffering and death was God's divine will for Jesus's life (i.e., "it is necessary" [δεῖ], in 16:21). Jesus resolutely submitted to God's plan of suffering and death through his

---

self-denial even onto death.

acceptance of his fate (26:39, 42, 45b–56). Second, Judas would decide to betray Jesus into human hands, and they would have him killed (10:4; 26:2–4, 14–16, 23–25, 46–56). The purpose of the Son of Man's suffering and death was to restore humanity's relationship with God through the forgiveness of their sins (26:28). However, his demise would occur due to human betrayal. Jesus came to save humanity from their sins even though they would betray him and lead him to his suffering and death. The Son of Man mediates God's grace and mercy to all of humanity. Jesus voluntarily accepted and endured costly self-denial in order to obey God's will. The Son of Man mediated for his disciples the importance of submitting to God's will even in suffering persecution and the costly sacrifice of one's life.

The Son of Man demonstrated that self-sacrificial servanthood on behalf of others is necessary in obeying God's will (20:17–28). In 20:17–19, Jesus revealed in greater detail the events surrounding his upcoming suffering and death. Jesus's rejection would be universal. He would be handed over to the chief priests and scribes (i.e., Jewish authorities; by Judas in 10:4; 26:14–16, 47–56) to be condemned to death, and they will hand Jesus over to the Gentiles (cf. 27:26–50) to be physically persecuted and crucified (20:18–19). In their parallel versions, Mark and Luke do not mention crucifixion as the manner of Jesus's death. However, Matt 20:19 states that the Gentiles will crucify him. Jesus's insistence that he and his disciples go to Jerusalem (20:17–18) accentuated his willingness to obey God's will of suffering and death (cf. 16:21; 17:22–23). Jesus wanted his disciples to go with him to Jerusalem so they could witness his voluntary obedience to God's will. Through experiencing his costly sacrifice for the sake of others (cf. 1:21; 20:28), the Son of Man would mediate the need for willing self-sacrifice of life in obeying God's will for their future ministry (cf. 16:24–26). Genuine disciples must be servants/slaves by putting others first (20:26–27), just as the Son of Man did when he gave his life as a ransom for the many (20:28). The Son of Man mediated for his disciples that obedience to God's will must be demonstrated through sacrificial suffering and death for the sake of others (adhering to the command to love one's neighbors in 22:39). The request of the mother of the sons of Zebedee for status and position in the kingdom of heaven is contrasted with Jesus's instructions relating to lowliness and servanthood (20:20–27). Instead of status and position, Jesus was concerned that his disciples obediently follow God's will (20:22–23). The term *cup* (ποτήριον) is also used in 26:27–28, 39 (indirectly v. 42) relating to: (1) a symbol of Jesus's death, the blood of the covenant shed for the forgiveness of sins, and (2) Jesus's voluntary acceptance of death in obedience to God's will. Jesus's willingness to succumb to self-sacrificial death fulfills Isa 52:13—53:12 regarding the suffering servant who would die to forgive the sins of the many according to God's will (e.g., 53:10–12). Instead of status and position, Jesus was focused on suffering and death, which was the culmination of God's will for his life. The previous passion predictions indicate the divine necessity of suffering and death and Jesus's willingness to obey God's will through his voluntary self-sacrifice (16:21; 17:22–23; 20:17–19). Similarly, the sons of Zebedee would be killed in the future as they continued to follow God's will faithfully in their mission (cf. 28:18–20). In 20:25–28, Jesus taught that honor is given to those who are willing to be a servant and slave for others. Rather than emulating the Gentiles's thirst for status and position, being great and first in God's kingdom requires serving others (cf. 23:11–12). Jesus's teaching on servanthood is compared with his future action in 20:28. Jesus the Son of Man's ministry as a servant found its fulfillment when he gave his life as a ransom for many (cf. 1:21 [i.e., shedding his blood for the forgiveness of sins for the many in 26:28[7]]). The result of the ransom that Jesus's death mediated is God's grace and mercy which would provide the forgiveness of humanity's sins, restore their relationship with the Father in the heavens, and enable them to receive eternal salvation. Jesus's ultimate act of servanthood in obedience to God's will would be demonstrated to his disciples through his sacrificial death, mediating for them the important need to serve others even onto death in obedience to God's will.

The Son of Man demonstrated the importance of accepting rejection and death as requirements for obeying God's will (26:1–5, 14–56). Unlike Mark and Luke, Matthew has a fourth passion prediction recorded in 26:2, which serves as a general statement to the events outlined in chapter 26, specifically, Judas's handing over of Jesus the Son of Man to the religious leaders and Roman soldiers to be arrested and ultimately killed. In 26:6–13, the woman who anointed Jesus's feet stands in contrast with Judas's willingness to betray Jesus in 26:14–16. As an act of worship, the woman sacrificially poured expensive ointment contained in an alabaster jar over Jesus's head. In contrast, Judas's selfishness is accentuated in the thirty silver pieces paid to Judas to betray Jesus. In light of Jesus's teaching on money in 6:24, 33, the woman represented a genuine follower of Jesus while Judas represented a hypocrite who claimed fidelity to Jesus but lived in opposition to God's will (see also 7:21–23; 23:27–28). Both Judas (26:14–16) and the Roman soldiers (28:11–15) accepted the payment of silver from the chief priests, aligning themselves with those against Jesus and his followers. In contrast to Judas's action of betrayal, the disciples obeyed Jesus's command to go into the city

---

7. Only Matthew provides the result of Jesus's paying the ransom for the many, namely, the forgiveness of sins. Mark and Luke do not mention the atonement for sin as directly in their accounts.

and make preparations for the supper (20:17–19), an important detail not mentioned in Mark and Luke. Their obedience to Jesus characterized them as genuine disciples who fulfill God's will. However, Judas disobeyed Jesus's command not to accept silver from others (cf. 10:9), which, consequently, led him to reject God's will. In 26:26, Jesus specifically identified Judas as his betrayer, a detail not included in the parallels in Mark and Luke. Judas's hypocrisy is also emphasized in the following ways in chapter 26. First, in 26:25, 49 he called Jesus "Rabbi" instead of "Lord"; genuine disciples in Matthew call Jesus "Lord" (e.g., 8:18–23). Usually "Teacher" and "Rabbi" were titles given by those in opposition to Jesus and/or his mission. Second, he is grouped with other sinners (e.g., Pharisees and scribes) who opposed Jesus and his mission and sought after his death (cf. 17:22; 23; 26:23, 45, 50). Therefore, like them, they will receive judgment for rejecting (in Judas's case, betraying [also 10:4; 26:46, 48; 27:3]) the Son of Man (26:23–25). Judas disobeyed God's will for a genuine disciple to remain faithfully committed to Jesus. In 26:24, the Son of Man will be betrayed by *that human* (i.e., Judas), and consequently, he proclaimed judgment on human sin; betrayal. In 26:26–28, Jesus's death makes the forgiveness of sins possible and provides eternal life for those who seek the forgiveness of sins. However, in 26:45–56, Judas chose to carry through with his sinful behavior even though forgiveness of sins would have been possible if he repented of his sin and sought forgiveness. Jesus the Son of Man mediates God's grace and mercy to humanity—the forgiveness of sins is available through his obedient death to humans who repent of their sins, seek forgiveness, and receive eternal salvation. Third, Judas was the cause for Jesus's arrest. He led the religious leaders/Roman soldiers to the area of Gethsemane; he welcomed Jesus, kissed him fervently, called him "Rabbi" and then allowed the Roman soldiers to arrest him (26:47–50). Throughout chapter 26, Judas represented those who are disobedient to God's will.

In sharp contrast to Judas, Jesus and his other disciples represented those who obey God's will. In 26:18, 45–46, Jesus said the time was near for his upcoming death. Jesus continued moving forward to his suffering and death by celebrating Passover with his disciples, going to Gethsemane to pray and submit to God's will, and telling his disciples to go with him, the Son of Man, to meet his betrayer and be arrested. Jesus's obedient desire to fulfill God's will even unto death mediated for his disciples the importance of fidelity to God's will even when it results in suffering and death. In 26:26–29, the disciples's obedience is implied as they appear to follow Jesus's directions during the Passover supper: to take, eat the bread, and drink the cup. In addition, the disciples would drink the cup when they would be required to sacrifice their lives for Jesus's sake and the mission of the kingdom (cf. 10:16–39; 16:24–26; 20:20–28). The Son of Man's desire to fulfill God's will was symbolized in the Passover supper. The representative elements of bread and cup which he shared with his disciples, symbolized his self-sacrificial suffering and death and mediated for them God's requirement of sacrificial obedience in their future ministry, even if it meant suffering and death. In 26:28 (also 1:21), Matthew uses the term *sins* (ἁμαρτιῶν), highlighting the purpose of Jesus the Son of Man's mission—his blood shed for the forgiveness of sins for the many (20:28). The Son of Man willingly obeyed God's will through his sacrificial death for all humans, so they could seek forgiveness for their sins and inherit eternal life. He will celebrate with his followers in his Father's kingdom the meaning behind his sacrifice— namely, God's grace and mercy mediated through Jesus's suffering and death. In Gethsemane, Jesus's prayer to his Father emphasized his willingness to submit to God's will. When he asked his Father if the cup could be taken from him, he willingly expressed his desire to follow God's will above his own (26:39, 42). These two references of Jesus's desire to obey God's will emphasized his total submission to his Father; a detail only mentioned once in Mark and absent in Luke. In Matthew, the ultimate proof of genuine discipleship and commitment to God is one's dedication to yield completely to God's will (cf. 7:21; 12:50; 21:31–32). Jesus told his disciples that the time had come for the Son of Man to be betrayed and arrested, and commanded them to *rise up* (ἐγείρεσθε) and go with him so he could be betrayed into the hands of sinners (26:45b–46). Jesus's acceptance of God's will (26:39, 42) and his insistence to go to the place of his arrest, which would result in his subsequent suffering and death (26:45b–46), mediated for his disciples the importance of complete obedience to God's will through resolutely drinking the cup of suffering and death according to the Father's plan (cf. 16:21; 17:21–23; 20:17–19; 26:2). In 26:50–53, the Roman soldiers laid their hands on Jesus and arrested him (cf. 17:22; 26:45). One of Jesus's disciples took a sword and cut off the servant of the high priest's ear. Jesus commanded his disciple to stop the violent behavior because such actions were in opposition to God's will. As seen earlier in Matthew, words or actions against Jesus's fate are of satanic origin and, consequently, were not aligned with God's plan (cf. 4:1–11; 16:23). Jesus stated that he could have asked for angelic help, but his resilient focus to suffer and die was demonstrated when he mentioned the scriptures and the prophets to emphasize that obedience to God's will must always come first (26:53–54, 56; see also 16:21; 26:24). Mark and Luke do not stress Jesus's foreknowledge of God's will revealed in the scriptures and his unwillingness to seek divine aid as Matthew does. Matthew grounds Jesus's voluntary death with his obedience to God's will in a different way from the other Synoptic Gospels. Matthew 26 clearly demonstrates the Son of Man's complete submission to God's will through his committed obedience to follow the road to suffering and death. Similarly, genuine disciples must choose to put God's will above all else even unto their own suffering (persecution) and death (emphasized in 16:21–27). Jesus the Son of Man fulfilled God's will through obedience when he knew it would lead to his arrest and death, which mediated for his disciples the kind of obedient self-sacrificing ministry expected from them and other future followers who are resolutely focused on fulfilling God's will for their lives.

3.4. The Son of Man's Parousia: The Mediator of Promised Vindication and Reward for Faithful Obedience to God's Will in Matthew

In chapter 4, I demonstrated that the Son of Man functioned as the mediator of the Father's judgment, vindication, and reward for faithful disciples who have obeyed God's will throughout their lives and ministry. At Jesus's parousia, he will judge individuals based on whether they have lived obediently, and remained faithful to him.

The Son of Man will separate the children of the kingdom from the children of the evil one at his parousia, rewarding faithful disciples and punishing the evil ones (13:24–30, 36–43). At the Son of Man's parousia, he will separate his faithful disciples from those who practice evil and cause others to sin. Before the parousia, the children of the kingdom and children of the evil one will be mixed together. With the evil ones among them, Jesus warned the children of the kingdom that they might uproot them. However, Jesus provided opportunity for the unfaithful to remain with the righteous, as an act of patience, mercy, and grace by God (13:27–30). Earlier in Matthew, Jesus stated his concern for the great harvest of people who had not heard the good news or experienced the itinerant ministry of his disciples (9:37–38), a ministry directed both to Jews and Gentiles (10:5–7, 18, 23). As Jesus and John the Baptist proclaimed, the good news centered on repenting for one's sins because the kingdom of the heavens is near (3:2; 4:17; 10:7). In addition, the Son of Man's mission was to mediate God the Father's grace and mercy towards humanity by providing the means of the forgiveness of sins through his sacrificial suffering and death (e.g., 20:17–19, 28; 26:28). The disciples's ministry to the Israelite cities was to continue until after Jesus's resurrection (10:23). Then Jesus would commission them to minister to all the nations (28:18–20). In 24:14, Jesus said that the good news would be preached to all the nations before his parousia. Therefore, while warning the believers that others will try to lead them away from their faith, Jesus called his genuine disciples to influence sinners through

CONCLUSION: THE SON OF MAN AS MEDIATOR IN MATTHEW 215

preaching and teaching the good news. God's mercy and compassion for the unrighteous are accentuated in the time before the Son of Man's parousia (cf. 9:9–13; 12:7). In 13:36–40, Jesus described the Son of Man's role as the one who revealed and demonstrated the good news, and, consequently, produced children of the kingdom. In contrast, the children of the evil one are under the devil's authority. At the parousia, the angels will gather together the sons of the evil one and throw them into the fire where there will be weeping and gnashing of teeth. The evil ones are characterized by (1) lawlessness, or acts that demonstrate disobedience to God's word (cf. 7:21–23, 26–27; 23:2–3, 27–28), and (2) acts against others, such as causing others to fall away from their faith, preventing them from receiving the gospel message, or hating others and demonstrating a lack of love in violation to the command to love God and others (cf. 18:6–7, 23:13–15; 24:10–12 [22:37–40]). In contrast, the righteous ones are characterized as slaves of the master (13:27–30), who obey his commands as revealed in the scriptures (cf. 7:21–25). Specifically, these righteous ones are servants/ slaves who are willing to love and sacrifice their lives for others, especially in their care and help for the needy, obeying the commands to love God and others (cf. 20:26–28; 22:37–40). In the parable of the wheat and weeds, the Son of Man is the judge who has complete authority over his angels and the fate of the children of the kingdom and children of the devil. The evil ones, who disobey God's will, receive eternal separation from God, the ultimate torment, which causes weeping and gnashing of teeth. In contrast, the righteous ones will inherit eternal life for their faithful obedience to God's will (cf. 16:24–27). As judge, the Son of Man will mediate individuals's eschatological fate based on whether they have faithfully obeyed God's will in their lives. The children of the kingdom are vindicated and rewarded for their commitment to living according to God's will.

The Son of Man will vindicate and reward faithful disciples for their lifelong renunciation of temporal possessions and people and for life in obedience to God's will (16:21–27; 19:16–30). In 16:21–26, the comparison between Jesus and his disciples provides the reason for the Son of Man's eschatological reward for faithful followers at his parousia in 16:27. The phrase *it is necessary* (δεῖ) in 16:21 accentuates Jesus's understanding that self-sacrificial suffering and death was required in obeying God's will. Similarly, faithful disciples will recognize that they will be expected to deny themselves, take up their cross, and continually follow Jesus. The disciples are called to emulate Jesus's ministry by being willing to obey God's will faithfully even if doing so means suffering and death (cf. 5:10–12; 10:16–22). In 10:37–39, faithful disciples are those who put Jesus above everyone else and pick up their cross and follow him; they are worthy of him and will be rewarded with eternal life (cf. 19:27–29). In 16:27, the Son of Man will come with his angels in the glory of his Father at the parousia, and he will vindicate and reward each person based on his or her actions, specifically, voluntary sacrifice of life in allegiance to Jesus and God's will.[8] Jesus will receive vindication and reward through his resurrection from death (16:21), and so will faithful disciples be promised vindication and eternal life as their reward for sacrificing their lives for Jesus's sake. Jesus the Son of Man mediated promised reward to genuine disciples who, like him, are willing to give up their lives even onto death in obedience to God's will. In addition, the Son of Man will mediate the Father's promised reward of eternal life for those who practice self-denial and who continue to follow God's will obediently throughout their lives. At his parousia, the Son of Man will vindicate genuine disciples for the suffering, persecution, and reproach they have experienced in fulfilling God's will.

In 19:16–20, the rich young man is contrasted with genuine disciples of Jesus. Jesus offered the rich young man an opportunity to be morally complete by following his commands to go, sell his possessions, and give to the poor to attain treasure in the heavens (19:21–22). However, the rich young man heard Jesus's word and chose to disobey it. Only through God's power could the rich man be saved and considered a genuine disciple (19:26). The choice to keep his earthly possessions proved that this rich young man was unwilling to accept Jesus's offer of salvation and receive the gift of eternal life (19:23–26). Peter stated that he and the other disciples gave up everything to follow Jesus and inquired on their reward for faithfulness (19:27). Jesus promised that those who continued to persevere in following him throughout their lives or until his parousia, would be rewarded with eternal life when the Son of Man establishes his renewed world after his eschatological judgement has been completed (cf. 19:28; 25:31). In other words, after sinners are sent to eternal torment and evil has been destroyed, the faithful followers of Jesus will be given their reward in his regenerated world. When the Son of Man comes as judge at his parousia, vindication and eschatological reward will be given to his committed followers (cf. 13:43; 16:27; 24:13, 30–31, 46–47; 25:19–23, 34, 46b). In the Son of Man's renewed world, his twelve apostles will sit on twelve thrones ruling over the twelve tribes of Israel. In Matthew, only the Son of Man has the authority to judge (cf. 13:40–43; 16:27; 24:30–31; 25:31–32, 46). Therefore, the disciples will have some kind of administrative, governmental authority over the tribes of

---

8. Mark and Luke emphasize that the Son of Man will reject those who are ashamed of him and his words at his parousia. However, Matthew's account is different. The Son of Man will come with his angels for the purpose of recompense—rewarding genuine disciples for faithful self-denial.

Israel but will not share the role of judging, which is reserved for the Son of Man alone. In addition, they will be rewarded because they have willingly relinquished possessions (home, land) and family relationships (i.e., brothers, sisters, father, mother, and children) on account of Jesus's name (19:29).[9] In 5:10–11, 10:18, 39, and 16:25, the disciples will have endured persecution and even possible death on Jesus's behalf (see also 10:37–39; 16:24–26). At his parousia, the Son of Man will mediate promised vindication and reward for faithful disciples who have emulated the kind of persecution, reproach, and even possible death that he experienced (16:24–26) and who have relinquished earthly possessions and family relationships (19:27, 29) all in obedience to God's will for their lives and ministry.

The Son of Man will vindicate and reward faithful disciples for their endurance of lifelong persecution and their obedient watchfulness until his parousia (24:3–51). Matthew 24:3–51 solely relates events preceding the Son of Man's parousia (24:4–28) and the circumstances surrounding his return as judge (24:29–51). Matthew 24:1–2 connects specifically to 23:37–39, emphasizing the rejection and persecution of Jesus's messengers (23:32–36) and the consequent judgment of the destruction of Jerusalem and its temple in AD 70. The connection between 24:1–2 and 23:37–39 is not a concern in the contexts of Mark 13:1–2 and Luke 21:5–6. Jesus left the temple, signifying its future destruction due to the Pharisees's, other religious leaders's, and Jerusalem residents's rejection of God's will (23:37—24:2). Jesus began his eschatological discourse by warning his disciples of future opposition to him and their ministry. False prophets and false christs will emerge to deceive people, wars will occur among nations, and the disciples will be hated and undergo persecution due to their allegiance to Jesus (also 7:15–20; 10:16–23; 11:12). Those who oppose the disciples will also lead many people into sin and will be characterized by lawlessness, which, consequently, will cause them to behave in unloving ways towards others (24:10–12). Mark and Luke do not mention these important areas of sinful disposition demonstrated by those who are against Jesus's followers. In Matthew, false prophets, the Pharisees, and scribes exemplify those who are lawless (cf. 7:23; also hypocritical and impure, 23:27–28) and, therefore, are disobedient to God's will, which is represented through Jesus and

---

9. Matthew's emphasis on reward for faithfulness is developed more than in Luke. The rich man's refusal to obey Jesus's command of self-renunciation meant he was unwilling to become perfect (Matt 19:21–22). In addition, the recompense of the disciples's administrative authority in the Son of Man's renewed world stresses the Son of Man's mediation of vindication and reward for faithful disciples (19:25, 28–29). Luke does not mention the Son of Man's call for perfection nor the eschatological benefit of a governmental role for the disciples in this context.

the disciples's itinerant ministry. However, genuine disciples who endure in their loyalty to Jesus and their obedience to the mission Jesus required of them demonstrate God's will (cf. 10:1–40 [esp. 10:22]; 24:13). In commitment to God's will, the disciples would announce the good news in the cities of Israel after the Son of Man's resurrection (10:23) and to the entire world until the Son of Man's parousia (24:14; 28:18–20).[10] When the Son of Man comes, he will be the mediator of vindication and reward for his future disciples because they have fulfilled God's will. He will grant them eternal life for their enduring loyalty to Jesus especially in times of persecution and their commitment to announce the good news throughout the world until his parousia. In 24:15–31, Jesus spoke about the events that will immediately precede the Son of Man's parousia. Matthew 24:15 specifically warns about the abomination of desolation spoken about in Daniel the prophet, which would stand in the holy place. An antichrist figure will emerge and be the epitome of opposition to both Jerusalem and the church, and he will lawlessly desecrate the temple (cf. Dan 12:1–13; 2 Thess 2:1–17). In Dan 12:1–13, Matt 24, and 2 Thess 2:1–17, the importance of faithful endurance until the end, judgment on evil and especially the antichrist, and the vindication for those who continually follow Jesus are accentuated. The Son of Man is mediator of God's promised vindication and reward for his future disciples who chose to endure during the increase of persecution, the rise of lawlessness, and the period of the antichrist by remaining faithful to him. Genuine disciples must be willing to relinquish temporal attachments and pleasures (24:17–19, 37–44) and focus more attentively on being ready when the Son of Man returns (cf. 6:19–21, 24, 33; 19:16–30).[11] They were to disregard the Sabbath legal requirements of not traveling in obedience to Jesus's command to leave all behind and prepare themselves for the eschaton (24:20). The increase of persecution and false teaching will shorten the days of the Son of Man's return (24:21–26); therefore, future disciples must be focused solely on preparing themselves for his arrival (24:42–44). Future disciples who choose to obey God's will during the difficult times of persecution and loss will be vindicated and rewarded by the Son of Man

---

10. Matthew's emphasis of preaching the good news throughout the present and the future ministry of the disciples (cf. 10:23; 24:14; 28:18–20) is not found in Mark and Luke. In Matthew, the Son of Man will judge based on whether his followers have proclaimed the good news in obedience to God's will.

11. Matthew's eschatological discourse emphasizes the Son of Man's imminent return more than Mark and Luke (cf. 24:27, 30, 44). The emphasis on the parousia in Matthew is intended to encourage faithful disciples to remain committed throughout these perilous times, so they will be ready to receive the promised vindication and reward when the Son of Man returns.

at this parousia. Jesus the Son of Man is the mediator of vindication and reward for faithful, enduring disciples.

In 24:27-35, Jesus spoke about the imminent signs and events of his parousia as the Son of Man. No one will be able to deny the eschatological signs of his return, which are manifested in the celestial changes in the skies (24:27-29). Jesus himself will be the sign of the Son of Man in heaven who appears returning on the clouds of heaven with power and great glory (cf. 16:27; 19:28; 25:31). The tribes of the earth will mourn due to their rejection of the Son of Man. In contrast to the tribes's sorrow, the Son of Man's angels will gather the chosen ones (24:30-31). As all humanity witnesses the Son of Man's glorious parousia, they will recognize that only faithful disciples will be gathered for future reward. The Son of Man is the mediator of the promised reward to those genuine disciples who have lived fulfilling God's will through their enduring faith and obedience. In contrast, false prophets (24:11, 24), false christs (25:5, 24), false disciples (24:48-51), the tribes of the earth (24:30), and many others (24:37-41) will not be prepared when the Son of Man returns. As in the days of Noah, judgment will fall on all humanity. Like Noah, genuine disciples will be saved because they obeyed God's will (24:13), but the wicked will perish because they neglected to obey God by continuing in sinful living (24:38, 48-51). Jesus further defined what he meant by staying awake and being ready in his analogy between a wise and faithful slave and a wicked slave (24:42-51). The wise and faithful servant is blessed because he continually did his job of managing the master's household, thereby obeying the will of God (cf. 24:46; cf. 7:21; 12:50). The faithful servant is compared with genuine disciples who are committed to obeying Jesus, enduring in their faithful allegiance to God and his will to the end (10:22; 24:13). In contrast, the wicked servant acted sinfully towards others and with others and was not prepared at the master's unexpected hour. Like the Pharisees and the scribes, the wicked servant lived lawlessly, led others into sin, and did not love others (13:41; 23:28; 24:10-12). Such behavior is incongruent with genuine disciples who are called to obey God's will by loving him entirely and loving others (even one's enemies; 22:37-40; 5:48). Consequently, the wicked slave is considered a hypocrite and will be sent to eternal torment, the place reserved for all offensive things and the ones practicing lawlessness (not loving others; 23:28, 33; 24:10-12).[12] Throughout the eschatological discourse, Jesus emphasized that at the Son of Man's parousia

---

12. Luke's reference to the parable of the wise and wicked servant is not contained in his eschatological discourse (cf. 12:42-46). Once again, Matthew's emphasis is on being ready (i.e., faithful and obedient) when the Son of Man returns. Judgment includes both reward and punishment based on how genuine and prepared disciples are at the time of the imminent parousia.

he will be the mediator of vindication and promised reward for those faithful disciples who obediently follow the God's will.

The Son of Man will separate the righteous ones from the evil ones based on their love for God and for neighbors according to God's will (25:31–46). The judgment scene in 25:31–46 begins with the Son of Man's parousia. As in 16:27, 19:28, and 24:30, 25:31 emphasizes the eschatological return of the Son of Man, specifically as it relates to reward (cf. 13:43; 16:27; 19:28; 24:31) and judgment (13:40–42; 24:30). Matthew 25:31–46 is the climax of Jesus's eschatological discourse (24:3–51). At judgment, a nondescript universal group of people (i.e., all the nations) will appear before the Son of Man either to be rewarded or punished based on their acts of love and mercy to the needy (24:30, 37–39; 25:32; 28:19). As in 13:36–43, the Son of Man will gather together the nations and separate them—the sheep on his right and the goats on his left (25:32–33). As in 20:20–28, the right and left are viewed as places relating to status. In contrast to the mother of the sons of Zebedee's request of an elevated positions in God's kingdom, Jesus spoke about what was essential and more important—being a servant and slave to others, like the Son of Man who would endure suffering and death to ransom the many (cf. 23:11–12). Jesus identified himself as a lowly criminal (with other criminals on his left and right) before others, even though he was, in reality, sacrificing himself as a servant according to God's will (27:38). Therefore, exalted positions at the parousia will be given to those who have fulfilled God's will by being a servant and slave to others, emulating the sacrificial servanthood of Jesus.

Similarly to 20:26–28, Jesus the Son of Man mediated God's will to his disciples by teaching them the importance of servanthood as the ethics of God's kingdom and by demonstrating servanthood through his self-sacrificial death. The six deeds of servanthood in 25:35–36 represent acts of mercy for others, which, as demonstrated in Jesus's ministry, were mandatory for those who practice God's will (cf. 5:7; 9:9–13; 11:19; 12:1–13; 20:26–34; 23:23). Jesus quoted Hos 6:6, "I desire [will; θέλω] mercy not sacrifice," to emphasize that mercy for others is grounded in God's will. The sheep are considered righteous because they are committed to obeying God's will as outlined in the six acts of servanthood. In Matthew, people prove their love for God through loving others, even one's enemies (22:37–40; 5:43–48). The identity of the recipients of the six acts of servanthood is all who are in need, a universal understanding of the least of my brothers and the least ones (25:40, 45). In Matthew, *brother* (ἀδελφός) is not specifically spoken of as a disciple or a Christian person (e.g., 5:21–26, 43–48) and is found in contexts that relate to demonstrating one's love to God through one's love for neighbors (22:37–40). These righteous ones emulate Jesus by extending his merciful acts to all people not just to a particular group of people (e.g., 4:23–25; 9:1–35; 15:21–39). Similarly to Jesus, the righteous ones will be merciful and loving to all the needy (25:34–40), fulfilling the command to love their neighbors (22:39), and will be rewarded by shining as the sun in the Father's kingdom (13:43; i.e., eternal life in 25:46). In contrast to the righteous ones, the ones on the Son of Man's left will be judged for their lifelong rejection of those in need. These unmerciful people demonstrate their lack of concern and love for others by not attending to human needs (25:41–43). They might consider themselves Jesus's followers, but their lack of love and mercy towards others is demonstrated in their unconcern to practice acts of servanthood and, consequently, disobedience to God's will (cf. 7:21–23; 13:49; 23:27–28; 24:11, 45–51). At judgment, the Son of Man will send them away to eternal punishment (25:46). The Son of Man will return at judgment to mediate the promised reward of eternal life for those righteous ones who have obeyed God's will by practicing loving, merciful deeds towards others in the needy world.

The Son of Man will vindicate and reward all faithful disciples who put God's plans above those who are in opposition to God and his will (26:63–66). Before Caiaphas, Jesus did not defend himself before his accusers or correct Caiaphas's statement, "You are the Christ, the Son of God" (26:63), but remained silent and added to Caiaphas's remark concerning Jesus's divine identity (26:64).[13] In 26:64, Matthew combined Ps 110:1 and Dan 7:13 in Jesus's response to Caiaphas: "From now on [ἀπ' ἄρτι] you will see [ὄψεσθε] the Son of Man." Jesus was referring to two separate periods: (1) to his resurrection and exaltation (time of Jesus's vindication; Ps 110:1) and (2) indicating his parousia (time of Jesus's judgment; Dan 7:13). In all three Son of Man passion predictions, both Jesus's death in obedience to God's will and his vindication through his resurrection are emphasized (cf. 16:21; 17:22; 20:17–19). In Matthew, Jesus's vindication from death through his resurrection and exaltation are emphasized in the events surrounding his crucifixion and resurrection (cf. 27:51–53, 62–66; 28:11–18). In 16:27–28, Jesus's vindication from death provided hope and promise for the disciples; they will be vindicated and rewarded at the Son of Man's parousia for their faithful endurance, love for others, and, generally, vigilant obedience to God's will (see also 19:28; 24; 25:14–46). Jesus the Son of Man is the mediator of promised vindication and reward for his faithful

13. In Matthew, Jesus's answer to Caiaphas is constructed more as a need for further explanation: "You have said it; but I say to you, from now on you will see the Son of Man ... " (26:64). The emphasis on an accurate assessment of the Son of Man's role as judge appears more essential in the Matthean account than what is recorded in Mark 14:62 and Luke 22:67–69.

followers who do his Father's will. Caiaphas stated Jesus's revelation in 26:64 was blasphemous speech. In his estimation, Jesus spoke against God and his temple/ordained leaders, intruded into God's divine prerogatives, and called God's uniqueness into question (26:61–62; cf. 27:40; 9:1–9; 12:1–14; 15:1–14; 23 [where Jesus urged the crowds and his disciples not to emulate the practices of the Pharisees and scribes]). Jesus the Son of Man's vindication through resurrection, his reward through exaltation, and role as judge mediated for his future disciples their vindication over death and reward for faithful obedience to God's will.

Bibliography

Agbanou, Victor Kossi. *Le Discours Eschatologique de Matthieu 24-25: Tradition et Rédaction*. Études bibliques 2. Paris: J. Gabalda, 1983.
Aland, Kurt, and Barbara Aland. *The Text of the New Testament*. Translated by Erroll F. Rhodes. Grand Rapids: Eerdmans, 1987.
Albright, W. F., and C. S. Mann. *Matthew: Introduction, Translation, and Notes*. Anchor Bible 26. New York: Doubleday, 1971.
Allen, E. L. "On This Rock." *Journal of Theological Studies* 5 (1954) 60–62.
Allen, Willoughby C. *A Critical and Exegetical Commentary of the Gospel according to St. Matthew*. 3rd ed. International Critical Commentary 25. Edinburgh: T. & T Clark, 1912.
Allison, Dale C., Jr. "Elijah Must Come First." *Journal of Biblical Literature* 103 (1984) 256–58.
———. "Torah, Urzeit, Endzeit." In *Resurrecting Jesus: The Earliest Christian Traditions and Its Interpreters*, 49–97. New York: T. & T. Clark, 2005.
———. "Two Notes on a Key Text: Matthew 11:25–30." *Journal of Theological Studies* 39 (1988) 477–85.
Anderson, Joel Edmund. "Jonah in Mark and Matthew: Creation, Covenant, Christ, and the Kingdom of God." *Biblical Theological Bulletin* 42 (2012) 172–86.
Bacchiocchi, Samuele. "Matthew 11:28–30: Jesus' Rest and the Sabbath." *Andrews University Seminary Studies* 22 (1984) 289–316.
Bahnsen, Greg L. "The Theonomic Reformed Approach to Law and Gospel." In *Five Views on Law and Gospel*, edited by Greg L. Bahnsen et al., 102–15. Counterpoints. Grand Rapids: Zondervan, 1996.
Baldwin, Joyce D. *Daniel*. Tyndale Old Testament Commentaries. Downers Grove, IL: InterVarsity, 1978.
Banks, Robert. *Jesus and the Law in the Synoptic Tradition*. Society for New Testament Studies Monograph Series 28. Cambridge: Cambridge University Press, 1975.
Barbour, R. J. "Gethsemane in the Tradition of the Passion." *New Testament Studies* 16 (1970) 231–51.
Barnett, Paul. "Who Were the *Biastai* (Mt 11:12–13)?" *Reformed Theological Review* 36 (1977) 65–70.
Barrett, C. K. "The Background of Mark 10:45." In *New Testament Essays: Studies in Memory of Thomas Walter Manson 1893–1958*, edited by A. J. B. Higgins, 1–15. Manchester: Manchester University Press, 1959.
———. *The Holy Spirit and the Gospel Tradition*. London: SPCK, 1966.

Barth, Gerhard. "Matthew's Understanding of the Law." In *Tradition and Interpretation in Matthew*, by Günther Bornkamm et al., 58–159. London: SCM, 1982.

Bauer, David R. "Son of David." In *Dictionary of Jesus and the Gospels*, edited by Joel B. Green and Scot McKnight, 766–69. Downers Grove, IL: InterVarsity, 1992.

———. *The Structure of Matthew's Gospel: A Study in Literary Design*. Journal for the Study of the New Testament Supplement Series 31. Bible and Literature Series 15. Sheffield: Almond, 1989.

Baur, Ferdinand Christian. *Kritische Untersuchungen über die Kanonischen Evangelien*. Tübingen: Fues, 1847.

Bayer, Hans F. *Jesus' Predictions of Vindication and Resurrection: The Provenance, Meaning, and Correlation of the Synoptic Predictions*. Wissenschaftliche Untersuchungen zum Neuen Testament 2/20. Tübingen: Mohr Siebeck, 1986.

Beare, Francis W. *The Gospel according to Matthew: Translation, Introduction, and Commentary*. Peabody, MA: Hendrickson, 1981.

Beasley-Murray, George R. *Jesus and the Kingdom of God*. Grand Rapids: Eerdmans, 1985.

———. *Jesus and the Last Days: The Interpretation of the Olivet Discourse*. Peabody, MA: Hendrickson, 1993.

Bennett, W. J., Jr. "The Son of Man Must . . . " *Novum Testamentum* 17 (1975) 113–29.

Benoit, Pierre. *L'Évangile selon Saint Matthieu*. La Sainte Bible traduite en fraçais sous la direction de l'école biblique de Jérusalem Bible. Paris: Les Éditions du Cerf, 1961.

Betz, Hans Dieter. "The Logion of the Easy Yoke and of Rest (Matt 11:28–30)." *Journal of Biblical Literature* 86 (1967) 10–24.

———. *The Sermon on the Mount: A Commentary on the Sermon on the Mount, including the Sermon on the Plain (Matthew 5:3—7:27 and Luke 6:20–49)*. Hermeneia. Minneapolis: Fortress, 1995.

Beyer, Herman Wolfgang. "βλασφημέω, βλασφημία, βλάσφημος." In vol. 1 of *Theological Dictionary of the New Testament*, edited by Gerhard Kittel and translated by Geoffrey W. Bromiley, 621–25. Grand Rapids: Eerdmans, 1964.

Bird, Michael F. "Jesus as Law-Breaker." In *Who Do My Opponents Say that I Am? An Investigation of the Accusations against Jesus*, edited by Scot McKnight and Joseph B. Modica, 3–26. Library of New Testament Studies 327. London: T. & T. Clark, 2008.

Blomberg, Craig L. *Matthew: An Exegetical and Theological Exposition of Holy Scripture*. New American Commentary 22. Nashville: Broadman, 1992.

Bock, Darrell L. *Blasphemy and Exaltation in Judaism: The Charge against Jesus in Mark 14:53–65*. Biblical Studies Library. Grand Rapids: Baker, 2000.

———. *Blasphemy and Exaltation in Judaism and the Final Examination of Jesus*. Wissenschaftliche Untersuchungen zum Neuen Testament 2/106. Tübingen: Mohr Siebeck, 1998.

———. *Luke*. Vol. 2. Baker Exegetical Commentary on the New Testament 3. Grand Rapids: Baker, 1996.

Bonnard, Pierre. *L'Évangile selon Saint Matthieu*. 2nd ed. Commentaire du Noveau Testament 1. Neuchâtel: Éditions Delachaux & Niestlé, 1970.

Boring, M. Eugene. "The Gospel of Matthew." In vol. 8 of *The New Interpreter's Bible*, edited by Leander E. Keck, 87–506. Nashville: Abingdon, 1994.

Bornkamm, Günther. "End-Expectation and Church in Matthew." In *Tradition and Interpretation in Matthew*, by Günther Bornkamm et al., 15–51. 2nd ed. London: SCM, 1982.

———. *Jesus of Nazareth*. Translated by Irene and Fraser McLuskey. New York: Harper, 1960.

———. "The Stilling of the Storm in Matthew." In *Tradition and Interpretation in Matthew*, by Günther Bornkamm et al., 52–57. 2nd ed. London: SCM, 1982.

Brandenburger, Egon. *Das Recht des Weltenrichters: Untersuchung zu Matthäus 25, 31–46*. Stuttgarten Bibelstudien 99. Stuttgart: Katholisches Bibelwerk, 1980.

Broer, Ingo. "Redaktionsgeschichtliche Aspekte von Mt 24:1–28." *Novum Testamentum* 35 (1993) 209–33.

Brown, Raymond E. *The Death of the Messiah: From Gethsemane to the Grave: A Commentary on the Passion Narratives in the Four Gospels*. 2 vols. New York: Doubleday, 1994.

Brown, Raymond E., et al., eds. *Peter in the New Testament: A Collaborative Assessment by Protestant and Roman Catholic Scholars*. Minneapolis: Augsburg, 1973.

Brown, Schuyler. "The Matthean Apocalypse." *Journal for the Study of the New Testament* 4 (1979) 2–27.

Bruner, Frederick Dale. *Matthew: A Commentary*. 2 vols. Rev. ed. Grand Rapids: Eerdmans, 2004.

Büchsel, Friedrich. "δέω (λύω)." In vol. 2 of *Theological Dictionary of the New Testament*, edited by Gerhard Kittel, 60–61. Translated by Geoffrey W. Bromiley. Grand Rapids: Eerdmans, 1964.

———. "λύτρον." In vol. 4 of *Theological Dictionary of the New Testament*, edited by Gerhard Kittel, 340–56. Translated by Geoffrey W. Bromiley. Grand Rapids: Eerdmans, 1967.

Bultmann, Rudolf. *History of the Synoptic Tradition*. Translated by John Marsh. Rev. ed. Peabody, MA: Hendrickson, 1963.

———. *Theology of the New Testament: Complete in One Volume*. Translated by Kendrick Grobel. Scribner Studies in Contemporary Theology. New York: Scribner's, 1951, 1955.

Burnett, Fred W. "Παλιγγενεσία in Matt 19:28: A Window on the Matthean Community?" *Journal for the Study of the New Testament* 17 (1983) 60–72.

———. *The Testament of Jesus-Sophia: A Redaction-Critical Study of the Eschatological Discourse in Matthew*. Washington, DC: University Press of America, 1979.

Byrskog, Samuel. *Jesus the Only Teacher: Didactic Authority and Transmission in Ancient Israel, Ancient Judaism, and the Matthean Community*. Coniectanea Biblica: New Testament Studies 24. Stockholm: Almqvist and Wiksell, 1994.

Calvin, John. *Commentary on a Harmony of the Evangelists, Matthew, Mark, and Luke*. Translated by William Pringle. 3 vols. Grand Rapids: Eerdmans, 1949.

Cameron, Peter Scott. *Violence and the Kingdom: The Interpretation of Matthew 11:12*. Arbeiten zum Neuen Testament und Judentum. Frankfurt am Main: Peter Lang, 1984.

Campbell, J. Y. "The Origin and Meaning of the Term 'Son of Man.'" *Journal of Theological Studies* 48 (1947) 145–55.

Caragounis, Chrys C. *Peter and the Rock*. Beihefte zur Zeitschrift für die neutestamentliche Wissenschaft und die Kunde der älteren Kirche 58. Berlin: de Gruyter, 1990.

———. *The Son of Man: Vision and Interpretation*. Wissenschaftliche Untersuchungen zum Neuen Testament 38. Tübingen: Mohr Siebeck, 1986.

Carey, Holly J. "Judas Iscariot: The Betrayer of Jesus." In *Jesus among Friends and Enemies: A Historical and Literary Introduction to Jesus in the Gospels*, edited by Chris Keith and Larry W. Hurtado, 249–67. Grand Rapids: Baker Academic, 2011.

Carroll, John T. *Response to the End of History: Eschatology and Situation in Luke-Acts*. Society of Biblical Literature Dissertation Series 92. Decatur, GA: Scholars, 1988.

Carson, D. A. "Jesus and the Sabbath in the Four Gospels." In *From Sabbath to Lord's Day: A Biblical, Historical, and Theological Investigation*, edited by D. A. Carson, 57–98. Grand Rapids: Zondervan, 1982.

———. *Matthew*. The Expositor's Bible Commentary: With New International Version. 2 vols. Grand Rapids: Zondervan, 1995.

Carter, Warren. *Matthew and the Margins: A Sociopolitical and Religious Reading*. The Bible & Liberation Series. Maryknoll, NY: Orbis, 2000.

Carter, Warren, and John Paul Heil. *Matthew's Parables: Audience-Oriented Perspectives*. The Catholic Biblical Quarterly Monograph Series 30. Washington, DC: Catholic Biblical Association of America, 1998.

Casey, Maurice. *The Solution to the "Son of Man" Problem*. The Library of New Testament Studies 343. London: T. & T. Clark. 2007.

———. *Son of Man: The Interpretation and Influence of Daniel 7*. London: SPCK, 1979.

Catchpole, David R. "The Answer of Jesus to Caiaphas (Matt xxvi 64)." *New Testament Studies* 17 (1971) 213–26.

———. "John the Baptist, Jesus, and the Parable of the Tares." *Scottish Journal of Theology* 31 (1978) 557–70.

———. "On Doing Violence to the Kingdom." *Journal of Theology for South Africa* 25 (1978) 50–61.

———. "The Poor on Earth and the Son of Man in Heaven: A Re-Appraisal of Matthew 25:31–46." *Bulletin of the John Rylands University Library of Manchester* 61 (1979) 355–97.

Charette, Blaine. *The Theme of Recompense in Matthew's Gospel*. Journal for the Study of the New Testament Supplement Series 79. Sheffield: JSOT, 1992.

———. "'To Proclaim Liberty to the Captives': Matthew 11:28–30 in the Light of OT Prophetic Expectation." *New Testament Studies* 38 (1992) 290–97.

Chilton, Bruce. *God in Strength: Jesus' Announcement of the Kingdom*. The Biblical Seminar 8. Sheffield: JSOT, 1987.

Chow, Simon. *The Sign of Jonah Reconsidered: A Study of Its Meaning in the Gospel Traditions*. Coniectanea Biblica: New Testament Series 27. Stockholm: Almqvist and Wiksell, 1995.

Combs, William W. "The Blasphemy against the Holy Spirit." *Detroit Biblical Seminary* 9 (2004) 57–96.

Cooke, Bernard. "Synoptic Presentation of the Eucharist as Covenant Sacrifice." *Theological Studies* 21 (1960) 1–44.

Cope, Lamar. "Matthew XXV 31–46: 'The Sheep and the Goats' Reinterpreted." *Novum Testamentum* 11 (1969) 32–44.

Cotter, Wendy J. "The Parable of the Children in the Market-Place, Q (LK) 7:31–35: An Examination of the Parable's Image and Significance." *Novum Testamentum* 29 (1987) 289–304.

Court, J. M. "Right and Left: the Implications for Matthew 25:31–46." *New Testament Studies* 31 (1985) 223–33.
Cranfield, C. E. B. "Who Are Christ's Brothers (Matthew 25:40)?" *Metanoia (Prague)* 4 (1994) 31–39.
Cullmann, Oscar. *The Christology of the New Testament*. Translated by Shirley C. Guthrie and Charles A. M. Hall. New Testament Library. Philadelphia: Westminster, 1963.
———. *Peter: Disciple, Apostle, Martyr*. Translated by Floyd V. Filson. 2nd rev. ed. Waco, TX: Baylor University Press, 2011.
Cyril of Jerusalem. *The Catechetical Lectures*. In vol. 7 of *Nicene and Post-Nicene Fathers, Second Series*, edited by Philip Schaff and Henry Wace. Translated by Edwin Hamilton Gifford. Buffalo, NY: Christian Literature, 1894. Revised and edited for New Advent by Kevin Knight. Online. http://www.newadvent.org/fathers/310115.htm.
Davies, W. D. "'Knowledge' in the Dead Sea Scrolls and Matthew 11:25–30." *Harvard Theological Review* 46 (1953) 113–40.
———. *The Setting of the Sermon on the Mount*. Cambridge: Cambridge University Press, 1964.
Davies, W. D., and Dale C. Allison Jr. *A Critical and Exegetical Commentary on the Gospel according to Matthew*. 3 vols. International Critical Commentary. Edinburgh: T. & T. Clark, 1988–97.
Davison, James E. "*Anomia* and the Question of an Antinomian Polemic in Matthew." *Journal of Biblical Literature* 104 (1985) 617–35.
Depont, Jacques. "Le logion des douze trônes (Mt 19, 28; Lc 22, 28–30)." *Biblica* 45 (1964) 355–92.
Derrett, J. Duncan M. "A Camel through the Eye of a Needle." *New Testament Studies* 32 (1986) 465–70.
———. *Law in the New Testament*. London: Darton, Longman & Todd, 1970.
———. "Palingenesia (Matt 19:28)." *Journal for the Study of the New Testament* 20 (1984) 51–58.
———. "Thou Art the Stone and upon This Stone." *Downside Review* 106 (1988) 276–85.
Deutsch, Celia. *Hidden Wisdom and the Easy Yoke: Wisdom, Torah, and Discipleship in Matthew 11:25–30*. Journal for the Study of the New Testament Supplement Series 18. Sheffield: JSOT, 1987.
Dienes, Roland. "Not the Law but the Messiah: Law and Righteousness in the Gospel of Matthew: An Ongoing Debate." In *Built upon the Rock: Studies in the Gospel of Matthew*, edited by Daniel M. Gurtner and John Nolland, 53–84. Grand Rapids: Eerdmans, 2007.
Dodd, C. H. "The Fall of Jerusalem and the 'Abomination of Desolation.'" *Journal of Roman Studies* 37 (1947) 47–54.
———. *The Parables of the Kingdom*. Rev. ed. New York: Scribners, 1961.
Donahue, John R. *The Gospel in Parable: Metaphor, Narrative, and Theology in the Synoptic Gospels*. Philadelphia: Fortress, 1988.
———. "Recent Studies on the Origin of 'Son of Man' in the Gospels." *Catholic Biblical Quarterly* 48.3 (1986) 484–98.
Donaldson, Amy M. "Blasphemy against the Spirit and the Historical Jesus." *Society of Biblical Literature Seminar Papers Series* 42 (2003) 157–71.

Draper, J. A. "The Development of the 'Sign of the Son of Man' in the Jesus Tradition." *New Testament Studies* 39 (1993) 1–21.

Dunn, James D. G. *Jesus and the Spirit: A Study of the Religious and Charismatic Experience of Jesus and the First Christians as Reflected in the New Testament.* Grand Rapids: Eerdmans, 1997.

———. *Jesus, Paul, and the Law: Studies in Mark and Galatians.* Louisville: Westminster John Knox, 1990.

Edanad, Antony. "Institution of the Eucharist according to the Synoptic Gospels." *Bible Bhashyam* 4 (1978) 322–32.

Edin, Mary H. "Learning What Righteousness Means: Hosea 6:6 and the Ethic of Mercy in Matthew's Gospel." *World and Word* 18 (1988) 355–63.

Edwards, Richard Alan. *The Sign of Jonah: In the Theology of the Evangelists and Q.* Studies in Biblical Theology Second Series 18. Napperville: Alec R. Allenson, 1971.

Eubanks, Nathan. *Wages of Cross-Bearing and the Debt of Sin: The Economy of Heaven in Matthew's Gospel.* Beihefte zur Zeitschrift für die neutestamentliche Wissenschaft und die Kunde der älteren Kirche 196. Berlin: de Gruyter, 2013.

Evans, Craig A. "In What Sense 'Blasphemy': Jesus Before Caiaphas in Mark 16:61–64." *Society of Biblical Literature Seminar Papers* 30 (1991) 215–34.

———. *Matthew.* New Cambridge Bible Commentary. New York: Cambridge University Press, 2012.

Fenton, John C. *The Gospel of St. Matthew.* The Pelican Gospel Commentaries. Harmondsworth: Penguin, 1964.

Feuillet, André. "Les Origines et la Signification de Mt 10, 23b: Contribution a L'Étudie du Problème Eschatologique." *Catholic Biblical Quarterly* 23 (1961) 182–98.

———. "Le Triomphe du Fils de L'Homme: D' Après la Dèclaration du Christ aux Sanhédrites (Mc., xiv, 62, Mt. xxvi, 64; Lc. xxii, 69)." In *La Venue du Messie: Messianisme et Eschatologie,* edited by Édouard Massaux, 149–71. Recherches bibliques 6. Lovanii: Descleé de Brouwer, 1962.

Foerster, Werner. "βδελύσσομαι, βδέλυγμα, βδελυκτός." In vol. 1 of *Theological Dictionary of the New Testament,* edited by Gerhard Kittel, 598–600. Translated by Geoffrey W. Bromiley. Grand Rapids: Eerdmans, 1964.

Ford, Desmond. *The Abomination of Desolation in Biblical Eschatology.* Washington, DC: University Press of America, 1979.

Foster, Paul. *Community, Law, and Mission in Matthew's Gospel.* Wissenschaftliche Untersuchungen zum Neuen Testament 2/177. Tübingen: Mohr Siebeck, 2004.

France, R. T. *The Gospel of Matthew.* The New International Commentary on the New Testament. Grand Rapids: Eerdmans, 2007.

———. *Jesus and the Old Testament: His Application of the Old Testament Passages to Himself and His Mission.* 1st ed. Grand Rapids: Tyndale, 1971.

———. "The Servant of the Lord in the Teaching of Jesus." *Tyndale Bulletin* 19 (1968) 26–52.

Fuller, Reginald H. "The Double Origin of the Eucharist." *Biblical Research* 8 (1963) 60–72.

———. *The Foundations of New Testament Christology.* New York: Scribners, 1965.

Gaechter, Paul. *Die literarische Kunst im Matthäus-Evangelium.* Stuttgarter Bibelstudien 7. Stuttgart: Katholisches Bibelwerk, 1965.

Galot, Jean. *Theology of the Priesthood.* Translated by Roger Balducelli. San Francisco: Ignatius, 1984.

Gaston, Lloyd. *No Stone on Another: Studies in the Significance of the Fall of Jerusalem in the Synoptic Gospels.* Supplements to Novum Testamentum 23. Leiden: Brill, 1970.

Geist, Heinz. *Menschensohn und Gemeinde: Eine redaktionskritische Untersuchung zur Menschensohnprädikation im Matthäusevangelium.* Forschung zur Bibel 57. Würzburg: Echter, 1986.

Gempf, Conrad. "Birth-Pangs in the New Testament." *Tyndale Bulletin* 45 (1994) 119–35.

Gerhardsson, Birger. "Sacrificial Service and Atonement in the Gospel of Matthew." In *Reconciliation and Hope: Essays on Atonement and Eschatology: Presented to L. L. Morris on His Sixtieth Birthday,* edited by Robert Banks, 25–35. Grand Rapids: Eerdmans, 1974.

Getty-Sullivan, Mary Ann. *Parables of the Kingdom: Jesus and the Use of Parables in the Synoptic Tradition.* Collegeville, MN: Liturgical, 2007.

Gibbs, Jeffrey A. *Jerusalem and Parousia: Jesus' Eschatological Discourse in Matthew's Gospel.* Saint Louis: Concordia Academic, 2000.

———. *Matthew 1:1—11:1.* Concordia Commentary 1. Saint Louis: Concordia, 2006.

———. *Matthew 11:2—20:34.* Concordia Commentary 2. Saint Louis: Concordia, 2010.

Giblin, Charles H. "Theological Perspective and Matthew 10:23b." *Theological Studies* 29 (1968) 637–61.

Glasson, T. Francis. "The Ensign of the Son of Man." *Journal of Theological Studies* 15 (1964) 299–300.

———. "The Reply to Caiaphas (Mark xiv. 62)." *New Testament Studies* 7 (1960) 88–93.

———. *The Second Advent: The Origin of the New Testament Doctrine.* 2nd rev. ed. London: Epworth, 1945.

Glazener, Clyde G. "An Investigation of Jesus' Usage of the Term Son of Man: A Possible Interpretive Key to the Gospel of Matthew." ThD diss., Southwestern Baptist Theological Seminary, 1974.

Gnilka, Joachim. *Das Mattäusevangelium.* 2 vols. Herders theologischer Kommentar zum Neuen Testament. Freiburg: Herder, 1986, 1988.

Goodacre, Mark. *The Case Against Q: Studies in Markan Priority and the Synoptic Problem.* Harrisburg, PA: Trinity, 2001.

Goulder, Michael. "Psalm 8 and the Son of Man." *New Testament Studies* 48 (2002) 18–29.

Gray, Sherman W. *The Least of My Brothers: Matthew 25:31–46: A History of Interpretation.* Society of Biblical Literature Dissertation Series 114. Atlanta: Scholars, 1989.

Green, Joel B. *The Death of Jesus: Tradition and Interpretation in the Passion Narrative.* Wissenschaftliche Untersuchungen zum Neuen Testament 2/33. Tübingen: Mohr Siebeck, 1988.

———. *The Gospel of Luke.* The New International Commentary of the New Testament. Grand Rapids: Eerdmans, 1997.

Green, Joel B., ed. *Hearing the New Testament: Strategies for Interpretation.* Grand Rapids: Eerdmans, 1995.

Green, Joel B., and Scot McKnight, eds. *Dictionary of Jesus and the Gospels.* Downers Grove, IL: InterVarsity, 1992.

Grimm, Werner. *Weil Ich dich liebe: Die Verkündigung Jesu und Deuterojesaja.* Arbeiten zur Neuen Testament und Judentum. Frankfurt: Peter Lang, 1976.

Grundmann, Walter. *Das Evangelium nach Matthäus*. Theologischer Handkommentar zum Neuen Testament. Berlin: Evangelische Verlagsanstalt, 1972.

Guelich, Robert A. *Not to Annul the Law Rather to Fulfill the Law and the Prophets: An Exegetical Study of Jesus and the Law in Matthew with an Emphasis on 5:17-48*. Hamburg: Universität Hamburg, 1967.

Gundry, Robert H. *Matthew: A Commentary on His Handbook for a Mixed Church under Persecution*. Grand Rapids: Eerdmans, 1994.

―――. *The Use of the Old Testament in St. Matthew's Gospel: With Special Reference to the Messianic Hope*. Supplements to Novum Testamentum 18. Leiden: Brill, 1967.

Gurtner, Daniel M. "Matthew's Theology of the Temple and the 'Parting of Ways.'" In *Built upon the Rock: Studies in the Gospel of Matthew*, edited by Daniel M. Gurtner and John Nolland, 128-53. Grand Rapids: Eerdmans, 2007.

Gutbrod, W. "νόμος." In vol. 4 of *Theological Dictionary of the New Testament*, edited by Gerhard Kittel, 1022-85. Translated by Geoffrey W. Bromiley. Grand Rapids: Eerdmans, 1967.

Hagner, Donald A. *Matthew*. 2 vols. Word Biblical Commentary 33A-B. Dallas: Word, 1993, 1995.

Hahn, Ferdinand. "Die Eschatologische Rede Matthäus 24 und 25." In *Studien zum Matthäusevangelium Festschrift für Wilhelm Pesch*, edited by Ludger Schenke, 116-23. Stuttgarter Bibelstudien. Stuttgart: Katholisches Bibelwerk, 1988.

―――. *The Titles of Jesus in Christology: Their History in Early Christianity*. Translated by Harold Knight and George Ogg. London: Lutterworth, 1969.

Ham, Clay. "The Last Supper in Matthew." *Bulletin for Biblical Research* 10 (2000) 53-69.

Hammerton-Kelly, Robert G. *Pre-Existence, Wisdom, and the Son of Man: A Study of the Idea of Pre-Existence in the New Testament*. Society for New Testament Studies Monograph Series 21. Cambridge: Cambridge University Press, 1973.

Hampel, Volker. *Menschensohn und historischer Jesus: Ein Rätselwort als Schlüssel zum messianischen Selbstverständnis Jesu*. Beiträge zur evangelischen Theologie 33. Neukirchen-Vluyn: Neukirchener, 1990.

Hare, Douglas R. A. *Matthew*. Interpretation: A Bible Commentary for Teaching and Preaching. Louisville: Westminster John Knox, 2009.

―――. *The Son of Man Tradition*. Minneapolis: Fortress, 1990.

―――. *The Theme of Jewish Persecution of Christians in the Gospel according to Matthew*. Society for the New Testament Studies Monograph Series 6. Cambridge: Cambridge University Press, 1967.

Harnack, Adolf von. "Hat Jesus das alttestamentliche Gesetz abgeschafft?" In *Aus Wissenschaft und Leben*, by Adolf von Harnack, 227-36. Reden und Aufsätze 2. Giessen: Alfred Töplemann, 1911.

―――. *Sprüche und Reden Jesu: Die Zweite Quelle des Matthäus und Lukas*. Leipzig: J. C. Hinriches'sche Buchhandlung, 1907.

―――. *Zwei Worte Jesu: Matth. 6,13=Luk. 11,4; Matth. 11,12f=Luk. 16,16*. Berlin: Königlichen Akademie der Wissenschaften in Commission bei G. Reimer, 1907.

Harrington, Daniel J. *The Gospel of Matthew*. Sacra pagina 1. Collegeville, MN: Liturgical, 1991.

Hauerwas, Stanley. *Matthew*. Brazos Theological Commentary on the Bible. Grand Rapids: Brazos, 2006.

Hay, David M. *Glory at the Right Hand: Ps 110 in Early Christianity*. Society of Biblical Literature Monograph Series 18. Nashville: Abingdon, 1973.

Heil, John Paul. *The Death and Resurrection of Jesus: A Narrative-Critical Reading of Matthew 26-28*. Minneapolis: Fortress, 1991.

———. "The Double Meaning of the Narrative of Universal Judgment in Matthew 25:31-46." *Journal for the Study of the New Testament* 69 (1998) 3-14.

———. "Final Parables in the Eschatological Discourse in Matthew 24-25." In *Matthew's Parables: Audience-Oriented Perspectives*, by Warren Carter and John Paul Heil, 177-209. Catholic Biblical Quarterly Monograph Series 30. Washington, DC: Catholic Biblical Association of America, 1998.

Herntrich, Volkmar. "κρίνω." In vol. 3 of *Theological Dictionary of the New Testament*, edited by Gerhard Kittel, 923-33. Translated by Geoffrey W. Bromiley. Grand Rapids: Eerdmans, 1965.

Hertig, Paul. *Matthew's Narrative Use of Galilee in the Multicultural and Missiological Journeys of Jesus*. Mellen Biblical Press Series 46. Lewiston, NY: Edwin Mellen, 1998.

Hicks, John Mark. "The Sabbath Controversy in Matthew: An Exegesis on Matthew 12:1-14." *Restoration Quarterly* 27 (1984) 79-91.

Hiers, Richard. "'Binding' and 'Loosing': The Matthean Authorizations." *Journal of Biblical Literature* 104 (1985) 235-50.

Higgins, A. J. B. "Is the Son of Man Problem Insoluble?" In *Neotestamentica et Semitica: Studies in Honour of Matthew Black*, edited by E. Earle Ellis and Max Wilcox, 70-87. Cambridge: Cambridge University Press, 1969.

———. *Jesus and the Son of Man*. Philadelphia: Fortress, 1964.

———. *The Lord's Supper in the New Testament*. Studies in Biblical Theology 6. Chicago: Henry Regnery, 1952.

———. "The Sign of the Son of Man (Matt XXIV.30)." *New Testament Studies* 9 (1963) 380-82.

———. *The Son of Man in the Teaching of Jesus*. Society for New Testament Studies Monograph Series 39. Cambridge: Cambridge University Press, 1980.

Hill, David. *The Gospel of Matthew*. New Century Bible. London: Oliphants, 1972.

Hoffmann, Paul. *Studien zur Theologie der Logionquelle*. Neutestamentliche Abhandlungen 8. Münster: Aschendorff, 1972.

Hooker, Morna. *Jesus and the Servant: The Influence of the Servant Concept of Deutero-Isaiah in the New Testament*. London: SCPK, 1959.

———. *The Son of Man in Mark: A Study of the Background of the Term "Son of Man" and Its Use in St. Mark's Gospel*. London: SCPK, 1967.

Howton, Dom John. "The Sign of Jonah." *Scottish Journal of Theology* 15 (1962) 288-304.

Hummel, Reinhart. *Die Auseinandersetzung zwischen Kirche und Judentum im Matthäusevangelium*. Beitrage zur evangelischen Theologie 33. Munich: Kaiser, 1963.

Hunter, A. M. "Crux Criticorum—Matt 11:25-30—A Re-Appraisal." *New Testament Studies* 8 (1962) 241-49.

Janzen, J. Gerald. "The Yoke That Gives Rest." *Interpretation* 41 (1987) 256-68.

Jeremias, Joachim. *The Eucharistic Words of Jesus*. Translated by Norman Perrin. Philadelphia: Fortress, 1977.

———. "Ηλ(ε)ίας." In vol. 2 of *Theological Dictionary of the New Testament*, edited by Gerhard Kittel, 928-41. Translated by Geoffrey W. Bromiley. Grand Rapids: Eerdmans, 1964.

---. "Ἰωνᾶς." In vol. 3 of *Theological Dictionary of the New Testament*, edited by Gerhard Kittel, 406–10. Translated by Geoffrey W. Bromiley. Grand Rapids: Eerdmans, 1965.

---. *New Testament Theology: Part One, The Proclamation of Jesus*. London: SCM, 1971.

---. *The Parables of Jesus*. New Testament Library. Rev. ed. London: SCM, 1962.

Johnson, Luke Timothy. *The Gospel of Luke*. Sacra pagina 3. Collegeville, MN: Liturgical, 1991.

Jones, Ivor Harold. *The Matthean Parables: A Literary and Historical Commentary*. Supplements to Novum Testamentum 80. Leiden: Brill, 1995.

Juel, Donald. *Messiah and Temple: The Trial of Jesus in the Gospel of Mark*. Society of Biblical Literature Dissertation Series 31. Missoula, MT: Scholars, 1977.

Keener, Craig S. *The Gospel of Matthew: A Socio-Rhetorical Commentary*. Grand Rapids: Eerdmans, 2009.

Kertelge, Karl. "Der dienende Menschensohn (Mk 10, 45)." In *Jesus und der Menschensohn: Für Anton Vögtle*, edited by Rudolf Pesch and Rudolf Schnackenburg, 225–39. Freiburg: Herder, 1975.

Kevan, Earnest F. *The Grace of Law: A Study in Puritan Theology*. London: Carey Kingsgate, 1964.

Kiilunen, Jarmo. "Der Nachfolgewillige Schriftgelehrte: Matthäus 8.19–20 im Verständnis des Evangelisten." *New Testament Studies* 37 (1991) 268–79.

Kik, J. Marcellus. *Matthew Twenty-Four: An Exposition*. Swengel, PA: I. C. Herendeen, 1948.

Kim, Ki Kon. *The Signs of the Parousia: A Diachronic and Comparative Study of the Apocalyptic Vocabulary of Matthew 24:27–31*. Korean Sahmyook University Monographs Doctoral Dissertation Series 3. Seoul: Korean Sahmyook University, 1994.

Kingsbury, Jack Dean. "The Christology of Mark and the Son of Man." In *Unity and Diversity in the Gospels and Paul: Essays in Honor of Frank J. Matera*, edited by Christopher W. Skinner and Kelly R. Iverson, 55–70. Early Christianity and Its Literature 7. Atlanta: Society of Biblical Literature, 2012.

---. "The Figure of Peter in the Gospel of Matthew." *Journal of Biblical Literature* 98 (1979) 67–83.

---. *Jesus Christ in Matthew, Mark, and Luke*. Philadelphia: Fortress, 1981.

---. *Matthew as Story*. 2nd and rev. ed. Philadelphia: Fortress, 1988.

---. *Matthew: Structure, Christology, Kingdom*. Minneapolis: Fortress, 1975.

---. "On Following Jesus: The 'Eager' Scribe and the 'Reluctant' Disciple (Matthew 8:18–22)." *New Testament Studies* 34 (1988) 45–59.

---. *The Parables of Jesus in Matthew 13: A Study in Redaction-Criticism*. Richmond, VA: John Knox, 1969.

Kirchhevel, Gordon D. "He That Cometh in Mark 1:7 and Matt 24:30." *Bulletin for Biblical Research* 4 (1994) 105–11.

Kirk, J. R. Daniel. *A Man Attested By God: The Human Jesus of the Synoptic Gospels*. Grand Rapids: Eerdmans, 2016.

Klassen, William. *Judas: Betrayer or Friend of Jesus?* Minneapolis: Fortress, 1996.

Klein, Leonard. "Who are the 'Least of the Brethren'?" *Dialog* 21 (1982) 139–42.

Klostermann, Erich. *Das Matthäusevangelium*. 4th ed. Handbuch zum Neuen Testament 4. Tübingen: Mohr Siebeck, 1971.

Knight, George A. F. *Law and Grace: Must a Christian Keep the Law of Moses?* Religious Book Club 146. London: SCM, 1962.
Konradt, Matthias. *Israel, Church, and the Gentiles in the Gospel of Matthew*. Translated by Kathleen Ess. Baylor-Mohr Siebeck Studies in Early Christianity. Waco, TX: Baylor University Press, 2014.
Kümmel, Werner Georg. "Jesus und der jüdische Traditionsgedanke." In *Heilsgeschehen und Geschichte: Gesammelte Aufsätze 1933–1964*, 15–35. Marburger Theologische Studien Band 3. Marburg: N. G. Elwert, 1965.
———. *Promise and Fulfillment: The Eschatological Message of Jesus*. Translated by Dorothea M. Barton. 2nd ed. Studies in Biblical Theology 23. London: SCM, 1961.
Künzi, Martin. *Das Naherwartungslogion Mattäus 10, 23: Geschichte seiner Auslegung*. Beiträge zur Geschichte der biblischen Exegese. Tübingen: Mohr Siebeck, 1970.
Kynes, William L. *A Christology of Solidarity: Jesus as the Representative of His People in Matthew*. Lanham, MD: University Press of America, 1991.
Ladd, George E. "The Parable of the Sheep and the Goats in Recent Interpretation." In *New Dimensions in New Testament Study*, edited by Richard N. Longenecker and Merrill G. Tenney, 191–99. Grand Rapids: Zondervan, 1974.
Lagrange, M.-J. *Évangile selon Saint Matthieu*. Paris: Lecoffre, 1948.
Lambrecht, Jan. *Out of the Treasure: The Parables in the Gospel of Matthew*. Louvain Theological and Pastoral Monograph Series 10. Louvain: Peeters, 1991.
———. "The Parousia Discourse: Composition and Content in Mt. XXIV-XXV." In *L'Évangile selon Matthieu: Rédaction et théologie*, edited by M. Didier, 309–42. Bibliotheca ephemeidum theologicarum lovaniensium 29. Beligique: J. Duculot, SA, Gembloux, 1972.
Yang, Yong-Eui. *Jesus and the Sabbath in Matthew's Gospel*. Journal for the Study of the New Testament Supplement Series 139. Sheffield: Sheffield Academic, 1997.
Lenski, R. C. H. *The Interpretation of St. Matthew's Gospel*. Columbus: Wartburg, 1943.
Lietzmann, Hans. *Der Menschensohn: Ein Beitrag zur Neutestamentlichen Theologie*. Freiberg: Mohr Siebeck, 1896.
Lindars, Barnabas. *Jesus Son of Man: A Fresh Examination of the Son of Man Sayings in the Gospels in the Light of Recent Research*. Grand Rapids: Eerdmans, 1983.
Linton, Olof. "The Parable of the Children's Game." *New Testament Studies* 22 (1976) 159–79.
———. "The Trial of Jesus and the Interpretation of Ps cx." *New Testament Studies* 7 (1960–61) 258–62.
Loader, William R. G. *Jesus' Attitude towards the Law: A Study of the Gospels*. Wissenschaftliche Untersuchungen zum Neuen Testament 2/97. Tübingen: Mohr Siebeck, 1997.
Lohse, Eduard. *History of the Suffering and Death of Jesus Christ*. Translated by Martin O. Dietrich. Philadelphia: Fortress, 1967.
———. *Märtyrer und Gottesknect: Untersuchungen zur urchristlichen Verfündigung vom Sühntod Jesu Christi*. Forschungen zur Religion und Literatur des Alten und Neuen Testaments 64. Göttingen: Vandenhoeck & Ruprecht, 1963.
Lövestam, Evald. *Spiritual Wakefulness in the New Testament*, translated by W. F. Salisbury. Lunds universitets årsskrift. N.F. Avd. 1. Bd. 55. Nr. 3. Lund: CWK Gleerup, 1963.
Luz, Ulrich. *Matthew 21–28: A Commentary*. Hermeneia. Minneapolis: Fortress, 2005.
———. *Matthew 8–20: A Commentary*. Hermeneia. Minneapolis: Fortress, 2001.

———. "The Son of Man in Matthew: Heavenly Judge or Human Christ." *Journal for the Study of the New Testament* 48 (1992) 3–21.

Lybaek, Lena. *New and Old in Matthew 11–13: Normativity in the Development of Three Theological Themes.* Forschungen zur Religion and Literatur des Alten und Neuen Testaments 198. Göttingen: Vandenhoeck & Ruprecht, 2002.

Maddox, Robert. "Who Are the 'Sheep' and the 'Goats': A Study of the Purpose and Meaning of Matthew xxv 31–46." *Australian Biblical Review* 13 (1965) 19–28.

Manson, Thomas W. "Jesus, Paul, and the Law." In *Law and Religion*, edited by E. L. J. Rosenthal, 25–41. Judaism and Christianity 3. London: Macmillan, 1938.

———. *The Sayings of Jesus: As Recorded in the Gospels according to St. Matthew and St. Luke.* London: SCM, 1957.

———. *The Teaching of Jesus: Studies in Its Form and Content.* Cambridge: Cambridge University Press, 1967.

Marcus, Joel. "Entering into the Kingly Power of God." *Journal of Biblical Literature* 107 (1988) 663–75.

———. "The Gates of Hades and the Keys of the Kingdom (Mt. 16:18–19)." *Catholic Biblical Quarterly* 50 (1988) 449–55.

Marguerat, Daniel. *Le Jugement dans l'Évangile de Matthieu.* 2nd ed. Le Monde de la Bible 6. Genève: Labor et Fides, 1995.

Marshall, I. Howard. *The Gospel of Luke: A Commentary on the Greek Text.* The New International Greek Testament Commentary. Grand Rapids: Eerdmans, 1978.

———. *Last Supper and Lord's Supper.* The Didsbury Lectures. Carlisle: Paternoster, 1980.

McArthur, Harvey K. *Understanding the Sermon on the Mount.* London: Epworth, 1961.

McKnight, Edgar V. "Literary Criticism." In *Dictionary of Jesus and the Gospels*, edited by Joel B. Green and Scot McKnight, 473–81. Downers Grove, IL: InterVarsity, 1992.

McKnight, Scot. *Jesus and His Death: Historiography, the Historical Jesus, and Atonement Theory.* Waco, TX: Baylor University Press, 2005.

McNeile, Alan H. *The Gospel according to St. Matthew: The Greek Text with Introduction, Notes, and Indices.* London: MacMillan, 1915.

Meier, John P. "John the Baptist in Matthew's Gospel." *Journal of Biblical Literature* 99 (1980) 383–405.

———. *Law and History in Matthew's Gospel: A Redactional Study of Mt. 5:17–48.* Analecta Biblica 71. Rome: Biblical Institute, 1976.

———. *Matthew.* New Testament Message 3. Collegeville, MN: Liturgical, 1980.

———. "Nations or Gentiles in Matthew 28:19?" *Catholic Biblical Quarterly* 39 (1977) 94–102.

———. *The Vision of Matthew: Christ, Church, and Morality in the First Gospel.* Theological Inquiries. 1979. Reprint, Eugene, OR: Wipf & Stock, 1991.

Merklein, Helmut. *Die Gottesherrschaft als Handlungprinzip: Untersuchung zur Ethik Jesu.* Forschung zur Bibel 34. Würzburg: Echter, 1978.

Metzger, Bruce M. *The Text of the New Testament.* 3rd ed. New York: Oxford University Press, 1992.

———. *A Textual Commentary on the Greek New Testament.* 2nd ed. Stuttgart: Deutsche Bibelgesellschaft, 1994.

Michael, J. Hugh. "The Sign of John." *Journal of Theological Studies* 21 (1920) 146–59.

Moo, Douglas J. "Jesus and the Authority of the Mosaic Law." *Journal for the Study of the New Testament* 20 (1984) 3–49.

———. *The Old Testament in the Gospel Passion Narratives*. Sheffield: Almond, 1983.

Morris, Leon. *The Gospel according to Matthew*. The Pillar New Testament Commentary. Grand Rapids: Eerdmans, 1992.

Moule, C. F. D. "Neglected Features in the Problem of the Son of Man." In *Neues Testament und Kirche: Für Rudolf Schnackenburg*, edited by Joachim Gnilka, 413–28. Freiburg: Herder, 1974.

Mounce, Robert H. *Matthew*. Good News Commentary. Peabody, MA: Hendrickson, 1991.

Müller, Mogens. *The Expression "Son of Man" and the Development of Christology: A History of Interpretation*. Copenhagen International Seminar. London: Equinox, 2008.

Mussner, Franz. "Der nicht erkannte Kairos (Mt 11, 16–19/Luke 7, 31–35)." *Biblica* 40 (1959) 599–613.

Nau, Arlo J. *Peter in Matthew: Discipleship, Diplomacy, and Dispraise—with an Assessment of Power and Privilege in the Petrine Office*. Good News Studies 36. Collegeville, MN: Liturgical, 1992.

Neander, Augustus. *The Life of Jesus Christ in Its Historical Connection and Historical Development*. Translated by John McClintoak and Charles E. Blumenthal. 4th ed. London: George Bell, 1880.

Nel, Marius. "What Is the 'Sign of the Son of Man in Heaven' (Mt. 24:30)?" *In die Skriflig* 49 (2015) 1–9.

Nolland, John. *The Gospel of Matthew: A Commentary on the Greek Text*. The New International Greek Testament Commentary. Grand Rapids: Eerdmans, 2005.

O'Neill, J. C. "The Charge of Blasphemy at Jesus' Trial Before the Sanhedrin." In *The Trial of Jesus: Cambridge Studies in Honour of C. F. D. Moule*, edited by Ernest Bammel, 72–77. Second Series. Studies in Biblical Theology 13. London: SCM, 1970.

Osborne, Grant. *Matthew*. Zondervan Exegetical Commentary on the New Testament 1. Grand Rapids: Zondervan, 2010.

Otto, Rudolf. *The Kingdom of God and the Son of Man: A Study in the History of Religion*. Translated by Floyd V. Filson and Bertram Lee Woolf. Lutterworth Library 9. London: Lutterworth, 1938.

Overman, J. Andrew. *Church and Community in Crisis: The Gospel according to Matthew*. New Testament in Context. Valley Forge, PA: Trinity, 1996.

Pamment, Margaret. "The Son of Man in the First Gospel." *New Testament Studies* 29 (1983) 116–29.

Park, Eung Chun. *The Mission Discourse in Matthew's Interpretation*. Wissenschaftliche Untersuchungen zum Neuen Testament 2/81. Tübingen: Mohr Siebeck, 1995.

Paschal, R. Wade, Jr. "Service." In *Dictionary of Jesus and the Gospels*, edited by Joel B. Green and Scot McKnight, 747–51. Downers Grove, IL: InterVarsity, 1992.

Patsch, Hermann. *Abenmahl und historischer Jesus*. Calwer theologische Monographien: Reihe A. Biblewissenschaft 1. Stuttgart: Calwer, 1972.

Patte, Daniel. *The Gospel according to Matthew: A Structural Commentary on Matthew's Faith*. Philadelphia: Fortress, 1987.

Perrin, Norman. "The Use of *(Para)didonai* in Connection with the Passion of Jesus in the New Testament." In *A Modern Pilgrimage in New Testament Christology*, by Norman Perrin, 94–103. Philadelphia: Fortress, 1974.

Pesch, Rudolf. "Die Passion des Menschensohnes: Eine Studie zu den Menschensohnworten der vormarkinischen Passionsgeschichte." In *Jesus und der Menschensohn: Für Anton Vögtle*, edited by Rudolf Pesch and Rudolf Schnackenburg, 166–95. Freiburg: Herder, 1975.

———. "Eschatologie und Ethik." *Bibel und Leben* 11 (1970) 223–38.

Plummer, Alfred. *An Exegetical Commentary on the Gospel according to S. Matthew*. Grand Rapids: Eerdmans, 1953.

Pond, Eugene W. "Who Are 'the Least' of Jesus' Brothers in Matthew 25:40?" *Bibliotheca Sacra* 159 (2002) 436–48.

———. "Who Are the Sheep and the Goats in Matthew 25:31–46?" *Bibliotheca Sacra* 159 (2002) 288–301.

Powell, Mark Alan. "The Plot to Kill Jesus from Three Different Perspectives: Point of View in Matthew." *Society of Biblical Literature Seminar Papers* 29 (1990) 603–13.

Reicke, Bo. *Die Zehn Worte Geschichte und Gegenwart: Zählung und Bedeutung der Gebote in den verschiedenen Konfessionen*. Beiträge zur Geschichte der biblischen Exegese 13. Tübingen: Mohr Siebeck, 1973.

———. "Synoptic Prophesies on the Destruction of Jerusalem." In *Studies in New Testament and Early Christian Literature: Essays in Honor of Allen P. Wilkgren*, edited by David Edward Aune, 21–34. Supplements to Novum Testamentum 33. Leiden: Brill, 1972.

Reiser, Marius. *Jesus and Judgment: Eschatological Proclamation in Its Jewish Context*. Translated by Linda A. Maloney. Minneapolis: Fortress, 1997.

Rengstorf, Karl Heinrich. "βρύχω, βρυγμός." In vol. 1 of *Theological Dictionary of the New Testament*, edited by Gerhard Kittel and Gerhard Friedrich, 641–42. Translated by Geoffrey W. Bromiley. Grand Rapids: Eerdmans, 1964.

———. "σημεῖον." In vol. 7 of *Theological Dictionary of the New Testament*, edited by Gerhard Kittel and Gerhard Friedrich, 200–261. Translated by Geoffrey W. Bromiley. Grand Rapids: Eerdmans, 1971.

Ridderbos, Herman. *The Coming of the Kingdom*. Edited by Raymond O. Zorn. Translated by H. de Jongste. Philadelphia: Presbyterian and Reformed, 1962.

Rigaux, Béda. "Βδελυγμα της ερημωσεως." *Biblica* 40 (1959) 675–83.

Robinson, Bernard P. "Peter and His Successors: Tradition and Redaction in Matthew 16:17–19." *Journal for the Study of the New Testament* 21 (1984) 85–104.

Rowland, C. C. "Apocalyptic, Poor, and the Gospel of Matthew." *Journal for Theological Studies* 45 (1994) 505–18.

Sabourin, Leopold. "'You Will Not Have Gone Through All the Towns of Israel Before the Son of Man Comes' (Matt 10:23b)." *Biblical Theology Bulletin* 7 (1977) 5–11.

Sanders, E. P. *Jesus and Judaism*. Philadelphia: Fortress, 1985.

Schaberg, Jane. "Daniel 7–12 and the New Testament Passion-Resurrection Predictions." *New Testament Studies* 31 (1985) 208–22.

Schmitt, Götz. "Das Zeichen des Jona." *Zeitschrift für die Neutestamentliche Wissenschaft und die Kunde der Älteren Kirche* 69 (1978) 123–29.

Schnackenburg, Rudolf. *The Gospel of Matthew*. Translated by Robert R. Barr. Grand Rapids: Eerdmans, 2002.

———. *Jesus in the Gospels: A Biblical Christology*. Translated by O. C. Dean. Louisville: Westminster John Knox, 1995.
———. *The Moral Teaching of the New Testament*. Translated by J. Holland-Smith and W. J. O'Hara. Frieburg: Herder, 1965.
Schneider, Walter. "κρίμα." In vol. 2 *The New International Dictionary of New Testament Theology*, edited by Colin Brown, 362–67. Regency Reference Library. Grand Rapids: Zondervan, 1976.
Schniewind, Julius. *Das Evangelium nach Matthäus*. 2 vols. Das Neue Testament Deutsch. Göttingen: Vandenhoeck & Ruprecht, 1952, 1954.
Schrenck, Gottlob. "βιάζομαι, βιαστής." In vol. 1 of *Theological Dictionary of the New Testament*, edited by Gerhard Kittel and Geoffrey W. Bromiley, 609–14. Translated Geoffrey W. Bromiley. Grand Rapids: Eerdmans, 1964.
Schweitzer, Albert. *The Kingdom of God and Primitive Christianity*. Edited by Ulrich Neuenschwander. Translated by L. A. Garrard. New York: Seabury, 1968.
———. *The Mystery of the Kingdom of God: The Secret of Jesus' Messiahship and Passion*. Translated by Walter Lowrie. New York: Macmillan, 1950.
———. *The Quest of the Historical Jesus*. Edited by John Bowden. Minneapolis: Fortress, 2001.
Schweizer, Eduard. *Erniedrigung und Erhöhung bei Jesus und seinen Nachfolgern*. Abhandlungen zur Theologie des Alten und Neuen Testaments 28. Zürich: Buchdruckerei Schürch, 1955.
———. *The Good News according to Matthew*. Translated by David E. Green. Atlanta: John Knox, 1975.
Scroggs, Robin. "The Exaltation of the Spirit by Some Early Christians." *Journal of Biblical Literature* 84 (1965) 359–73.
Senior, Donald P. "Between Two Worlds: Gentiles and Jewish Christians in Matthew's Gospel." *Catholic Biblical Quarterly* 61 (1999) 1–23.
———. *Matthew*. Abingdon New Testament Commentaries. Nashville: Abingdon, 1998.
———. *The Passion Narrative According to Matthew: A Redactional Study*. Bibliotheca Ephemeridum Theologicarum Lovaniensium XXXIX. Leuven: Leuven University Press, 1982.
———. *The Passion of Jesus in the Gospel of Matthew*. Passion Series 1. Wilmington, DE: Michael Glazier, 1985.
Shaw, Frances. *Discernment of Revelation in the Gospel of Matthew*. Religions and Discourse 30. Oxford: Peter Lang, 2007.
Sigal, Phillip. *The Halakhah of Jesus of Nazareth according to the Gospel of Matthew*. Studies in Biblical Literature 18. Atlanta: Society of Biblical Literature, 2007.
Sim, David C. *Apocalyptic Eschatology in the Gospel of Matthew*. Society for New Testament Studies Monograph Series 88. Cambridge: Cambridge University Press, 1996.
Simonetti, Manlio, ed. *Matthew 1–13*. Ancient Christian Commentary on Scripture 1. New Testament Ia. Downers Grove, IL: InterVarsity, 2001.
Stanley, David M. *Jesus in Gethsemane: The Early Church Reflects on the Sufferings of Jesus*. An Exploration Book. New York: Paulist, 1980.
Stanton, Graham N. "The Gospel of Matthew and Judaism." *The Bulletin of John Rylands University Library of Manchester* 66 (1984) 264–84.

———. "Once More: Matthew 25:31–46." In *A Gospel for a New People: Studies in Matthew*, by Graham N. Stanton, 207–31. Edinburgh: T. & T. Clark, 1990.

———. "Pray That Your Flight May Not Be in Winter or on a Sabbath (Matthew 24:20)." *Journal for the Study of the New Testament* 37 (1989) 17–30.

Stein, Robert H. *Jesus, the Temple, and the Coming Son of Man: A Commentary on Mark 13*. Downers Grove, IL: IVP Academic, 2014.

Strecker, Georg. "The Passion and Resurrection Predictions in Mark's Gospel (Mark 8:31; 9:31; 10:32–34). *Interpretation* 22 (1968) 421–42.

Streeter, Burnett H. *The Primitive Church: Studied with Special Reference to the Origins of the Christian Ministry*. Hewett Lectures 1928. New York: Macmillan, 1929.

Suggs, M. Jack. *Wisdom, Christology, and Law in Matthew's Gospel*. Cambridge, MA: Harvard University Press, 1970.

Swete, Henry B. *The Holy Spirit in the New Testament*. Grand Rapids: Baker, 1976.

Swetnam, James. "Some Signs of Jonah." *Biblica* 68 (1987) 74–79.

Tasker, R. V. G. *The Gospel according to St. Matthew: An Introduction and Commentary*. Tyndale New Testament Commentaries. Grand Rapids: Eerdmans, 1961.

Taylor, Justin. "The Coming of Elijah: Mt. 7:10–13 and Mk. 9:11–13: The Development of the Texts." *Revue Biblique* 98 (1991) 107–19.

Taylor, Vincent. *Jesus and His Sacrifice: A Study of the Passion-Sayings in the Gospels*. London: MacMillan, 1951.

Theophilos, Michael P. *The Abomination of Desolation in Matthew 24:15*. The Library of New Testament Studies 437. London: T. & T. Clark, 2012.

Thielman, Frank. *The Law and the New Testament: A Question of Continuity*. Companions to the New Testament. New York: Crosswood, 1999.

Tisera, Guido. *Universalism according to the Gospel in Matthew*. European University Studies 462. Frankfurt am Main: Peter Lang, 1993.

Tödt, H. E. *The Son of Man in the Synoptic Tradition*. Translated by Dorothea M. Barton. New Testament Library. Philadelphia: Westminster, 1965.

Trilling, Wolfgang. *The Gospel according to St. Matthew*. Translated by Kevin Smyth. 2 vols. New Testament for Spiritual Reading 1–2. New York: Crossroad, 1981.

Turner, David L. *Matthew*. Baker Exegetical Commentary on the New Testament. Grand Rapids: Baker Academic, 2008.

Vadakumpadan, Sabastian. "The Parousia Discourse: Mt 24–25: Tradition and Redaction." PhD diss., Pontificium Institutum Biblicum, 1976.

Vanhoozer, Kevin J. "The Reader in New Testament Interpretation." In *Hearing the New Testament: Strategies for Interpretation*, edited by Joel B. Green, 301–28. Grand Rapids: Eerdmans, 1995.

Vermes, Geza. *Jesus the Jew: A Historian's Reading of the Gospels*. Philadelphia: Fortress, 1981.

———. "The Son of Man Debate Revisited (1960–2010)." *Journal of Jewish Studies* 61 (2010) 193–206.

———. "The Use of בר נש/בר נשא in Jewish Aramaic." In *An Aramaic Approach to the Gospels and Acts*, by Matthew Black, 310–30. 3rd ed. Peabody, MA: Hendrickson, 1998.

Verseput, Donald. *The Rejection of the Humble Messianic King: A Study of the Composition of Matthew 11–12*. European University Studies: Europaeische Hochschulschriften 23/291. Frankfurt am Main: Peter Lang, 1986.

Via, Daniel O. "Ethical Responsibility and Human Wholeness in Matthew 25:31-46." *Harvard Theological Review* 80 (1987) 79-100.
Viviano, Benedict T. "Revelation in Stages (Matthew 11:25-30 and Numbers 12:3, 6-8)." In *Matthew and His World: The Gospel of the Open Jewish Christians: Studies in Biblical Theology*, by Benedict T. Viviano, 95-101. Novum Testamentum et Orbis Antiquus, Studien zur Umwelt des Neuen Testaments 61. Fribourg: Academic; Göttingen: Vandenhoeck & Ruprecht, 2007.
Vögtle, Anton. "Der Spruch vom Jonaszeichen." In *Das Evangelium und die Evangelien*, by Anton Vögtle, 103-36. Düsseldorf: Patmos, 1971.
Waetjen, Herman C. *The Origin and Destiny of Humanness: An Interpretation of the Gospel according the Matthew*. Contre Madera, CA: Omega, 1976.
Walck, Leslie W. *The Son of Man in the Parables of Enoch and in Matthew*. Jewish and Christian Texts in Contexts and Related Studies 9. London: T. & T. Clark, 2011.
Walker, Rolf. *Die Heilsgeschichte im ersten Evangelium*. Forschungen zur Religion und Literatur des Alten und Neuen Testaments 91. Göttingen: Vandenhoeck & Ruprecht, 1967.
Watts, Rikki. *Isaiah's New Exodus and Mark*. Wissenschaftliche Untersuchungen zum Neuen Testament 2/88. Tübingen: Mohr Siebeck, 1997.
Weaver, Dorothy Jean. *Matthew's Missionary Discourse*. Journal of the Study of the New Testament Supplement Series 38. Sheffield: JSOT, 1999.
Weber, Kathleen. "The Image of Sheep and Goats in Matthew 25:31-46." *Catholic Biblical Quarterly* 59 (1997) 657-78.
Weiss, Johannes. *Die Predigt Jesu vom Reiche Gottes*. 3rd ed. Göttingen: Vandenhoeck & Ruprecht, 1964.
———. *Jesus' Proclamation of the Kingdom of God*. Edited and translated by Richard Hyde Hiers and David Larrimore Holland. Lives of Jesus Series. Philadelphia: Fortress, 1971.
Wellhausen, Julius. *Einleitung in die Drei Ersten Evangelien*. 2nd ed. Berlin: Georg Reimer, 1911.
Wenham, David. *The Parables of Jesus*. Downers Grove, IL: IVP Academic, 1989.
———. *The Rediscovery of Jesus' Eschatological Discourse*. Gospel Perspectives 4. Sheffield: JSOT, 1984.
Wenham, John W. *Our Lord's View of the Old Testament*. Tyndale New Testament Lecture 1953. London: Tyndale, 1953.
Weren, Wim. "Children in Matthew: A Semantic Study." *Concilium* 2 (1996) 53-63.
Westerholm, Stephen. *Jesus and Scribal Authority*. Coniectanea Biblica: New Testament Series 10. Lund: CWK Gleerup, 1978.
Wilson, Alistair I. *When Will These Things Happen? A Study of Jesus as Judge in Matthew 21-25*. Paternoster Biblical Monographs. Carlisle: Paternoster, 2004.
Wilson, Walter T. *Healing in the Gospel of Matthew: Reflections on Method and Ministry*. Minneapolis: Fortress, 2014.
Wink, Walter. *John the Baptist in the Gospel Tradition*. Society for New Testament Studies Monograph Series 7. Cambridge: Cambridge University Press, 1968.
Witherington, Ben, III. *Matthew*. Smyth & Helwys Bible Commentary 19. Macon: Smyth & Helwys, 2006.
Witte, Brendon Robert. "'Who Do You, Matthew, Say the Son of Man Is?': Son of Man and Conflict in the First Gospel." PhD diss., University of Edinburgh, 2016.

Wong, Eric K.-C. "The Matthean Understanding of the Sabbath: A Response to G. N. Stanton." *Journal for the Study of the New Testament* 44 (1991) 3–18.
Wouters, Armin. " . . . *wer den Willen meines Vaters tut": Eine Untersuchung zur Verständnis vom Handeln in Mattäusevangelium*. Biblische Untersuchungen 23. Regensburg: Friedrich Pustet, 1990.
Wrede, William. *Das Messiasgeheimnis in den Evangelien: Zugleich ein Beitrag zum Verständnis des Markusevangeliums*. 4th ed. Göttingen: Vandenhoeck & Ruprecht, 1969.
Wright, G. F. "The Term 'Son of Man' as Used in the New Testament." *Bibliotheca Sacra* 44 (1887) 575–601.
Wright, N. T. *Jesus and the Victory of God*. Christian Origins and the Question of God 2. Minneapolis: Fortress, 1996.
———. *The Resurrection of the Son of God*. Christian Origins and the Question of God 3. Minneapolis: Fortress, 2003.
Yates, John E. *The Spirit and the Kingdom*. London: SPCK, 1963.
Zeller, Dieter. "Die Bildlogik des Gleichnisses Mt 11, 16/Lk 7, 31f." *Zeitschrift für die neutestamentliche Wissenschaft und die Kunde der älteren Kirche* 68 (1977) 252–57.
Zumstein, Jean. *La Condition du Croyant dans L'Évangile selon Matthieu*. Orbis Biblicus et orientalis 16. Fribourg: Editions Universitaires Fribourg; Göttingen: Vandenhoeck & Ruprecht, 1977.

www.ingramcontent.com/pod-product-compliance
Lightning Source LLC
Chambersburg PA
CBHW050851230426
43667CB00012B/2237